Time and Tide

Time and Tide

The Feminist and Cultural Politics
of a Modern Magazine

Catherine Clay

EDINBURGH
University Press

Edinburgh University Press is one of the leading university presses in the UK. We publish academic books and journals in our selected subject areas across the humanities and social sciences, combining cutting-edge scholarship with high editorial and production values to produce academic works of lasting importance. For more information visit our website: edinburghuniversitypress.com

Edinburgh University Press Ltd
The Tun – Holyrood Road,
12(2f) Jackson's Entry,
Edinburgh EH8 8PJ

First published in hardback by Edinburgh University Press 2018

Typeset in 11/13 Adobe Sabon by
IDSUK (DataConnection) Ltd, and
printed and bound in Great Britain by
CPI Group (UK) Ltd, Croydon, CR0 4YY.

A CIP record for this book is available from the British Library

ISBN 978 1 4744 1818 8 (hardback)
ISBN 978 1 4744 5481 0 (paperback)
ISBN 978 1 4744 1819 5 (webready PDF)
ISBN 978 1 4744 1820 1 (epub)

Contents

List of Illustrations

Acknowledgements

I have spent many years researching and writing this book, and it would never have reached completion without the generous help and support of numerous organisations and individuals. The first of three British Academy Small Research Grants started the whole project off as early as 2005, and an AHRC Research Fellowship in 2011 enabled me to complete the primary research and produce a first draft of the book. I am grateful both to these funding bodies and their external assessors who recognised *Time and Tide*'s significance and the value of this research, and enabled me to conduct the numerous visits to archival collections in the UK and the US which were essential for reconstructing for the first time the history and workings of this fascinating periodical. The book expanded significantly beyond its original remit, and I am indebted to Nottingham Trent University, too, for the two research sabbaticals I was awarded to work on this project.

I am also grateful to all the archivists and librarians who have assisted me in my research. Andy Simons of the British Library provided much practical assistance in my searches of the newspaper and periodical archive, and I thank the following libraries and archives for their assistance and permission to quote from their collections: Ball State University Archives and Special Collections; the Beinecke Rare Book and Manuscript Library, Yale University; the Bodleian Library; Cambridge University Library; Cornell University Library (Division of Rare and Manuscript Collections); Fales Library and Special Collections, New York University Libraries; Girton College Library, Cambridge; Harry Ransom Center, The University of Texas at Austin; the Houghton library, Harvard University; Hull History Centre; King's College Library, Cambridge; Mass Observation Archive, University of Sussex; McFarlin Library, University of Tulsa (Department of Special Collections and University Archives); McMaster University Library (The William Ready Division of Archives and Research Collections); the National Library of Scotland; the Schlesinger Library, Radcliffe

Institute, Harvard University; the Women's Library Archives (which I consulted first at the purpose-built Women's Library on Old Castle Street, London, and latterly at its new location in the London School of Economics). The illustrations from *Time and Tide* which appear in the book are reproduced by kind permission of the Syndics of Cambridge University Library, and of The William Ready Division of Archives and Research Collections, McMaster University Library.

This book also owes much to many individuals, among them colleagues, readers and friends. I am particularly indebted to Jim Clayson and Anne Harvey for the knowledge they have shared with me regarding Eleanor Farjeon, and to Angela V. John for the knowledge and biographical material she has shared with me about Lady Rhondda. I am also grateful to all three for reading and commenting on drafts of Chapter 2. My very deep gratitude extends to Maria DiCenzo, Barbara Green and Fiona Hackney with whom I have had not only many fruitful conversations about *Time and Tide*, but about women's periodicals more generally in our collaborative work on another volume for Edinburgh University Press: *Women's Periodicals and Print Culture in Britain, 1918–1939: The Interwar Period.* The opportunity to work together on this edited volume has been one of the most pleasurable offshoots of my *Time and Tide* research. I am also grateful to both Maria and Barbara for reading and commenting on draft chapters of this book. Faith Binckes, whom I first met at a conference on women's literary networking, has been another source of intellectual inspiration and friendship, and I thank her for reading and commenting on draft chapters at both the early and later stages of writing. Other friends and colleagues who read draft chapters were Anna Ball, Katharine Cockin, Lucy Delap, Faye Hammill, Ben Harker and Sharon Ouditt, and I thank them too for their invaluable feedback. I would also like to thank Jackie Jones and anonymous readers for Edinburgh University Press for their useful comments and suggestions. Last, but not least, I extend special thanks to Mary Joannou for her intellectual generosity, hospitality and friendship over the years. Returning to her home at the end of long days in the West Room of Cambridge University Library became another source of great pleasure attached to this research.

Every effort has been made to contact copyright holders. I thank The Institution of Engineering and Technology Archives for permission to quote from the letters of Caroline Haslett. The extract from the unpublished letter from Wyndham Lewis to John Beevers is reprinted by permission of The Wyndham Lewis Memorial Trust (a registered charity), and the extract from the unpublished letter from Edith Sitwell to John Beevers by Edith Sitwell is reprinted by permission of Peters Fraser & Dunlop (www.petersfraserdunlop.com) on behalf of the Estate of Edith Sitwell. The extract from the Unpublished Diary of Rebecca West by Rebecca West is reprinted by permission of Peters Fraser & Dunlop (www.petersfraserdunlop.com) on behalf of the Estate of Rebecca West, and material from the Mass Observation Archive is reproduced with permission of Curtis Brown Group Ltd, London on behalf of The Trustees of the Mass Observation Archive © The Mass Observation Archive. Quotations from unpublished Vera Brittain material are included by permission of Mark Bostridge and T. J. Brittain-Catlin, Literary Executors for the Estate of Vera Brittain 1970. For permission to quote from unpublished letters by Ezra Pound I am grateful to New Directions Pub. acting as agent, copyright © 2017 by Mary de Rachewiltz and the Estate of Omar S. Pound. These extracts are reprinted by permission of New Directions Publishing Corp. I also thank the Trustees of the Ezra Pound Literary Property Trust, and the Estates of Gwen Raverat and Edmond X. Kapp, for permission to reproduce visual material that appeared in *Time and Tide*; full credit is given where the illustrations appear in the book. Excerpts from the poems of Eleanor Farjeon are reproduced with permission from the Eleanor Farjeon Trust and David Higham Associates.

I would also like to thank all those whose responses to parts of the book I have presented at various research events have enriched the ideas it contains. In particular the book benefits from the stimulating discussions I have had at conferences of the British Association of Modernist Studies, the Middlebrow Network, the Modernist Studies Association, the Space Between Society, and the Women's History Network. I would also like to thank Erica Brown for her invitation to present my research in a seminar series organised to launch the Readerships and Literary Cultures 1900–1950 Special Collection at Sheffield Hallam University, Kristin Ewins for her invitation to address the Fourth International Conference of the European Society of Periodical Research (ESPRit) in Stockholm, Ben Harker for his invitation to speak at a Radical Studies Network seminar at the Working Class Movement Library in Salford, Naomi Hetherington for her invitation to present at a seminar of the History of Feminism network, and Chris Mourant for his invitation to deliver a session on *Time and Tide* at the Modernist Magazines Research Seminar at the Institute for English Studies, London. The fruitful conversations I had at all these events have left their mark in one way or another on this book. None of the content in this book has been previously published, with the exception of the first part of Chapter 1 which appeared in an article for *Women: A Cultural Review*, Winter 2016, copyright Taylor & Francis.

Finally, I would like to thank all my friends and family who have sustained me through the long writing of this book, and everybody at Edinburgh University Press who has helped see it to completion: Jackie Jones for responding so positively to the proposal and early manuscript material, Christine Barton, James Dale, Ersev Ersoy and Adela Rauchova for their practical assistance during the end-stages of producing the typescript, and Rebecca Mackenzie for her terrific design for the cover.

Abbreviations

Archives

BFUW Papers	British Federation of University Women Papers, The Women's Library, London School of Economics and Political Science.
DS Papers	Doris Stevens Papers, Schlesinger Library, Radcliffe Institute, Harvard University, Cambridge, MA.
EP Papers	Ezra Pound Papers. American Literature Collection, Beinecke Rare Book and Manuscript Library, Yale University.
ER Papers	Elizabeth Robins Papers, Fales Library and Special Collections, New York University Libraries.
ES Collection	Dame Edith Sitwell Collection, Harry Ransom Humanities Research Center, The University of Texas at Austin.
GBS Collection	George Bernard Shaw Collection, Harry Ransom Humanities Research Center, The University of Texas at Austin.
JMK Papers	John Maynard Keynes Papers, King's College Archive Centre, Cambridge University.
MB Papers	Mary Butts Papers. General Collection, Beinecke Rare Book and Manuscript Library, Yale University.
MOA	Mass Observation Archive, University of Sussex.
NA Papers	Sir Normal Angell Papers, Ball State University.
RW Tulsa	Rebecca West Collection. McFarlin Library, Department of Special Collections and University Archives, University of Tulsa.
RW Yale	Rebecca West Collection. General Collection, Beinecke Rare Book and Manuscript Library, Yale University.

TB Harvard	Theodora Bosanquet Papers, Houghton library, Harvard University.
TB SPR	Theodora Bosanquet Papers, Society for Psychical Research Archive, Cambridge University Library.
VB Papers	Vera Brittain Papers. The William Ready Division of Archives and Research Collections, McMaster University Library.
WCML	Working Class Movement Library, Salford.
WH Collection	Winifred Holtby Collection, Hull History Centre.
WL Cornell	Wyndham Lewis Collection, Division of Rare and Manuscript Collections, Cornell University Library.
WL HRC	Wyndham Lewis Collection, Harry Ransom Humanities Research Center, The University of Texas at Austin.

Organisations

APOWC	Association of Post Office Women Clerks
AWKS	Association of Women Clerks and Secretaries
BFUW	British Federation of University Women
FWCS	Federation of Women Civil Servants
ILP	Independent Labour Party
IFUW	International Federation of University Women
LNU	League of Nations Union
NUSEC	National Union of Societies for Equal Citizenship
NUWSS	National Union of Women's Suffrage Societies
NUWT	National Union of Women Teachers
PPU	Peace Pledge Union
SPG	Six Point Group
SPR	Society for Psychical Research
TUC	Trade Unions Council
UDC	Union of Democratic Control
WAAC	Women's Auxiliary Army Corps
WES	Women's Engineering Society
WFL	Women's Freedom League
WI	National Federation of Women's Institutes
WILPF	Women's International League for Peace and Freedom
WSPU	Women's Social and Political Union

To my parents, Nick and Di Clay,
and in loving memory of
Peter R. Armstrong (1948–2007).
For opening up to me the world of books.

Introduction: *Time and Tide* – Origins, Founders and Goals

'PERHAPS some day a future historian will unearth the legend that Saint Bernard came to bless the offices of a paper, which was in its day not without importance, on All Saints Day, 1929.'[1] Thus spoke Lady Margaret Rhondda, founder and editor of the influential weekly review *Time and Tide* (1920–79), at a house-warming luncheon held on 1 November 1929 in the paper's new offices at 32, Bloomsbury Street, London, and presided over by the literary giant George Bernard Shaw. If I may identify myself as that 'future historian', the aim of this book is precisely to unearth the material history of this modern feminist magazine and to establish its 'importance' not only for its contribution to the political and cultural landscape of its day, but also for re-thinking our current critical narratives about both literature and feminism in Britain during the interwar period. The 'ceremony' at which Shaw officiated, as one of *Time and Tide*'s star contributors, marked a 'new chapter' in the history of the periodical following its move from Fleet Street to Bloomsbury in May that year (8 Nov 1929: 1332). From its unapologetic feminism of the early 1920s *Time and Tide* had begun to rebrand itself as a less woman-focused, general-audience review, and by the end of its second decade there was very little, on the surface, to distinguish it from such male-edited rivals as the *New Statesman and Nation*.[2] Concluding its house-warming feature *Time and Tide* asks: 'And will it matter so much, in a hundred years' time, whether the review was founded by men or women?' (1334). The question speaks to the public attention *Time and Tide* attracted as a paper known to be directed and staffed by women, and is characteristic of the periodical's tendency to downplay sexual difference. As we shall see, an equalitarian feminist emphasis on women's common humanity with men (which tended to submerge the category of 'women') informed a great many of *Time and Tide*'s strategies and manoeuvres as it worked to secure its position among the leading weekly reviews. But for historians today (nearly one hundred years on as I write) it does matter immensely that *Time and Tide* was founded by women. As the only female-controlled periodical of its kind it is unique in the history of Britain's periodical press, and as such it is a landmark for both feminist and cultural histories of the interwar period.

Launched on 14 May 1920 *Time and Tide* was the brainchild of the Welsh suffragette Lady Rhondda (1883–1958), a wealthy businesswoman who inherited her title and business interests (principally, in coalmining, shipping, and newspapers) from her father, the industrialist and Liberal politician David Alfred Thomas (John 2013: 14–15). As Rhondda narrates in later accounts, ever since she was a small child she had wanted to edit a newspaper, and by her early twenties she knew that it was a weekly review she wanted to edit, for though 'read by comparatively few people [. . .] they are the people who count, the people of influence' (Lejeune 1956: 11). In the autumn of 1918, as she surveyed the wreckage caused by the First World War and considered how narrowly civilisation had escaped complete destruction, Rhondda's ambition to edit a weekly paper that would 'change customs and [. . .] influence ideas' was renewed (Rhondda 1933: 300–1). She first discussed her idea for a new periodical with Mrs Chalmers Watson, founder and first commandant of the Women's Army Auxiliary Corps (WAAC) and with whom Rhondda had worked in the Ministry of National Service during the war. (Watson would become *Time and Tide*'s first chairman.) But as Angela V. John recounts, before establishing her paper Rhondda 'sought to expose the unfair treatment of women by the mainstream press' and organised a deputation of women, including the veteran feminist Elizabeth Robins, to protest to national newspaper owners 'about their coverage – or lack of it – in their papers' (John 2013: 292). In a letter circulated to papers including the *London Times*, *Daily Dispatch*, *Daily Sketch*, *Evening Standard*, *Sunday Chronicle*, *Sunday Herald* and *Daily Telegraph*, Rhondda's delegation was particularly concerned about the apparent backlash against women workers after the war, claiming that the press was turning public opinion against women workers and leading the government 'to get rid of women as quickly as possible, without reference either to the expedience or injustice of the methods employed' (Tusan 2005: 223).

This early engagement with leading newspapers is an important indication of the way that Rhondda and her core feminist collaborators would make the press itself a subject of ongoing debate in the pages of *Time and Tide*, not only regarding its coverage of women's issues, but also in terms of its responsibilities to the wider public. As Patrick Collier has discussed, the period after the war was marked by a perceived 'crisis in journalism' (2006: 11) following the so-called 'Northcliffe Revolution' which was seen to have transformed journalism 'from its imagined artistic or public service mission into the (feminine) realm of the commodity' (Collier 2007: 188–9). In various ways *Time and Tide* repeatedly differentiated itself from women's newspapers and a feminised popular press. But as I show in this book, *Time and Tide*'s feminist writers and critics were also more optimistic about the mainstream press than many of their male contemporaries, and at key moments the periodical enthusiastically harnessed strategies used by popular newspapers both to advertise its name more widely and to campaign for a more serious and intelligent journalism for politically and culturally engaged readers. This modern feminist magazine thus challenges narratives of journalistic decline circulating in the interwar period, and in its willingness to embrace techniques identified with popular media forms evidences the continuation of an 'optimism about the power of mass market technologies and institutions to transform and rejuvenate contemporary culture' that Mark S. Morrisson identifies with an earlier, pre-war modernist moment (2001: 6). Indeed, for the woman journalist whose professional identity was closely tied to women's entry to modernity, opportunities for employment increased as the newspaper and periodical market expanded during the interwar years. However, as Sarah Lonsdale has documented, journalism in this period was still organised into very gendered spheres, and while by the outbreak of the Second World War women made up approximately 20 per cent of journalists (doubling their participation in mainstream journalism since the turn of the twentieth century) they were mostly employed by women's magazines, precariously freelance, or confined to the newspaper 'Women's Page' (Lonsdale 2018: 463).

As a periodical run by women but founded along more general-audience lines, *Time and Tide* negotiated a difficult tension from its very first issue over its feminist designation and association with the 'women's paper' category. As I discuss in Chapter 1, the periodical wore its feminism overtly during its early years, and relied on the support it drew from suffrage networks and other women's organisations to build its readership base. But from the beginning it sought to

extend beyond feminist audiences, and in its early marketing strategies the periodical also distinguished itself from its immediate feminist competitors and former suffrage organs, the *Woman's Leader*
and the *Vote*. As it expanded, *Time and Tide* continued to cater for
a core target group of (largely middle-class) women readers well into
the 1930s. But by 1928 (when women finally won the vote on equal
terms with men) *Time and Tide* was already accelerating its efforts
to move out of the women's paper category. As I show in Chapter 4,
Time and Tide's disavowal of the 'feminist' and 'women's' label was
necessary for the periodical's expansion into a new marketplace in
the field of political journalism and public affairs; rebranding itself
as a leading 'journal of opinion' it firmly secured a place among
the most prestigious weekly reviews of its day (a position it would
retain throughout the Second World War and beyond). *Time and
Tide*'s reorientation has been seen negatively in early accounts of the
periodical which suggest that 'in the 1930s [its] feminism gradually
faded away' (Doughan and Sanchez 1987: 45). However, it is my
chief argument in this book that, despite surface appearances, feminism remained a central motivating and shaping force on *Time and
Tide*'s editorial policy and content. Even when, by the late 1930s, the
periodical most visibly distanced itself from feminist organisations
and women's genres it had by no means abandoned its feminist principles, and it remained committed to the ordinary intelligent woman
reader it addressed from its earliest years.

As such this book contributes to recent revisionary scholarship
that challenges the 'narratives of "failure and disappointment"'
which figure so prominently in the history of interwar feminism
(DiCenzo 2014: 423). While the disappearance of an overt feminism
from *Time and Tide*'s pages in the second half of the 1930s has often
been read as evidence for these demise narratives, a closer and more
sympathetic analysis of this periodical reveals a picture much more
complex.[3] As Maria DiCenzo observes, 'critics have underestimated
the extent to which the concerted efforts of feminists met with sustained opposition' (2014: 423), and this opposition became particularly pronounced as *Time and Tide* moved into the traditionally male
territory of foreign policy and international affairs. As I discuss in
Chapters 5 and 8, the periodical's more international focus in the
1930s is reflective of a wider shift among feminists after the war
'to argue for the importance of [women's] presence, influence and
input in international and world affairs' (Gottlieb 2010: 102), but
to preserve women's participation in this sphere it was necessary for
Time and Tide's female political journalists to work without drawing

attention to their sex, often by writing anonymously. That *Time and Tide* did establish itself as a platform for women to 'influence ideas', however invisibly, on such important issues as war and peace is, however, incredibly important. As Benny Morris states, in a study of the British weekly press during the 1930s, the weekly reviews were 'influential in moulding public opinion and that public opinion affected, and was reflected in, the foreign policy of the National Government. In this respect, the quality weekly press was of especial importance inasmuch as it influenced and reflected the thinking of the nation's intellectual and political elite' (1991: 1). Morris's study of the attitudes of the British weekly and Sunday papers towards Nazi Germany during the 1930s is a rare example of scholarship that includes the female-edited *Time and Tide* among its range of sources. As Maria DiCenzo and Leila Ryan observe, in most historical scholarship there is 'a tendency to ghettoize feminist media [. . .] limiting the scope and impact of these discursive arenas and obscuring their contribution to wider political discourses' (2007: 248). While it is beyond the scope of this book to evaluate in any detail *Time and Tide*'s contribution to political debates in such an extremely complex period of international history, the periodical's importance in this sphere should not be ignored. As DiCenzo further notes, even in feminist historical scholarship 'international and peace movement activities after the war are often regarded [. . .] as part of the fragmentation process rather than an extension of the feminist movement' (2014: 438, note 25). But *Time and Tide*'s reorientation towards international movements and causes was for its feminist core collaborators a natural extension of their rights as global as well as national citizens, and, I argue, entirely consistent with the feminist agenda espoused by the periodical from its earliest years.

That feminist agenda belonged squarely to an equal rights tradition and was pursued vigorously in *Time and Tide*'s pages during its early years. Articles on topics ranging from women's education and employment, to marriage, motherhood and birth control, along with the ongoing campaign for equal franchise, evidence 'the proliferation of issues and changing opportunities confronting feminists after the war (DiCenzo 2014: 422).[4] A vehicle for feminist news and comment *Time and Tide* was also a key platform for major debates in interwar feminism, most notably the debate between 'Old' and 'New' feminists which was conducted in the pages of *Time and Tide* and its competitor the *Woman's Leader*.[5] It is not my primary purpose in this book, however, to analyse *Time and Tide*'s constitutive role in, and mediation of, feminism as a social movement. While I do discuss (in Chapter 1) *Time and Tide*'s launch of Britain's leading equalitarian feminist organisation in the interwar years, the Six Point Group, my focus throughout is directed more towards the ways in which the presentation of *Time and Tide*'s feminism adapted in accordance with the redefinition of the periodical's own goals and changing external circumstances, and in relation to the multiple readerships it sought to reach. As such, my discussion of *Time and Tide* is influenced by key insights and methodologies developed in the field of modern periodical studies as well as feminist media history. Lucy Delap, in her work on *Time and Tide*'s feminist precursor, the *Freewoman*, uses the term 'periodical community' to refer to the 'material, cultural, and intellectual milieu of a periodical or group of related periodicals' (2000: 234), and Jason Harding (2002), in his study of T. S. Eliot's *Criterion*, has also emphasised the importance of attending to the interactions between periodicals and periodical networks to interpret any single magazine. In each part of this book I pay attention to *Time and Tide*'s close interdependence, and competition, within a changing set of interlocking periodical networks (from feminist papers and socialist media to intellectual weeklies and elite literary journals) as the periodical worked to secure its status as Britain's only female-controlled weekly review and to address both men and women readers. In the feature on Shaw's visit to *Time and Tide*'s new Bloomsbury offices, quoted above, *Time and Tide* states that '[a] weekly review is also a social animal' (8 Nov 1929: 1332), a reminder that when we're dealing with periodicals we're concerned not only with printed words and image on a page, but also with living, breathing organisms with complex social structures. By attending to *Time and Tide*'s networks and core personnel I also restore to view its unique female culture which, indirectly as well as directly, brought a feminist perspective to bear upon the periodical.

This female culture was nowhere more prominent in the pages of *Time and Tide* than in the visibility it afforded to a network of modern women writers spanning pre- and post-war generations. One of *Time and Tide*'s first directors was the famous suffrage playwright and actress Elizabeth Robins, who as well as informing editorial policy provided contacts and advice on literary matters.[6] By 1923 *Time and Tide* had recruited two more well-known literary figures from the women's suffrage movement, Cicely Hamilton and Rebecca West, both of whom would be among the periodical's longest-serving board members.[7] Hamilton, co-author of the famous suffrage play *How the Vote Was Won* (1909), became a close friend of Rhondda and wrote regularly for the paper throughout the interwar years.[8]

West, formerly the literary editor of the *Freewoman*, was *Time and Tide*'s first drama critic and would play a significant role in *Time and Tide*'s expansion into the literary highbrow sphere, as will be discussed in Chapter 4. In the mid-1920s, two modern women writers of a post-suffrage generation joined *Time and Tide*'s board of directors: Winifred Holtby, the novelist and journalist whose best-known work *South Riding* was published posthumously in 1936, and E. M. Delafield, author of the bestselling *Diary of a Provincial Lady* (1930) which was first serialised in *Time and Tide*. Each played an instrumental role in the development of *Time and Tide*'s political and lighter content respectively, as will be discussed in Chapters 5 and 6. Another very significant staff writer from the early years was the socialist poet and children's author Eleanor Farjeon, whose weekly column of topical verse (published under the pseudonym 'Chimaera') was a much-loved feature and had a shaping influence on the periodical's identity (see Chapter 2). As well as contributions from these key figures *Time and Tide* published creative work (including short fiction, sketches and poems) by a large number of women writers, some familiar, many forgotten or neglected. They include: Valentine Ackland, Rose Allatini, Iris Barry, Stella Benson, Elizabeth Bowen, Kay Boyle, Frances Cornford, Richmal Crompton, Helen Cruickshank, E. M. Delafield, Susan Ertz, Eleanor Farjeon, Helen Friedlaender, Stella Gibbons, Susan Glaspell, Beatrice Harraden, Winifred Holtby, Pamela Hansford Johnson, Marganita Laski, Louisa I. Lumsden, Sylvia Lynd, Cynthia Maguire, Ethel Mannin, Viola Meynell, 'Susan Miles,' Naomi Mitchison, Kate O'Brien, Hilda Reid, Jean Rhys, Mary Richardson, May Sarton, Helen Simpson, Margaret Stanley-Wrench, Sylvia Thompson, Grace Tollemache, Doreen Wallace, Sylvia Townsend Warner, Vera Wentworth, Dorothy Whipple, Vita Sackville-West, E. H. Young and E. Ayrton Zangwill.

This long roll call of names illustrates *Time and Tide*'s gravitational pull for women writers representing a range of political and aesthetic interests. From suffrage and socialist networks, and from 'high' and 'middlebrow' spheres, they are a reminder of authors 'left in the wide margin of the [twentieth] century' as Raymond Williams puts it in his influential essay 'What Was Modernism?' (1989: 35). In light of the continuing sway that modernism holds in current literary scholarship, another of my central arguments is that an analysis of the cultural politics of this modern feminist magazine necessitates a re-thinking of our critical frameworks for mapping British literary culture in the interwar period. As will become clear in the course of this book, modernism was not a primary concern in *Time and*

Tide's arts pages, but this does not mean that the periodical was uninterested in its movements. In early fiction reviews *Time and Tide* responded to the literary experimentation of Katherine Mansfield, Dorothy Richardson and Virginia Woolf, and in 1928 it solicited contributions from Britain's leading female modernists in fiction and poetry respectively, Woolf and Edith Sitwell. As I discuss in Chapter 4, *Time and Tide* actively contributed to staging what Bonnie Kime Scott describes as the 'second rise of modernism' identified with 'the women of 1928' (1995: xxxvii), and forged important links with Woolf and Bloomsbury in this year. But the periodical was also an important publicity vehicle for women writers working outside the parameters of modernism, at a time when the processes of canon formation were already consecrating a small group of modernist male authors. In January 1927 *Time and Tide* inaugurated a new sub-division in the paper under the heading 'Miscellany' which, I argue in Chapter 6, created and legitimised a place for the 'feminine middlebrow' and, as well as promoting many of the authors listed above, offered publishing space to aspiring women writers. *Time and Tide*'s wide and inclusive approach to literary culture in this period contrasts with the narrow and exclusive editorial practices of such influential literary reviews as T. S. Eliot's *Criterion/New Criterion* (1922–39), Edgell Rickword's *Calendar of Modern Letters* (1925–7), and the Cambridge quarterly *Scrutiny* (1932–53) edited by F. R. and Q. D. Leavis. A participant in what Christopher Hilliard has described as the 'democratization of writing in Britain' (2006) *Time and Tide* is a rich archive for exploring contested models of authorship (both 'professional' and 'amateur') and calls into question existing definitions of literary value.

As Collier has observed, much of the expanded field of modern periodical studies 'has remained conceptually framed by aesthetic modernism', leaving 'much larger, nonmodernist locales of the vast landscape of early twentieth-century print culture' invisible or underexplored (2015: 95; 99). As one such 'nonmodernist locale' *Time and Tide* opens up the field of literary production in this era substantially. It also opens up the field of literary criticism. In a compelling discussion of Rebecca West's critical book, *The Strange Necessity* (1929) Laura Heffernan asks: 'What would it mean to position West as a forgotten critic of modernism? How might we think about the institutional formation of modernism as eclipsing not only literary styles, but alternative modes of interpretation and critical practice?' (2008: 310). In Chapter 4 I identify a series of essays West wrote for *Time and Tide* between 1928 and 1930 as a neglected archive of feminist modernist criticism in which her deliberate use of the personal voice resists T. S. Eliot's famous doctrine of impersonality. But in this book, I also make newly visible the contributions to *Time and Tide*'s review pages of even more sorely neglected women reviewers and critics, whose writing on music, theatre, film and literature further supports Heffernan's point that 'New Critical reading practices emerged as but one mode of interpretation among many' (312). In Chapter 3 I revisit the well-known 'Classicism versus Romanticism' debate through the columns of one of *Time and Tide*'s regular staff writers, Christopher St John (née Christabel Marshall), and show how John Middleton Murry's 'Romantic' principles of criticism were more amenable to *Time and Tide*'s feminist mediation of culture than the 'Classical' principles espoused by Eliot. Also in this chapter, I examine the early fiction reviews contributed by poet Sylvia Lynd and novelists Rose Macaulay and Naomi Royde-Smith, which, engaging in a contemporary debate about pleasure (recently examined by Laura Frost), unsettle cultural hierarchies in modernist criticism. It was, of course, precisely during the interwar period that the institutions of modernism secured this movement's cultural ascendancy and academic institutionalisation, and *Time and Tide*'s writers and critics were not unaware of modernist critical discourses. The periodical's conversation with modernism thus not only highlights the limits of modernism as a lens for assessing culture in the interwar period, but also the perspicuity of its key staff writers who 'talked back' to the very modernist paradigms by which they would themselves be eclipsed.

The contest between different systems of literary value reached its zenith in the early 1930s in what Virginia Woolf famously described as the 'Battle of the Brows'.[9] As I discuss in Chapter 6, *Time and Tide* steered an ingenious course through these debates, and succeeded, during the years of its expansion, in straddling both 'high' and 'middlebrow' spheres. At the same time the quick succession of the periodical's first two literary editors, R. Ellis Roberts (1933–4), a critic in the belles-lettres tradition, and John Beevers (1934–5), a recent graduate of Queens College, Cambridge, registers the difficult balance *Time and Tide* tried to strike as it negotiated what Melba Cuddy-Keane describes as 'an increasing gap between professional study and the general public' (2003: 1). As Josephine M. Guy and Ian Small have discussed, the first decades of the twentieth century saw the gradual professionalisation of literary criticism, as the critical authority of the Victorian 'man of letters' began to give way to that of the academic specialist or 'expert' in the institutionalisation of English literature as a university subject (2000: 378). *Time and Tide* provides fertile ground for an exploration of growing tensions between 'amateur' and 'professional' modes of criticism in the inter-war period, and in Part Three of this book I examine the significant contribution made to the periodical by another neglected female critic, Theodora Bosanquet. A highbrow intellectual and author-ity on Henry James (she served as his amanuensis during the last years of his life) Bosanquet was *Time and Tide*'s literary editor from 1935 to 1943. As I discuss in Chapter 7, Bosanquet was also, from 1933, the close companion of *Time and Tide*'s political editor, Lady Rhondda, and the new partnership forged between the two women is a further example of the strong female culture which continued to underpin and shape this modern feminist magazine. Indeed, as I show in Chapter 8, while *Time and Tide*'s book criticism under Bosan-quet's literary editorship appears to conform to male professional standards (significantly, in early 1935 the periodical began issuing a monthly Double University Number in addition to its monthly Lit-erary Supplements) a fascinating unpublished archive of automatic writing Bosanquet produced in association with her reviewing for the periodical reveals an unorthodox practice beneath. Further evi-dence of the female and feminist perspective that continued to shape the paper even as it avoided the feminist label, this material also demonstrates *Time and Tide*'s occupation of what Carol Atherton describes as an 'ambivalent space between the values of the amateur and the institutional status of the professional' in this period (2005: 6) that questions the authority of the university to be the sole arbiter and distributor of knowledge.

As Anne Fernald and Jane Garrity have each argued, in recent issues of *Modern Fiction Studies* and *Literature Compass* respec-tively, academic scholarship on the first decades of the twentieth century has continued to display a 'lack of serious interest in women writers' (Fernald 2013: 229), a marginalisation that can be linked to a 'larger cultural disenchantment with feminism' (Garrity 2013: 16). The history of *Time and Tide*'s reception in historical and literary scholarship loudly evidences a persistent reluctance to redraw the map of Britain's early twentieth-century landscape in favour of rec-ognising women as full participants in the politics and culture of this period as feminists, activists, writers, journalists and critics. Despite the best efforts of Rhondda and her core collaborators, the periodi-cal has not enjoyed its rightful place at the centre of media history or modern periodical studies where it has been overshadowed by modernist 'little magazines' including short-lived experiments like

Blast. This book, the first in-depth study of *Time and Tide*, aims to fill this gap.[10] Along the way individual chapters take up some key issues in interwar feminist and cultural history, from debates about work and professionalism (Chapters 1, 2 and 7) to women's responses to war and fascism (Chapters 5 and 8), and from modernism's 'problem with pleasure' (Chapter 3) to the cultures of literary celebrity (Chapter 4), middlebrow culture (Chapter 6), and radical 'modernist commitments' (Chapter 7). These chapters are not, however, designed to stand alone, but contribute to a larger narrative arc exploring the feminist and cultural politics of this important modern magazine. As such the book is organised chronologically in three parts, tracing *Time and Tide*'s evolution from its 'Early Years' as an overtly feminist magazine (Chapters 1 to 3, 1920–8), to its 'Expansion' and rebranding in the late 1920s as a more general-audience weekly review (Chapters 4 to 6, 1928–35), and, finally, to its 'Reorientation' in the mid-1930s in response to a world in crisis (Chapters 7 and 8, 1935–9). Unarguably *Time and Tide* is one of the richest archives for exploring British feminism and women's writing between the wars, and it would be impossible in one book to examine all its fascinating aspects. But it is my hope that readers will also find this book a necessary resource for pursuing the many new avenues of enquiry it opens up.

Notes

1. *Time and Tide* 8 November 1929: 1332. Further references to the periodical will be provided parenthetically in the text.
2. The *New Statesman* was founded by Shaw in 1913 with Beatrice and Sidney Webb, and absorbed the Liberal *Nation and Athenaeum* in 1931.
3. Susan Kent, for example, reproduces the line taken by Doughan and Sanchez, writing that '*Time and Tide* by the 1930s had so lost its feminist perspective that it could run a regular weekly feature under the heading "Men and Books," to which such writers as Cicely Hamilton and Elizabeth Robins contributed' (1993: 125).
4. The women's suffrage movement won a partial victory in 1918 when, under the Representation of the People Act, women over the age of thirty were able to vote if they were householders, the wives of householders, occupiers of property with an annual rent of £5 or more, or graduates of British universities. It was not until 2 July 1928 that women, when they reached the age of twenty-one, could vote on equal terms with men (Purvis and Holton 2000: 3–4).

5. See Maria DiCenzo with Alexis Motuz (2016) for a discussion of this debate.

6. The General Correspondence files in the Elizabeth Robins papers contain letters from Rhondda and *Time and Tide*'s first editor, Vera Laughton, showing that Robins provided connections with such figures as Alice Meynell, Rose Macaulay and Margaret Macnamara, and that she acted as literary advisor on poetry submitted to the periodical.

7. West joined *Time and Tide*'s board of directors in 1922; both she and Hamilton are listed in a notice of *Time and Tide*'s directors printed in the periodical in its issue of 27 July 1923 (750). According to auditors' reports preserved among Rebecca West's papers at the University of Tulsa, Hamilton was still serving on *Time and Tide*'s board of directors in the mid-1940s, while West remained on the board until 1958, the year of Rhondda's death.

8. See Lis Whitelaw (1990) on Hamilton's friendship with Rhondda.

9. Woolf uses the phrase in her letter written but never sent to the *New Statesman and Nation* in 1932. See Melba Cuddy-Keane (2003: 22–34) for a discussion of this essay.

10. The only volume dealing exclusively with *Time and Tide* is Dale Spender's *Time and Tide Wait for No Man* (1984), an edited anthology of articles published in the periodical during the 1920s. Other discussions of *Time and Tide* include Alberti (1994b); Clay (2006; 2009; 2010; 2011; 2018); DiCenzo with Motuz (2016); Dowson (2009); Green (2017); Alvin Sullivan (1986, vol. 4); Melissa Sullivan (2011).

Part I

The Early Years,
1920-1928

Chapter 1

A New Feminist Venture: Work, Professionalism and the Modern Woman

Time and Tide made its first appearance before the public on 14 May 1920 and attracted a high degree of media interest; both national and provincial newspapers complimented the new weekly on its independent outlook, its interesting and readable content, and its fine list of contributors.[1] Curiosity in the new venture was aroused particularly by its all-female board of directors; as one contemporary reader later recalled, '[a]s a journalistic innovation made exclusively by women the experiment intrigued us' (Brittain 1940: 142). This perception that *Time and Tide* was doing something new in contemporary journalism is important. According to its founder, Lady Rhondda, *Time and Tide* was 'a paper of a class that has never been run by women before', and from the outset it sought to distinguish itself not only from mainstream organs of the press but from other feminist periodicals too.[2] Yet, for all its appearance as a new feminist venture, in the history of feminist publishing *Time and Tide* in fact drew on a long tradition of periodicals run by women, including 'movement and advocacy papers, avant-garde periodicals, literary reviews aimed at feminist readers, and more' (Green 2009: 191). The early years of the twentieth century saw an upsurge of feminist periodicals published in association with the women's suffrage movement, and many of *Time and Tide*'s first contributors were drawn from these periodical networks. As this chapter will show, *Time and Tide*'s early promoters were keenly aware of their competitors in the feminist periodical market and savvy in their use of existing traditions at the same time as they departed from them. Michael North reminds us that '[t]o innovate is, in Latin at any rate, to renew or to reform, not to start over afresh', and arguably peri-odicals have a particularly strong purchase on what North describes as 'the complex nature of the new' (2013: 3; 69). As Faith Binckes discusses:

> The very periodicity of magazines implies a textual culture with an almost infinite capacity to renew itself and an equally prodigious capacity to reproduce itself. It is hard to imagine a form more suited to the construction of newness, but a newness consistently contested, competitive and remade. (2010: 55)

Time and Tide was remarkably adept at reinventing itself over the course of its long lifespan; during its first two decades, this modern feminist magazine repeatedly updated and renewed its image, and worked competitively to extend into new markets. In the opening section of the present chapter I examine *Time and Tide*'s 'construc-tion of newness' in the context of early twentieth-century feminist print culture, and explore the ways in which it established its mod-ern identity as a successor to an earlier feminist press. In particular, I begin to grapple with the paradoxical idea that the 'new' thing that *Time and Tide* was doing was to disavow identification with the 'feminist' or 'women's periodical' category at the same time as it remained both of these things. Ambitious to compete with the lead-ing intellectual weeklies of its day (papers such as the *New States-man* and the *Nation and Athenaeum*) *Time and Tide* succeeded in overtaking its immediate competitors in the feminist periodical mar-ket, and worked actively from the outset to address male as well as female readers. Discussing women's suffrage print media Maria DiCenzo has argued that 'the tendency to focus on a "separate press" that spoke to and for women has obscured how actively these publications sought to address a wider readership which included men' (2011: 83), and in the second section of this chapter I examine the editorial and textual strategies through which *Time and Tide* expanded its reach beyond female and feminist audiences. The chap-ter concludes with reference to a series of articles contributed pseud-onymously by the periodical's new editor in 1926, and demonstrates just how sophisticated *Time and Tide* was in exploiting modern media forms and techniques to circulate its name more widely, and make its own interventions in public debates about work, profes-sionalism and the 'modern woman'.

Feminist networks and cultures of the new

In its first leading article *Time and Tide* stated that: 'Only one thing surely can justify the production of a newspaper – that those responsible for it are convinced that there is a definite gap in the ranks of the Press which none of the present organs are able to fill.' It went on:

> TIME AND TIDE has, in the view of its promoters, come into being to supply a definite need. The great whirlwind which has just passed has left us standing in a new and unknown world. It follows natu-rally enough that those who have served us as guides in the past are in certain directions ill equipped to help us understand our strange surroundings, or to supply the new needs which we find ourselves to have acquired. This is perhaps specially true of the Press; bred for the most part in Victorian or Edwardian days, tethered inevitably to its own past, it would often seem to find great difficulty in interpreting the changed conditions that lie – still but half realised – around us. (14 May 1920: 4)

In this bold, declarative paragraph *Time and Tide*'s 'promoters' announce the paper's arrival in the periodical marketplace in rhetoric resonant of the manifesto.[3] The language used is very modernistic ('new', 'unknown', 'strange', 'half realised') and registers the politi-cal and social uncertainties of a landscape defamiliarised by the First World War. Occupying a world still traumatised by the 'great whirl-wind' which has just passed, *Time and Tide* stakes its claim to 'supply a definite need' by asserting its newness against the existing Press which, 'tethered [. . .] to its own past', is stuck in outworn Victorian or Edwardian attitudes and conventions. Through this act of differ-entiation *Time and Tide* constructed its newness. But the leader was much more circumspect about the most obvious thing that set *Time and Tide* apart from other organs of the press: the fact that it was controlled, edited and staffed entirely by women. Asserting that there is 'a demand to-day for a more independent Press' it continued:

> That the group behind this paper is composed entirely of women has already been frequently commented upon. It would be possible to lay too much emphasis upon the fact. The binding link between these people is not primarily their common sex. On the other hand, this fact is not without its significance. (4)

The see-saw rhythm of this prose reveals a key tension at the heart of *Time and Tide*'s first address to the public and one that the periodical would continue to negotiate over the next two decades: a tension between its unavoidable identification with women and its desire to escape the limitations of that category.

Unpublished evidence reveals that considerable work went into striking the right balance with this first leader in order not to lay 'too much emphasis' on women. In a letter to Elizabeth Robins dated 30 April 1920, Margaret Rhondda enclosed a draft of the leader asking her to 'please deal firmly with it from every point of view' and explaining that she was most concerned about 'whether I have stressed women too much at the end'.[4] Four days later Rhondda thanked Robins for correcting the leader which, revised further 'with a view to less emphasis on women', had now met with the general approval of the Board.[5] *Time and Tide*'s decision not to emphasise women was a significant departure from earlier feminist and suffrage periodicals such as the *Woman's Leader* and the *Englishwoman* which, as their titles indicate, deliberately framed their identities and goals in terms of representing women's interests and concerns. Deliberately avoiding the 'feminist' or 'women's' tag the leader constructed *Time and Tide* as a paper which, as it went on to state, 'is in fact concerned neither specially with men nor specially with women, but with human beings' (4). However, this framing of *Time and Tide* in gender-neutral terms also reveals the periodical's connections with suffrage print culture. As Cheryl Law summarises: 'Suffragists had struggled to escape from the confinements of the "woman's sphere" and establish that the interests of men and women were identical in order to accord women the right to an equal place in the world. This had been the purpose of the feminists' insistence on their designation as "human beings" in order to claim their rights' (1997: 166). *Time and Tide*'s assertion of newness is thus carefully balanced with an awareness of the actual heritage of feminist periodical publishing it was building on. Both participating in and distancing itself from the women's movement and a separate press for women, from the start *Time and Tide* navigated a difficult tension over its feminist designation, one that it would continue to negotiate well into its second decade.

Time and Tide's direct debt to the women's suffrage movement was manifest at multiple levels of the periodical's first issue. Among the seven directors listed on the back of its opening number was one of the most inspirational figures of the women's suffrage campaign, the aforementioned Elizabeth Robins. Rhondda had also been an active member of the Women's Social and Political Union (WSPU), as had another of *Time and Tide*'s first directors, Helen Archdale, a Scottish militant who had worked previously on the WSPU paper, the *Suffragette*, and would become *Time and Tide*'s editor until 1926.[6] Another veteran of the women's suffrage movement, Cicely Hamilton, joined *Time and Tide*'s board of directors in 1921; Rebecca West, one of the best-known names in feminist journalism and literary editor before the war of the avant-garde feminist magazine the *Freewoman*, joined the Board in 1922.[7] Many of the periodical's early contributors were also drawn from suffrage networks. Among those listed in the contents bill of the first issue were the poet and essayist Alice Meynell, and Christopher St John (Christabel Marshall), co-author with Cicely Hamilton of the famous suffrage play, *How the Vote Was Won* (1909). A significant amount of creative work published in *Time and Tide* was contributed by writers who had been active in the women's suffrage movement (Clay 2009: 21–2), including male supporters of the cause such as Laurence Housman and Gerald Gould. In appearance and content, too, *Time and Tide* had much in common with the official suffrage organs. Its strong feminist mandate was evident in the prominence afforded in its pages to the ongoing campaign for equal franchise as well as other feminist issues (ranging from education, employment and equal pay, to the rights of married women, child welfare and birth control) and even more minor features in the paper point to feminist intertexual relationships.[8] 'Time Table', a weekly calendar of political and cultural events, echoes Robins's collection of writings on the women's movement, *Way Stations* (1913) which was organised under section headings 'Time Tables'. 'In the Tideway', a weekly news comment column in the style of titbits, first appeared as 'Under the Clock', recalling the famous 'Votes for Women' clock outside the WSPU's flagship shop at 156 Charing Cross Road (Murray 2000: 206–7), then as 'Echoes and Re-Echoes', literally reproducing the title ('Echoes') of a regular column in the *Englishwoman*.

Time and Tide thus drew extensively on the networks, material cultures and iconography of women's suffrage. At the same time, further unpublished evidence shows that from the start *Time and Tide* sought to do things differently by reducing the emphasis on women seen in the former suffrage organs. For example, with reference to its regular 'Personalities and Powers' feature which used the illustrated biographical sketch to discuss 'women as well as men of achievement' (14 May 1920: 7), Rhondda stated explicitly in a letter to Robins that 'we don't want only women'.[9] Another regular feature from the first issue, 'The World Over', created space for an international feminist perspective but this feature was not always focused on women.[10] That *Time and Tide* deliberately sought to differentiate itself from what its directors perceived as the narrower, propagandist slant of the official suffrage organs is thrown into sharp relief when we compare the Prospectus of *Time and Tide* with that of its chief competitor in the feminist periodical market, the *Woman's Leader*. The first issue of the *Woman's Leader* appeared just three months before *Time and Tide*, in February 1920, and was successor to the *Common Cause*, the official organ of the National Union of Women's Suffrage Societies (NUWSS) which had been reconstituted in March 1919 as the National Union of Societies for Equal Citizenship (NUSEC). Rhondda had served on the board of the *Common Cause* from 1918, but resigned early in 1920 after criticising the way the paper was run (Tusan 2005: 223). By this time her own plans for a rival publication were well underway, and in February 1920 *Time and Tide*'s Prospectus was being fully discussed by its board of directors.[11] Meanwhile, the *Woman's Leader* was reframing its agenda, and in its Prospectus declared that the 'official connection' that existed formerly between the *Woman's Leader* and the NUWSS/NUSEC had been 'discontinued by mutual agreement in order that the paper may reach a wider public' (16 Apr 1920: 256). As DiCenzo notes, the *Woman's Leader* was one of several periodicals which 'began as suffrage organs, but went on to embrace issues beyond enfranchisement' (2011: 45). However, the unofficial connections that remained between the *Woman's Leader* and the NUSEC are precisely what *Time and Tide* renounced in the way that it framed its own identity and goals. While the Prospectus of the *Woman's Leader* went on to explain that the journal would 'continue to promote the objects and programme of the National Union of Societies for Equal Citizenship' and 'follow its general lines and policy on those questions which affect the status and opportunities of women' (256), *Time and Tide*'s Prospectus made no reference to women as a special category, stating simply that it would 'deal with all interesting topics of the day in Politics, Industry, and Art' (14 May 1920: 24).

In the initial framing of its identity and goals, therefore, *Time and Tide* deliberately neutralised the strong connections it actually had with the women's movement. However, within months of its first issue the periodical's directors changed direction following a decision made in the summer of 1920 to 'make a more definite appeal to women, be more frankly feminist than we have yet been'.[12] The prime motivator for this change of editorial policy was financial, with the running costs of the magazine (far in excess of initial forecasts) necessitating a drive to increase circulation.[13] But, as Rhondda's letters to

Robins reveal, *Time and Tide*'s core collaborators had already been discussing a 'Women's Programme' which Rhondda hoped would give the periodical 'a big boom'.[14] This 'Programme' was made public on 19 November 1920 in a leading article which outlined 'six much needed reforms, which especially concern women as women, and which they themselves must press for if they want them settled' (560). As *Time and Tide* later confirmed, the 'Programme' was the genesis of the Six Point Group (SPG), Britain's leading equal rights feminist organisation of the interwar years.[15] Drawing much support from readers it provided *Time and Tide* with a clear feminist manifesto absent from early numbers of the paper, and played a crucial role in increasing *Time and Tide*'s readership base.[16] Winning the support of twenty-four major women's organisations including the National Union of Women's Teachers and the Federation of Women Civil Servants (Eoff 1991: 70), the programme also attracted attention in the national press.[17] *Time and Tide*'s change of direction is evidence of the periodical's ability to capitalise on the dynamism of the interwar women's movement through effective feminist marketing; the Six Point Group appears to have provided the magazine with an identifiable 'cause' to sell to potential feminist audiences. It is also evidence of *Time and Tide*'s rivalry with other feminist periodicals. As Johanna Alberti remarks, Rhondda 'must surely have known that the NUSEC was also working towards six points, and that there was a striking similarity in the two programmes' (1989: 139). In June 1921 Rhondda faced-off a proposal from Ray Strachey, editor of the *Woman's Leader*, to amalgamate the two journals, and, in a revealing glimpse of the competition between feminist periodicals, concluded: 'I'm all for carrying on as we are. I believe we can beat Mrs Strachey every time.'[18] Rhondda was right. The *Woman's Leader* struggled to increase its subscription base and over the next few years gradually shrank in size and circulation as *Time and Tide* increased in prestige and influence.[19]

Overtaking the *Woman's Leader*, *Time and Tide* thus emerged as the leader of the feminist periodicals. The *Englishwoman* also appears to have been squeezed out of the market at round this time; it published its final issue in January 1921.[20] A large part of *Time and Tide*'s success was its ability to appeal to women representing a wide range of political and personal interests. The early agenda of the Six Point Group programme brought together two major strands in the post-war women's movement, equal rights and welfare feminism, and alongside this *Time and Tide* deployed tactics from the commercial end of women's periodical publishing in order to make its 'more definite appeal to women'. For example, on 19 January 1923 *Time and Tide* launched a series of Six Point Group Supplements, and in the same issue introduced a new competition feature with cash prizes, a staple of mass-market women's magazines.[21] In May 1923 *Time and Tide* reported 'a continual and steady rise in its circulation' (11 May 1923: 487), and by the mid-1920s the journal had become very attractive to advertisers who saw *Time and Tide*'s largely middle-class female readership as a lucrative target group for marketing a range of commodity products (Clay 2011). With the addition on *Time and Tide*'s board of directors from 1926 of Miss Marion Jean Lyon, advertising manager of *Punch*, *Time and Tide* became increasingly savvy in marketing itself among new and larger audiences, as will be discussed in Chapter 4.[22] But what also emerges from an analysis of *Time and Tide*'s early years is that its core target audience was an expanding class of professional working women, and arguably even more important than the links *Time and Tide* sustained with women's suffrage periodical networks were the new connections it created with what Alice Staveley (2008) identifies as an as yet virtually unexplored genre of women's interwar publishing, the women's professional magazine.

Print organs of women's employment organisations, women's 'professional' or 'trade' magazines flourished after the 1919 Sex Disqualification (Removal) Act opened up the professions for the first time to women. They include such titles as the *Woman Teacher* (1919) of the National Union of Women Teachers (NUWT), the *Woman Clerk* (1919) of the Association of Women Clerks and Secretaries (AWKS), and *Opportunity* (1921) of the Federation of Women Civil Servants (FWCS). *Time and Tide* actively promoted itself in these magazines, advertising in their pages, and forming alliances with the organisations they represented. For example, an advertisement in the *Woman Teacher* for *Time and Tide*'s special Programme number in January 1921 bore the strapline 'Women Teachers – Support the Paper which Supports You' (21 Jan 1921: 128), and, in an article printed in its organ *Opportunity*, the FWCS agreed to advise the Six Point Group on 'all matters connected with equal pay and conditions in the Civil Service' (Mar 1921: 27). Perhaps the most striking relationship is that which was established between *Time and Tide* and the *Woman Engineer* (1919), the quarterly organ of the Women's Engineering Society (WES), and arguably the most 'professional' product in this market.[23] The WES was founded in 1919 to protect the right to work of all women employed in the engineering trades during the war who were being routinely dismissed to make way for returning male engineers under the government's Restoration of Pre-War Practices Bill.[24] Its magazine was edited by the Society's secretary, Caroline Haslett, who as one of the first executive members of the Six Point Group inhabited the same feminist networks as Archdale and Rhondda. For several years the two periodicals regularly exchanged advertisements, suggestive of a far more symbiotic relationship than that between *Time and Tide* and any other women's professional magazine.[25] In the examples that follow I show how the *Woman Engineer* promoted *Time and Tide* in acts of representation which differentiated it from other organs of the feminist press, and offered a particular model of work and professionalism that resonated with *Time and Tide*'s own idea of the 'modern woman'.

Time and Tide placed an advertisement in the *Woman Engineer* in September 1921, less than a year after it first drew attention to the WES in its own columns.[26] Advertising itself as 'The Cheapest Fourpennyworth Published' it explicitly targeted women, stating: 'All women who wish for a clean and impartial review of current affairs should subscribe to "Time and Tide"' (105). Occupying a full half-page beneath the *Woman Engineer*'s main feature (an article on women compositors), the positioning of the advertisement is suggestive of a shared feminist discourse (the article is devoted to the 'difficulties' and 'possibilities' faced by industrial women). However, another item printed in the same issue deliberately removes the 'feminist' tag:

> We would commend to our subscribers the bright and progressive Weekly Review *Time and Tide* [. . .]. While not a 'feminist' paper, *Time and Tide* does manage to keep to the fore the fact that this world is made up of men *and* women [. . .] and in our opinion fills a very great need in our public life. (96)

The *Woman Engineer* was not alone in promoting *Time and Tide* within women's print culture while at the same time distinguishing it from other 'feminist papers'. A 'misunderstanding' which arose the following year in the pages of *Opportunity* also points to the growing perception within professional women's networks that *Time and Tide* was different from other feminist magazines. According to an item printed in its issue of November 1922, a reader had objected to a paragraph in the previous number which implied (by omission) that *Time and Tide* did not devote itself to the championship of women's causes. The editor of *Opportunity* justified its representation of the *Woman's Leader* and the *Vote* as 'the two "feminist" weeklies', explaining that: 'We have never regarded *Time and Tide* as belonging to that category. It does devote considerable space to women [. . .] but it is a publication on much wider lines, and on its literary and dramatic side should rank rather with general weeklies, *New Statesman* or *Saturday Review*' (126). Evidence that *Time and Tide* was already developing a reputation as a publication competitive with the leading 'general weeklies' of the day, these representations of *Time and Tide* in two professional women's magazines demonstrate how significant a role women's print media played in defining and differentiating between a variety of women's periodicals. The importance for *Time and Tide* of such promotional work within feminist print culture is further illustrated by two advertisements it placed in the *Woman Engineer* towards the end of 1925.

The first of these, printed on the inside back cover of the *Woman Engineer*'s September 1925 issue, boldly presents *Time and Tide* as 'The Modern Weekly for the Modern Woman' (Figure 1.1). Exploiting a media fascination with the 'modern woman' in the interwar

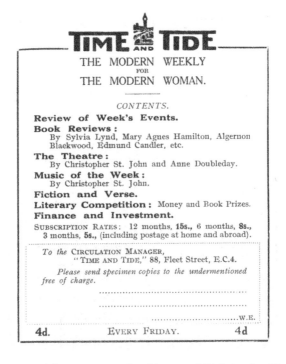

Figure 1.1 Advertisement for *Time and Tide* in the *Woman Engineer* Sep 1925. Reproduced with the permission of the Women's Engineering Society and the Institution of Engineering and Technology Archives.

popular press (Bingham 2004), this striking strapline also echoes a new title in the popular women's magazine market, *Modern Woman*, which published its first issue in June the same year. Among the most prominent of the so-called 'service magazines' which sprang up in the 1920s in imitation of the pre-eminent publication of this kind, *Good Housekeeping*, *Modern Woman* (with its subtitle 'the journal with the new spirit of the age') was launched 'to appeal to the new interest in all things modern, and particularly, the latest developments in the home' (Hackney 2008: 117). The intertextual relationship between this new publication and the advertisement *Time and Tide* placed in the *Woman Engineer* is a reminder of *Time and Tide*'s responsiveness to developments at the commercial as well as non-commercial end of women's periodical publishing. But it is the professional context of the *Woman Engineer*'s periodical environment that provides the symbolic grounding for the advertisement, and which sets *Time and Tide* apart from its competitors in the women's magazine market. In contrast with the domestic focus of commercial magazines, the *Woman Engineer* addressed readers as economic workers eager to seize new professional opportunities.[27] Significantly, the issue in which this advertisement appeared was a special number devoted to 'The First International Conference of Women in SCIENCE, INDUSTRY and COMMERCE' (Sep 1925: front cover) which had taken place at the British Empire Exhibition at Wembley in July that year. Caroline Haslett was the chief organiser of the conference (Messenger 1967: 37–8) which, as she stated in the leading article of the *Woman's Engineer*'s special issue, emphasised women's 'responsibility for service and citizenship in the world's work' (51–3). The issue also printed speeches given by a number of prominent women invited to speak at the conference, among them Lady Rhondda who used the platform to advocate commerce as a career for women.[28] In this context the 'modern woman' of *Time and Tide*'s strapline is imbued with a feminist discourse shared by both magazines in relation to new fields of work for women, emphasising a range of occupational and professional opportunities which extended beyond women's more traditional employment in the teaching profession and the civil service. *Time and Tide* also drew attention in its columns to the 'Women's Week at Wembley' (25 July 1924: 723) and published several articles in the summer and autumn of this year on the subject of business and commerce as new fields for university-educated women.

The advertisement for *Time and Tide* as 'The Modern Weekly for the Modern Woman' appeared in the *Woman Engineer*, however, only once; on the inside back cover of its next issue Haslett's magazine carried an advertisement with the more neutral strapline 'Read *Time and Tide*, the Non-Party Weekly' (Dec 1925). This removal of the woman-tag speaks, I suggest, to the continuing tension *Time and Tide* negotiated over its feminist designation and identification with the 'women's paper' category, but apparently, too, to a conversation taking place within these periodical communities about feminist strategies as well as goals. In the lead-up to the 'Women in Science, Industry and Commerce' conference Rhondda and Haslett were also discussing a new feminist enterprise, a 'Business and University Committee' set up by Rhondda and Professor Caroline Spurgeon, President of the International Federation of University Women (IFUW), to promote opportunities for university-educated women to enter commerce and business, and to which Haslett became Honorary Secretary. Commenting, in November 1925, on the letterhead Haslett had drafted for the new committee's notepaper, Rhondda questioned Haslett's choice of nomenclature and remarked: 'I do not see why we need to insert "Women," it is such a comfort to get away from the word sometimes. What do you think?'[29] In her reply Haslett admitted to 'an oversight on [her] part to continue to call it the Business and University <u>Women's</u> Committee' and agreed 'that it will be quite a good thing to get away from the word "Women"'.[30] Whether or not Rhondda directly instructed *Time and Tide*'s advertising manager to remove the 'modern woman' tagline from the advertisement placed in the December 1925 issue of Haslett's periodical, the promotion of her own magazine in more gender-neutral terms undoubtedly reflected her desire to 'get away from' the word women sometimes in order to realise her goal of a female-run but general-audience review. As we have seen, while the 'modern woman' was emblematic of the 'new' in popular post-war culture (Bingham 2004: 48), the 'new' thing that *Time and Tide* was doing was *not* being a 'women's paper', for all its identification with a predominantly female contributor and readership base.

Evidence that *Time and Tide* was continuously monitoring and updating its image, these advertisements clearly demonstrate *Time and Tide*'s deliberate self-positioning in multiple sectors of the print media marketplace. But the *Woman Engineer*'s placement of the *Time and Tide* advertisement in its December 1925 issue, alongside advertisements for the *Woman's Leader* and the *Vote* (see Figure 1.2), is also important in this respect. In contrast with *Time and Tide*'s gender-neutral strapline, the advertisements for these feminist periodicals specifically target women readers ('A Non-Party, Political Paper, indispensable to Every Woman'; 'The Progressive Non-Party Paper

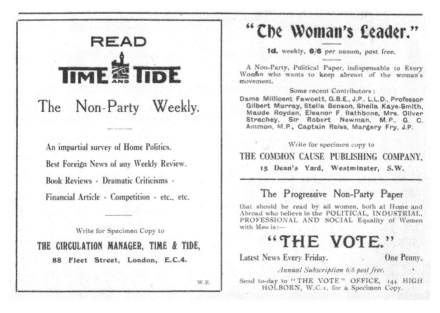

Figure 1.2 Advertisement for *Time and Tide* in the *Woman Engineer* Dec 1925. Reproduced with the permission of the Women's Engineering Society and the Institution of Engineering and Technology Archives.

that should be read by all women'), and through this juxtaposition Haslett's magazine performed another important act of differentiation. Significantly, it is *Time and Tide* that dominates the advertising space, assisted by the bold border – characteristic of poster-advertising – designed to grab readers' attention. But most striking of all are the typographical differences across the titles of these magazines. With their decorative flourishes, the serif typefaces of the former suffrage organs speak to an age that has been superseded by the modernist era. In contrast, the sans-serif type used in the instruction to 'READ' *Time and Tide* introduces this magazine as modern, as does the experimentation in the masthead itself where the extension of the crossbar on the letter 'T' accentuates the strong, modernistic lines of its design.[31] In an era which saw a vogue for 'self-expression via typography [. . .] and other material aspects of texts' (Collier 2016: 13), *Time and Tide* emerges visually as the most 'modern' product alongside its immediate competitors in the feminist periodical market, without the 'modern woman' signifier. This careful framing of the magazine to avoid the women's paper category was crucial to *Time and Tide*'s success beyond a feminist and female readership, as I discuss next.

Male readers and textual performances

Just two months before *Time and Tide*'s 'Modern Weekly for the Modern Woman' advertisement appeared in the *Woman Engineer*, a debate which began in its correspondence columns reveals the highly self-conscious ways in which this periodical was also constructing its relationship with male readers. The debate was started by a reader whose letter printed in *Time and Tide*'s issue of 12 June 1925 opened: 'Madam, – It would be interesting to know why (since readers of TIME AND TIDE must know its Editor to be a woman) they address their letters "Sir"' (576). In a note appended to the bottom of the letter, *Time and Tide* responded: 'Addressing an Editor as "Sir" is an editorial custom. We think the use of such words as Editress, Authoress, Sculptress is much to be deprecated' (576). This editorial note glosses over what was in fact a deliberate change of policy early in the periodical's life to adopt this 'editorial custom'. Following the convention used in other woman-run periodicals, including the *Woman's Leader* and the *Vote*, until mid-November of its first year all letters to the editor were printed with the female appellation 'Madam'; it was only from 26 November 1920 that *Time and Tide* began printing all letters with the male appellation 'Sir'. Crucially, *Time and Tide*'s adoption of the 'editorial Sir' took effect at the precise moment it launched its feminist programme, thus concealing its female editorial identity at the very moment it was making a more direct appeal to women. But if this use of the male appellation was part of a strategy to reassure male readers, it also propagates the problematic idea that professional women should adopt male standards. In the mid-1920s, deepening tensions between 'old' and 'new' feminists centred on whether they should assert women's 'difference' or 'sameness' in relation to men; as Law summarises, ('old') equalitarians perceived the welfare feminists' insistence on women's difference as 'playing into the opposition's hands', while the new feminists saw the equalitarians' position 'as that of aping male values' (1997: 166–7). As *Time and Tide* continued to compete for audiences both within and beyond feminist periodical communities, this was a debate that it would have to face in its own columns.

One week after the question of the 'editorial Sir' was raised in *Time and Tide*'s pages, *Time and Tide* printed another reader's letter which endorsed its editorial policy:

> Sir, – I am pleased to note in the current issue of TIME AND TIDE that you are not anxious to be addressed as Madam. I am one of your male readers, and although I know your journal is conducted

by women, I have always admired the clever way in which you have avoided making it a women's periodical. I like it because it is readable and bears no sex label. (19 June 1925: 598)

Pointing to the journal's success in transcending the 'women's periodical' category, this letter also provides valuable evidence of *Time and Tide*'s early male readers. However, the compromise involved in this successful elision of female editorial identity produced the following response from another correspondent:

Why should a woman editor be addressed as 'Sir'? 'Editress' and 'Authoress' are abominations, but surely 'Madam' is on a different plane? Might all women not as well insist on being described as men, and is the insistence on 'Sir' not a small insult to one's sex? Can one only become a reasonable being by taking over male appellations?' (26 June 1925: 623)

This letter echoes the complaints of new feminists against old feminists' 'slavish acceptance of masculine standards' (Law 1997: 165) and reveals the risk *Time and Tide* ran in alienating some of its female readers. But *Time and Tide*'s response was firm, effectively closing down the debate in a note appended to the letter which read: 'On [this] point we expressed our opinion on June 12 – *Editor*, TIME AND TIDE' (623). However, two weeks later *Time and Tide* published a feature which reignited the debate in the periodical's correspondence columns. At once an acknowledgement of the thorniness of the issue, this feature also worked to manage the debate, and to justify its editorial policy to its readers.

The feature, which appeared on 10 July 1925, comprised excerpts from a speech made by the well-known playwright and dramatic critic St. John Ervine at *Time and Tide*'s recent annual staff dinner.[32] Ervine began contributing regularly to *Time and Tide* in the mid-1920s and later gained 'the title of *provocateur*' in the periodical (13 Oct 1934: 1292). Taking up the question of the 'editorial Sir' that had been raised in *Time and Tide*'s correspondence columns, Ervine mused:

I wonder what the editor of *The Times* would say if one of his readers addressed him as 'Madam'. [. . .] I think he would feel a little odd about it and I am not sure that I do not agree with the writer of the letter to TIME AND TIDE, and that this tradition [. . .] is not a tradition at all but merely an idle habit due chiefly in this case to the fact that most people do not know that TIME AND TIDE is edited by a woman. (10 July 1925: 669)

Ervine's use of double-negatives makes it very unclear whether he does agree with the writer of the letter to *Time and Tide*, or not. But by shifting attention from *Time and Tide*'s editorial policy to readers' assumptions 'that an editor must be a man' he cleverly refocuses the terms of the debate and goes on to assert (with another double-negative): 'I am not sure that it would not be rather a fine thing if everybody who wrote to the paper were compelled to address the editor as "Madam" [. . .] Why not in TIME AND TIDE alter the contributors' style of addressing the editor and make a convention of "Madam"' (669). In what might be read as a feminist argument for challenging sex-prejudice, Ervine's suggestion also reminds us that periodicals are gendered not by the sex of their editors but by textual performances. In the 1890s male editors commonly feminised the journalistic space of women's magazines by assuming female identities (Beetham 1996: 188); now *Time and Tide*'s female editor masculinises the periodical's journalistic space by adopting the male appellation in its Letters to the Editor. *Time and Tide*'s manoeuvres in this debate are canny. By printing Ervine's speech *Time and Tide* allows a dissenting voice to be heard in the paper while maintaining its editorial position. It also promotes the periodical's distinctiveness, for as the continuation of his speech makes clear, Ervine was in fact working *with* the paper's promoters in another important act of differentiation:

> The thing I have noticed about TIME AND TIDE which I have never noticed about another paper is this. [. . .] I am still waiting for the burst of hysteria. Every newspaper is entitled to one burst of hysteria a year and many papers take more than their fair share of hysteria, but TIME AND TIDE has never yet indulged in any hysteria – and that is not right. (669)

Appreciation of the humour here – and the compliment (however patronising readers may have found it) – relies on familiarity with contemporary narratives about journalistic decline and a 'feminised' popular press: the absence of 'hysteria' in *Time and Tide* implies its (masculine) self-control and upholding of professional standards.[33]

Sexual difference, as Bingham has shown, had become 'a central organising feature of the whole newspaper [. . .] operation' in the interwar years (2004: 42), and *Time and Tide*'s *un*feminine character is reinforced by Ervine in a series of further questions and provocations:

> Where is the column giving advice to the young woman whose young man is wavering? Where is the column advising on the proper way in

which to keep your husband's affection, and all those things which are common features of newspapers for women edited by men. It is a violent breach of this tradition which makes adherents of the 'Sir' instead of 'Madam' look childish, and I suggest that if there is going to be any following of tradition, that the aged tradition of a newspaper for women dealing entirely in slop should be followed. (10 July 1925: 669)

Essentially, Ervine suggests, *Time and Tide*'s use of '"Sir" instead of "Madam"' is of very little consequence compared with its departure from the conventions for women's newspapers, and he concludes with further accolades and endorsements: 'I do not know any other paper which succeeds in making me read so much of it as TIME AND TIDE does. [. . .] Perhaps the time will come, and that time will be Utopia, when there is only TIME AND TIDE to read' (669). Providing more evidence of *Time and Tide*'s attractiveness to male as well as female readers, Ervine's speech also enacts another important construction of the new. It is precisely because it is modern that *Time and Tide* departs from 'the aged tradition of a newspaper for women dealing entirely in slop', a characterisation of women's newspapers which, however blunt, works rhetorically to distinguish *Time and Tide* from the popular women's magazine market.[34]

Further correspondence published in *Time and Tide*'s columns shows that its strategic adoption of the 'editorial Sir' did not win the support of all readers.[35] But a letter printed one week following the publication of Ervine's speech also suggests that *Time and Tide* may have had other tactical uses for the male appellation. This letter opens: 'Sir, – by so addressing you may I be allowed to express my complete agreement with your decision to remain editorially concealed as "Sir" rather than exhibited and labelled as "Madam"' (17 July 1925: 705). The sympathy expressed by this correspondent for *Time and Tide*'s decision highlights a key context for this debate: the huge amount of attention focused on women in the interwar popular press. As Bingham has shown, women provided endless 'talking points' for newspaper editors looking to drum up interest, and the 'modern young woman' was 'one of the most prominent characteristic figures of post-war culture' (2004: 42; 48). In December 1920 *Time and Tide* commented in its 'In the Tideway' column:

Surely most people will agree most cordially with the writer in one of the Sunday papers that women are too much talked about. He complains of the absurd articles which are so numerous, headed, do women do this, that or the other well, and the persistent seeking for and analysis of the woman's point of view. It would be much more comfortable all round if women were considered as human beings, and praised or condemned their merits as such. (17 Dec 1920: 668)

Time and Tide's impatience with the treatment of women as news in the popular press reflects its own desire to be read and evaluated as a periodical created by 'human beings' and not be 'exhibited and labelled' as a publication run by women. Arguably, for *Time and Tide*'s female editor the 'editorial Sir' worked as a kind of bulwark against the kinds of assumptions and prejudices associated with the term 'Madam'. Indeed, as will be seen below, the disadvantages of visibility may have been felt even more keenly in the context of *Time and Tide*'s early editorial problems, and, later, of its need to re-establish the periodical's identity unhindered by its new editor's public image.

It is not insignificant that *Time and Tide*'s adoption of the 'editorial Sir' in November 1920 followed closely upon the departure of the periodical's first editor who was not – as is commonly documented – Helen Archdale, but Vera Laughton. In an early appraisal of Laughton Rhondda described her as 'young and keen', but only weeks later she reported that Laughton's performance on the paper was 'quite dreadful' and at the end of July 1920 Laughton was given two months' notice.[36] From this point the paper was effectively edited by Archdale who played a key role in establishing *Time and Tide* during its early years. However, by 1925 it appears that Rhondda and Archdale – who had been close companions since 1922 – no longer saw eye to eye on how the paper should be run. As revealed by Rhondda's recent biographer, Angela V. John, in June 1926 an action plan was drawn up stating that *Time and Tide* was to be 'tried for one year more from October 1926' with a number of measures aimed at reducing costs (2013: 302). Archdale had been resisting the changes proposed under these 'Terms of Arrangement' for a year and when in July they were 'proved, in practice, unworkable' Archdale was, in her words, 'blamed and sacked'.[37] This period represented a moment of crisis for *Time and Tide*, and when Rhondda took over from Archdale in the summer of 1926 the change of editorship passed unannounced in the periodical's columns. While sensitivity towards Archdale provides one explanation for this, it is likely that there were strategic reasons too.[38] A prominent businesswoman and public figure Rhondda was, as John notes, 'featured frequently in the Society columns of newspapers and magazines' (2013: 331), and any notice of her new editorial responsibility would undoubtedly have attracted immediate attention. At this critical moment when *Time and Tide* was looking to secure its future, such challenges the periodical faced both internally and externally would need to be managed very carefully.

A series of articles published by *Time and Tide* in the autumn of 1926 on the subject of 'Women of the Leisured Classes' reveals just how sophisticated this periodical was in managing and controlling its image, and in using the media to extend its influence within existing and new readerships. Published under a pseudonym, 'Candida', the articles were in fact written by Rhondda, and her choice of signature (borrowed from the title of one of George Bernard Shaw's early plays) encodes a feminist agenda.[39] With conscious reference to Olive Schreiner's bible of the women's movement *Woman and Labour* (1911), the series condemned a large class of 'leisured' women and underlined the most central theme of *Time and Tide*'s feminist discourse: that a woman's work was of the utmost importance for her and for society.[40] Economic independence through self-supporting professional work was a key value for middle-class feminists of the post-war period, building on the efforts of nineteenth-century feminism to free women from the private sphere. Rhondda's articles thus re-advertised *Time and Tide*'s feminist identity, and reaffirmed the periodical's 'old' feminist position based on an equal rights tradition at a time of deepening divisions within the women's movement. Earlier the same year the NUSEC had moved family endowment and birth control to its immediate feminist programme, as well as the highly controversial issue of protective legislation, all 'new feminist' reforms which emphasised women's 'difference' from men, particularly in their traditional roles in the home.[41] *Time and Tide* had responded rapidly in its columns to these developments, which were also reported and debated in the *Woman's Leader* (Alberti 1989: 166–80), but its widely advertised series was also designed to take its feminism into a wider public arena. Anticipating that the articles were 'likely to make something of a stir', in a letter to Robins Rhondda explained: 'We are most anxious to get up a correspondence and if possible a controversy about these articles and I should be so grateful [. . .] if you would enter into it.'[42] The series generated a huge correspondence in *Time and Tide*'s own columns and made headlines 'throughout the country'; towards the end of November *Time and Tide* reported in its 'Review of the Week' that the articles had been quoted in a variety of newspapers and journals including *The Daily Express*, *The Daily Chronicle*, the *Tatler*, the *Sphere*, *The Morning Post* and *Public Opinion* (19 Nov 1926: 1047).

Deliberately provocative, the series successfully exploited an obsession with 'women as news' in the popular press in order to circulate *Time and Tide*'s own name more widely; at the same time, the periodical made a clear intervention in public debates about the 'modern woman'. Reflecting on the media interest the articles had generated, *Time and Tide* remarked:

> Curiously enough the tendency in the general press has been to attempt to classify the articles as an attack on the 'modern girl' when they are in fact the very opposite of that. [. . .] they are not attacking anything modern for the leisured woman belongs to no new category. There have been leisured women since the time of Cnossos. It is one of the oldest professions of the world. (19 Nov 1926: 1047)

In this fascinating echo of the media attention ignited by Eliza Lynn Linton's famous attack on the 'Girl of the Period' in the nineteenth-century press, *Time and Tide*'s exploitation of 'woman' as a hot media topic reveals the more commercial orientation of this periodical compared with the more organisationally based social movement papers such as the *Woman's Leader* and the *Vote*.[43] Inverting the terms in which popular newspapers 'contrasted "old" and "new" versions of femininity and emphasized the challenge that "modern young women" posed to convention' (Bingham 2004: 49) *Time and Tide* represents the leisured young woman as positively archaic. Ostensibly *Time and Tide*'s critique is of the parasitic woman who is not involved in any form of labour, but the elevation of women's contribution to society through work in the public sphere could also imply a devaluation or disregard of women's domestic labour. In contrast with the 'new' feminists who, as DiCenzo and Motuz (2016) discuss, were engaged in politicising the home, *Time and Tide*'s emphasis was on liberating women from this sphere, as we have seen. As debates between 'old' and 'new' feminism continued to play out in the pages of *Time and Tide* and its chief rival the *Woman's Leader*, Rhondda's periodical chose this moment to reassert its claim to the 'modern' even as it eschewed the 'new' feminist label. Fuelled by the controversy ignited in its columns by the 'leisured women' series, *Time and Tide* went on to stage its own contest between 'old' and 'new' forms of femininity in which professional work and economic emancipation signalled the dawn of a new age.

This contest opened when, in December 1926, *Time and Tide* invited the popular journalist G. K. Chesterton to express his views in its columns. In his article Chesterton objected most particularly to 'Candida's' claim that motherhood was no longer a full-time job (3 Dec 1926: 1098–9). In a reply to her critics, Rhondda (still writing as 'Candida') noted that the 'most deeply felt and widely held objection' to the articles was that they failed to appreciate 'the sacredness of motherhood' and she went on to challenge Chesterton 'to come and debate the whole question with me in public, when, where, and how he chooses' (10 Dec 1926: 1135). Chesterton responded just as Rhondda must have hoped. In a notice printed in *Time and Tide*'s issue of 7 January 1927 (and which for the first time revealed 'Candida's' identity) readers were invited to attend a debate on 'The Menace of the Leisured Woman' between 'Mr. G. K. Chesterton and Lady Rhondda' which would be presided over by George Bernard Shaw on 27 January at the Kingsway Hall (9). Like the articles the debate attracted 'enormous interest' from the public (4 Feb 1927: 103). The Kingsway Hall was full, and while hundreds of people were unable to get seats, thousands more were able to listen in as it was broadcast live around Britain.[44] For nearly two months the subject of the 'leisured woman' again occupied *Time and Tide*'s correspondence columns, and a large space was also devoted to it in the general press.[45] The success of *Time and Tide*'s media stunt is hugely significant. According to Rhondda the debate resulted in a 50 per cent increase in sales of *Time and Tide*, and the radio broadcast, as well as coverage in provincial newspapers, took the periodical to new regional audiences.[46] One reader from King's Lynn wrote in to describe her experience of 'listening in' while a storm raged outside: 'Yes, TIME AND TIDE had actually found its way to a remote Norfolk Fen' (4 Feb 1927: 116).

The debate played an important role, therefore, in increasing *Time and Tide*'s circulation and making the periodical better known. But it was also significant for the interventions it made in public discourse about the 'modern woman'. Known for his public anti-suffragism before the war, Chesterton spent much of his journalistic career railing against modernity and believed that women's primary place was in the home (Corrin 1989: 27; Sewell 1990: 18). More recently, in March 1925, he had founded *G. K.'s Weekly* which served as an organ for Distributism, a social and economic theory that favoured small-scale economic and manufacturing enterprises and looked back to the Middle Ages as a model for social life. The Distributist League had held its inaugural meeting at the Essex Hall, London, just one month before *Time and Tide* launched its series on 'Women of the Leisured Classes' (Corrin 1989: 107). While its philosophy was 'centrally committed to work as the main enjoyment of life' Distributism opposed commercial and industrial progress and 'particularly [. . .] the concentration of power [. . .] brought about by the increasing role of international finance' (Shiach 2004: 224). Chesterton thus stood for everything that *Time and Tide* positioned itself against. As we have seen in *Time and Tide*'s association with the *Woman Engineer*, for members of these feminist periodical communities science, industry and commerce represented the future, and they were fields Rhondda and her colleagues wanted women to inhabit. By making Chesterton her chief antagonist Rhondda had set the stage for a contest between the forces of conservatism and the forces of progress, and, in the media coverage this debate generated, *Time and Tide* forged its own modern identity in Britain's feminist and interwar press.

By the end of 1926 *Time and Tide* had emerged as the leader in the feminist periodical market, both distinguishing itself from other feminist weeklies and making itself known to a much wider public. Participating in debates about work, professionalism and the 'modern woman' both within and beyond feminist communities, *Time and Tide* advertised its own brand of feminism in terms of a feminist 'duty' to work, and forged its own modern identity in contemporary journalism. However, the politics of work and leisure looked very different from the perspective of the labour movement, especially in 1926, the year of the General Strike. As *Time and Tide*'s discourse on professionalism makes clear, the periodical had come to represent the interests of middle-class women most strongly, and it is not insignificant that the only trade unionist representative on *Time and Tide*'s first board of directors, Christine Maguire, resigned before the end of its first year.[47] In the next chapter I examine the contributions to this periodical of a critically neglected socialist poet of the 1920s, Eleanor Farjeon, and explore the relationships *Time and Tide* was negotiating internally as well as externally during its early years, and also its interactions with periodicals and periodical networks associated with radical culture and the socialist press.

Notes

1. 'Press Comments on "Time and Tide"' were printed in the periodical in its issue of 11 June 1920.
2. Letter from Rhondda to Rebecca West, 1 June 1931. RW Tulsa.
3. For a discussion of the manifesto as a form, see Janet Lyon (1999).
4. MR to ER, 30 April 1920. ER Papers.

5. MR to ER, 4 May 1920. ER Papers.
6. *Time and Tide*'s remaining first directors were: Mrs Chalmers Watson and Dame Helen Gwynne-Vaughan, both leading figures during the war in the Women's Army Auxiliary Corps; Miss Christine Maguire, a trade unionist and Honorary Organiser of the Association of Women Clerks and Secretaries; and Mrs H. B. Irving (née Dorothea Baird), an actress and playwright well known for her interests in baby welfare and housing for the poor.
7. Founded in 1911 by the militant suffragette Dora Marsden, the *Free-woman* (later the *New Freewoman*, and then the *Egoist*) can also be considered part of the history of feminist periodical publishing *Time and Tide* was building upon. However, *Time and Tide*'s democratic and egalitarian commitment to the ordinary woman (see Chapter 4) contrasts with Marsden's 'elitist conception of the "freewoman"' only attainable by the few (Delap 2007: 116). Under Rhondda's editorship *Time and Tide* also remained committed to its feminism throughout the period discussed here, unlike Marsden's periodical which saw the 'progressive erasure of feminism in favour of individualism' through its successive titles (Rabaté 2009: 271). For more on the *Freewoman* see Joannou (2002) and essays on the Modernist Journals Project Website.
8. See Dale Spender (1984) for an overview and selection of *Time and Tide*'s overtly feminist content.
9. MR to ER, 6 May 1920. ER Papers.
10. The second issue carried an article by the leader of the Australian women's suffrage movement, Vida Goldstein, on 'Australian Women and Politics' (21 May 1920: 30). In the next issue, an article on colonisation in Palestine did not have a special focus on women.
11. In a letter to Robins dated 22 February 1920 Rhondda refers to the Board's decision to have 'a full discussion of the Prospectus before issuing it' even though this meant delaying the first issue by a week. ER Papers.
12. MR to ER, 13 August 1920. ER Papers.
13. In the absence of subscription lists and records it is impossible to firmly establish circulation figures for the periodical. In its first year *Time and Tide* calculated costs for producing 5,000 and 10,000 copies (ER Papers, *Time and Tide* Subject File). Shirley M. Eoff estimates that *Time and Tide* reached between twelve and fifteen thousand readers in the 1920s, and cites evidence suggesting that it increased its circulation to over 30,000 copies per week during the Second World War (1991: 121; 128). William Berry, Viscount Camrose, *British Newspapers and Their Controllers* (London: Cassell, 1948) places *Time and Tide*'s wartime circulation higher at around 40,000 (Eoff: 144 and n.99). These are respectable figures for an intellectual weekly review targeting a select public. In the early 1920s the *New Statesman*'s circulation averaged 6,000 to 8,000 a week, with net sales growing to around 14,500 following its merger with

the *Nation and Athenaeum* in 1931 and reaching a circulation of 29,000 by 1939 (Hyams 1963: 75; 122; 227).

14. MR to ER, 13 August 1920. ER Papers.
15. An item printed early the following year confirms that the programme outlined on 19 November 'has now become the charter of the Six Point Group' (25 Feb 1921: 176). The Six Points on which the Six Point Group campaigned for satisfactory legislation were: Child Assault, the Widowed Mother, the Unmarried Mother and her Child, Equal rights of Guardianship for Married Parents, Equal Pay for Teachers, and Equal opportunities for Men and Women in the Civil Service.
16. *Time and Tide* reported in December 1920 that it had received a 'large number of letters' showing 'a very widespread demand among women for a clearly defined and practical programme' (3 Dec: 604), and in a letter dated 4 April 1921 Rhondda told Robins that 'The circulation continues to mount.' ER Papers.
17. Rhondda communicated to Robins in a letter dated 13 January 1921 that the programme had been 'reported on at some length in the *Telegraph*, the *Manchester Guardian*, and one or two other papers'. ER Papers.
18. MR to ER, 15 June 1921. ER Papers. The proposal was made during a lunch arranged by Strachey and J. C. Squire who was expanding his empire at the *London Mercury* offices. According to Rhondda, Strachey and Squire planned to make the *Woman's Leader* into a 6d paper 'very much on "Time and Tide" lines' and the proposed amalgamation was based on the assumption that Strachey would be editor.
19. Tusan records the 'falling circulations' of both the *Woman's Leader* and the *Vote* during the 1920s (2005: 216). The *Woman's Leader* began, like *Time and Tide*, as a 24-page magazine, but by October 1924 it was only eight pages and had dropped its price from 2d to 1d. It published its last issue in 1932.
20. DiCenzo notes that 'the demise of the *Englishwoman* occurred around the same time as the appearance of *Woman's Leader* and *Time and Tide*' (2011: 130).
21. The competition offered money and book prizes and remained a fixture in *Time and Tide*'s pages for years to come.
22. Miss Marion Jean Lyon is first listed among *Time and Tide*'s board of directors in its issue of 13 August 1926 (748).
23. The *Woman Engineer* was printed on a far higher quality of paper than any of the other trade magazines I have looked at, allowing for the high-quality reproduction of photographic and other visual material as well as clean, stylish print.
24. See Caroll Pursell (1993) for a discussion of the WES.
25. I am indebted to Alice Staveley for first alerting me to advertisements for *Time and Tide* carried by the *Woman Engineer*.

26. In its fifth issue *Time and Tide* drew attention to a resolution recently passed by the WES 'call[ing] upon all leaders of industry and trade unions to act in the best interests of the nation by uniting with women in overcoming the artificial barriers to progress and development in productions' (11 June 1920: 114).

27. Hackney notes that the version of modern womanhood envisioned by *Modern Woman* 'was by no means restricted to domestic pursuits' and like *Good Housekeeping* the magazine 'envisioned a public agenda for its readers' (2008: 118). Bridging political, cultural and domestic life, it addressed women primarily as housewives nonetheless.

28. This was a significant theme in Rhondda's public engagements and her writing in this period which included a section on 'Business and Commerce' in a book on careers for girls (John 2013: 277).

29. MR to CH 17 November 1925. BFUW Papers.

30. CH to MR 25 November 1925. BFUW Papers.

31. Jeremy Aynsley observes that: 'In the 1920s the sans-serif typeface in general was interpreted as a modern design solution' and was advocated, particularly in Europe, 'as international and fulfilling the Zeitgeist, or the spirit of the age' (2007: 41).

32. The dinner was held on 3 July 1925.

33. Adrian Bingham identifies the 'feminization' of the press as 'the most striking development in popular journalism between the wars' (2004: 38). For an extended discussion of this perceived crisis in contemporary journalism, see Patrick Collier (2006), especially Introduction and Chapter 1.

34. One indignant female reader, who identified herself as the Controlling Editor of *Home Notes* and Leach's Publications, challenged Ervine's inference 'that all Women's papers are edited by men, or conducted on traditions laid down by them' (24 July 1925: 728).

35. Helena Normanton, who identified herself as a former editor of a colonial magazine in India, wrote to express her 'hearty support' for Evine's suggestion 'that women editors should be addresses *as women*' (24 July 1925: 728).

36. MR to ER, 14 June and 27 July 1920. ER Papers.

37. Helen Archdale to Winifred Cullis, 27 July 1926. Material in private hands sourced via Angela V. John.

38. John notes that Winifred Holtby told Vera Brittain in April 1927 that Rhondda was keeping the change of editorship 'as quiet as possible' (2013: 340).

39. John notes that Rhondda 'borrow[ed] the title of [George Bernard] Shaw's early comedy with its eponymous heroine who challenged conventional representations of marriage and gender roles' (2013: 410).

40. Schreiner's famous cry 'Give us labour and the training that fits us for labour!' was printed at the start of the second article.

41. See DiCenzo and Motuz (2016) for a re-examination of this central debate in interwar feminism.
42. MR to ER, 5 April 1926. ER Papers.
43. I am indebted to Maria DiCenzo for this observation. For a discussion of Linton see Andrea L. Broomfield (2004).
44. A notice that the debate would be broadcast was printed in *Time and Tide*'s issue of 21 January 1927.
45. Correspondence on the 'leisured woman' ran until 22 April 1927.
46. Letter from Rhondda to Doris Stevens, 27 March 1927. DS Papers.
47. Rhondda reported to Robins in a letter dated 24 November 1920 that Miss Maguire had resigned from the board. ER Papers.

Chapter 2

'The Weekly Crowd. By Chimaera': Collective Identities and Radical Culture

As founder and, from 1926, editor of *Time and Tide* Lady Rhondda indisputably influenced the development and identity of this periodical more than any other single figure. As Angela V. John observes, the creation of this publishing venture was Rhondda's 'most cherished undertaking' and she would place it before all other concerns until the end of her life (2013: 261). Rhondda's commitment was financial as well as ideological; inheriting her father's business empire as well as his title she became one of Britain's wealthiest women, and from the outset she controlled 90 per cent of *Time and Tide*'s company shares and subsidised the paper heavily (John: 264; 281).[1] John's biography of Rhondda has underlined the importance for Rhondda's feminism of her experiences in industry and commerce. As chair during the interwar years of 'thirteen different boards [. . .] a director of at least forty-eight companies, and a shareholder in many others' (264) Rhondda held an 'exceptional' position in the business world; newspapers described her as 'the Queen of Commerce' and 'the leading businesswoman of the western hemisphere' (281). A pioneer in this traditionally male world, in articles for the press and in her work for numerous women's organisations and committees after the war Rhondda energetically promoted opportunities for educated middle- and upper-class girls to enter business (John 2013: 275–7), and these professional and class-based interests came to shape *Time and Tide*'s early alliances and identity, as we have seen. However, an editor's influence on a magazine is never uniform or total; as Jason Harding states '[t]he overall profile of any periodical is a complex blend of the signatures of the individual contributors, ordered and articulated by innumerable editorial decisions' (2002: 7). This chapter explores the internal dynamics of *Time and Tide*'s 'inside' relationships between editors, staff and contributors, and shows how a set of concerns seemingly antithetical to Rhondda's business interests also played an important shaping role in the periodical's early identity. This discussion will be advanced with reference to a pseudonymous feature which was printed regularly in *Time and Tide*'s pages for nearly ten years, 'The Weekly Crowd'.

First appearing in *Time and Tide*'s issue of 19 May 1922, 'The Weekly Crowd. By Chimaera' comprised a weekly summing-up of the news in verse and was later revealed to be contributed by the poet and short story writer Eleanor Farjeon.[2] Farjeon's choice of pseudonym – that mythical creature, part lion, part snake, part goat – might usefully symbolise the nature of the periodical genre itself: a publication composed of very disparate parts. Likewise, the 'crowd' in the feature's title foregrounds what Harding describes as the 'multiple subject positions and interplay of voices often exhibited simultaneously' in a periodical's pages (2002: 5). In this column, I argue, Farjeon negotiated a difficult tension between *Time and Tide*'s middle-class professional and business interests and those of another constituency from which it drew support during the early years: labour women and networks associated with a socialist periodical press. Officially *Time and Tide* was affiliated to no political party, though in general terms it occupied a position on the liberal-left, and Rhondda, for all her identification with business and capital, was in fact instrumental in securing the continued representation of Labour on *Time and Tide*'s board of directors. Soon after the resignation of its only trade unionist board member, Christine Maguire, Rhondda reported to Robins that she wanted to recruit the novelist, journalist and future Labour MP Mary Agnes Hamilton to the board but 'fear[ed] it may not be easy to manage' as its Conservative members (Mrs Chalmers Watson and Dame Helen Gwynne-Vaughan) knew her to be a pacifist.[3] Hamilton did become one of *Time and Tide*'s directors later in 1921, and also contributed regular book reviews to the periodical for more than a decade.[4]

Farjeon, also a socialist and a pacifist, was one among several writers on the 'literary left' who would contribute to *Time and Tide* over the years. While her name continues to be associated with the hymn 'Morning Has Broken' and with the world of children's literature, the poems she wrote under pseudonyms for socialist newspapers and journals reveal an undeservedly forgotten radical poet.[5] For years she contributed topical poems to socialist newspapers and journals, including the *Daily Herald*, the *New Leader* (formerly the *Labour Leader* and official organ of the Independent Labour Party) and to George Lansbury's socialist and pacifist *Labour Weekly*.[6] According to Jim Clayson, Farjeon was 'the most important poet of the labour movement in the 1920s' and her contributions to *Time and Tide* are a clear demonstration of the overlapping feminist and socialist periodical networks *Time and Tide* inhabited.[7] 'The Weekly Crowd' in particular presents a fascinating case study for exploring how the periodical managed to hold radically different voices together within its pages, and channel potentially destabilising elements into a resource that benefited and augmented the paper.

'No more war!': Ireland, pacifism and the First World War

Farjeon's first 'Weekly Crowd' (Figure 2.1) might easily serve as a model for the multivocality of periodical texts and intrinsic heterogeneity of their contents. The poem is structured around an array of voices in a 'crowd'; among them 'A Schoolboy', 'A Musician', and 'A Politician' provide lively comment on the latest news in sport, culture and politics. As a microcosm for the periodical itself, the poem usefully demonstrates that reading interwar periodicals 'requires a sensitive ear for the allusions and references to the larger cultural conversation' in which they participate (Harding 2002: 2–3). For present-day readers one of the poem's most obscure topical references is the question posed by 'Dr Casey Wood' ('Was that the Nightingale?') and it is only when we return to the poem's original and wider textual environment that the allusion is explained: in newspapers that week it was reported that Dr Wood, an American ornithologist, had at last heard the English nightingale in song.[8] Farjeon's marginal position in the history of British poetry is in no insignificant way due to the fugitive status of her topical verses in a print medium – journalism – that is itself already 'subjugated'.[9] Her first 'Weekly Crowd' was published in the same year as T. S. Eliot's landmark modernist text, *The Waste Land*, but her work has not attained the kind of literary status required by Ezra Pound's famous maxim: 'literature is news that STAYS news'.[10] Yet I want to suggest that in this first poem for *Time and Tide* Farjeon's reference to the nightingale deliberately invokes an important symbol for poets, and that through this she very self-consciously placed herself within a

THE WEEKLY CROWD.

BY CHIMAERA.

The Sands run on, the Waters flow,
With Time and Tide the Crowd must go.

A TRAMP : Cowslips! Sweet Cowslips from tho fields for sale!

A CHILD : Oh, Mother, let me wear my sandals, do! It's Summer now!

DR. CASEY WOODS : Was that the Nightingale?

A SCHOOLBOY : I say! Hot stuff! Fender hit fifty-two off fourteen balls! Fry caught him when he stood at one-eight.five! He swiped three sixes! Good old Fender!

THE TRAMP : Bluebells! Bluebells from a wood. . . .

MADAME POMPOM : Rip out last Season's hems, and let all frocks Down to the ankle.

THE CHILD : Mother, its so cold! It's Winter now— I want my woolly socks.

BOB : It left 'im with a bad black eye, I'm told.

BILL : It left 'im fair knocked-out!

BOB : It never did! 'E 'ad it stitched, that's all.

BILL : Bet you a quid 'E didn't!

BOB : Who? The Prince?

BILL : Not 'arf! the Kid!

A MUSICIAN : Were you at Albert Hall? That Choir's not sung Outside the Vatican for five hundred years.

MISS BEAUMONT : How *interesting*! And they look so *young*— Mere boys

A SPORTSMAN : In three months—

A POLITICIAN : Yes, by all one hears, when this three-months Commission's had its whack, Russia and France may both have changed their tack at Genoa—

SPORTSMAN : Bah! In three months Carp meets Jack.

NORA : Curfew at noine in Belfast! Oh, ochone! When will the shootin' stop?

A WOMAN : Before he came From France, the King upon a soldier's stone Laid flowers from Wiltshire in a mother's name.

A TEACHER : Looks bad for the Continuation School.

THE CHILD : Mother, it's Spring again. I want my cool frock!

THE TRAMP : Yellow Iris! Iris from a pool. . . .

With Time and Tide the Crowd is gone—
The Waters flow, and the Sands run on.

Figure 2.1 'The Weekly Crowd. By Chimaera', *Time and Tide* 19 May 1922: 468. Reproduced with the permission of The William Ready Division of Archives and Research Collections, McMaster University Library.

native tradition that Peter Howarth traces from 'Wordsworth and Clare through Hardy' to a group of non-modernist poets including Edward Thomas (2005: 11).[11] Significantly, Dr Wood's question immediately follows utterances from 'A Tramp' and 'A Child', voices which recur twice more in the poem and, I propose, bear the imprint of Farjeon's four-year friendship with the poet Edward Thomas.[12] Specifically, her 'Tramp' recalls the tramps, vagrants and wayfarers in Thomas's poetry, as well as Thomas's friend W. H. Davies (himself actually a beggar and tramp), and also Douglas Goldring's magazine the *Tramp* to which Thomas and Davies both contributed; her 'Child' invokes another central figure in this group of modern English poets, the children's poet Walter de la Mare, also a friend of Thomas.[13] Farjeon's ear for the actual sounds and rhythms of the speaking voice throughout the rest of the poem further evidences the influence of Thomas, and of his great mentor the American Robert Frost whose ideas about the pure sound of speech sought to revolutionise English poetry.[14] Existing in competitive dialogue with a metropolitan modernism identified with Eliot and Pound, the voices of 'The Tramp' and 'The Child' thus connect Farjeon to a native 'non-modernist' tradition that has exerted an equal influence on the development of British poetry in the twentieth century.[15]

It is with Farjeon's status as a 'forgotten radical' in London's interwar print culture, however, that this chapter is primarily concerned.[16] Over time Farjeon developed a number of patterns for the feature, including single-voiced poems (spoken by, for example, 'A Ballad Singer' or 'A Patter Artist') as well as alphabet frames and more formulaic multi-voiced poems such as 'A Family at Breakfast (Reading its Papers)'. Given the feature's intrinsically topical nature the poems were wide-ranging in their content, but there was one unchanging element which appeared every week, the four lines in italics which open and close the very first poem: '*The Sands run on, the Waters flow, / With Time and Tide the Crowd must go. [...] With Time and Tide the Crowd is gone – / The Waters flow, and the Sands run on*'. This frame provides a unity to the feature, inviting us to read Farjeon's 'Weekly Crowd' poems in relation to each other and in relation to their larger textual environment. In particular, the motif of flowing waters and running sands binds the poems to the periodical's title imagery and to the drawing in its masthead, where 'time' and 'tide' are figured in the familiar face of Big Ben towering above the River Thames (Figure 2.2a). As a visual metaphor for women's relationship to modernity this editorial artwork is arresting. Invoking the arrival of women as voters and Members of Parliament, it also registers a turning of the tide of opinion on women's role in

Figure 2.2a *Time and Tide* Masthead, 14 May 1920. Reproduced with the permission of The William Ready Division of Archives and Research Collections, McMaster University Library.

public life. In October 1920, *Time and Tide*'s introduction to a new feature extended the metaphor:

> It is proposed in 'The Minute Hand' to [. . .] give especial notice to the ebb and flow of that tide, which, in its advance, opens new opportunities of service and achievement to those hitherto excluded. In the past, opportunities in Parliament, in public office, in education, in business, have opened in turn to Jews, to Roman Catholics, and to working-men. To-day they are opening to women. So, in our watch on this tide, we shall be concerned very largely with this specially characteristic feature of our times. (8 Oct 1920: 454)

The advances of women appeared occasionally in 'The Weekly Crowd'; for example, in *Time and Tide*'s issue of 16 March 1928 (the week the Equal Franchise Bill was introduced to Parliament) a 'Daughter' states: 'that a girl should be a voter / At the same age as men we *have* made plain' (244). However, in the main the feature contained little in the way of feminist news and comment, and experimentation in the periodical's masthead shortly after the first appearance of 'The Weekly Crowd' suggests that the feature played an important part in shaping *Time and Tide*'s early identity along different lines.

In July 1922, just two months after the inaugural 'Weekly Crowd', *Time and Tide* introduced a significant new element to the drawing of Big Ben and the River Thames emblazoned in its title banner: a crowd which passes to and fro over Westminster Bridge (Figure 2.2b). In the context of *Time and Tide*'s feminist identity this crowd may represent the arrival of women as voters and as Members of Parliament, but given its development from Farjeon's weekly contribution it

Vol. 3. No. 28. [REGISTERED AT THE G.P.O. AS A NEWSPAPER] FRIDAY, JULY 14, 1922 [3½d. Post Free to Yearly and Half-Yearly Direct Subscribers] Weekly. Price 4d.

Figure 2.2b *Time and Tide* Masthead, 14 July 1922. Reproduced with the permission of The William Ready Division of Archives and Research Collections, McMaster University Library.

might equally represent publics served by a radical press. 'The Weekly Crowd' was always printed between or immediately following *Time and Tide*'s leading articles, sharing with the socialist press a refusal to divide aesthetics and politics.[17] Indeed, the very first poem was printed between an unsigned leader on the nursing profession and an article by Mary Agnes Hamilton on Russia, perhaps a deliberate positioning of content by two socialist contributors. But it is the frame uniting Farjeon's poems that carries special significance. With its four-beat oral stress pattern set against the five-beat structure of print culture this element sustains links with a nineteenth-century socialist aesthetic. Symbolically, therefore, the crowd newly depicted in *Time and Tide*'s masthead could represent socialist as well as feminist readers, working with the framing lines of Farjeon's weekly poem to create a 'collective identity that might generate loyalty and mobilization' across different constituencies.[18] However, the radicalism of socialist print culture also introduced the possibility for discord among *Time and Tide*'s early collaborators. As I discuss below, while the second line in the frame declares the periodical's role as a leader of public opinion ('With *Time and Tide* the Crowd must go'), *Time and Tide*'s editorial position was not one that Farjeon's verse would always follow.

Farjeon appears to have been radicalised by the First World War and its memory haunts 'The Weekly Crowd' from her first poem in the voice of 'A Woman' whose notice of 'the flowers from Wiltshire' laid by the King 'upon a soldier's stone' refers to King George V's pilgrimage in May 1922 to visit the First World War Graves Commission. Significantly, this woman's voice immediately follows the voice of an Irish woman, 'Nora', who exclaims: 'Curfew at noine in Belfast! Oh, ochone! / When will the shootin' stop?'

The Irish Troubles brought to the fore the question of when and in what circumstances it might be necessary to use force which, as June Hannam and Karen Hunt explain, caused tensions for socialists too between anti-militarism and pacifism.[19] The subject of Irish Home Rule had dominated British politics since the 1870s, and in the summer of 1920 *Time and Tide* published a series of articles on 'Various Aspects of the Irish Problem' demonstrating the periodical's engagement from the outset with a broad political agenda extending far beyond a ghetto of 'women's issues'.[20] Indeed, at the same time that *Time and Tide*'s board of directors was discussing its 'feminist programme', 'A Good Irish Policy' was listed at the top of 'a number of general questions' which the board considered 'sufficient to make a really good and effective programme for any Government'.[21] But unpublished evidence reveals divisions on the board as to what line on Ireland *Time and Tide* should take. In a letter to Robins written three days after 'Bloody Sunday', Rhondda observed wryly that 'we are indeed a Board of varying opinions'.[22] One of the board's Conservative members, Mrs Chalmers Watson, was the principal source of discord; her hard-line approach was 'to proclaim Marshal Law and suppress the rebellion'.[23] For a while Rhondda managed to steer *Time and Tide* down a more liberal line advocating that the Irish should select their own form of government, but in January 1921 she reported to Robins that a new 'crisis' had been reached placing 'the whole future of the paper [. . .] at stake'.[24] *Time and Tide*'s other Conservative board member, Dame Helen Gwynne-Vaughan, had joined Watson in wanting the paper to take their line of backing the government, and Rhondda feared that if it came to a vote 'this fundamental cleavage' placed the paper in 'serious danger'.[25]

By the time Farjeon began contributing to the periodical in May 1922 it appears that *Time and Tide*'s board of directors had found a more unified stance on Ireland following the ratification of the Anglo-Irish treaty in December 1921.[26] But a 'Weekly Crowd' poem published just days after the start of the Irish Civil War foregrounds the possibility for friction that remained between *Time and Tide*'s editors and contributors. The poem is spoken (or sung) by 'The Ballad-Singer (Passing down the Street)' and the first stanza is allotted to the conflict:

> The White Flag's bein' hoisted now in Dublin,
> And day by day the Rebel Strongholds fall,
> O'Connor's reached the limit of his troublin',

And De Valera's is near, God help us all.
For tho' Sackville Street be taken,
Still the country will be shaken
With the Civil Wars which ravage and appal –
Though why men call 'em civil
When they issue from the Divil
Is more than I can say, God help us all! (7 July 1922: 636)

This verse is significant for the emphasis it places upon the violent suppression of anti-treaty fighting in Dublin in June and July 1922. *Time and Tide*'s editorial in the same issue offered unqualified support for the military force used by the Provisional Government (which, it claimed, 'only struck when the Republicans forced its hand'), and, counting the greater security of the Anglo-Irish Treaty to be 'one good result' of the battles *Time and Tide* credited its signatories with 'know[ing] how to fight for peace' (7 July 1922: 633). Farjeon's poem unsettles this position by immediately inviting sympathy for the fallen 'Rebel Strongholds'; the unusual inversion of the second foot in the first line creates an unexpected stress on 'Flag's' expressing the undue force with which the Provisional Government quelled opposition. The poem also withholds judgement concerning the rebels' own use of violence. In lines three and four the defeat of the anti-treaty leaders Rory O'Connor and Éamon De Valera produces no note of triumphalism, but the more woeful cry (repeated at the very end of the stanza) 'God help us all!' Finally, the poem accurately anticipates the prolonged nature of the Irish Civil War which would 'ravage and appal' the country for many months to come, and the shifting rhythm between five and three metrical feet in these lines both accentuates the misnomer in the description of any war as 'civil' and quickens the poem's urgent desire for peace.

Farjeon deserves to be remembered as an important anti-war poet of the 1920s and it is notable that she often used the ballad (commonly identified with a labouring-class oral tradition) for her most incisive political protest and comment. In other 'Weekly Crowd' poems of 1922 a ballad-singer reports the deaths of leading figures in the Irish conflict: for example, the revolutionary leader Michael Collins who was shot in August 1922, and his follower Sean Hales who was killed four months later in reprisal for the Free State's execution of anti-Treaty prisoners.[27] Another 'Weekly Crowd' of 1922, also spoken in the voice of a ballad-singer, opens with the following strident stanza:

No more War!
No more War!
That was the cry their banners bore,
That was the message they sent forth,
East and West and South and North,
Who on Saturday did fare
On the World's face everywhere –
Pilgrims, with their Slogan plain:
'Not again, oh not again,
Tear our children as you tore
Us! For men are stricken sore,
And earth has suffered at the core –
No more War,
No more, no more!' (4 Aug 1922: 782)

This poem was written on the occasion of No More War demonstrations held in London and around the world on Saturday, 29 July 1922 marking the anniversary of the outbreak of the First World War. One of the most overtly political poems Farjeon wrote for *Time and Tide*, it proclaims its radicalism with the rallying cry 'No more War!' carried by the 'banners' and voices of anti-war demonstrators. The dramatic pause on 'Us!' towards the end of this first stanza is a forceful reminder of the human suffering experienced not only by combatants but the whole collective body during 1914–18, and it is the memory of this that drives the anguished plea 'Not again, oh not again'. Towards the end of the second stanza, the names of the Irish border towns Dundalk and Greenore remind readers of the ongoing civil war in Ireland. But these are preceded by a series of questions relating to other issues which threaten international security and peace: uncertain developments in the Greco-Turkish War (1919–22) which followed the partitioning of the Ottoman Empire; Britain's expansion of its air force, reflecting increased spending on armaments in many European countries after the war; and the severity of German reparations under the terms of the Versailles Treaty. In the third stanza, topical references to 'Champions' in cricket, chess and a theatrical appearance of the military 'Saint George' at London's 'Old Vic' introduce some light relief to the poem ('no man will deplore' their victories). But chiefly these diversions serve to reinforce the underlying message that war is not a game.

Farjeon's pacifism connects her to a large female constituency between the wars. As Pamela Graves notes, '[w]omen were the great peace crusaders of the postwar decade, active in the No More War movement and ever-vigilant watch dogs against militarism' (1994: 209). 'The Weekly Crowd' admits the presence of a pacifist strand in British feminism in the pages of *Time and Tide*, but comparison of two poems Farjeon wrote less than two months later, at the height of a fresh crisis in the Near East, illustrates the editorial constraints she was working under in this periodical compared with her contributions to the socialist press. This new crisis was the threatened attack by Turkish troops on British and French troops in Constantinople in the neutral zone in September 1922, an incident referred to by historians as the Chanak Crisis and which raised the very real fear of Britain going to war again. Britain's leading socialist newspaper, the *Daily Herald*, widely proclaimed Labour's 'No War' slogan in its daily coverage of the crisis, and beneath an editorial on 20 September 1922 warning readers of the British Cabinet's 'warlike mood', it printed a poem by Farjeon under her pseudonym in this paper, 'Tomfool'. The poem is entitled 'Gallipoli' (famous for the failed Allied offensive on Turkey in 1915) and from its opening question 'Have you not had your toll, Gallipoli?' it moves, in three stanzas, with mounting horror at the possibility of England making 'so soon the old mistake / Again'. It concludes unequivocally:

> For the great feast
> Of battle in the East
> Shall we prepare the flesh again? No, no,
> Gallipoli! (20 Sep 1922)

Time and Tide's position on the conflict was quite different from that of the *Daily Herald*'s. In its editorial columns *Time and Tide* acknowledged that the British government was 'largely to blame' for the escalation of the crisis, but did not go as far as the *Daily Herald* in its criticism of Lloyd George's Cabinet, stating rather that 'it may be that war will prove to be the only way out' (22 Sep 1922: 897). Farjeon's 'Weekly Crowd' in the same issue (just two days after her 'Gallipoli' poem was published in the *Daily Herald*) opens with reference to the situation in the Greece. Characteristically it focuses on the victims of war, specifically the thousands of Greeks and Armenians who died in 'massacre and fire' during the repossession of Smyrna by Mustafa Kemal Ataturk, leader of the Turkish national movement.[28] This poem does not carry the 'No more War!' slogan of her earlier anti-war verse in this periodical, or the unequivocal pacifism of her 'Gallipoli' poem printed in the *Daily Herald*. But through a succession of unanswered questions it registers anxiety about the developing crisis, and its topical references clearly convey Farjeon's radical sympathies. The second and third stanzas read:

> In Downing Street the War Chiefs lay their plans,
> While Labour cries, 'No ship! no gun! no man!'
> Will Nansen's plea for power to intervene
> Be listened to, or placed beneath the ban?
>
> Meanwhile her troops from Asia France recalls,
> And Italy avoids the Eastern brawls:
> Will Britain speed her soldiers to new wars
> If on her back alone the burden falls? (22 Sep 1922: 900)

If less openly defiant than her 'Gallipoli' poem, Farjeon's desire for peace is clear in the reference to Dr Nansen, the Norwegian diplomat, Arctic explorer and Nobel Peace Prize laureate, who in 1922 spearheaded the Russian Relief campaign and negotiated on behalf of European Relief agencies with Soviet Russia. (The League of Nations, fearful of the Bolsheviks, rejected his appeal in the press and elsewhere for international support.) But it is the quoted phrase in the second line presented here that provides the most direct link to radical cultures associated with the socialist press: just three days earlier a front-page headline in the *Daily Herald* read 'LABOUR SAYS: "NOT A MAN, NOT A GUN, NOT A SHIP"' (19 Sep 1922). The reiteration of this headline could read as simply one more item in the poem's weekly assortment of topical comment, but it is also evidence of how closely Farjeon identified with the anti-war stance of the Labour movement.

Cryptic references in Rhondda's correspondence with Elizabeth Robins suggest that *Time and Tide* may have found Farjeon's radicalism a liability. Early in October 1922 Rhondda reported that she would be raising 'the question [. . .] of Chimaera' at *Time and Tide*'s board meeting on 16 October.[29] After the meeting Rhondda informed Robins that 'Chimaera' was discussed but no formal board decision was arrived at. The matter was clearly very delicate; she writes 'of course, nothing was recorded in the minutes'.[30] As John Lucas reminds us, the increased circulation of left-wing papers like the *Daily Herald* reflected 'a quite new sense of militancy, of tangible radicalism, which could be traced to recent events in Russia and with which these newspapers and journals plainly sympathised' (2000: 141). However, if Farjeon's poems unsettled some of *Time and Tide*'s directors by working against the periodical's editorial position, one thing couldn't be ignored: their popularity with readers. According to one subscriber, quoted in *Time and Tide*'s pages, 'The Weekly Crowd' was 'worth the whole price of the paper' (9 Feb 1923: 166). In the next section of this chapter I examine a strategy of 'comic militancy' Farjeon adopted in her 'Weekly Crowd' poems to negotiate editorial constraints, and argue that by 1926 *Time and Tide* was able to harness Farjeon's radicalism in ways that benefited and augmented the paper.

'Far from the Weekly Crowd': work, holidays, and the General Strike

In May 1922, the month Farjeon began contributing her 'Weekly Crowd' poems to *Time and Tide*, the *Daily Herald* published in its May Day supplement a poem by Farjeon called 'The Next Holiday'. Printed under her 'Tomfool' pseudonym the poem is a song for all 'Lads and Lasses' pledged to meet their sweethearts 'every May'.[31] Traditionally a workers' holiday, May Day was regularly marked and celebrated in socialist print culture of the period. For example, a special May Day issue of the *New Leader* in 1926 explicitly names May Day as a 'Socialist festival' which shares with 'those ancient merry-makings' of Celtic tradition 'the interests of labouring men' (30 Apr 1926: 15). This article in the official organ of the Independent Labour Party (ILP) was published just four days before the start of the General Strike, which involved nearly two million workers following a long period of conflict within Britain's coal industry.[32] In radical culture the 'general strike' and the 'holiday' have been part of a shared discourse ever since the Radical William Benbow made his case for the cessation of labour for one month in his 1832 revolutionary pamphlet *Grand National Holiday* (Prothero 1974: 134).[33] In 1926 the General Strike was defeated after only nine days, but throughout this and the following decade trade unions continued to campaign for greater leisure time in the form of the shorter working week and paid holidays. At no point did Farjeon make May Day the occasion for socialist comment in her contributions to *Time and Tide*. However, in several 'Weekly Crowd' poems marking other festival days including Easter and Whitsun, and in poems published during the month of August, Farjeon drew attention to the holiday season with a regularity reflecting the repeated demand for universal holidays made by representatives of the industrial working class

(Jones 1986: 27). In significant ways Farjeon's socialist approach to leisure undercut *Time and Tide*'s feminist approach to work discussed in Chapter 1. However, these holiday poems also appear to have strengthened *Time and Tide*'s editor-staff relations, and paved the way for brokering new relationships as the periodical worked to gain the attention of a wider public.

Farjeon's first holiday poem appeared in *Time and Tide*'s issue of 18 August 1922, and its title 'Far from the Weekly Crowd' immediately announces the poem's departure from the feature's usual format. Apparently composed during a holiday in Dorset, Big Ben is replaced by 'The Chimes of Cattistock' and a note explains that the poem refers to the gathering of people 'from far and wide [. . .] to hear the playing of the famous Cattistock Carillon by M. Joseph Denyn of Malines' (18 Aug 1922: 780). The following week Farjeon's regular contribution was again printed under the title 'Far from the Weekly Crowd'. It begins: 'Where are they all, the crowds that press / City and town on business or idleness? How many faces / Are gone from their familiar places! [. . .] Can they have melted in thin air, / These people who were everywhere?' The poem continues:

> Melted? Oh no! look out o'doors –
> Look to the mountains and the moors,
> The Norfolk Broads, the Wilds of Wales,
> The Sussex Downs, the Yorkshire Dales,
> The Highlands and the Lakes – but most,
> Look all along the English coast
> Where, like a surf left by the tide,
> Framing the isle on every side,
> Weathered by bursts of sun, and clouds
> Of rain – you'll find the holiday crowds. (25 Aug 1922: 804)

Once again, the familiar 'crowd' of Farjeon's poems is dislodged from its usual metropolitan environment, dispersed here across Britain's countryside and coast. But by making the holiday season its central subject the poem remains very topical: August was the month when thousands of holidaymakers left the city, served by Britain's rapidly growing leisure industry.[34] Farjeon herself shared with *Time and Tide*'s largely middle-class contributor and readership base the resources to enjoy more holidays than the workers' annual May Day festival. But I want to suggest that the poem's focus on 'holiday crowds' creates a link to socialist movements which sought to 'reduce work and increase leisure' in this period (Shiach 2004: 224). Significantly, while

Farjeon regularly took holidays she was never released from the contract of her weekly contribution, and her customary practice was to
run off verses in advance (Annabel Farjeon 1986: 156). The following
year she invented an elaborate conceit for managing her absence from
London in the month of August and her distance from the daily newspapers on which her weekly contribution relied. As I will discuss, this
conceit would also become a vehicle for more radical comment on
industrial capitalism in the context of ongoing trade union disputes
over the hours of human labour.

Farjeon's new idea involved making her pseudonym one of the
voices in 'The Weekly Crowd'. The first of these poems appeared in
Time and Tide's issue of 27 July 1923; it begins:

> CHIMAERA (settling down to its job):
> Where are the papers? Let me scan the news
> And see what in the world at present passes,
> What things transpire to put men in the blues,
> And what to make them look through rosy glasses.
> Let's see – hum! Fashion – Politics – and Sport –
> The Court – and the Police-Court – and the Weather –
> The usual topics here for me to sort
> And put into the stewpan all together,
> Then gorge upon the tasty seven-days' era – (27 July 1923: 754)

Here Chimaera's 'job' (and by extension Farjeon's) is neatly sum-
marised, but immediately following these lines a 'A Stern Voice' cries
'Desist!' and announces the arrival of 'Bellerophon' who, as in the
Greek myth, has come to 'slay' Chimaera.[35] A verbal battle ensues
between the two characters, and with dexterous wit Chimaera turns
the 'hour' of her death to a 'month' explaining that 'then from the
dust / I'll re-create myself'. The poem ends with Bellerophon's command 'Chimaera, die!' and Chimaera's reply: 'Good-bye – until
September'. Over the next four weeks *Time and Tide* printed verses
'by Chimaera' under the title 'Far from the Weekly Crowd' which
feature nymphs and fauns in woodlands and on seashores, and the
goddess 'Cereus' who surveys the world with her sickle.[36] Finally,
on 24 August, 'Morpheus' (the god of dreams) declares: 'The Pag-
eant's ended' and Chimaera is 'reborn' (850). On 31 August 'The
Weekly Crowd' was back with its customary format marking Farjeon's return to London and the resumption of her usual duties. With
this new device Farjeon neatly resolved the problem of how to fulfil
her weekly contract during the holiday season, and from this point

on 'Chimaera' regularly features as a character in Farjeon's holiday poems. However, with her next appearance Chimaera cuts a more rebellious figure and I argue that, in the context of continuing efforts within the labour movement to keep the issue of paid holidays in the public eye (Jones 1986: 18), Farjeon's holiday poems invite readers' recognition of a radical agenda.

In late 1923 *Time and Tide*'s future editor became publicly embroiled on the question of paid holidays. As John recounts, in December of this year Rhondda added her voice in *The Times* 'to a plea for shop assistants to be given three consecutive days off over the Christmas holiday'; a few days later the *Daily News* printed a letter from a man of the Rhondda valley who 'pointedly suggested that Lady Rhondda lead a movement for the payment of statutory holidays including a fortnight each summer for miners' (2013: 274).[37] In August 1924, the year that saw the formation of the first Labour government, Chimaera appeared in Farjeon's 'Weekly Crowd' alongside two new characters, an 'Editor' and a 'Printer's Devil'. The poem begins:

THE EDITOR (In his office, on the eve of publication):
The copy's late! There is no time to waste –
Let someone to Chimaera in all haste
And see what's happening. No doubt the creature
Is following its triple-headed nature
And nosing out the News – but let it know
It's nearly time for us to Press to go. (8 Aug 1924: 762)

The subtle transformation here from Chimaera's obedience in the last poem, which depicted the creature 'settling down to its job', to her neglect in this one, which results in the copy being 'late', heralds a new note of conflict between employer and employee during the holiday season. On reaching Chimaera's dwelling the Printer's Devil finds that far from 'nosing out the News' 'the Creature' is busy packing to go on holiday, and pressed to 'send along some copy of some sort' Chimaera responds:

But I don't *know* the News, boy! I've not read
The papers for a week. Take back instead
This interview verbatim; and from me
Tell them that from the fields of Normandy
And Breton shores I'll send them news of bliss
Far from The Weekly Crowd. I mustn't miss
My boat. Goodbye.

The poem ends comically with the Printer's Devil exclaiming:

> Good riddance, you uncouth
> Monstrosity! Now for the bitter truth.
> (*He goes and breaks the Bitter Truth to the Editor. Being out of earshot,*
> *Chimaera cannot report the effects.*) (762)

Once again, the poem works to manage Farjeon's absence from the London newspapers on which her weekly contribution relies; in the next issue her poem is printed under the now familiar heading 'Far from the Weekly Crowd' and is spoken in the voice of 'A Wanderer' in northern France (15 Aug 1924: 786). But the poem's recasting of Chimaera as a Caliban-like 'creature' defying its master ('uncouth / Monstrosity') introduces a new sense of militancy, albeit comic. In the final line, we delight in the unreported 'effects' of Chimaera's defiance upon the Editor, whose response to the 'Bitter Truth' is presumably unprintable.

This poem marks the beginning of a running joke in 'The Weekly Crowd' about an errant Chimaera whose regular disappearance from the workplace during the holiday season causes increasing levels of disruption and annoyance to 'The Ed'. Through a strategy of 'comic militancy' the joke keeps alive the issue of workers' rights to a holiday, but a poem published early the following year suggests that the joke was also directed towards *Time and Tide*'s own office environment.[38] This poem, published in *Time and Tide*'s issue of 30 January 1925, deployed the iconography of the periodical's masthead to stage a conversation between 'Father Thames' and 'Big Ben'. It begins:

Father Thames:	Come, what's the matter, Father Time?
Big Ben:	I'm tired. I've stopped.
Father Thames:	Oh, this won't do!
	You never catch *me* stopping. I'm
	Waiting for no man; why should you?
Big Ben:	Tush! All men have a holiday
	In season. Why can't I? I will! (30 Jan 1925: 102)

The quip often attendant on *Time and Tide*'s title – 'waiting for no man' – is an obvious in-joke that invokes the businesslike efficiency of *Time and Tide*'s own professional environment. According to John, 'efficiency' was an important word in Rhondda's vocabulary, and in the early 1920s she 'helped to set up and was president of the Efficiency Club, a support group for increasing cooperation among business and professional women' (2013: 284; 280). The joke trades on the implied reader's sympathy for Big Ben's insistence on his right to 'a holiday / In season', but the Great Bell of Westminster is startled into a new position when he observes: 'Heavens! What's this? The Sun – he slips / From sight! It's black as midnight!' The poem concludes:

Father Thames:	Till
	Old Time comes out of his Eclipse,
	Behold, the Sun himself stands still!
Big Ben:	I'm coming back to work. Tick! tick! . . .
Father Thames:	(I fancied that would do the trick!)

Here the total solar eclipse on 24 January 1925 (which was the subject of newspaper headlines around the world that week) becomes a vehicle for wider political comment on the changes in working practices that accompanied the shift from 'Old Time' (measured by the sun) to the time of modernity (measured by the clock) when, especially following the introduction of standard time at the end of the nineteenth century, time became 'exploitable, suffused with the value of capital' (Armstrong 2005: 7). In another 'Weekly Crowd' composed for the Whitsuntide holiday in May 1925, comedy turns on *Time and Tide*'s request for Chimaera's copy 'For our issue of June 5th by May 28th' which leads Chimaera to exclaim:

Upon my word! Of all the shabby tricks!
How without straw, pray, can I make my bricks?
How write the week's news up a week too soon,
Before it happens, for the Fifth of June? (5 June 1925: 542)

Again the delight for readers is in Chimaera's resourcefulness, as she proceeds to 'invent' a conversation between Jove, Apollo and several other gods from classical mythology. But the implication in these poems is that *Time and Tide*'s own working environment is not immune from the 'tyranny of the clock'.

The radicalism of socialist movements thus continued to make its mark upon 'The Weekly Crowd'. But while in 1922 the subversive energies of Farjeon's poems appear to have created tensions between *Time and Tide*'s directors, by the mid-1920s her 'in-jokes' seem to have strengthened relationships between *Time and Tide*'s in-crowd of staff and regular contributors. In July 1925 a 'Weekly Crowd' poem indicates that she was among 'the Staff, the Ed., / The Guests, and the Contributors' present at *Time and Tide*'s fifth birthday dinner (10 July

1925: 670),[39] and her contribution to a publicity drive towards the end of the same year confirms that by this time she had become one of the periodical's core collaborators.[40] However, a 'Weekly Crowd' poem written at the end of her summer holiday in August that year suggests that Farjeon's radicalism also placed her at some distance from the company of women who worked on the paper. The poem is spoken in the voice of a ballad-singer and begins:

> It's far far I've been from the towns and the cities,
> It's far from the streets where the great engines sound,
> From the tale of men's sorrows, their joys and their pities,
> It's far from the wheels that make the world go round.
> Lone have I gone as the slow heron winging
> Back in the twilight to the home-marsh again,
> And as for the songs that I've been a-singing,
> They weren't for the hearing of maids or of men. (21 Aug 1925: 814)

The plaintive quality of this verse contrasts strongly with the comic poems discussed above. The repetition of 'far' accentuates the distance travelled away from the 'Weekly Crowd', and the phrase 'lone have I gone' suggests a separation from *Time and Tide*'s inner circle of core collaborators. As previously noted, Farjeon often used the ballad-singer as a vehicle for her most radical verse, and in the 'songs that [. . .] weren't for the hearing of maids or of men' we might read an allusion to a radicalism that cannot be expressed in *Time and Tide*'s pages. The next stanza begins with references to 'War', 'sorrow', and 'scars', and speaks of communing with 'coney' and 'wren': a retreat into the natural world which continues into the third stanza where 'out of sight' and 'out of hearing' the ballad-singer hears only 'the wordless voice of the hill and the fen'. In the final stanza, the ballad-singer describes coming 'back [. . .] to the facts and the rumours' and the world of 'the street', and the last lines read:

> But never a rhyme or a tune I'll be bringing
> To tell where I've been and what I've seen again,
> Yet it lies out of earshot at the root of my singing
> Of songs for the hearing of maids and of men.

The poem appears to convey a suppressed radicalism that lies 'at the root' of her contributions to *Time and Tide*, but which due to editorial constraints must be kept 'out of earshot'. In 1926, the year of the General Strike, Farjeon's 'Weekly Crowd' took on a new form of artistic militancy.

The General Strike was called by the Trade Unions Council (TUC) in May 1926 in response to the announcement by coal owners of wage cuts and increases in working hours. Farjeon's 'Weekly Crowd' poems contain frequent references to the miners' plight from as early as 1922, and *Time and Tide* also paid attention in its editorial columns to this developing national crisis. However, when the strike was called *Time and Tide* was unsympathetic. In an abridged issue published on 7 May (three days into the strike) its editorial declared: 'In our view the Government was entirely right in its decision to refuse to attempt to negotiate while the pistol of the General Strike was held to its head. [. . .] Tyranny remains tyranny whencesoever [*sic*] it emanates' (7 May 1926: 2). The Leftist press of course refused to print their papers and journals during the strike, and while *Time and Tide*'s strike issue contained contributions from some regular writers, significantly 'The Weekly Crowd' did not appear. Farjeon did contribute that week, however, to the *British Worker*, the official bulletin of the TUC published daily from the *Daily Herald* offices for the duration of the strike. Using her *Daily Herald* pseudonym 'Tomfool' Farjeon composed poems voicing deep sympathy with the strikers, including 'We Have Not Chosen Lightly' (5 May 1926: 4), and 'Stand By!' (8 May 1926: 4), a poem which, as Morag Shiach observes, in its echo of the war finds resonances of government betrayal (2004: 233).[41] Another poem, 'The Great, Great Trek' expresses unity with 'the Workers' (6 May 1926: 4), while a fifth compares the 'Skeleton Service' put in place by the government to maintain a basic transport system with the 'live flesh and blood' of the 'body of Labour' and asks: 'who [. . .] Can blame him for blunting the Capital Knife / That would pare him to a Skeleton Service for life?' (11 May 1926: 4).

The radicalism of Farjeon's *British Worker* poems places beyond doubt the fact that the non-appearance of her weekly contribution in *Time and Tide*'s strike issue represented a withdrawal of her services in solidarity with the industrial working class. Rhondda, in contrast, allowed her business premises at 92 Victoria Street to be used by the government's supply and transport organisations (John 2013: 271), and *Time and Tide* produced a second issue under strike conditions. This was published on 14 May, two days after the strike was called off. This time Farjeon's weekly contribution did appear, but her poem is radically different from her usual 'Weekly Crowd' (see Figure 2.3).

For regular readers of *Time and Tide*, the most striking aspect of Chimaera's poem this week is its departure from its usual format. In place of 'The Weekly Crowd' we have 'The Striking Week', a title

The Striking Week

By CHIMÆRA

All the Crowd a listens in
At Ten O'clock and One.
" Any fresh news to-day ? "
Practically none.

Here there were disturbances,
There things were still ;
Such and such newspapers
Printed—just a bill ;
Bus-routes and train times
Repeated o'er again .   .   .   .
Hark, hark ! the Signal—
There goes Big Ben.

All the Crowd a listens in
At One O'clock and Four.
" Any fresh news to-day ? "
Very little more.
When will the Strike end ?
That's still in doubt,
Some men are going back,
Most staying out ;
Volunteers still working in
The places of the men .   .   .   .
Hark, hark ! the Signal—
There goes Big Ben.

All the Crowd a listens in
At Four O'clock and Seven.
" New reports from Newcastle,
Fresh news from Devon."
What were the rights of it ?
Folk split on those.
What will be the end of it ?
God only knows.
And afterwards—afterwards ?
What will happen then ? .   .   .   .
Hark, hark ! the Signal !
There goes Big Ben.

All the Crowd a listens in
At Seven O,clock and Ten.

Figure 2.3 'The Striking Week. By Chimaera', *Time and Tide* 14 May 1926: 18. Reproduced with the permission of The William Ready Division of Archives and Research Collections, McMaster University Library.

that not only marks the week's events as noteworthy, but also carries connotations of the week being on strike in an extraordinary rupture of time itself. As such the poem belongs to what Shiach identifies as a body of literature which draws on 'the complex temporalities of the General Strike' (2004: 230). Its preoccupation with the linear progression of clock-time (as Big Ben strikes 'One', 'Four', 'Seven', and 'Ten') is disrupted by repetition producing stasis, and the suspense-inducing absence of news (registered in the ellipsis in each stanza) is, to borrow Shiach's words, 'an unsettling marker of the disruption of temporality' (2004: 230). The succession of unanswered questions inscribes anxieties about the future bred by a radical consciousness ('And afterwards – afterwards? / What will happen then?') But it is arguably the silent omission of the feature's usual framing device that encodes Farjeon's radicalism most strongly: opposed to *Time and Tide*'s position on the strike Chimaera cannot endorse the line 'With *Time and Tide* the Crowd must go'. Significantly the absence of the frame in 'The Striking Week' connects this poem with Farjeon's holiday poems written 'Far from the Weekly Crowd'; with one exception, each of these poems also omit the four-line frame.[42] Shiach has observed that 'release from the repetitions and compulsions of labour was part of the meaning of the strike' (2004: 241), and in this formal link between the poems we might read an echo of William Benbow's *Grand National Holiday*. Indeed, while Labour's case for leisure between the wars was 'essentially reformist and social democratic in nature' (Jones 1986: 137), Benbow's holiday 'was to be a revolution' (Prothero 1974: 153) and it is this history of radicalism that makes its imprint on Farjeon's poem.

In *Time and Tide*'s next issue, published on 21 May, a full bill of contents was restored and 'The Weekly Crowd' represented the return of normal working conditions. The poem's usual title and frame were reinstated, and it ended with a mother's voice (in response to the news that 'the Printers' terms are settled') saying: 'Ah, then / We *will* have our old *Time and Tide* this week!' (21 May 1926: 450). The following week, however, the ongoing coal dispute was the subject of *Time and Tide*'s leading article, and for this issue Farjeon wrote a poem which, with its stark exposure of human suffering, is much closer in style and content to her poems in the *British Worker*. This poem begins with a characteristic celebration of the Whitsun holiday in the voice of a ballad-singer who cries: 'Golden Whitsun! Golden Whitsun! / Whitsun on a tide of gold!' But in the fourth stanza, after scenes of holidaymakers enjoying leisure pursuits in the country and in the city, there is a sudden shift in tone:

Ah, but was it golden Whitsun
Where the miner's pickaxe fails,
And the shadow of the Hunger
Creeps across the Monmouth Vales!
There the mother by the cradle
Sees the coming of her grief –
Can the Funds save *all* the children,
Being raised for their relief?
At the month's end, Baldwin's promise
Of new subsidies expires –
Sure, it was not golden Whitsun
By the miner's unlit fires. (28 May 1926: 474)

Here the Whitsun holiday is overshadowed by the bitter experiences of miners and their families in Wales; for them the 'unlit fires' mean that Whitsun is 'not golden' and the future portent is not happiness but 'grief'. This is an overt expression of Farjeon's sympathy with the miners, but the poem's most unexpected development comes at the very end:

Summer, careless of the gold-dross
With its human stranglehold,
Changes with her living sunshine
Whitsun time and tide to gold.

With its unmistakable reference to the publication in which it is printed, the closing line of this poem is extraordinarily ambiguous. Interpretation hinges on whether we treat the last word as an adjective or a noun: as an adjective, 'gold' functions as it has done in the rest of the poem to denote the colours of summer transforming time as well as tide into a golden hue, but if we read 'gold' as a noun, the line takes on a whole new inflection. Not only does the introduction of the word 'time' alongside 'tide' invite the capitalist notion 'time is money', but by invoking the title *Time and Tide* it also implicates the paper in the exploitation of human labour. Some lines from another of Farjeon's poems published in the *British Worker* lend support to this more radical reading:

WE have a dream [. . .]
Where life's rich cornfields turn from green
To gold for all men's hands to glean:
Where, since each man may glean the gold,
Contentment gives back sevenfold
Joy to the harvest. (16 May 1926: 4)

Here the changing colour of the corn from green to gold is linked to a socialist vision in which everyone benefits equally from the earth's resources. This radicalism is suppressed in the more oblique lines of Farjeon's Whitsun poem for *Time and Tide*, but it is hard not to infer a critique of the periodical's operation within the economic structures of capitalist society. Crucially, the wealth of *Time and Tide*'s founder and soon-to-be editor, Lady Rhondda, was largely derived from coal; her father had been the most powerful coal owner in South Wales (John 2013: 242). Admittedly, *Time and Tide* was far from making 'gold'; it in fact ran at a loss for most of its lifetime. However, heavily subsidised by Rhondda *Time and Tide* relied in a very material way upon labour in the pits.[43]

Editorial constraints limited the extent to which Farjeon's poems could openly condemn capitalism in the pages of *Time and Tide*, but May 1926 seems to have heightened a socialist approach to leisure in her contributions to this periodical. In a 'Weekly Crowd' at the beginning of August 1926 comic militancy is replaced by campaigning vigour in a rallying call that summons readers to abandon work for the holiday season:

> Holidays have come about!
> Get your easy garments out,
> Leave your offices behind you,
> Go where they will never find you. (6 Aug 1926: 714)

But if Farjeon's radicalism was perceived as a liability at the end of 1922, by 1926 it appears that *Time and Tide* was able to harness it as part of its strategy for generating debate and attracting new audiences. Significantly, among the publications in which *Time and Tide* placed advance notices of its series on 'Women of the Leisured Classes' in the autumn of 1926 (see Chapter 1) was the ILP organ, the *New Leader*.[44] In radical as well as feminist discourses 'useful members' and 'idle classes' were familiar terms (Prothero 1974: 157), and William Benbow himself divided the world between the useful worker and the parasite (Shiach 2004: 201). The series presented an opportunity, therefore, to draw socialists as well as feminists into the controversy over 'The Menace of the Leisured Woman', as the figures who joined Rhondda on a public platform in January 1927 further demonstrate (both Chesterton and Shaw were prominent spokespersons in the Labour movement). In an article on the debate published in the *New Leader* the following week, A. Fenner Brockway (editor of the ILP organ under its former title, the *Labour Leader*) accepted Rhondda's charges against the Leisured Woman, but he also stated that her critique did not go far enough: 'Lady Rhondda's indictment cannot be limited to the leisured woman; it extends to the whole leisured *class* – that leisured class which is a menace to society, both because it exists by robbing the *working* classes, and because it is still the ruling class' (4 Feb 1927: 15). Identified with the interests of Labour rather than capital the *New Leader* went further in its denunciation of capitalism than *Time and Tide* would ever do in its columns. Brockway concluded his article as follows:

> And at the other end of the social scale we see another tragedy, a tragedy as terrible, but with heroism and nobility in it – the wife of the working man old before she is young, living an existence of unending anxiety, contriving to make her pittance clothe and feed her family, starving herself to do it, whose home is one or two rooms into whose life come little of colour and beauty. This is surely the worst of Capitalism's contrasts. (15)

Brockway's article in the *New Leader* is evidence of *Time and Tide*'s success in attracting attention from the socialist press; the *Daily Herald* also carried a report of the debate in its issue of 28 January 1927. But it also reveals the wide gulf that remained between Rhondda's world and that of the working classes; as John points out, '[Rhondda] does not seem to have voiced much specific concern about the women in Welsh mining families whose lives were dependent on the collieries she helped to control' (2013: 274). This gap posed a risk for *Time and Tide* as it worked to secure its future under its new editor, particularly in so far as it needed the continued support of women readers. During the 1920s, as Pamela Graves discusses, 'labour women came to associate feminism with "leisured" women who had no understanding of the problems of the poor' and tended to characterise middle- and upper-class feminists as 'rich, but idle, ladies' (1994: 119; 124). In this context, *Time and Tide*'s 'leisured women' debate can be read as an important public relations exercise as well as a publicity stunt in which the periodical sought to manage Rhondda's image and sell feminism to a new post-war generation of women who had not been involved in the suffrage movement. As reported in *G. K's. Weekly*, Chesterton identified the fundamental difference between himself and Rhondda in terms of his opponent's belief in a 'modern commercial capitalist and ultimately monopolist civilisation' and his own total and utter disbelief in it. Equating Rhondda's mandate for work as a mandate for 'serving a rich capitalist society', he recommended that both men and women 'retire into their homes to think more often' and address the capitalist problem by 'cultivat[ing] a sense of individual liberty, a creative power from within' (5 Feb 1927: 224). The verbatim report of the entire debate was printed in his magazine under the provocative title 'The Menace of the Busybody'. At once asserting Chesterton's elevation of leisure over work, this riposte to *Time and Tide* also implied that feminist social reformers were interfering amateurs meddling in affairs they ought to stay out of. This was, of course, an image that *Time and Tide* was intent on dismantling in its discourse of professionalism, and in its feminist advocacy of women's rights to full participation in political and public life. Indeed, the year 1926 had been one of renewed efforts by feminists to secure this goal through an Equal Political Rights Campaign Committee set up to coordinate the activities of the women's organisations (Alberti 1989: 187). As chair of this committee Rhondda was, as always, far from 'idle', and her controversial articles constructed the responsible female citizen as the very opposite of the 'leisured woman' model.

As Faith Binckes observes, controversy is often 'the life and breath' of periodicals (2010: 9), and in its own reporting of the debate *Time and Tide*'s positioning of 'The Weekly Crowd' directly alongside a 'verbatim report' of George Bernard Shaw's speech seems deliberately designed to foreground competing discourses around work and leisure. The poem begins with a dialogue 'at Midnight' between two familiar speakers, Big Ben and Father Thames, which seems to replay an in-joke about *Time and Tide*'s work ethic:

> Big Ben: Are you asleep, Old Thames?
> Thames: Not I. Are you?
> Big Ben: I never sleep. With so much work to do
>   Keeping the seconds moving on, I find
>   I have no time to sleep. (4 Feb 1927: 106)

Here, Big Ben (who in Farjeon's solar-eclipse poem two years earlier had insisted on his right to a holiday) now appears to have become completely enslaved to the ticking of the clock; following a summary of the week's events the poem concludes:

> Big Ben: Sleep, Thames.
> Thames: Sleep, Time.
> Big Ben: River, I cannot, while
>   These empty forces drive across the Isle.
>   When men and women cease to laugh and weep,
>   Idle and work and love and hate – I'll sleep.

However, the allusion in Big Ben's last lines to Charles Kingsley's popular ballad 'The Three Fishers' preserves a socialist vision, and the oppositions in the last line ('idle and work', 'love and hate') are perhaps deliberately designed to stoke the coals of controversy, invoking the terms and passions aroused on both sides of the 'Leisured Woman' debate.[45] Significantly, and unlike Farjeon's earlier poem, there is a humanising of Big Ben's ceaseless activity here that conveys not deadening labour in the service of capital, but vital work in the service of 'men and women' in a world where there is still so much to be done. As such, the poem supports *Time and Tide*'s feminist agenda, and suggests that a certain understanding had been reached between Farjeon and the periodical's new editor.

Indeed, Farjeon's collaboration with Rhondda seems to have licensed an escalation of Chimaera's rebellion in subsequent 'Weekly Crowd' poems. In a holiday poem of April 1927, published on the eve of the Easter weekend, Chimaera's flight from work and pursuit of leisure is constructed in overtly defiant terms:

> I'm running away! I'm running away!
> I don't care *what* my Editors say!
> While my Editors fume and fuss and fret,
> I'm running away to Somerset!
> Topical news will pass me by
> While I browse on the grass and drink the sky.
> I shan't do work! I shall take it slack!
> I'm running away – till I come back. (22 Apr 1927: 374)

This poem appeared in *Time and Tide* just one week before the *Daily Herald* printed an elaborate diagram identifying Rhondda as one of five key individuals at the heart of a monopoly combining the interests of employers in heavy industry and the press who were lined up to take more powerful and insidious action than proposed anti-union legislation (28 Apr 1927: 10).[46] Yet Chimaera's open disregard for editorial authority does not, I suggest, point to a breakdown of real editor-staff relations, but the very opposite. 'The Weekly Crowd', as I have shown, was a core part of *Time and Tide*'s early identity, and by the mid-1920s it had become an accepted home for Farjeon's radical voice in the paper. Stories of Chimaera's rebellion were now a staple part of the feature in the holiday season, and the in-jokes worked to entertain, and strengthen bonds between, members of *Time and Tide*'s readership that is both feminist and socialist. Another poem, published in August 1927, presents the 'Editor' discussing with his 'Sub' the problem faced by the office every August:

```
Ed:                    It's then
        The only tricky member of our staff
        Plays false with us, packs up, and with a laugh
        Sheers off, and leaves the paper in the lurch.
Sub:    You mean Chimaera?
Ed:                    Naturally. Search
        The creature's lodgings, and if it is there
        Handcuff it, bind it, drag it by the hair
        Straight here, where under pain of execution
        We'll force from it its weekly contribution. (12 Aug 1927: 738)
```

As usual this poem functions as a conceit for managing Farjeon's absence from London in the month of August; at its conclusion, the 'Editor' receives a telegram from 'Chimaera' announcing: 'Am / taking my holiday in ancient Greece / and good queen bess's england will send piece each week from there.'[47] But the use of handcuffs and torture in the disciplining of the errant Chimaera extends Farjeon's representation of the tyranny to which 'the creature' is subject. In a now familiar two-layered commentary, the in-joke is almost certainly directed towards *Time and Tide*'s new editor, Rhondda, who was by all accounts very demanding of her staff,[48] while the tightening of industrial legislation following the General Strike provides fresh impetus for the poem's comic militancy.[49]

Farjeon continued to contribute 'Weekly Crowd' poems under her pseudonym Chimaera until May 1931.[50] But from May 1927, as the 'Leisured Women' debate drew to a close, a new feature replaced Farjeon's usual contribution in the first issue of every month. Under the title 'The Monthly Calendar' this feature was still signed 'Chimaera' and it carried an almost identical frame to that used in 'The Weekly Crowd': '*The Sands run on, the Waters flow, / With Time and Tide the Year must go. // With Time and Tide the Year is gone – / The Waters flow, and the Sands run on*' (6 May 1927: 422). In all other respects, however, Farjeon's 'Monthly Calendar' was completely different from her 'Weekly Crowd' poems. Positioned in a new 'Miscellany' section introduced by *Time and Tide* in the same issue (see Chapter 6) it was separated from the periodical's political content. With no topical news in sight, the poem is a song to 'May' with its white hedgerows, crooning doves, contented cows and woodland streams. The poem was illustrated by Gwen Raverat whose drawing of an idyllic outdoor scene reinforces the pastoral mode of this new feature (Figure 2.4). Two children absorbed in play at the riverbank signify time for leisure, while the languorous pose of the girl lying under the tree recalls Chimaera's intention two weeks earlier to 'browse on the grass and

422   **TIME AND TIDE**   MAY 6, 1927

Drawing by Gwendoline Raverat

The Monthly Calendar

May

By CHIMÆRA.

The Sands run on, the Waters flow,
With Time and Tide the Year must go.

In May the hedge is white above
  And green below,
And in the wood the mated dove
  By day croons low,
And there the nightingale all night
  Shaking the deep-
Leaved branches with its own delight
  Forgets to sleep.

In May the children lie and play
  Under the trees,
And cows in deep content all day
  Crop the fresh leas;
The purple flag amid her blades
  By the new streams
Watches her face until it fades.
  To twilit dreams.

The oak is golden still and young,
  Cuckoo still sings
In tune, the fledgling finds its tongue
  Before its wings,
The apple-bloom across the branch
  Spreads rosy nets
That turns to a pale avalanche
  Before it sets.

The Queen in every cot and town
  Chosen again
Has worn her silver parsley-crown
  And daisy-chain;
And Proserpine, her olden bliss
  Recapturing,
Has once again forgotten Dis
  And found the Spring.

With Time and Tide the Year is gone—
The Waters flow, and the Sands run on.

Figure 2.4 'The Monthly Calendar', *Time and Tide* 6 May 1927: 422. © Estate of Gwen Raverat. All rights reserved, DACS 2017.

drink the sky'. Indeed, in contrast with Farjeon's unsleeping Big Ben, enslaved to the regular rhythms of clock time, here her 'nightingale all night [. . .] with its own delight / Forgets to sleep', accountable only to the pleasures of its own creation. Subsequent 'Monthly Calendar' poems and illustrations also dwelt on scenes from rural life: haymaking in June; river bathing in July; a village dance in August; apple picking in September.[51]

Farjeon's use of the conventions of rural idyll in this feature may at first appear to represent a retreat from the politically engaged verse of her 'Weekly Crowd' contributions. However, in the context of debates about work and leisure in the pages of this periodical it is possible to read 'The Monthly Calendar' not as nostalgia, but as an attempt to recover a space for leisure within the calendar of modern life and as a radical counter-discourse to *Time and Tide*'s feminist duty to work. Producing a new rhythm in Farjeon's weekly contributions the feature literally gave her a 'holiday' every month from the business of summing up the news in verse, and introduced variety to her labour, the loss of which was a key feature of socialist discourses around work. Furthermore, its use of the lyric mode, which Anne Janowitz (1998) has recovered in its communitarian form as a site of collective engagement and recuperation, offers a way for thinking about this feature as a continuation of Farjeon's socialist aesthetic. Raverat (who would later join *Time and Tide*'s staff as an art critic) was also a frequent contributor to the *New Leader*, which under H. N. Brailsford's editorship between 1922 and 1926 published drawings and woodcuts in every issue (Leventhal 1974: 98). The new 'Monthly Calendar' feature may be read, therefore, as evidence of how connections with socialist print culture literally reshaped the content of *Time and Tide*, and brought fresh ideas into the development of the paper. Indeed, according to F. M. Leventhal, 'one of the hallmarks of the *New Leader* was its illustrations', and in its literary content 'Brailsford was determined not only to draw upon prominent figures in the movement for the political columns, but also to solicit contributions from the best authors of the day' (1974: 98). This was undoubtedly an ambition shared by Rhondda, and in Part Two of this book I examine the ways in which an increased use of illustration as well as writing by celebrated literary figures aided *Time and Tide*'s expansion at the end of the decade. First, I turn in the next chapter to the periodical's cultural criticism, and discuss the ways in which *Time and Tide*'s reviews of music, theatre, film and books addressed and constructed the paper's readership during its early years.

Notes

1. Rhondda's father, the Liberal MP D. A. Thomas, was a highly successful and wealthy industrialist with business interests in coalmining, shipping and newspapers. He was given a peerage, becoming Lord Rhondda, in 1916.

2. Farjeon's identity as 'Chimaera' was revealed in *Time and Tide* in a review of her book *The Soul of Kol Nikon* (23 Nov 1923: 1173).

3. MR to ER, 13 January 1921. ER Papers.

4. An advertisement placed in the *Woman Engineer* in September 1921 lists Hamilton as one of *Time and Tide*'s directors. Hamilton contributed book reviews to *Time and Tide* from August 1920 to January 1932.

5. The Children's Book Circle annually presents an Eleanor Farjeon Award for distinguished service to the world of British children's books. Mary Ashraf acknowledges Farjeon as a socialist poet in her edited collection *Political Verse and Song from Britain and Ireland* (1975). Farjeon's diverse output is represented in a new selection of her poetry edited by her literary executor, Anne Harvey (2013).

6. Farjeon had been contributing poems to the *Daily Herald* under the pseudonym 'Tomfool' since 1916. She began contributing poems to H. N. Brailsford's *New Leader* in October 1922 as 'Merry Andrew', and used her 'Tomfool' pseudonym in Lansbury's *Labour Weekly* (which ran from February 1925 to July 1927).

7. Private correspondence. I am indebted to Jim Clayson for the knowledge he has shared with me regarding Farjeon's contributions to the socialist press.

8. Dr Wood's arrival in England to hear the nightingale sing had been reported in national newspapers the previous week: 'Atlantic Journey to Hear the Nightingale' (*Manchester Guardian*, 6 May 1922: 11); 'The County of the Nightingale. A Surrey Guide for Dr. Casey Wood' (*Observer*, 7 May 1922: 15). On Tuesday 16 May the *Daily Express* carried an article on its front page entitled: 'Nightingale in Chorus. Dr. Wood Hears Them At Last'.

9. Laurel Brake (1994) discusses a 'literature/journalism' divide which became more pronounced in the modernist era.

10. Pound's oft-quoted phrase comes from his *ABC of Reading* published in 1934.

11. The nightingale is immortalised in John Keats's 'Ode to a Nightingale'.

12. Farjeon met Thomas through her brother, Bertie, in 1912; Thomas was killed at the Front in 1917. See Farjeon (1958) for an account of these years.

13. Farjeon shared with Thomas a popular passion for hiking or 'tramping' in the English countryside before the war.

14. As Matthew Hollis discusses, Thomas wrote a glowing review of his friend Robert Frost's second poetry collection, *North of Boston* (1914),

in which most of the poems resemble short dramas or dialogues and give fullest expression to Frost's early poetics and what he called 'the sound of sense'. When the Thomases joined the Frosts for a holiday in Gloucestershire in August 1914, Farjeon rented rooms nearby and joined Thomas and Frost in walks and talks about poetry (2011: 73–4).

15. Howarth makes the compelling argument that 'a good deal of great twentieth-century British, Irish and Commonwealth poetry owes as much or more to Thomas and Hardy's example than it does to Pound and Eliot' (3).

16. Farjeon deserves a place alongside the figures recovered by Angela Ingram and Daphne Patai in *Rediscovering Forgotten Radicals: British Women Writers 1889–1939* (1993).

17. See Ruth Livesey (2004) for a discussion of Socialism and Victorian poetry.

18. Lucy Delap discusses the multiple collective identities offered by feminist periodicals (DiCenzo 2011: 167).

19. Hannam and Hunt define this tension as one between 'absolute pacifism versus "war against war"' (2002: 184).

20. The first article was contributed by Robert Lynd, an Irish nationalist and regular writer for the *New Statesman*. The series ran from 2 July to 27 August 1920.

21. Letter from Margaret Rhondda to Elizabeth Robins, 10 November 1920. ER Papers.

22. MR to ER, 24 November 1920. ER Papers. The first Bloody Sunday took place in Dublin during the Irish War of Independence on 21 November 1920.

23. MR to ER, 24 November 1920. ER Papers.

24. MR to ER, 13 January 1921. ER Papers.

25. MR to ER, 27 January 1921. ER Papers.

26. The Anglo-Irish Treaty was signed on 6 December 1921.

27. Michael Collins's death is recorded in the voice of 'A Ballad-Singer' in 'The Weekly Crowd' published in *Time and Tide*'s 1 September issue. The death of Sean Hales on 7 December 1922 is also recorded by 'A Ballad-Singer' in 'The Weekly Crowd' published in *Time and Tide*'s issue of 15 December 1922.

28. Mustafa Kemal first came to fame at Gallipoli.

29. MR to ER, 3 October 1922. ER Papers.

30. MR to ER, 17 October 1922. ER Papers.

31. The poem is printed on page 2 of the *Daily Herald*'s 1922 May Day Supplement, which is preserved in the Working-Class Movement Library (WCML).

32. The General Strike began on 4 May 1926.

33. I am indebted to Jen Morgan for this connection at a seminar of the Radical Studies Network, Salford, where I presented an earlier version of this chapter.

34. Stephen G. Jones notes that 'the seaside holiday habit [. . .] extended in the inter-war years' (1986: 39).
35. Bellerophon was a hero of Greek mythology whose greatest feat was killing the three-headed monster Chimaera. Though not formally educated Farjeon was very widely read, and classical mythology provides material for many of her poems.
36. The title is almost certainly a reference to Thomas Hardy and his novel *Far from the Madding Crowd* (1874). Farjeon would pay homage to Hardy in a 'Weekly Crowd' poem published after his death in January 1928.
37. Miners received no pay when not working. Jones notes that prior to the Holidays with Pay Act of 1938 paid holidays covered only a small proportion of workers throughout the interwar period (1986: 17).
38. I borrow the term 'comic militancy' from Susan Carlson who, in an essay on suffrage journalistic drama, uses it to define a comic mode that 'rarely operates as a radical tool, but performs a militancy of its own' (2000: 212).
39. In this poem, an 'Office-Girl' rouses a sleepy Chimaera whose hangover is magnified on account of having not one head but '*three*'!
40. For twenty-six weeks from 2 October 1925 *Time and Tide* published a '*Time and Tide* Alphabet. By Chimaera' which was 'Dedicated to all our Friends and Helpers'. With each letter of the alphabet this advertising-cum-verse feature issued fresh appeals to readers to help make the periodical more widely known and was later printed as a booklet to raise funds for the periodical.
41. The poem is included in Hamilton Fyfe's *Behind the Scenes of the Great Strike* (1926) and reprinted (under the title 'Promises') in Mary Ashraf (1971: 347).
42. Farjeon's first 'Far from the Weekly Crowd' poems in August 1922 both omit the usual frame, as do all her 'Far From the Weekly Crowd' poems in 1923. A 'Far from the Weekly Crowd' poem in August 1924 is untypical in retaining the frame.
43. The situation changed a lot after the 1920s as Rhondda withdrew from most of her links with mining companies. This was not from principle, but because these companies were making large losses.
44. The *New Leader* carried an advertisement for *Time and Tide*'s series in its issue of 15 October 1926.
45. A reformer rather than a revolutionary Charles Kingsley (1819–75) was active in the new Christian socialist movement; the line 'men must work and women must weep' became a catchphrase and has been taken up by subsequent radical writers and artists.
46. The diagram is reproduced in John (2013: 272).
47. Poems in the rest of August were set in ancient Greece and Elizabethan England.

48. Lorna Lewis, who joined *Time and Tide*'s staff in the 1930s, recalls that Rhondda 'extracted the last ounce from her staff [and] tore strips off us freely and frequently' (Deakin 1984: 112). Other contemporaries would be less good-humoured in their assessment of Rhondda; Vera Brittain believed Rhondda exploited her close friend Winifred Holtby, 'overworking a woman who was seriously ill' (John 2013: 315).

49. The Trade Disputes and Trade Unions Act of 1927 declared strike action unlawful.

50. The last 'Weekly Crowd' was printed in *Time and Tide*'s issue of 30 May 1931. For a further three years from June 1931 to 1934 Farjeon contributed a new monthly verse feature called 'The Broadsheet'.

51. The feature ran until December 1930.

Chapter 3

Mediating Culture: Modernism, the Arts and the Woman Reader

Time and Tide arrived in the cultural landscape at the start of a propitious decade for British modernism. Two of modernism's landmark texts, T. S. Eliot's *The Waste Land* and James Joyce's *Ulysses*, appeared in 1922, the *annus mirabilis* of modernism which also saw the launch of Eliot's literary review, the *Criterion*, 'an institution crucial to the dissemination and consolidation of modernist writing' in the early processes of modernism's canonisation (Harding 2009: 349). Modernism remains the dominant cultural force in most critical accounts of the period, though a growing body of scholarship has done much to recover and explore a broad spectrum of writing that existed alongside and in competition with it.[1] *Time and Tide* has much to contribute to revisionary accounts of the period. From its first issue the periodical carried several pages of cultural content, including reviews of music, theatre and books, as well as original creative contributions (short fiction, poems). None of the early creative work can be described as modernist, and in its reviewing of contemporary literature *Time and Tide* was completely silent during its early years on the canonised male trio of Wyndham Lewis, Eliot and Joyce, although it did regularly review female modernists, including Katherine Mansfield, Dorothy Richardson and Virginia Woolf. For *Time and Tide*'s early writers and critics literary modernism was not the most central or important aspect of modern culture, but this does not mean that they were unfamiliar with its key texts and discourses, or that the literary and artistic trends it did examine were unimportant. Indeed, I will argue that *Time and Tide*'s conversation with modernism in its review pages highlights both the limits of the modernist lens for assessing culture in this period, and the perspicuity of this periodical's female writers and critics in their analysis of cultural hierarchies already in the process of being established.

This chapter examines how a select group of *Time and Tide*'s regular female columnists mediated culture in the early years of this modern feminist magazine from 1920 to 1926. Demonstrating that contributors to its review columns were in close touch with a wide range of literary and artistic developments after the war, it argues that the periodical's mediation of culture is identifiably feminist, both in its promotion of women in the arts, and in its response to developments in criticism in the interwar years. I begin by discussing the contributions to the paper of the writer, historian and translator Christopher St John (née Christabel Marshall, 1871–1960), an important figure in the women's suffrage movement and a central figure in the London-based play-producing subscription society, the Pioneer Players, founded in 1911 by her partner Edith Craig.[2] St John contributed weekly music criticisms to *Time and Tide* from its first issue for more than ten years, and from September 1921 she contributed fortnightly theatre reviews, succeeding Rebecca West as the paper's first dramatic critic, and sharing the column with Cicely Hamilton, Margaret Rhondda (writing as 'Anne Doubleday') and Velona Pilcher, an American thespian who became a close friend of St John after meeting at a party given by Rhondda in 1922 (Purkis 2011: 123). St John also wrote occasional book reviews for the paper, and was very likely the author of more than thirty film criticisms which were published under a pseudonym between 1924 and 1926. Her reviews display a catholic taste that is used to educate the reader in the appreciation of art wherever it may be found, though film becomes a kind of test-case in *Time and Tide*'s columns for how broad or highbrow the periodical could be in its search for its own identity and audience. In the second part of this chapter I discuss *Time and Tide*'s fiction reviews through the columns of three female critics: Rose Macaulay (1881–1958), Sylvia Lynd (1888–1952) and Naomi Royde-Smith (1875–1964). Macaulay, *Time and Tide*'s first fiction reviewer, told Rhondda that she considered *Time and Tide* 'far superior' to the *Woman's Leader*, a reminder of the close competition between these periodicals which frequently shared contributors.[3] Lynd joined the paper in October 1922 and contributed regular fiction reviews for the best part of a decade, while Royde-Smith, who would later succeed Thomas Moult as *Time and Tide*'s chief reviewer of 'New Poetry', also reviewed novels and other books when she joined the periodical's columns in January 1925. With reference to the vulnerable status of the 'woman's novel', and to an interwar debate about pleasure, this section recovers a shared cultural discourse that emphasises delight in modern fiction and privileges the experience of women readers.

Educating the reader: *Time and Tide*'s music, theatre and film reviews

One cultural consequence of the First World War was the new importance attached to education, and the missionary zeal ascribed to English literature in the rebuilding of national life (Baldick 1983: 94). In
1921 the Newbolt Report placed English at the heart of the school
curriculum, and this Arnoldian view of literature's high cultural value
was at the centre of T. S. Eliot's literary-critical programme which, as
Peter Widdowson discusses, 'promoted literature [. . .] as a spiritual-
aesthetic "stay" against the destructive mass civilization of the
post-war "wasteland"' (1999: 50). Regarded not only as one of the
greatest poets of his generation but also as the period's pre-eminent
critic, Eliot has exerted far-reaching influence on our understanding of the interwar cultural landscape. His ideas about authorship,
creativity, impersonality and tradition have dominated the critical
discourse of modernism, yet, as David Goldie has argued, there is 'a
case that his contemporaries tend to suffer neglect in the shadow of
that achievement, and that as a consequence we have only a partial
understanding of the critical undergrowth out of which Eliot sprang'
(1998: 5). Goldie's purpose, in his influential study of Eliot's critical
dialogue with his colleague and rival John Middleton Murry, is to
restore the balance between two men who, in the years immediately
following the First World War, drew equal respect from their contemporaries until their public disagreements over the nature and function
of criticism left Eliot the winner and Murry the loser in the famous
classicism versus romanticism debate. Goldie's study has important
implications for other writers and critics who have suffered neglect
under the shadow of 'Eliotic modernism'. As Sydney Janet Kaplan
has discussed, boundaries shift and new participants enter the conversation when Murry rather than Eliot is used as the fulcrum for
modernism, enlarging the parameters of the literary-cultural field
(2010: 9–10). Christopher St John was one such participant, whose
contributions to *Time and Tide* bring new light to bear on this post-
war conversation about culture, and emphasise an interdisciplinar-
ity of modernism that is often overlooked. St John was vehemently
opposed to the narrowing of English culture around the literary.
In an early music criticism for *Time and Tide* she lamented the fact
that 'the bulk of educated people are not trained to appreciate music
as they are trained to appreciate literature' and, espousing a view
deriving from Schopenhauer that music *'coming from within* as
no other art does [. . .] is rightly considered the most spiritual of

all expressions of the genius of man', she stated: 'no one can claim to possess culture of the highest kind if music has no place in in it (10 Sep 1920: 372). Writing in the same column a few months later she asserted even more emphatically, in the year of the Newbolt Report, 'music [. . .] should be given its proper place in the training of the intellectual citizen', and argued that to teach people Beethoven is 'exactly of the same importance' as teaching Shakespeare (5 Aug 1921: 751).

In many ways, as we shall see, St John's criticism echoes Walter Pater's famous pronouncement that 'all art aspires to the condition of music', supporting Simon Shaw-Miller's contention that the literary or visual bias in many accounts of modernism 'fails to acknowledge the profound interaction between the arts, and to recognise the leading role that music plays both as a technical model and an ideological paradigm for emerging modernist sensibilities' (2010: 600). However, unlike those interpreters of Pater for whom music's abstraction became the paradigm for art viewed in isolation from the world, St John consistently opposed the idea of the autonomous art-object which became central to formalist models of criticism. Writing in her theatre column in 1925 she stated that 'I have learned one or two lessons from music which I find helpful when I am writing about the theatre', and explains:

> Perhaps the most important is that the effect of music on any given individual is determined in the first place by that individual's temperament. Knowledge, culture, and experience come into play only as auxiliaries. This explains the puzzlingly contradictory opinions we read of the same piece of music, and of the same performance of it. [. . .] music is essentially subjective, it takes different shapes in different minds [. . .]. In the theatre we are dealing with something less intangible than music [. . .] the critic has more excuse for saying 'This is.' If I prefer to say 'It is so to me,' it is because contact with music has made me more cautious, and perhaps more sensible of the element in drama which reacts to every colour in the temperamental spectrum. (13 Feb 1925: 153)

This is one of St John's clearest position-statements on the nature of the art object, and of criticism. Her assertion that 'music is essentially subjective' corresponds closely with Pater's definition of aesthetic experience as lying within the act of perception rather than the art object itself, and the importance she attaches to the individual's 'temperament' also echoes Pater and his emphasis on the effect of the art object 'on me' (Atherton 2005: 106; 130). In this St John stands in stark contrast to Eliot, whose literary criticism emphasises the place of both text and reader within a much more objective system, that of the critical tradition. In essays including 'The Function of Criticism' (1923) Eliot was searching for an impersonal evaluative standard, based on what he called an 'Outside Authority' and the critic's 'sense of fact'. As Goldie discusses, this essay amounted to 'a manifesto for his new classicism' which was defined in relation to Murry's romanticism and evocation of the 'inner voice' (1998: 103). For Murry, criticism was always 'an entirely subjective discipline, varying its worth according to the sensibility of the intuitive capacities of the critic himself' (Goldie: 88).

Although Eliot's and Murry's respective classical and romantic positions did not become fully defined and polarised until their public disagreements in 1923 and 1926, St John's first music criticism for *Time and Tide* in May 1920 locates her firmly on the Romantic side of this debate. The greater part of this review is devoted to a recital at London's Wigmore Hall by Miss Jelly d'Aranyi (1893–1960), a Hungarian violinist esteemed as a performer of Romantic music, and it concludes with a shorter review of a performance at the London Hippodrome by Spanish music hall star Racquel Meller. Her commentary on both female performers refuses a formalist position that would separate music as 'sound-structure' from music as 'play and performance' (Shaw-Miller 2010: 604). Writing effusively of d'Aranyi's 'powerful tone' and strong 'physical movement' she declares '[p]ersonality counts on the concert platform as much as elsewhere', and, of Meller she writes: 'She has chosen the singing of Spanish airs as her medium, and through it she makes the human heart visible. [. . .] She proves, if proof be needed, that the word is only an element, and not the most important one, in expression' (14 May 1920: 22). Repudiating Eliot's doctrine of impersonality (articulated most famously in his 1919 essay 'Tradition and the Individual Talent') St John is much closer to Murry who, in his essays for the *Athenaeum*, 'was consistent in stressing the importance of personality in the creation of art' (Goldie: 85). The similarities between St John's cultural criticism and Murry's critical discourse have important political implications. While Eliot's classicism is identified with conservative and anti-democratic politics (Beasley 2007: 47), Kaplan has suggested that Murry's romanticism, and his suspicion of hierarchical authority, allowed more space for women, and was closer to feminism and women's interests than Eliot's critical programme.[4] In view of these differences, St John's first music review takes on a double-layered significance. Not only does she place two female artists centre stage, but the attention she focuses on d'Aranyi's virtuoso performance speaks indirectly to a controversy over the employment of women in orchestras which raged in 1920 following the Hallé Orchestra's dismissal of women players who had been admitted during the war. St John would later record the controversy in her biography of the composer, writer and suffragist Ethel Smyth, comparing the Hallé's conduct with the progressive Sir Henry Wood, the first conductor to openly acknowledge the value of female orchestra players, and who considered that women had a particular talent for the violin (1959: 191–2).

This would be the first of many reviews which display what might be described as a distinctly feminist mediation of culture, pointing to the important role *Time and Tide* played in the reception of women as 'creative artists of all types', as St John later put it in a music column of 1926. In this piece her subject was the British Women's Symphony Orchestra, and the need for this and women's art corporations in general in order to afford women opportunities to show their work and 'to break down the *parti-pris* of the male umpires in "the wider arena"' (19 Mar 1926: 285). In 1928, the year that women finally won the vote on the same terms as men, St John identifies sex-prejudice as the thing that 'shocked [her] into independence' as a critic, asking: 'Could anything but a *parti-pris* against women composers explain why those accustomed to speak with authority about music in England spoke of Ethel Smyth's as if they had never heard it?' (16 Mar 1928: 264). St John reviewed for *Time and Tide* all of Smyth's major works performed in the 1920s, including the revival of her popular comic opera *The Boatswain's Mate* (20 Oct 1922: 1009–10) and her Mass in D which she describes as 'A Forgotten Masterpiece' (22 Feb 1924: 178). This promotional work is a reminder of the strong connections between feminism and the arts fostered by the women's suffrage movement. In April 1928, as the Equal Franchise Act approached its passage in Parliament, *Time and Tide* announced that 'DAME ETHEL SMYTH [. . .] is celebrating this year as a kind of Jubilee' (27 Apr 1928: 399) and the following month printed a full-page spread containing the words and music of Smyth's famous 'March of the Women' (Figure 3.1) along with details of a card being reprinted (with the words and tune only) expressing the hope 'that the March will be sung on various occasions this year' (18 May 1928: 487).[5] St John thus worked with a wider feminist discourse in the periodical to publicise women's achievements in the arts, and this is evident in her theatre as well as music columns. For example, in a review of Edith Craig's new production as Art Director at the Leeds Art Theatre (*The Great World Theatre*, a morality play

Figure 3.1 'March of the Women', *Time and Tide* 18 May 1928: 487. Reproduced with the permission of The William Ready Division of Archives and Research Collections, McMaster University Library.

adapted by Hugo von Hofmannsthal) she identified Craig as 'one of the finest stage-managers in the world' and commented on 'the irony of her not being in control of a single one of London's many stages' (1 Feb 1924: 106).

Katharine Cockin has observed that prejudices other than sexism limited the opportunities in commercial theatre of a feminist and lesbian theatre director like Craig (1998: 160). As Maggie B. Gale has shown, while London's commercial theatre was a system still largely controlled by men this was a period of expanding opportunities for women in British theatre history (1996: 61–6). Women's creative involvement in commercially oriented theatre, however, has been left out of the modernist historical record which, as Kirsten Shepherd-Barr points out, 'has barely allowed for the significance of theatrical performances' at all (2005: 59). In her writing for *Time and Tide* St John spoke out repeatedly against what Martin Puchner has described as the 'anti-theatrical impulse within the period of modernism' attributed to 'the perceived affinity between the theatre and the public sphere' (2002: 2; 11). Observing in one book review 'the general tendency of professors of literature to study the drama apart from the theatre', St John refers again to the condition of music to point out that 'drama resembles music in having to go through a process, usually called performance, before it can be given to the world [. . .] Its value can be no more appreciated by reading it in silence than the value of music can' (2 Sep 1927: 788). Changes in theatre audiences after the First World War, and especially theatre's seeming popularity among women, made it 'fashionable for theatre critics to adhere to the fearful view that the theatre [. . .] was becoming feminised' (Gale 2000: 114), but St John confronted these trends from her first theatre review where she praised a new melodrama, *The Legion of Honour*, by the novelist and playwright Baroness Orczy (2 Sep 1921: 840–1).[6] Melodrama has long been associated with the feminine and was the dominant popular form of nineteenth-century theatre. In the early twentieth century, it gradually gave way to another kind of theatre with music, the revue, recognised today as the most 'vital, innovative, and influential form of musical theatre' in this era (Moore 2007: 88). Against a general debasement in contemporary theatre criticism of this new form of popular entertainment, St John again bucked the trend. In one theatre column, she declared that she was 'as happy' in the company of melodrama and revue 'as in that of the intellectual aristocrats of comedy or tragedy' (26 Oct 1923: 1077); in another: 'My taste happens to be catholic enough for me to appreciate musical comedy, revue and other pastiches as well as pure drama' (31 Dec 1926: 1209).

St John does not, therefore, reproduce in her theatre reviews any of the anxieties about a feminised mass culture that is so familiar to modernist criticism. However, there is an emphasis in her columns on educating and elevating the reader to the (perceived) higher culture; as she stated in an early theatre review, 'one of the duties of the critic is to guide public taste' (27 Apr 1923: 445).[7] Significantly, this expression of the critic's duty comes in a review of 'Three American Plays' in which St John took up the subject of the commercial theatre and promoted the latest offering of one of the best-known theatrical managers, and impresarios, Charles B. Cochran. As one of the new 'business' theatre managers and producer of some of the most successful revues in the interwar years, Cochran was a prime target for attack by critics who believed that the commercialisation of the West End was antithetical to art.[8] In an earlier review St John had come to Cochran's defence when he was slated for his new production *Mayfair and Montmartre*, stating that in her opinion 'we owe a great debt to Mr. Cochran for having raised a popular form of entertainment [. . .] to a level which has not been reached before in this country or in any other' (31 Mar 1922: 308). In her 1923 review she declared that 'Mr. Cochran, I know, holds that commerce often reinforces art', and as evidence that commercialism may be an incentive to artistic enterprise went on to discuss the latest 'Cochran flair', his importation from New York of *Anna Christie* by America's leading playwright Eugene O'Neill. O'Neill became known in the 1920s as a daring, experimental playwright, and this was the first time a play of his was seen in the West End. For St John, Cochran's success in bringing this play to London not only disproves the argument that commercial enterprises cannot be artistic, but also evidences:

> the existence of a large body of playgoers in London who long to escape from literal representation on the stage of the externals of a life with which they are familiar. This is what they are offered here as an alternative to the romance of the dramatised novelette, and all they are likely to be offered as long as this country remains indifferent to the new theatre movement against realism and naturalism. (27 Apr 1923: 446)

St John goes on to identify as one of the leaders of this 'new theatre movement' the modernist theatre director and designer Edward Gordon Craig. Lamenting the 'obstinate obscurantism' that characterises the critical response to Craig in England, she applauds the greater receptivity to his ideas in America, evidenced in the influence she discerns in the scene-design of *Anna Christie*. In this promotion of the modernist avant-garde associated with Craig, her public expression of faith in British theatre audiences in the quote presented above is significant: reversing the terms in which they were frequently demonised, here London's playgoers do not 'long to escape' from the supposedly stultifying realities of their everyday lives, but from the uninspiring representation of life in the more conservative and claustrophobic plays of this period that were realist in mode and focused on the middle-classes.

From the mid-1920s St John became increasingly preoccupied with challenging the cultural dominance of realist drama and thus engaged in one of the most important debates in twentieth-century theatre history. As David Krasner summarises, the central question for theatre theory in this period was 'should theatre remain faithful to real-world representation or challenge the veracity of mimesis by cutting against the grain of realistic presentation?' (2008: 2). In the late summer of 1926 St John locked horns on this issue with the dramatic critic St John Ervine, who 'trounced' St John in his *Observer* column after reading a review St John had written for *Time and Tide* of John Galsworthy's new play, *Escape*. In her review St John called into account 'critics [. . .] who make it their business to question the accuracy of a dramatist's predications', stating that this kind of 'pettifogging criticism' makes her 'see red' (27 Aug 1926: 777). Recognising himself as one of the critics implicated in the review, Ervine quoted the offending passage and asserted that the dramatist cannot be allowed 'to fly in the face of all fact and probability' or 'to make his characters behave in a fashion which is entirely contradictory to their nature'. Challenging St John's authority as a critic, Ervine held that 'Mr. Galsworthy's plays should be subjected to close scrutiny' and accused St John of holding up a 'distorting mirror' to nature (19 Sep 1926: 13). St John responded, in her next theatre criticism for *Time and Tide*, with an article which defended theatre that does not aim to be '*representational*', and which makes 'frank admission of the nature of the medium, and of the artistic conventions which must govern its presentation of life'. Denouncing, in her turn, critics including Ervine as 'Our Complacent Realists', she pointed out that in his advice to the players Hamlet 'did not [. . .] speak of holding the mirror up to nature, but of holding the mirror "as t'were," up to nature' and suggested that Shakespeare perhaps interpolated the phrase 'because the idea occurred to him that in a mirror we don't see reality as it is, but reversed' (8 Oct 1926: 905–6). St John's interest in theatre that disrupts illusion and conventional realism foregrounds her modernist sensibility and close association with the theatrical avant-garde.[9] But what is also interesting here is her interest in communicating these ideas to a wide audience; welcoming the exposure Ervine's column gave her, she states that she is 'very grateful to Mr. St John Ervine' for having put her conception of the theatre 'before a larger public than [she] can command' (905).

St John's desire to reach a wide public contrasts with the position of critics like Eliot who retreated into 'minority journalism' (Collier 2006: 68) and illustrates the democratic impulse behind *Time and Tide*'s commitment to educating the reader through its review columns. In the mid-1920s this mediation of culture extended to film which, from mid-1924 to mid-1926, was reviewed in a monthly (later fortnightly) column called 'Films – and Films'. The feature appeared under a pseudonym, 'Hecate', an indication, perhaps, of the uncertain status of this newest of art forms at a 'time of enquiry about the cinema's artistic significance' (Low 1997: 26). In the early 1920s film received scant attention in the newspapers in relation to other arts, and in trade papers was 'treated primarily as an entertainment' (Sexton 2002: 292), and given this low status 'daring to be a film critic in the early 1920s was to be rather déclassé' (Hankins 2004: 507). The period over which *Time and Tide*'s film criticisms appeared, however, is crucial. According to Leslie Kathleen Hankins, the years between 1924 and 1926 represent a 'pivotal two year period' in which 'intellectuals became eager to engage with film' (2004: 494), and *Time and Tide* was among the first intellectual weeklies to engage seriously with the medium.[10] The biggest challenge for critics seeking to engage with film as an art form was the cinema's rapid commercialisation, presenting the writer on film with difficult choices regarding her choice of language in relation both to the medium, and the audience. This difficulty is highlighted in *Time and Tide*'s first 'Films – and Films' article:

> Shall we speak of the industry or of the art? Shall we be metaphorical with the 'shadow-show,' colloquial with the 'movies,' technical with the 'kinematograph,' or ambiguous with the 'pictures'? Shall we risk the accusation of pedantry with 'kinema,' or accept the French 'cinema' [. . .]? (6 June 1924: 546)

The variety of terms here reflects the 'proliferation of discourses about cinema in 1920s Britain' which ranged from newspapers to books, trade journals to fan magazines, as well as intellectual weekly periodicals, and which in turn reflect the variety of audiences for writing on film in this period (Wasson 2002: 322). As *Time and*

Tide's film critic further identifies, '[t]he next difficulty is to decide on our attitude':

> Shall it be high-brow or low-brow, idealistic or realistic? Are we to judge films by the standard of the million, an international million too, whose training in the appreciation of any form of art is elementary, or by the standard of the hundred whose tastes and opinions have been refined by general culture? (546)

Privately considering itself as a 'high-class women's weekly', *Time and Tide* unsurprisingly supported a 'high-brow' attitude in its 'Films – and Films' column.[11] The first film selected for review was *Die Nibelungen* (1924), a historical fantasy by the German director Fritz Lang. This choice anticipates the interest taken in German cinema by early Film Society members, for whom German cinema came to 'define an "alternative" film culture and an art of the film' beyond the commercial norm represented by America (Marcus 2007: 268), and it shows the direction the column would take over the next twelve months. As well as containing references to *The Cabinet of Dr Caligari* (Robert Wiene, 1919), the German expressionist film which came to be viewed by intellectuals as 'the pinnacle of film art' (Sexton 2002: 295), the column includes discussions of *The Street* (Karl Grune, 1923), and *The Last Laugh* (F. W. Murnau, 1924), and regularly extols German film-making over Hollywood. The film that makes the greatest impression of all on *Time and Tide*'s film critic, however, is one that is less commonly mentioned in film histories of the period, *Warning Shadows* (1923) by Arthur Robison, an American director living in Berlin. 'Hecate' describes this film as 'indisputably a masterpiece' in terms that must have sounded familiar to any regular reader of *Time and Tide*'s columns:

> Nothing quite like it [*Warning Shadows*] has ever been seen before, although in other German films, *Caligari* and *The Street*, for example, a similar effort has been made to put on the screen not an illustrated story, not a photographed drama, but something subjective, the effect of which on each individual onlooker is determined more by his psychic disposition than by his knowledge or by his experience. It is rare to find two people upon whom the same piece of music produces an identical impression, because music has to pass through an individual consciousness before it can be said to have an objective existence. The screen art which the Germans are seeking to develop seems to have much in common with music. It is quite as difficult to describe the

subject-matter of *Warning Shadows* as to describe the subject-matter of a symphony. Form and contents are unified. And my reaction to it, how elusive and incommunicable! How strictly my own, not to be shared with another! Must I fall back on such foggy abstractions as 'the technique is truly remarkable?' (5 Dec 1924: 1200)

Present readers will no doubt recognise the elements which suggest that Christopher St John was also the author of *Time and Tide*'s film reviews. First, the influence of Pater in the review's emphasis on the subjective nature of the aesthetic experience, and intangibility of the critic's response, and, second, its comparison with music which, as we have seen, functions as her 'technical model' and 'ideological paradigm' for writing about culture elsewhere in her columns. The passage quoted continues with reference to a conversation with 'a great lover of the Elizabethan drama who thinks that the screen in our day is very much like what the stage was in Shakespeare's', quite likely a reference to the great English actress (and mother of Edith Craig) Ellen Terry.

It is impossible to claim St John's authorship of this column with absolute certainty, but on earlier occasions she had used her theatre column to write about film, moving from an early sceptical stance (in a 1922 review that compared Clemence Dane's play *A Bill of Divorcement* with its adaptation for the screen), to a more active interest in film's artistic possibilities.[12] In March 1923, responding to a debate at London's Stoll Picture Theatre Club where St John Ervine moved the resolution 'that the film-play defeats the imagination', she defended the medium, concluding that it 'can stir the faculty of imaginative insight to full activity' (30 Mar 1923: 348). In another theatre criticism the following year she stated: 'I know at least one prophet who boldly foretells that the future is with the shadow-show' (14 Mar 1924: 250). St John may have had Ellen Terry in mind here, in whose company she forged her conviction of film's imaginative power one year earlier.[13] Or perhaps Edith Craig, who was making a film in Egypt at the very time St John was defending film from cinephobes like Ervine (Cockin 1998: 141). All three women would be on the original Council of the Film Society when it was founded in 1925.[14] *Time and Tide*'s 'Films – and Films' column also contains the occasional biographical clue pointing to St John.[15] But the most compelling evidence is the nature of the film criticism itself which often echoes the themes of St John's music and theatre criticisms. Another example is this response to the 'truculent abuse' of cinema among English intellectuals:

Is not their faculty of appreciation narrowly confined to literature? It is the dominance of the idea that being *well-read* is equivalent to being *well-educated*, which accounts in a great measure for all the arts in England having to struggle along without the support of the intellectual classes. [. . .] Kinematography which seeks to make ideas intelligible without the aid of literature at all is even more despised than theatrics which include it as an element. (2 Jan 1925: 10)

If this is not the voice of Christopher St John it is remarkably close to her complaint against the narrowing of culture around the literary in her signed music and theatre criticisms.

Whether or not St John was the author of these reviews, the culture of film appears to have tested how far *Time and Tide* could sustain a highbrow attitude in this column without alienating its core female readership. Film's popularity with women, who far outnumbered men in cinema audiences, was widely noted at the time in commentaries which frequently represented female fans as passive, mindless and dangerously susceptible to film's fantasies (Stead 2018: 105). While *Time and Tide*'s film criticism does extend to American cinema, and consciously resists the 'indiscriminate abuse of American work' (26 Feb 1926: 205), its discourse tends to reflect an avant-garde privileging of the director, as in the warm reception given to Charlie Chaplin who is praised for his 'genius' as 'author, producer and manager' (9 Oct 1925: 987).[16] There is also a general resistance to film's commercial development, for example, reservations about the introduction of sound (7 Aug 1925: 771), and criticism of Hollywood's star system (4 July 1924: 642–3). The most telling highbrow signature, however, is the self-distancing in this column from popular cinema audiences.[17] In one review *Time and Tide*'s columnist observes that 'there is a large public in England interested in film personalities' but 'the public which is interested in film principles is much smaller' (10 Oct 1924: 983), and the following year expresses disdain for the female fans who reportedly 'mobbed' film star Rudolph Valentino (after a screening of *The Eagle*) and who will remember nothing about the film 'except that his Cossack uniform was becoming' (4 Dec 1925: 1196–7). A review in May 1926 barely hides Hecate's contempt for the mass of cinemagoers:

Some people are best pleased when the story is good and well told. [. . .] They don't notice defects in the composition of the pictures, although they are acutely sensitive to defects in the composition of the story. [. . .] the majority of filmgoers do not trouble to analyse the source of their pleasure. If they are entertained they are satisfied. (21 May 1926: 455)

Here, writ large, is what Laura Frost has identified in her recent study of literary modernism and its aesthetics in the interwar period as modernism's problem with pleasure. Along with popular women's novels, cinema was frequently the foil for what Frost terms 'modernist unpleasure'; its 'passive and corporeal pleasures [. . .] posited as inferior to the deliberately chosen, cerebral, and *difficult* pleasures of modernism' (2013: 28; 19). In this review, *Time and Tide*'s columnist seems to have lost faith in 'the majority of filmgoers' who are only interested in cinema as entertainment, and whose non-analytical pleasure in the medium militates against its artistic development.

The commercialisation of film, therefore, seems to have become a kind of test case for *Time and Tide*'s own identity and audience in its mediation of culture. Despite film's popularity with women, *Time and Tide*'s 'Films – and Films' feature appeared for the last time in its issue of 16 July 1926. What does *Time and Tide*'s pulling of its film column mean? Does it mean that the periodical had given up on film, sharing with other intellectuals the idea that the growth of the cinema industry had stifled film's potential as art? It is significant, perhaps, that just ten days before the publication of *Time and Tide*'s last 'Films – and Films' feature Virginia Woolf had contributed to the *Athenaeum* an essay on the cinema which, in keeping with many modernist prose writers' tendency to sneer at the theatre and other popular media, suggested that film was a lesser art than literature.[18] Or did the highbrow attitude adopted in *Time and Tide*'s film column risk losing touch with the periodical's core audience of women readers? In the autumn of the same year the film critic Iris Barry published her popular book on film *Let's Go to the Pictures* (1926) where she defended 'story' in film over and against abstraction, and claimed that 'the cinema [. . .] exists for the purpose of pleasing women' (Marcus 2007: 290–3). Compared with Barry's firm commitment to cinema's populist appeal, the highbrow attitude in *Time and Tide*'s film column was perhaps now seen as a liability since, in an important sense, this periodical also existed 'for the purpose of pleasing women'. While continuously working to broaden its reach beyond the women's paper category, its primary target audience for at least a decade was female, and to fulfil its ambition for a place among the leading general-audience weeklies it would need to take this readership with it. Arguably the retraction of *Time and Tide*'s regular film column represents both a modernist and highbrow move, calculated to distance the periodical from a form that was perceived to have failed in sustaining its status as art, *and* a rejection of the periodical's highbrow attitude to film in order to remove the risk of alienating female readers who experienced pleasure in this popular medium. During the same period, *Time and Tide*'s reviews of new novels reveal a 'delight' in modern fiction that contrasts with the anxieties about the non-analytical pleasures of female cinema fans in its film reviews. According to Frost 'the interwar debate about pleasure clusters most intensely around cinema and popular literature' (2013: 33), and it is to a discourse on pleasure in *Time and Tide*'s book reviews that I turn next.

Delighting in modern fiction: *Time and Tide*'s book reviews

Book reviews were a staple of *Time and Tide*'s content from the beginning and represent one of the most significant areas for the paper's growth. During its early years the periodical typically carried one or two pages of book reviews covering such varieties of non-fiction as biography, economics, history, politics and travel, as well as new works in fiction and poetry. Initially the paper made no attempt to separate the types of books reviewed, which were all dealt with under the same general heading 'Book Reviews'; later there was more differentiation and use of sub-headings within the book reviews section, often with individual reviewers becoming associated with particular kinds of book.[19] As will be discussed in Chapter 6, the space *Time and Tide* devoted to literature expanded dramatically towards the end of the decade, presenting the periodical with new challenges in its negotiation of 'high' and 'middlebrow' cultures. The present discussion focuses on *Time and Tide*'s early reception of modern fiction in the reviews contributed by three of the periodical's principle critics in the 1920s: Rose Macaulay, Sylvia Lynd and Naomi Royde-Smith. Linked by personal friendship ties as well as professional interests, together these three women represent an alternative literary network to those associated with Bloomsbury and high modernist coteries. Royde-Smith, the eldest of the three and author of over forty novels, is distinguished for being the first woman literary editor of a general newspaper, the *Westminster Gazette*, and the Thursday evening literary salons she co-hosted with Rose Macaulay at her home in South Kensington were a focal point for many writers after the war (LeFanu 2003: 152). Macaulay first met Royde-Smith in the 1910s and by the time she entered *Time and Tide*'s columns in June 1920 she was the author of ten novels; the last, *Potterism*, had just been published to immediate success and her popularity made her a much sought-after figure by newspaper and journal editors during the interwar years

(Collier 2006: 158). Lynd, primarily a poet, also published two novels (the second, *Swallow Dive*, appeared in 1921, one year before she began reviewing for *Time and Tide*) and she would become one of the founding members of the Book Society, a cultural institution virtually synonymous with the middlebrow. All three writers have been positioned 'outside' modernism, yet – like Christopher St John – they were each familiar with its key texts and discourses even as they advanced different literary-critical agendas. Among these was the promotion of what critics have since defined in categories of fiction as the 'woman's novel'.[20] Sharing with *Time and Tide*'s readers their delight in women's fiction, these critics both engaged with an interwar debate about pleasure, recently examined by Frost, and unsettled cultural hierarchies constructed in contemporary criticism.

Time and Tide's first discussion of women's fiction in its book pages was a review by Rose Macaulay in June 1920 of E. M. Delafield's new novel *Tension*. Delafield, who contributed book reviews herself during *Time and Tide*'s early years and would later play a major role in the periodical's development (see Chapters 5 and 6), was a leading figure in middlebrow culture.[21] Macaulay's discussion of the latest offering from this popular author is revealing both of contemporary anxieties about the cultural status of the woman's novel, and of the important cultural work performed by critics like Macaulay in promoting this kind of modern fiction. Most striking is Macaulay's use of the term 'sentimental', first, in her opening comments on Delafield's novel which she describes as 'wholly unmarred by sentiment', and, second, in her very last words, on the author's working out of the novel's tragic as well as comic situation 'entirely objectively [. . .] with [. . .] no sentimentality at all' (2 July 1920: 169). Macaulay's emphatic insistence on this point speaks to modernism's opposition to the sentimental which, as Suzanne Clark has shown, was explicitly gendered.[22] Writing against this discourse Macaulay describes Delafield's novel as 'coherent, well-constructed, and artistic' (169), deflecting an array of assumptions modernism linked to the feminine (disorderly, excessive, reflective not creative). Macaulay reviewed other women's novels in similar terms, including Mary Agnes Hamilton's *The Last Fortnight* (1921) which she also describes as 'artistic and coherent', as well as successful in 'avoid[ing] excess or hysteria' in its treatment of the extreme unhappiness of the inhabitants of a small suburban house (29 Oct 1920: 510). Hamilton, another central figure in *Time and Tide*'s early years (she contributed regular book reviews for more than a decade), has also been positioned 'outside' modernism, but Macaulay's review foregrounds her use of fictional methods that are recognisably modernist, observing that the fourteen days and nights over which the novel extends is part of the same contemporary 'tendency of novelists to concentrate on one crowded hour, or night, or week, or month [. . .] instead of taking their characters over an age' (29 Oct 1920: 510). Supporting the argument made by Lynne Hapgood and Nancy Paxton (2000) that a more inclusive context for understanding the development of English fiction in this period is needed, *Time and Tide*'s book review columns are themselves a reminder that the divisions constructed between 'modernist' and 'non-modernist' works of fiction are artificial. What we now recognise as classic modernist texts were reviewed alongside works dissociated from this category, as in Macaulay's review the following year of Dorothy Richardson's sixth volume in her *Pilgrimage* series, *Deadlock*, alongside a more traditional *Bildungsroman* by Gerard Hopkins.[23]

In this review Macaulay's comment that to turn from *Deadlock* to the simpler narrative of Hopkins's novel 'is like coming up from the depths of a running stream to the surface' (11 Mar 1921: 235) invokes one of the defining concepts in theorisations of the modernist novel: 'stream of consciousness', first used by May Sinclair in a review of Richardson's fiction. At the same time, it preserves the experience of total immersion in the world of fiction that is one of the defining features of the perceived dangers of reading in the history of the novel. As Kate Flint (1993) has shown, with reference to the Victorian and Edwardian eras, the private activity of reading with its tendency towards self-absorption was seen to be especially dangerous for women, and, as various critics have noted, from the turn of the twentieth century the expansion of book publishing (and the fiction market in particular) spawned similar concerns that popular novels were 'geared towards pleasure-seeking or thrills rather than moral edification' (Littau 2006: 21). In this context Macaulay's opening remark in a review of six novels in August 1920 under the heading 'Sensation' is deliberately provocative: 'There are good novels (a few), bad novels (many), indifferent novels (some) and sensational novels (not enough)' (27 Aug 1920: 329). Here, Macaulay invokes the evaluative terms 'good' and 'bad' novels only to subvert them in her esteem for a culturally devalued form, of which she further writes: 'the sensational story one reads every word of (excepting only the sentimental passages). One has to, of course, for if one misses any word it may be the one which matters, the master-key' (329). In this ingenious stroke Macaulay turns modernism's privileging of the 'word' back in on itself. As Karin Littau has documented, modernism introduced a bias towards reading as a 'predominantly mentalist activity', turning away from earlier theories of reading which were also concerned with readers' sensations, and demanding that readers be 'critically alert and active contributors in making meaning' as literature became more and more concerned with sense-making rather than sensation (2006: 10–11; 81). The implication in Macaulay's review that a despised form like sensation fiction could be made the occasion for hermeneutics undermines modernist critical discourses even as her rhetorical swipe at the 'sentimental passages' seems to reproduce a modernist turn against a once valuable cultural and aesthetic category. Indeed, in a flourish which relishes sensation in its reference to the popular Grand Guignol, Macaulay concludes: 'The chief test of this type of story is how far it curdles the blood, to what pitch it strings our horrified attention' (329).

Macaulay's skilful undermining of modernist discourses, while seeming to work within them, is characteristic of her reviews for *Time and Tide* which also display an ironic consciousness about the nature of criticism itself. Her review of two books of criticism, *The Art of Letters* by Robert Lynd and *Aspects of Literature* by John Middleton Murry, begins as follows:

> This is an age of writing about writing, and of writing again about that. There is probably more criticism, good and bad, of books old and new, of writers living and dead, than there has ever been before. And the criticism is certainly, in the main, better in its kind than most of the creative work. Creative work is, and has always been, in the main bad. And to-day more people can and do emit it than has been the case in past years. The good is produced, but among such a terrific swamp of the shoddy, the silly, the trumpery, as never before was. And the future gives little hope; the sky grows darker yet, and the sea rises higher. It behoves good critics, therefore, like the spirit of the Lord, to set up a standard in the flood. (17 Dec 1920: 665)

This review reveals Macaulay as an arch satirist at her best. Invoking modernist anxieties about a world of too much print, the irony of her own position as a critic called upon not only to 'writ[e] about writing' but also to 'writ[e] again about that' is all too clear. As Collier has discussed, rapid and dramatic changes in book reviewing as a cultural institution, including the emergence of newspapers as leading publishers of more and shorter reviews, produced fears not only that 'readers would get lost amidst the superfluity' but also that good writers 'might be perishing beyond the ken of reviewers and therefore of the public' (2006: 72–3; 80). Macaulay's assertion that 'creative work is [. . .] in the main bad' reproduces the modernist narrative of culture in decline, but this soon turns to mimicry of modernist hysteria about mass culture in her invocation of 'a terrific swamp of the shoddy, the silly, the trumpery, as never before was'. As Collier observes, the most obsessively recurrent note in Eliot's essays written between 1918 and 1922 was the need for 'standards of criticism' to combat the flood of critical writing aimed at 'the insurgent middle-class, [the] General Reading Public' (2006: 48). But in the mounting hyperbole of the closing sentences here, invoking the apocalyptic discourse at the end of the First World War, Macaulay's biblical recasting of familiar metaphors exposes the self-righteousness of modernist critics whose literary gate-keeping borders on the fanatical.

Less than two years after the publication of this review T. S. Eliot launched his quarterly journal the *Criterion,* a periodical which was concerned primarily with the 'maintenance of critical standards' (Harding 2002: 10), and through its association with the rise of University English (see Chapter 6) played an important role in what Nicola Humble has described as a 'gradual separation in this period of two modes of reading: the professional and the leisured' (2011: 48). Observing that modernism's leading critics shared 'a new insistence on the need to *study* a text rather than simply consume it', Humble proposes that 'it is the different ways in which the body is configured that provides one of the most powerful, if unconscious, contemporary modelling of the distinction between the high and the middlebrow [. . .] books are "highbrow" if read at a desk, pencil in hand, and middlebrow if read while "lolling in a chair or lying on a sofa, or in the train"' (2011: 45; 47). Sylvia Lynd, who began reviewing for *Time and Tide* in the same month that Eliot's *Criterion* was launched, unequivocally embodies the leisured, middlebrow reader in *Time and Tide*'s columns. In a review of two novels in 1923, Rose Macaulay's *Told by an Idiot* and Aldous Huxley's *Antic Hay*, she writes:

[T]o read him [Huxley] is rather like reading 'Fermé la Nuit' – one has to look up words in the dictionary. 'Imberb, rachitic, callipygous, stylobate, podium, coenobites' – There's a vocabulary to improve the mind. What it is to have a classical education! But is it fair, is it English to take advantage of it, to make a gentle reader arise from her sofa (not, alas, a white satin one), remember the order of the letters

of the alphabet, and make her fingers dusty? A plague upon these foreign ways. I simply shan't go on bothering, shall you? You don't have
to look up words in 'Told by an Idiot,' and it is even more amusing
than 'Antic Hay.' (9 Nov 1923: 1124)

Lynd's gentle mockery goes to the heart of the gendered dynamics
which turned reading from an activity primarily associated with leisure and pleasure to one that requires training and is expected to be
difficult. By 'tak[ing] advantage' of his male privilege of a 'classical
education', and requiring the 'gentle [female] reader' to get up from
her sofa and consult a dictionary, Huxley is figured as having broken
the chivalric codes of gentlemanly conduct. In contrast, Macaulay's
'more amusing' novel provides immediate and accessible delight, and
it is the corporeal rather than intellectual pleasures of reading that
Lynd foregrounds in her contributions to *Time and Tide*, illustrated
by the following comment in a review of Stella Benson's *The Poor
Man*: 'I took this book to bed as I once used to take a rag doll. I do
not like to let it out of my sight' (8 Dec 1922: 1185). Here, Lynd's
attachment to Benson's novel suggests an 'embodied, immediate pleasure [that] has long been associated with femininity' (Frost 2013: 12)
and is markedly different from highbrow reading practices which
'attempt to leave the body behind' (Humble 2011: 48).

In her reviewing for *Time and Tide* Lynd consistently favours novels which offer traditional reading pleasures over texts which demand
serious work or effort. This is best illustrated by her review, in March
1926, of Sylvia Townsend Warner's first and prize-winning novel
Lolly Willowes, alongside *The Making of Americans*, by Gertrude
Stein. Stein was one of the writers Eliot published in the first issue of
the *New Criterion* which had appeared just two months earlier, and
as 'one of modernism's most iconic experimenters' (James 2010: 85) it
is her self-constructed reputation as a genius that survives.[24] However,
in the opening sentence of this review it is Warner for whom Lynd
makes the greater claim: '*Lolly Willowes* is one of those rare books
that are not only works of genius, but also works of art.' Lynd's
appreciation of this novel lies in the conventional pleasures of realism
which encourage a close bond between characters and readers. Of the
novel's central protagonist she writes: 'From her first appearance until
her last, the figure of Laura Willowes is made real to us; we know
how she looked, and how she felt' (19 Mar 1926: 271). In contrast,
the stylistic methods of Stein in *The Making of Americans* discourage identification, and deliberately prevent another of fiction's traditional pleasures, immersion in the story. Admitting that '[Stein's] story

seems interesting whenever one comes on it' Lynd warns that: '[t]his is not very often for Miss Stein uses words as a sawmill uses sound, so that they get between her meaning and her reader's attention' (272). According to Frost, in modernism's redefinition of pleasure '[d]iffi-culty becomes an inherent value and is a deliberate aesthetic ambition set against too pleasing, harmonious reading effects' (2013: 20). Lynd resists this orthodoxy, and in her review of Stein's novel the difficulties of the text become sources of humour and critique in such statements as: 'Miss Stein's meaning could have been more concisely stated, one fancies. [. . .] Miss Stein has plenty of observation; but she has also and more conspicuously plenty of tediousness' (272). Categorically refusing the demand of modernist texts that readers 'embrace dis-comfort, confusion, and hard cognitive labour' (Frost 2013: 6) Lynd writes in exasperation: '*The Making of Americans* seems to me the sort of book that would produce its effect if the reader were hit over the head with it' (272).

Rejecting modernist critical paradigms Lynd repeatedly shared with *Time and Tide*'s readers her delight in modern fiction produced by an increasingly visible interwar generation of women novelists, among them – as well as Benson, Macaulay and Warner – such criti-cally neglected figures as Dorothy Canfield, Kathleen Coyle, Cicely Hamilton, Sheila Kaye-Smith, Beatrice Kean-Seymour, Margaret Kennedy, Ethel Mannin, F. M. Mayor, Sarah Millin, Naomi Mitchi-son, G. B. Stern, F. Tennyson Jesse, Amabel Williams-Ellis and Romer Wilson. Even this brief roll call is a reminder of the innumerable liter-ary works 'left in the wide margin of the century' by modernist his-toriography (Williams 1989: 35), but whose authors enjoyed a wide readership in their day, especially among women. Crucially, as this chapter has argued, women played a key role in the reception and promotion of women's fiction, as acknowledged in Lynd's review of a book published in 1926 by another female critic, *The Modern Novel* by Elizabeth Drew. Educated at Oxford University, Drew was a Res-ident Lecturer in English at Girton College, Cambridge, for three years from 1916 to 1919, and later provided lectures for the Faculty of English under her married name, Mrs E. Downs.[25] *The Modern Novel* was the first of a number of critical studies she published in the 1920s and 1930s, and the appeal of the book for Lynd was that its author 'does not speak as an oracle, but as a novel reader' and places 'the attention of the reader as the criterion of a novel's excel-lence'. While not agreeing with all her judgements, Lynd admires her 'unsusceptib[ility] to prestige values' and her 'brave [. . .] assertion of her personal tastes':

'Ulysses' and Dr Freud find her irreverent, while such charming books as *The Poor Man* [Stella Benson], *A Lost Lady* [Willa Cather], *The Rector's Daughter* [F. M. Mayor], *Dangerous Ages* [Rose Macaulay], with its destructive wit, fill her with delight. As a review of modern fiction this book covers a wide field. Not only has Miss Drew read an enormous number of modern novels, but she has apparently read them with pleasure. If the proof of the novel is in the reader, we need not fear the decay of fiction as long as there are readers of Miss Drew's intelligence and honesty to be entertained and interested by it. (16 July 1926: 644)

Appearing in the same year that saw the introduction of the English Tripos at the University of Cambridge, a key staging post in the institutionalisation of modernism, this book and Lynd's review are an important reminder of literary-critical voices that resisted the critical authority of a minority, and embraced 'delight' and 'pleasure' in modern fiction as key terms.

It is the freshness of these voices in *Time and Tide*'s pages that provides one of the chief delights in reading these columns today. Eschewing the stance of impersonal criticism, these female critics make themselves heard as 'flesh and blood' readers connected – as their reviews also sometimes make visible – to other flesh and blood writers, artists and critics.[26] The most vivid illustration of this is a review in November 1925 by Naomi Royde-Smith of two books: Sylvia Lynd's short fiction collection, *The Mulberry Bush and Other Stories*, and a collection of essays by Rose Macaulay, *A Casual Commentary*. Royde-Smith writes:

These two delightful books arrive for review in the same parcel, and as I cut their pages, it seems as if the voices and laughter of two of my most amusing friends are joining together in another happy fireside hour, or shouting through the wind of a long day's walk on the Downs or across some heather covered common. These two incomparable talkers [. . .] have each selected from their fugitive journalism enough pieces to make a volume. And I defy anybody reading either of these volumes to escape from an ultimate sensation of having read and re-read the thoughts of a friend. This is, of course, the feeling which any good essayist leaves in a reader's heart. (13 Nov 1925: 1116)

In this striking glimpse of the personalities and friendships of these three women, Royde-Smith flagrantly defies an objective critical standard and takes as much pleasure from promoting her two friends as she does from their books. Although Royde-Smith did not begin reviewing regularly for *Time and Tide* until January 1925, her first contribution to the periodical was a review of Rose Macaulay's novel *Potterism* (16 July 1920) and on other occasions each critic reviewed one or more of the other's work. As Collier had discussed, such reviewing practices (which were common in modernist circles too) fuelled a controversy in London's book-world over 'log-rolling' in which it was argued that 'writers gave positive reviews to their friends and influential colleagues, largely shutting out new or uncon- nected writers' (2006: 83). Royde-Smith's review (which is printed under the heading 'Rolled Logs') opens with 'the problem of log- rolling' in a 'small and friendly' literary world where for any writer 'the time must come when each of us is asked to review the book of a friend' (1116), but then resolves it by making her friendship with the authors a model for the ideal writer-reader relationship. In so doing she alludes to an earlier eighteenth-century salon and coffee-shop culture, with its idea of books entering into a dialogue with each other as if they are alive.[27] Significantly, this reader-author friend- ship concept imagines a social, cultural context for the reading and writing processes, and runs counter to the antagonistic relationship between writers and their audience that characterises the cultural producers of modernism.

The importance of *Time and Tide* in interwar London for the reception and promotion of women writers who have been posi- tioned 'outside' modernism will be the subject of further discussion in Part Two of this book. Despite Christopher St John's opposition in *Time and Tide*'s columns to the elevation of 'literature' above the other arts, the periodical became increasingly literary in emphasis, even as it continued to publish regular reviews of theatre and music. In its issue of 24 September 1926 *Time and Tide* carried the follow- ing announcement:

> In response to repeated requests for MORE BOOK REVIEWS, it has been decided considerably to enlarge the space devoted to the discussion of current literature. In addition to increasing the number of book reviews, we intend to publish, from time to time, articles on present-day literary tendencies and on the work of mod- ern writers, not only in this country, but in some of the principal foreign countries. (849)

In their request for 'more book reviews' *Time and Tide*'s readers were expressing the cultural aspirations of a whole interwar genera- tion for whom books acquired a new educational and democratic significance. From its next issue *Time and Tide* more than tripled the space it gave to book reviews, and this growth would accelerate further from 1928, as we shall see in Chapter 4.[28] Maintaining a vigilant eye on developments in literary journalism, the periodical provides a unique vantage point for examining the relationship between feminism and literary culture in the interwar years. Indeed, *Time and Tide*'s stated intention, in the announcement quoted above, to publish from time to time 'articles on present-day literary tendencies' carries an unmistakable echo of Eliot's assertion, in his essay 'The Idea of a Literary Review' (published in the first issue of the *New Criterion* in January 1926) that the literary review 'should attempt to illustrate [. . .] the tendencies of the time'. As Harding has discussed, 'the "modern tendency" [. . .] most obviously supported' by Eliot's magazine was 'a marked distaste for liberal democracy' and 'the restoration of authoritarian forms of political and social order' (2009: 353–4). *Time and Tide*'s cultural criticism reminds us that 'Eliotic modernism' was only one of several 'modern tendencies' that existed in this period, and did not have the kind of unchallenged cultural authority that has often been claimed for it.

Notes

1. For an overview and selection of this scholarship see Maroula Joannou (2012).
2. See Katharine Cockin (1998 and 2001) for an extended discussion of this artistic community.
3. MR to ER, 2 September 1920. ER Papers.
4. 'The "Outsiders" of British Modernism: John Middleton Murry, Katherine Mansfield, and D. H. Lawrence'. Paper given at the British Association for Modernist Studies (BAMS) international conference 2014, London.
5. *Time and Tide* explained that the first public performance of any work by Smyth had taken place fifty years ago. The periodical also alerted readers to a wireless concert of Ethel Smyth's works to be broadcast on the evening of 20 May, and printed an appeal in its correspondence columns for donations to an Ethel Smyth Jubilee Fund to raise money for a concert in Berlin.
6. See also Viv Gardner (2015) for a discussion of this perceived 'womanisation' of the theatre.
7. Katharine Cockin observes the commitment to 'inspiring, educating and elevating a mass audience to the (perceived) higher culture' in Edith Craig's circle (1998: 136).
8. Maggie B. Gale discusses the changes in ownership of commercial theatres after the war, when the running of theatres moved from actor-managers to the investor or financial speculator (1996: 39–43).

9. As Cockin (2001) has discussed, the Pioneer Players produced many modernist plays. Craig brought Russian Expressionist drama to London as early as 1915 with a play, co-translated by St John, which was banned by the manager of the Alhambra Theatre, André Charlot (Cockin 2015).

10. *Time and Tide* launched its 'Films – and Films' feature just one month after the *Spectator* introduced a regular film column, contributed by Iris Barry, on 3 May 1924. *Time and Tide* was ahead of the *Nation and Athenaeum* which introduced a film column in October 1925 (Marcus 2007: 275); the *New Statesman* carried regular reviews of books, music, drama and art, but not film.

11. Rhondda described *Time and Tide* as a 'High Class Women's Weekly' in an early letter to Elizabeth Robins. 13 August 1920. ER Papers.

12. In this review St John concluded that 'good live plays make bad dead films and [. . .] the arts of the kinema and the theatre are irreconcilable' (1 Sep 1922: 886).

13. St John describes viewing *Blood and Sand* (starring Rudolph Valentino) in the company of Ellen Terry, in the 1923 theatre column cited above.

14. See the *Oxford Dictionary of National Biography* entry on the Film Society.

15. In 'Films – and Films' published in *Time and Tide*'s issue of 3 July 1925 the writer mentions that 'long ago at the University of Oxford I was compelled to attend some lectures on political economy' (645); St John was a student at Somerville College, Oxford, from 1894 where she read Modern History.

16. Jamie Sexton notes that one of the characteristics of the Film Society programme notes was a 'privileging of the director as the creative intelligence guiding every aspect' (297).

17. In this respect *Time and Tide*'s column was typical of interwar journalistic discourse on film which was 'frequently mocking and dismissive of the female spectator' (Stead 2016: 130).

18. See Marcus (2007: 107–22) for a discussion of this essay.

19. For example, poetry was reviewed for some time by Thomas Moult, editor of the Georgian Poetry Anthologies, while children's writer Lydia Miller Mackay frequently contributed reviews of children's books.

20. In *Hysterical Fiction: The 'Woman's Novel' in the Twentieth Century* (2000) Clare Hanson notes that the term gained critical currency in the 1980s, a key example being Nicola Beauman's study of British interwar women novelists *A Very Great Profession: The Woman's Novel 1914–1939* (1983).

21. Delafield contributed book reviews for just over six months from May to November 1922.

22. Clark states: 'women [. . .] have a privileged (or fatal) relationship with the sentimental. From the point of view of literary modernism, sentimentality was both a past to be outgrown and a present tendency to be despised' (1991: 2).

23. Gerard Hopkins was the nephew of Gerald Manley Hopkins. *A City in the Foreground* (1921) was a university novel based on his experiences at Oxford.
24. Stein would ironically construct her reputation as a genius in *The Autobiography of Alice B. Toklas* (1933).
25. I am grateful to the archivists at Girton College Library, Cambridge, and at Cambridge University Archives, for their assistance in locating this biographical information.
26. Littau usefully distinguishes the 'flesh and blood reader' from the 'reader as abstraction' (2006: 155).
27. I am indebted to Katharine Cockin for this observation.
28. *Time and Tide*'s issue of 1 October 1926 carried three and a half pages of book reviews and reviewed seven books, compared with one page reviewing two books in its issue of 24 September 1926.

Part II

Expansion, 1928–1935

Chapter 4

'The Courage to Advertise': Cultural Tastemakers and 'Journals of Opinion'

The year 1928 marks the beginning of a new phase in *Time and Tide*'s development. With the passage in Parliament of the Equal Franchise Act, which for the first time granted votes to women on the same terms as men, the periodical gradually rebranded itself as a less woman-focused, more general-audience publication, and worked intensively to secure a position among the leading intellectual weekly reviews of its day. Early assessments of this periodical have intimated that *Time and Tide* became less feminist as it moved into its second decade.[1] However, this conclusion fails to understand *Time and Tide*'s more complex relationship with Britain's interwar political and cultural landscape as it sought to broaden its appeal while continuing to serve the needs of feminism and of its core female readership. In October 1926, not long after Lady Rhondda took over the periodical's editorship, Vera Brittain (a contributor since 1922) wrote to her husband warning him: 'if you ever talk of T.&.T. don't speak of it as a "women's paper." They are very anxious to get it out of that category.' Explaining that 'it [*Time and Tide*] is a weekly review of life and politics run by women' she differentiated it from such society magazines as the *Queen* and *The Gentlewoman* 'which people always think of when you say "women's paper"'.[2] As Margaret Beetham identifies, 'the definition of femininity as incompatible with engagement in public affairs' had become institutional in the nineteenth-century history of women's magazines (1996: 26). Rhondda was firm in her conviction that as a female-run weekly review *Time and Tide* was reinventing the category of 'women's journalism' and that as such it represented an important continuation of feminism in an equal rights tradition. In a letter to her friend and leading American feminist, Doris Stevens, she wrote in May 1927:

> There has never as far as I know been a serious weekly review run by women before. It's offering a new world of achievement to us if we succeed, & at the same time it's giving out week by week implicit & explicit feminism taken from the detached standpoint to thousands. There've been propaganda papers before – but never this. [. . .] If we succeed, it's in a way analogous (a smaller way of course) to what the women did who offered medicine to women or started the first big public schools for women. It's another definite step in a new direction. [. . .] I believe the day of the weeklies is at hand; I believe they could get it now if they would have the courage to advertise. (As I am trying to persuade them to do.) And when that day comes I want there to be a weekly run by women amongst them.[3]

In this clear differentiation of her periodical from 'propaganda papers', the suffrage organs on whose media history *Time and Tide* built (see Chapter 1), Rhondda highlights an important new set of interlocking periodical networks with which this modern feminist magazine interacted as it moved into its second decade. According to press historian Stephen Koss, the interwar period was the 'golden age' of the weekly review, and in her ambition for *Time and Tide* Rhondda was indeed pioneering a new professional field for women.[4] All the leading British weeklies (papers such as the *Spectator*, the *New Statesman*, and the *Nation and Athenaeum*) were edited by men, and while women were often employed as support staff at the level of production they had little to no influence over editorial policy and content.[5] Having overtaken its competitors in the feminist periodical market, and succeeded in attracting national attention through its 'leisured woman' debate (see Chapter 1), *Time and Tide* was now ready to stake its position alongside these male-edited rivals and seize in earnest women's rightful position alongside men in the world of public affairs. Far from abandoning its feminist position, feminism remained embedded at 'implicit and explicit' levels of the paper, as we shall see. In July 1928, just seven days after the Representation of the People (Equal Franchise) Act was passed into law, Rhondda wrote to Stevens: 'As I see it, feminism needs such a paper as "Time and Tide" more than it needs anything else. Getting equal rights is only one side of feminism. Equal rights are of little use to people whose hands are too feeble to hold them.' Conceptualising 'feminism today' as 'a kind of groping forward to find the new equal world and to try and discover how we can make its laws work', her goal, she explained, was to 'provide a common platform for the ones who are trying to think things out [. . .]; and by penetrating to the ordinary intelligent woman [. . .] get her to begin to think'.[6] As this letter shows, women readers remained *Time and Tide*'s core target audience, especially the newly emancipated 'ordinary intelligent woman' whose mobilisation into active citizenship was central to *Time and Tide*'s feminist agenda.

In October 1928 *Time and Tide* expanded, raising its price from fourpence to sixpence and increasing in size from twenty-four to thirty-two pages. As announced in its columns these changes brought the periodical 'into line with the other weekly reviews in respect both to size and to price' (5 Oct 1928: 813), thus completing its transition into the sixpenny weekly market. Rhondda's 'courage to advertise' was a key aspect of *Time and Tide*'s success, and in this chapter I explore a variety of ways in which the periodical engaged with publicity and the marketplace in order to strengthen its reputation for political and literary journalism. The first section examines the new relationships *Time and Tide* built with advertisers to reposition and expand its readership, and the internal and external marketing and publicity campaigns the periodical conducted in the lead-up to its size and price increase. In particular it explores *Time and Tide*'s contribution to contemporary debates about 'The Future of the Press' and the significance of a strategic alliance it forged with one of its closest competitors in the weekly review market, the *Nation and Athenaeum*. The second section discusses the value *Time and Tide* placed on publicity and advertisement in the literary sphere, and its participation in modern cultures of literary celebrity. With reference to *Time and Tide*'s new investment in graphic art content I show how the periodical pursued a feminist agenda in its promotion of women writers, both modernist and 'middlebrow', and, with reference to a new and widely advertised feature by Rebecca West, how *Time and Tide* also promoted the work of female critics. By the end of 1928 *Time and Tide* had significantly grown in stature and in an advertisement placed in the international feminist journal *Jus Suffragii* prided itself on being 'The only weekly review in the world edited and controlled solely by women' (Nov 1928: 32). Its importance for women writers and readers in the interwar period remained a key aspect of its identity, even as it rebranded itself as a more general-audience review.

'A new form': politics, the press and 'The function of the weekly review'

Time and Tide's expansion took place within a period of rapid growth in advertising and commercial culture. By the 1920s advertising had arrived as a recognised profession, and advertisers developed increasingly sophisticated techniques for selling products within a stratified marketplace organised into relatively well-defined segments or subgroups (Leiss et al. 2005: 68; 149). Importantly for this discussion, the emergence of advertising as an integral part of modern culture was intimately linked with the rise of the modern newspaper (attributed to the innovations of Lord Northcliffe, founder of the *Daily Mail*) for which display advertising became the main source of revenue. As Patrick Collier has discussed, 'the claim that Northcliffe and his imitators had transformed journalism from a profession to a branch of commerce' was central to the case made against the popular press in a cluster of commentaries which appeared after the war, feeding into a broad cultural narrative of journalistic decline in this period (2006: 23). Editors of the intellectual weeklies, which positioned themselves against a supposedly degraded and commercialised press, could be resistant to engaging with advertisers.[7] Rhondda, however, was 'a great believer in the power of advertising' (John 2013: 282), and her 'courage to advertise' is an important marker of the unique qualities she brought as an editor to *Time and Tide*. Active in the Women's Advertising Society, she recruited its president Marion Jean Lyon (advertising manager of *Punch*) to *Time and Tide*'s board of directors in 1926, and this additional expertise undoubtedly played an instrumental role in *Time and Tide*'s marketing strategies in the lead-up to its size and price increase in 1928, and beyond. In its last issue of 1926, *Time and Tide* announced that from the following week it would appear in 'a NEW FORM'. Explaining that the sheet would now be 'longer and narrower' and with the Table of Contents 'printed across both columns' (instead of occupying the left-hand column as it had done hitherto) it also informed readers that 'the paper on which it is printed will have a better finish'. The notice continued:

> It is our hope that these changes will benefit both readers and advertisers. [. . .] The surface finish of the new paper will enable us to reproduce not only the pen-and-ink drawings which we use at present, but also half-tone blocks and pencil drawings; and we, therefore, hope in the future to offer to our readers a certain variety in the matter of illustrations, and to our advertisers a wider scope for their advertisements. (31 Dec 1926: 1199)

These material changes to the paper would be of enormous consequence for *Time and Tide*'s expansion during this middle phase of its development. Its advertising content was one of the chief means by which *Time and Tide* gradually rebranded itself as a less woman-focused, more general-audience weekly review, and with attention to its own commodity status the new 'variety [. . .] of illustrations' it offered to readers made it the most distinctive and visually appealing product on the weekly review market.

During its first few years *Time and Tide* typically carried up to two pages of advertising, predominantly advertisements for cultural products (books, theatre announcements, for example) as well as companies of which Rhondda was herself a director, and classifieds.[8] Following a 'Publicity Week' in the autumn of 1924 *Time and Tide* dramatically strengthened its relationship with advertisers to whom the periodical offered itself as a lucrative outlet for products targeted at middle-class women consumers. For several years the biggest advertiser in *Time and Tide* was Debenham and Freebody, a leading retailer in the women's fashion market; from mid-October 1924, this London store bought full-page display advertising space in the periodical virtually every week. In March 1927, just two months after it adopted its new paper and format, *Time and Tide* offered even 'wider scope' to advertisers with the introduction of an advertising wrapper, a separately-numbered four-page sheet which more than doubled the periodical's advertising space. As Mark Morrisson notes, magazine publishing in this period saw a 'shift in the basis of profitability from subscription income to advertising revenue' (2001: 39), and *Time and Tide*'s survival became increasingly dependent on the relationships it built with advertisers. At the same time, *Time and Tide*'s advertising content was able to alter readers' 'horizon of expectations' for the magazine, and open the periodical up to multiple target groups.[9] Significantly, while from 1926 *Time and Tide* was working more intensively to move out of the 'women's paper' category, until late in 1929 the periodical presented itself for women readers: regular advertisements on the front cover for lingerie and frocks made from the British brand name fabric 'Viyella' addressed the female consumer (see Figure 4.1) in contrast with advertisements for motor cars and 'Luvisca' fabric for men on the front covers of the *Spectator* and the *Nation and Athenaeum*, each targeting a male readership. During this crucial period of transition into the sixpenny weekly market *Time and Tide* thus continued to package itself as the same product for its core female readership, but over time the periodical began to advertise on its inside pages commodity products marketed at male as well as female consumers and to introduce

Figure 4.1 *Time and Tide* front cover, 13 Dec 1929. Reproduced with
the permission of The William Ready Division of Archives and Research
Collections, McMaster University Library.

more gender-neutral advertisements on the front page of its advertising wrapper. By the end of 1930, advertisements for fashion and fabrics had completely disappeared from the periodical's front cover and this advertising space was increasingly bought up by publishers marketing books (see Figure 4.2).[10] According to Elizabeth Dickens it was with the intellectual weeklies that the book trade developed 'one of [its] most productive interwar relationships' (2011: 172), and by strengthening its links with publishers *Time and Tide* not only expanded an important source of revenue but also altered its identity and image.

In order to sell its journalistic space to this new group of advertisers, however, *Time and Tide* had to do more than adapt its format to meet advertisers' needs; it had to convince advertisers that it had the kind of public that these advertisers wanted to reach. Comparison of the inside front pages of *Time and Tide*'s first two advertising wrappers illustrates the ways in which this periodical continued to market itself to female readers while beginning to open itself up to a new and quite different audience. On the first, *Time and Tide* carried a full-page advertisement for one of the most successful of the new mass-market women's magazines catering to the middle and lower-middle classes, the British edition of *Good Housekeeping* launched in 1922 (Figure 4.3). Promoting the magazine's '5th Anniversary Number' (4 Mar 1927: ii) the advertisement was probably accepted in exchange for two smaller advertisements for *Time and Tide* which appeared in the February and March issues of *Good Housekeeping* the same year. Illustrating *Time and Tide*'s push beyond an existing feminist readership into new female markets, the exchange also demonstrates that in some contexts it was still strategic to advertise itself as a journal for women. Producing an allure of excitement in its bold use of capitals and alliteration, the first advertisement for *Time and Tide* in *Good Housekeeping* reads 'The weekly review for the woman of to-day [. . .] VIVID, VARIOUS, VIVACIOUS' (Feb 1927: 182) while the second more product-oriented advertisement concentrates on qualities that were likely to attract *Good Housekeeping*'s women readers: cultural criticism (books, theatre, music) and 'ORIGINAL literary competitions & acrostics' (Mar 1927: 238). Both advertisements offered a four-week free trial of the journal, and with its huge circulation *Good Housekeeping* offered *Time and Tide* the potential for reaching new female audiences. The inside front page of *Time and Tide*'s second advertising wrapper, however, directs us to a smaller and more select audience the periodical was equally eager to reach: that of the intellectual weeklies. Here, *Time and Tide* carried a full-page

TIME AND TIDE

THE REVIEW WITH INDEPENDENT VIEWS
POLITICS   LITERATURE   ART

Vol. XI. No. 52 [*Registered as a Newspaper*]   WEEK ENDING SATURDAY, DECEMBER 27, 1930.   Price 6d.

Principal Contents

THE MYSTERY OF TO-MORROW

Figure 4.2 *Time and Tide* front cover, 27 Dec 1930. Reproduced with the permission of The William Ready Division of Archives and Research Collections, McMaster University Library.

SPECIALLY ENLARGED

5th anniversary number

EVER since its inception, five years ago, *Good Housekeeping* has been the spirit of guidance and inspiration in more than 200,000 British Homes.

The March issue is the special enlarged 5th Anniversary Number. Amongst its features are :—

Serial Stories by :—
Anne Douglas Sedgwick
Gene Stratton Porter

Articles by :—
St. John Ervine
Lady Violet Bonham Carter
Margaret Bondfield, J.P., M.P.

Helena Normanton
Clemence Dane
J. D. Beresford
Basil Macdonald Hastings
Marion Cran

Also Fashion, Household Engineering and Cooking.

INSTITUTE OF GOOD HOUSEKEEPING
Every woman should write us for particulars of this Institute, carried on at 49, Wellington Street, Strand, W.C. Its laboratories and offices are constantly engaged upon research work connected with household management, and are always ready to solve the individual problems of *Good Housekeeping* readers.

260 PAGES, MANY IN COLOUR . . . **1/-** NET.   NOW ON SALE EVERYWHERE

Great New Serial by W.J. LOCKE
"The Kingdom of Theophilus" starts in this number

Figure 4.3 Advertisement for *Good Housekeeping* in *Time and Tide* 4 Mar 1927: ii. Reproduced with the permission of The William Ready Division of Archives and Research Collections, McMaster University Library.

advertisement for the *Nation and Athenaeum* (11 Mar 1927: ii) (Figure 4.4), the first of eight advertisements for this weekly review which appeared in *Time and Tide* between March 1927 and December 1928 and which were apparently placed in exchange for an equal number of advertisements for *Time and Tide* carried by the *Nation and Athenaeum* over the same period.[11] While it is impossible to calculate the benefit of this exchange in terms of actual new readers that may have been brought to either magazine, this strategic alliance played a key part in *Time and Tide*'s move into the forefront of the general-audience weekly reviews. Rebranding itself by association with the *Nation and Athenaeum* (advertising in the *Nation and Athenaeum* and promoting the *Nation and Athenaeum* in its own pages) *Time and Tide* was effectively paving the way for its own size and price increase in October 1928 which would complete its transition into the sixpenny weekly market.

The 1920s was a period of intense competition among the sixpenny weeklies. The *New Statesman*, which in circulation was second only to the *Spectator*, dominated the market on the left, but after the war it experienced a sharp decline under its first editor, Clifford Sharp, and by 1927 both halves of the paper (its front political end, and its back arts pages) were, according to Adrian Smith, 'rudderless' (1996: 186). In contrast, and despite a lower circulation, the *Nation and Athenaeum* was enjoying 'qualified success as a vibrant and revitalised journal' under the control of J. Maynard Keynes and its political editor, Hubert Henderson, and literary editor, Leonard Woolf (Smith 1996: 270). As discussed by Smith, the two papers would later see a reversal in fortunes when in 1931 the *Nation and Athenaeum* was swallowed up by its rival in the newly constituted *New Statesman and Nation*. But in 1927 the 'battle of survival' between the two papers was still to be played out (Smith 1996: 5), and it was at this moment that *Time and Tide* positioned itself as a new competitor in the field. As the most 'book-focused' of the intellectual weeklies (Dickens 2011: 167) the *Nation and Athenaeum* arguably represented the most promising target audience for *Time and Tide* to build its own reputation within Britain's weekly-review reading public. In early advertisements placed in the rival publication *Time and Tide* promoted its arts content most heavily, listing in the first advertisement short fiction and book review content in forthcoming issues (19 Mar 1927: 876) and in the third publicising an 'Autumn Books Number' (1 Oct 1927: 852). An endorsement from the influential French 'little magazine' *Mercure de France* further commended the periodical to the *Nation and Athenaeum*'s literary and highbrow readers, but in order to secure a position among the

ii. TIME AND TIDE MARCH 11, 1927

READ THE NATION AND BE WELL INFORMED

Readers of TIME AND TIDE will find in the columns of THE NATION well informed and authoritative comments on the economic, political, and international situation. THE NATION is the organ of a new school of Liberal thought which includes some of the ablest and most original economists and financial publicists in the country. The ably written book reviews have called forth this recent tribute, that they are "the cream of critical literary intelligence."

EXCLUSIVE FEATURES.

Foremost among the exclusive features of THE NATION are the frequent articles by J. M. Keynes, the noted author of "The Economic Consequences of the Peace," Mr. A. G. Gardiner says of him that he possesses "one of the keenest blades in contemporary literature"; certain it is that his articles are read throughout the world, his recent article on "The Position of the Lancashire Cotton Trade" being widely quoted." The Parliamentary Sketch: "At St. Stephen's" has been described as "the most brilliant political article in contemporary journalism," while "Life and Politics" is written by one who is obviously at the heart of things.

A REVISED OPINION.

Two years ago Mr. St. John Ervine, writing in "The World To Day" said of THE NATION: "Since the departure of Mr. Massingham for 'The Nation and Athenæum,' dullness has descended upon that review, and it is now nearly unreadable."

In October of last year, in a letter to the Editor of THE NATION, Mr. Ervine said: "Will you permit me to add, though they have nothing whatever to do with the subject of this letter, my congratulations on the great improvement which has taken place in THE NATION in the past month or two. I am not a Liberal, and I am unsympathetic to the rather arid intellectualism of some of your book reviewers, but I am bound to say that I find THE NATION as stimulating and provocative as ever it was."

Readers of TIME AND TIDE have been pleased with Mr. St. John Ervine's tributes to their own paper, and will readily appreciate the significance of this change of opinion.

SPRING BOOKS NUMBER.

All the above features come to you, with many others for but sixpence weekly. Order your copy Now. This week is an excellent introductory Number. There will be an article by J. M. Keynes titled "Are Books Too Dear," together with the Spring Books Supplement. Fill in the enclosed coupon and send a P.O. for a Trial Three Months' Subscription NOW.

F. B. HARGREAVES, *General Manager,*

THE NATION & ATHENÆUM,

38, GREAT JAMES STREET, BEDFORD ROW, W.C.1.

I enclose herewith 7/6 for a trial 3 months' subscription to "The Nation." PLEASE POST TO ME *at the address below.*

Signed..

....

Date

Cheques to be made payable to "THE NATION LTD."

T. & T., Mar., 1927.

Figure 4.4 Advertisement for the *Nation and Athenaeum* in *Time and Tide* 11 Mar 1927: ii. Reproduced with the permission of The William Ready Division of Archives and Research Collections, McMaster University Library.

leading weekly reviews *Time and Tide* would need to promote itself as a political as well as a literary magazine.[12]

Significantly, *Time and Tide*'s first advertisement printed in the *Nation and Athenaeum* carried an endorsement from a figure who (as discussed in Chapter 1) had already proved useful in differentiating the periodical from both mainstream and women's newspapers, St. John Ervine. Quoting Ervine in *The World To-day*, the endorsement reads: '*Time and Tide* offers a sane judgment of current events, and is sufficient in itself to justify the appearance of women in public affairs. . . . I do not know of any other paper which succeeds in making me read so much of it as *Time and Tide* does' (19 Mar 1927: 876). As a regular contributor to *Good Housekeeping*, Ervine would have been familiar to many of *Time and Tide*'s women readers, and in October 1927 (exactly one year prior to its size and price increase) *Time and Tide* published a leading article entitled 'Mr. St. John Ervine and The Press' which discussed a 'witty and provocative speech' Ervine had made at an 'Individualist Bookshop Luncheon' the previous week (28 Oct 1927: 955).[13] The subject of Ervine's speech was the huge growth in circulation of the London daily newspapers which, he argued, did not equate with influence. Identifying the big provincial newspapers (papers such as the *Manchester Guardian* and the *Yorkshire Post*) as the only organs of the press containing 'real news', he also pointed out, *Time and Tide* reported, 'that the weekly reviews were the papers that had political influence because they were read for their opinions'. Naming as examples the *Spectator*, the *New Statesman*, the *Nation and Athenaeum*, the *Saturday Review*, the *Outlook* and, significantly, 'TIME AND TIDE', Ervine's speech provided a useful vehicle for promoting the political value of the weekly reviews, and for advertising *Time and Tide*'s place among them. While not following wholeheartedly all of Ervine's conclusions (the article states that 'we do not regard the mammoth circulations of to-day with the same distrust that he does') *Time and Tide* found agreement in his suggestion that the journals with the most influence on public opinion are the weekly reviews. The article concludes:

> Here are papers taken by that minority of the public which enjoys new ideas and is prepared to take the trouble to read solidly – papers taken for their opinions [. . .] People take their daily papers for the news; but the educated public is beginning more and more to look to the weekly reviews for opinions. The day will come, we believe, when no house with any pretensions to culture will be found without one or other of the weekly reviews on its reading-table. (956)

This leading article (unsigned, but very likely written by Rhondda) marks the beginning of a carefully planned marketing campaign aimed as much to *Time and Tide*'s existing audience as to new readers. In language as sophisticated as any example of modern advertising, the text situates 'papers taken for their opinions' in a symbolic context (the cultured household with its 'reading-table'), bringing them into a meaningful relationship with more abstract values and ideas associated with a 'minority' and 'educated public'.[14] In this appeal to readers' cultural aspirations the leader invokes an audience and creates a demand among its own subscribers for this particular brand of journalism, demonstrating how adept *Time and Tide* was in exploiting modern advertising techniques not only to extend into new markets but to take its existing readership with it. At the same time, in the relationship the periodical constructed with its audience *Time and Tide* resisted a central component of the new consumer culture which placed irrationality at the heart of advertising practice, and challenged the 'persistent belief among advertisers that women are less rational consumers than men' (Leiss et al. 2005: 151; 202). In a testimonial printed in one of *Time and Tide*'s internal advertisements in 1926 the Labour MP Ellen Wilkinson states '*Time and Tide* tells us what women think and not what they wear' (19 Mar 1926: 289), and this idea of the 'thinking' woman (an activity traditionally associated with 'rational' masculinity) was central to the periodical's reframing of its goals amongst its existing readership. Immediately before its article on St. John Ervine and the press the last item in *Time and Tide*'s regular 'Review of the Week' invited readers to a 'TIME AND TIDE [. . .] AT HOME' where they would hear 'short speeches on the history and policy of the paper' by *Time and Tide*'s directors and have an 'opportunity for questions and comments and discussion' (28 Oct 1927: 955).[15] *Time and Tide* printed extracts from the directors' speeches in its issue of 9 December 1927 in a full-page feature called 'The Function of The Weekly Review' (1114). The heading alone, with its informative, 'function'-oriented discourse, communicates *Time and Tide*'s rationalistic image of human nature. The text, too, is anchored in rationality rather than suggestiveness, in arguments about a growing separation of the '*opinion*-paper' from the '*news*-paper' (Rhondda), and the irresponsibility of newspaper editors who fail to give the public the kind of solid reading matter they want (Rebecca West). Extracts from the concluding speech made by Professor Winifred Cullis further dismantle persistent characterisations of female readers as passive consumers, incapable of rational deliberation and thought: 'so many people like a good old partisan attitude, they cannot bear being asked to think and to make up their own minds. We, obviously, have picked up a group of readers that like it . . .' (1114).

This idea of the 'thinking' (woman) reader would also be central to *Time and Tide*'s public intervention in contemporary debates about journalism, developed in and around a series of articles which it published in February and March 1928 on 'The Future of the Press'. The series was planned towards the end of 1927, and as Rhondda explained to West (who contributed the fourth article in the series) '[w]e are going to advertise [. . .] and make a big stunt of it if we can'.[16] Appearing at the height of Lord Rothermere's anti-feminist campaign in the *Daily Mail* and *Daily Mirror* against the equalisation of the franchise, one might expect the series to have an explicit feminist agenda. Indeed, the notion that 'the influence of the daily press is detrimental to the position of women' was the subject of a Six Point Group debate in March 1928 at the Assembly Hall, Westminster, chaired by Rebecca West, evidence of the continued involvement of *Time and Tide*'s personnel in the organisational bases of interwar feminism. However, while a notice of this debate was printed in *Time and Tide*'s pages with the headline 'Women in the Press' (16 Mar 1928: 255) the feature series deliberately avoided the 'women' tag and seems to have been part of the periodical's strategy for extending beyond its immediate feminist readership. The first three articles were contributed by none other than St. John Ervine, and expanding upon the arguments made in his speech at the Individualist Bookshop Luncheon (reported earlier in *Time and Tide*'s pages) they mobilised a familiar narrative of journalistic decline with reference to the latest instance of amalgamations under the big press combines (the sale of the *Daily Telegraph* to the house of Berry). This critique was reinforced by four full-page cartoons accompanying the series. Taking full advantage of the new paper on which *Time and Tide* was printed they caricatured Britain's most powerful press barons under the title 'Our Dictators', graphically illustrating a popular view 'that the public [was] at the mercy of a degraded press' (Collier 2006: 139).[17] However, an unsigned leader published in *Time and Tide*'s issue carrying the second article in the series points to a more subtle agenda, one that was implicitly if not explicitly feminist and designed to jolt readers into active consideration of contemporary anxieties and debates.

This leading article, possibly written by *Time and Tide*'s youngest director, Winifred Holtby, opens with the following provocative gambit: 'We call the leaders of the great Press Industry "Our Dictators" and no-one challenges the title' (17 Feb 1928: 143). Moving beyond

a simplified view of the press barons as evil dictators, the article identifies reader passivity rather than press baron activity as the greater
threat to democracy, suggesting that to give in to 'the dictum that we
are ruled by [. . .] the Press' prevents a more active form of engagement in the debate about the state of contemporary journalism. The
consequences of such cultural pessimism about the press, the article
implies, are detrimental to the very interests that *Time and Tide*'s
feminist readers are assumed to share. Specifically addressing the supporters of 'movements for political, economic or social reform', the
article goes on to argue that the resignation of social reformers to a
view that the press is too degraded to represent their interests is in
itself partly to blame for the 'cold neglect' in the press of 'the causes
that really matter'. Reminding readers that the press 'must respond
to Good News Value', the article's author boldly asserts: 'let us see
to it that those things which are worthwhile put themselves into the
big headlines'. With this echo of tactics used by an earlier generation of feminists 'making news' at the height of the suffrage era, the
article then develops its most trenchant feminist analysis, noting the
current tendency of even those papers which nominally support the
Equal Franchise bill to 'underestimate the importance of the present
Session of Parliament'. Stating that the public was only 'startled to
a realisation of the most important issue of the day' when an enterprising Young Suffragist made headline news by making a 'Scene at
the Palace' the article concludes: 'The important thing for feminists
had become the important thing for everybody. Our dictators had
yielded again to their Dictator – the good news-value of a dramatised
idea' (145). At once an explicit assertion that the feminist issue is an
issue of general interest the piece also draws attention to the 'implicit'
feminism of *Time and Tide*'s own publicity stunt. While appearing to
subscribe to a dominant view of a moribund press, the series (with its
accompanying cartoons) was actually designed, this leader suggests,
to provoke readers to think for themselves about the current state of
journalism, and to question dominant and pessimistic narratives.

Time and Tide thus cleverly used a broader debate about the future
of the press to advertise its name more widely, and make a feminist
intervention in contemporary narratives about a perceived crisis in
journalism. As noted by Maria DiCenzo and Lucy Delap 'this was
not a period of decline for feminist activists and thinkers' (2008: 52),
and *Time and Tide*'s feminist writers were far more optimistic about
the press and the public than many of their male contemporaries.[18]
Continuing to align itself with the most progressive of the intellectual
weeklies, *Time and Tide* drew attention at the close of the series to
an article published in the *Nation and Athenaeum* the previous week

which 'attempts to estimate the kind of service that a paper of this class performs to politics in modern life'. Presenting a short excerpt from the article in which its author defined the weekly paper's 'most important function' as 'giving constructive ideas to politics', *Time and Tide* stated that it believed the quotation would be 'of especial interest to our readers at the present time in view of the definitions of the functions of the various sections of the Press recently given in TIME AND TIDE' (30 Mar 1928: 303). By promoting the qualities of the *Nation and Athenaeum*, *Time and Tide* again staked out its own territory as a journal of opinion capable of 'preparing political parties [. . .] for bold reform' through the contact it initiates between 'thinkers and politicians' (303). One week prior to its size and price increase *Time and Tide* placed an advertisement in Keynes's journal publicising the increased space it would devote 'to BOOKS AND LITERARY SUBJECTS' (6 Oct 1928: 23), but the following month it promoted both ends of the paper and introduced a new slogan: '*Time and Tide* is a journal for thinking men and women' (17 Nov 1928: 276) (Figure 4.5). At once advertising the periodical as a general-audience publication for male as well as female readers, the incorporation of the word 'thinking' here defines women as well as men as independent, rational subjects. Two weeks later an advertisement for the *Nation and Athenaeum* in *Time and Tide*'s pages carried a new strapline of its own: 'A Journal for Independent Thinkers' (30 Nov 1928: 1173). This 'thinker/thinking' tag remained a constant in the remaining advertisements exchanged by these two magazines, and provides further evidence of the close synergies involved in this strategic alliance.

Time and Tide's move into the highbrow sphere occupied by the intellectual weeklies would create new challenges for the periodical, as will be discussed in Chapter 6. More immediately, while rebranding itself by association with the *Nation and Athenaeum*, *Time and Tide* needed to retain the loyalty of its existing readership at the new price of sixpence, and increase its circulation within its core target group. Current subscribers were told that they would continue to receive the new *Time and Tide* at the present rates for at least two years, and the periodical also offered a four-week free trial which could be claimed at 'any address, at home or abroad [. . .] on receipt of 4d in stamps to cover postage' (28 Sep 1928: 901).[19] Other evidence suggests that *Time and Tide* was particularly anxious not to lose the support of professional working women whose periodical networks it had canvassed in earlier years (see Chapter 1). For example, an advertisement promoting *Time and Tide*'s 'Autumn Books Number' in the *Woman Teacher* one week following its size and price increase

Figure 4.5 Advertisement for *Time and Tide* in the *Nation and Athenaeum*
17 Nov 1928: 276. Reproduced by kind permission of the Syndics of
Cambridge University Library. Classmark: NPR.c.79.

asserted that the enlarged journal 'will now be more valuable than ever to the cultured Teacher' (19 Oct 1928: 23), while a reduced subscription offer, initially made to members of the Association of Post Office Women Clerks (APOWC) and extended to all members of the Federation of Women Civil Servants (FWCS), offered the periodical 'post free, at the very low rate of 6s. for a full year's subscription, a rate which only just covers the cost of postage' (*Opportunity*, Nov 1928: 169). Targeting both higher and lower income groups these advertisements and promotions show how actively *Time and Tide* continued to market itself within professional women's networks, and there is much evidence within the paper of the ways in which the periodical continued to serve the needs of the feminist movement. Features including its monthly 'Reports and Announcements' which publicised the feminist organisational activities of the National Union of Societies for Equal Citizenship (NUSEC), the Six Point Group (SPG), and the Women's Freedom League (WFL), and its 'Westminster' column which in 1928 contained regular reports on the Franchise Bill, provide examples of the 'explicit' feminism which remained in the paper even as it worked to broaden its appeal. Advertisements for other feminist periodicals also evidence *Time and Tide*'s continuing participation in overlapping feminist periodical communities, particularly those operating on an international level. Each of the following magazines were advertised frequently in *Time and Tide* beyond 1928: *International Woman Suffrage News* (*Jus Suffragi*), *Equal Rights* (the American feminist weekly and organ of the National Woman's Party), and *Woman's World* (a publication by and for Australian women). Holtby and Rhondda spoke at a series of weekly Six Point Group meetings on international feminism in the autumn of 1928 (John 2013: 396), and *Time and Tide*'s increasingly international outlook will be the subject of further discussion in Chapter 5. First, I consider *Time and Tide*'s renegotiation of the cultural landscape in and after 1928 with reference to its simultaneous self-promotion as a literary review.

From Fleet Street to Bloomsbury: literary celebrities and 'The function of literary criticism'

On the inside back cover of its first sixpenny issue, *Time and Tide* announced that the following week it would be publishing an Autumn Book Number (12 Oct 1928: iii). From its inception the periodical had been publishing two, later three, book issues a year (Autumn, Christmas and Spring); these ran to thirty-two instead of twenty-four pages, roughly quadrupling the space devoted to book reviews in a regular issue.[20] As *Time and Tide* explained in advance of its 'new departure' in October 1928, at the price of fourpence it had 'not been possible to deal as fully with all aspects of current affairs, *and especially with books and literary subjects* as the Editor would have wished' (5 Oct 1928: 905, my emphasis). Now the paper's book reviews section typically ran to five or six pages on a regular basis (compared with two or three previously) and in special Book Numbers to as many as fourteen pages, more than half the space available in the original twenty-four-page magazine. *Time and Tide*'s increasingly literary focus has been read as a dilution, even abandonment of its early feminist identity.[21] But this conclusion fails to appreciate the significance of *Time and Tide*'s extension of feminist analysis into areas of cultural critique, and the periodical's importance as a publicity vehicle for women writers (both modernist and 'middlebrow') at a time when the processes of canon formation were already consecrating a relatively small group of modernist male authors. As Aaron Jaffe identifies, it was during the interwar period that modernists and their allies worked 'with particular intensity [. . .] to create and expand a market for elite literary works' (2005: 3), capitalising on market forces they claimed to reject in the making of lasting reputations. In a review of Jaffe's book, Faye Hammill wonders 'to what extent so-called "minor" modernists contributed to their own marginality through ineffective negotiations with publicity and the marketplace' (2006: 390) and in her own study of *Women, Celebrity and Literary Culture Between the Wars* shows that certain women authors were no less savvy than their more famous modernist contemporaries in their engagement with the marketplace. In the remainder of this chapter I explore *Time and Tide*'s own involvement in modern celebrity culture, and the value it placed on publicity and advertisement in the literary as well as political sphere.

Time and Tide's new emphasis on the world of contemporary literature is illustrated quite literally by a series of cartoons billed as 'Lampoons of Literary Celebrities' which appeared over a four-month period from October 1927 to January 1928. Contributed by the poet and novelist Sylvia Townsend Warner in collaboration with artist Paul Bloomfield, the series featured in turn A. E. Housman, Virginia Woolf, Humbert Wolfe, David Garnett and Lytton Strachey. A reminder of how modernist names such as Woolf's circulated alongside such figures as the popular if now largely forgotten poet and civil servant Humbert Wolfe, the lampoons evidence *Time and Tide*'s new investment in parody as a form for promoting a variety of aesthetic discourses to its readership.[22] In each lampoon Bloomfield's artwork combines with Warner's parodic verse or prose to lightly satirise qualities popularly associated with the subject; in the case of Woolf, the supposed inaccessibility of her works (accentuated by the awkwardness of her pose) for the ordinary reader (Figure 4.6).[23] At the same time, these single-panel cartoons (to which entire pages are dedicated) demonstrate *Time and Tide*'s new investment in graphic art content enabled by the improved quality of its paper from January 1927. As forms of 'cultural advertisement' they evidence the periodical's growing visual appeal, and its use of comic genres in association with the serious weekly review format.[24] Indeed, in its use of illustration *Time and Tide* departed both from the intellectual weeklies which rarely incorporated any graphic art apart from advertising, and from the literary reviews associated with modernism. In 1926 the *New Statesman* had published a series of full-page pencil sketches of leading personalities by the cartoonist David Low, but on the whole this magazine 'was a singularly humourless product' (Smith 1996: 274); T. S. Eliot, preparing to launch the *Criterion*, was emphatic that his magazine should be 'simple and severe in appearance, without illustrations' (Harding 2002: 9–10).[25] By harnessing the 'dynamism of illustrative comedic forms' (Newton 2012: 67) *Time and Tide* deliberately courted a wider audience than that of these small-circulation publications, and the artists it employed worked across popular, commercial and 'middlebrow' markets. Earlier in 1927 Bloomfield had contributed literary caricatures to the women's weekly *Eve: The Lady's Pictorial*; another artist who contributed frequently to *Time and Tide* from 1928 was the caricaturist Powys Evans, a regular contributor to the *London Mercury*, J. C. Squire's literary monthly aimed at a broad readership.[26]

Not all of *Time and Tide*'s graphic content was comic. Eleanor Farjeon's new 'Monthly Calendar' feature (also dating from 1927, see Chapter 2) was illustrated with drawings and later woodcuts by Bloomsbury artist Gwendolen Raverat. *Time and Tide* also showcased work by another leading female woodcut artist, Clare Leighton, carried occasional graphic contributions from the modernist Wyndham Lewis, and from 1930 the artist Edmund Xavier Kapp (best known for his portraits or character studies, and whose sitters included Picasso and Matisse) frequently contributed drawings to the paper.[27] Promoting itself as an aesthetic as well as a commodity object *Time and Tide* emerged as the most visually appealing product on the weekly review market, its combination of text and image marking similarities not only with mass-market 'smart' magazines but also the book arts fostered by the Bloomsbury Group and the Hogarth Press.[28] The year 1928 saw a strengthening of *Time and Tide*'s connections with

Mrs. Woolf is Visited by some Uncommon Readers

A trail of smoke hung over Iowa, a scream from the engine awakened a child in Indianopolis, at Columbus an old woman had got out in a hurry, leaving her bag behind; but the train had started, it was too late to do anything about it and the negro boy was coming down the car with bananas. But it is impossible to fix the mind upon bananas, for in the harbour were streamers waving, steamers bathing, banded funnels with their sea-going tilt. Meanwhile the waxen fruit bought in the Caledonian Market remained perfectly immobile. And now, having passed the gloom and the felted silence of the archway at Euston, these young men were assuring her that they had read all her books and found them most congenial.

It was all rather confusing; but everything is confusing when one comes to think of it.

S.T.W.

Figure 4.6 'Lampoons of Literary Celebrities', *Time and Tide* 25 Nov 1927: 1057. Reproduced with the permission of The William Ready Division of Archives and Research Collections, McMaster University Library.

Bloomsbury. In this year Virginia Woolf's signature appeared for the first time in *Time and Tide*'s columns (her essay 'The Sun and the Fish' was published in the periodical's issue of 3 February) and the Hogarth Press published Rhondda's 'Leisured Women' articles in its Hogarth Essays series. In May of the following year *Time and Tide* moved from the offices it had occupied since May 1920 at 88 Fleet Street to what it described as 'a house of its own' at 32 Bloomsbury Street (10 May 1929: 547). Anticipating the language of Woolf's classic feminist essay *A Room of One's Own* (extracts from which were published in *Time and Tide* in November 1929) *Time and Tide*'s move from the heart of the newspaper industry to the centre of Bloomsbury's artistic community also signals the periodical's new ambitions in the cultural sphere.[29] The short article announcing the move was accompanied by a pen-and-ink drawing by Raverat who had recently been appointed as *Time and Tide*'s first regular art critic, and on the front cover of the same issue the periodical's coverage of the fine arts as well as literature was given visual emphasis in a new decorative border, in the art-deco style, surrounding *Time and Tide*'s masthead and list of principal contents (Figure 4.7).[30]

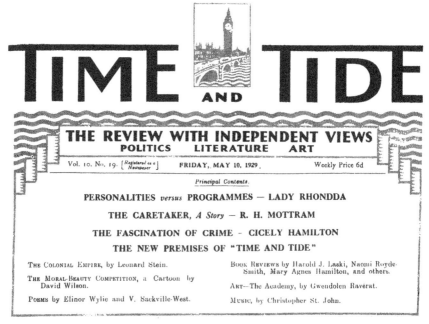

Figure 4.7 *Time and Tide* Masthead, 10 May 1929. Reproduced with the permission of The William Ready Division of Archives and Research Collections, McMaster University Library.

'Lampoons of Literary Celebrities' thus appeared on the cusp of a new orientation in *Time and Tide*'s pages towards Bloomsbury and modernist cultures. The celebrities depicted in the cartoons are predominantly Bloomsbury figures and evidence *Time and Tide*'s participation in the marketing of modernism. But in contrast with the popular press and mass-market magazines which parodied, discussed and circulated images of modernist celebrities but rarely published their work, *Time and Tide* also published original creative contributions by key female modernist figures.[31] In addition to Woolf's 1928 contribution, Edith Sitwell contributed an article on 'Modern Poetry' published in two parts in *Time and Tide*'s issues of 30 March and 6 April 1928, and in January 1929 *Time and Tide* published three of her poems.[32] With both the Bloomsbury and Sitwell entourages representing 'a growing force in literary London during the 1920s' (Harding 2002: 12–13), by harnessing their signatures the periodical was undoubtedly working to expand its own scope, readership and brow. But the publication of these authors' writing also points to the periodical's perceived value for reaching new and wider audiences, and its commitment to providing 'solid' reading matter in the realm of literature as well as politics. Melba Cuddy-Keane, in her study of the 'pedagogical Woolf', rejects an older image of Woolf as elitist and aloof, identifying her as a 'democratic highbrow' who 'took the intellectual into the border zone where professional and common reader/writer meet' (2003: 8). The article by Sitwell is explicit in its aim to make 'high' art available to all. Explaining what the modernist artist is seeking to do in poetry she uses examples from her own poems to help readers overcome their supposed 'insuperable difficulties': 'Now let us take the phrases one by one, and go into what appears at first as their queerness' (6 Apr 1928: 332). At once participating in modern celebrity culture *Time and Tide* thus also provided readers with direct access to writing by modernists widely marketed as inaccessible; later it would publish a contribution from another notoriously 'difficult' female modernist, Gertrude Stein.[33]

Time and Tide's publication in the late 1920s of Britain's two leading female modernists in fiction and poetry respectively points to the 'second rise of modernism' that Bonnie Kime Scott identifies with 'the women of 1928' (1995: xxxvii) and to the periodical's importance as a vehicle of promotion for female modernist celebrities. However, another illustrated feature published in *Time and Tide*'s last issue of 1928 demonstrates that the periodical was equally committed to promoting women writers who have been positioned outside modernism's movements. This feature, which appeared under *Time and Tide*'s familiar 'Personalities and Powers' heading, led with an article entitled 'Parnassus in Academe, Novelists at Oxford' which was contributed pseudonymously by one of the periodical's own directors and contributors, Winifred Holtby.[34] The article celebrates a 'shower of literary talent' (28 Dec 1928: 1271) scattered by Oxford over England since the war in the form of six female novelists, all former students at Oxford University, namely Hilda Reid, Margaret Kennedy, Naomi Mitchison, Vera Brittain, Sylvia Thompson and Winifred Holtby herself.[35] The most striking component, though, is the full-page drawing which accompanies the article and was provided by the artist Paul Bloomfield in the same style as his illustrations to the 'Lampoons of Literary Celebrities' discussed above (Figure 4.8). However, unlike these earlier cartoons this drawing does not make any of the women novelists featured here the target of satire, but rather the classical statue around which they triumphantly group and whose startled expression suggests an affront to decorum we are invited to dispute. A caricature of Venus de Milo, one of the most famous works of ancient Greek sculpture, the drawing places under scrutiny an archetypal femininity identified with a subject position that inspires rather than creates works of art.[36] Anticipating Woolf's assertion in *A Room of One's Own* that 'literature is open to everybody' the illustration suggests that women have as much right as men to share the proverbial home of poetry, literature and learning, a reading which gains further resonance in the context of an ongoing controversy over Cambridge University's refusal to grant degrees to women (Oxford University had been awarding degrees to women since 1921).[37] Implicitly positioning Oxford University as a progressive rival to its competitor Cambridge, the feature publicises a fraternity of women novelists neglected at the time and since by modernist critics, and that even an expanded canon of female modernism has played a part in obscuring.

Time and Tide's promotion of women writers identified with a 'middlebrow' as well as modernist sphere will be the subject of further discussion in Chapter 6. Another significant dimension of the periodical's expansion was its promotion of women critics. As Scott observes, women writers' literary criticism had also 'hit stride by 1928' (1995: 183) and in December of this year, three weeks before its 'Parnassus in Academe' feature, *Time and Tide* announced a new regular feature to be contributed monthly: 'Notes on Books and Writers by Rebecca West' (7 Dec 1928: 1212). West, who joined *Time and Tide*'s board of directors in 1922, wrote for the periodical from its first issue, contributing weekly theatre criticisms until August 1921,

DECEMBER 28, 1928   TIME AND TIDE   1273

Drawing by Paul Bloomfield.

Parnassus in Academe

Winifred Holtby—Hilda Reid—Margaret Kennedy—Naomi Mitchison—Vera Brittain and Sylvia Thompson.

Figure 4.8 'Parnassus in Academe', *Time and Tide* 28 Dec 1928: 1273. Reproduced with the permission of The William Ready Division of Archives and Research Collections, McMaster University Library.

then, less frequently, signed articles on a range of political and cultural subjects. A highly marketable journalist she was during these early years 'best known for being a feminist and for being shocking' (Pykett 2000: 177), but in 1928 West also emerged as an important modernist critic. In the summer of this year West published her first book of literary criticism, *The Strange Necessity*, which opens with an extended essay on James Joyce and, according to Margaret Stetz (1994), represents her fullest contribution to the cultural field as an aesthetic theorist. In correspondence with her publishers West requested that *The Strange Necessity* be marketed as 'a *technical, highbrow* book' (Scott 2000: 99), but, as Debra Rae Cohen summarises, the volume 'confused and upset most reviewers' who 'generally found its idiosyncratic melding of feminine and "highbrow" pursuits, its assault on conventional categories of analysis, incomprehensible, threatening, and offensively frivolous' (2006: 144). Cohen identifies West's 'increasing irritation with what she saw as [T. S.] Eliot's "pernicious influence"' as a critic. In a lecture delivered at London's City Literary Institute in early 1929 on 'Tradition in Criticism' West 'baited Eliot (the next speaker in the series) with reference to a form of criticism "of which [. . .] Mr. Eliot would disapprove and I would not . . . which takes almost the likeness and habit of imaginative work" – the form, that is, of "The Strange Necessity"'. As Cohen observes, West casts herself as 'a true inheritor of tradition' by representing 'The Strange Necessity' *as* traditional in its following of Addison, Lamb, De Quincey and others, 'both legitim[ising] her own critical enterprise and challeng[ing] the restrictive definitions of "tradition" promulgated by Eliot and his followers' (2006: 149–50). West later made her most sustained attack on Eliot in an article for the *Daily Telegraph* in September 1932 'What is Mr. T. S. Eliot's Authority as a Critic?'[38] Her contributions to *Time and Tide* further underline how important this periodical was in the authority it afforded to women journalists and critics, and whose mediation of culture (as we saw in Chapter 3) frequently resisted the formalist critical practices associated with an 'Eliotic modernism'.

West's 1928–30 articles for *Time and Tide*, which include discussions of Leo Tolstoy, Elinor Wylie, French and German literature, censorship,and Wyndham Lewis's *Paleface*, are indicative of West's wide literary and cultural interests in nineteenth-century and European literature as well as Anglo-American modernism, and represent a neglected archive of feminist modernist criticism. Several of the pieces share features with the personal and experimental criticism of *The Strange Necessity*. The first, which reads Tolstoy's last novel *Resurrection* (1899) alongside the recently published *Diary of Countess Tolstoy*, is a bold and passionate attack on one of Russia's celebrated literary figures, motivated by sympathy for the physical and emotional suffering of his cruelly treated wife (14 Dec 1928: 1229–31). Another fuses the enjoyment of reading a historical memoir found in a Parisian bookshop with the pleasures of shopping for hats, face cream, and 'brandied cherries' (26 July 1929: 904), suggestive of the relationship between art and commodity culture explored in *The Strange Necessity*'s title essay. Most interesting of all, in the context of the discussion of literary celebrity in the present chapter, is West's commentary on 'The High Cost of Personal Journalism' in her article on the recently deceased American poet Elinor Wylie. In this intensely emotional piece West represents the vulnerability that comes with being a celebrity, what Jonathan Goldman describes as the 'turn[ing] [of] the psychological subject into an object, something that lacks agency over itself' (2011: 1). Describing an occasion two years previously when she had invited Wylie to read to a small company of friends at her hotel rooms in New York, West recalls with 'agony' the sight of a misplaced newspaper near to where the poet was standing and covered with a 'lacerating' and entirely inaccurate account of Elinor Wylie's personal life (18 Jan 1929: 63). Pursued herself as a celebrity by the American press in the mid-1920s West described in a letter to her friend Fannie Hurst the experience of being 'crawled over' and 'eaten alive' by reporters (Bonnie Kime Scott 1995: 195). Her article on Wylie, which begins by presenting in full one of Wylie's poems, is a moving tribute to a woman writer whose work was often eclipsed by her beauty and personality in the popular press.[39]

Scott has noted the significance of attachments formed with female literary colleagues by the 'women of 1928' (1995: 184). While the American press provided West with the most lucrative outlet for her journalism, *Time and Tide* provided both a supportive context for the reception of her creative and critical work, and offered her a degree of agency unrivalled by other periodicals and newspapers with their customary editorial constraints.[40] Indeed, though West's name on *Time and Tide*'s contents bill in December 1928 undoubtedly added value to the paper during its transition into the sixpenny market, as one of *Time and Tide*'s directors she also left her mark on the paper as a subject rather than object.[41] Very few records of *Time and Time*'s board meetings survive, but in a distinct echo of West's assertion in 'The Strange Necessity' that 'Art is not a luxury, but a necessity' an advertisement *Time and Tide* placed in the *Nation*

and Athenaeum in April 1928 carried the strapline: 'A WEEKLY
REVIEW IS NOT A LUXURY – It is a necessity for everyone who
wishes to be informed upon current events' (14 Apr 1928: 60). The
increased space *Time and Tide* could devote to books and literary
subjects following its expansion in 1928 is consistent with West's
belief in the social and political relevance of art in the public sphere,
and in the importance to art of quality criticism (Collier 2006: 172–3;
199–200). In the light of West's contribution to *Time and Tide*'s
'Future of the Press' series discussed earlier in this chapter, where she
noted the tendency of most newspaper editors 'to cut down articles
to as far below a thousand words as possible and restrict the subjects to a certain frivolous and monotonous range' (2 Mar 1928:
194), the publishing space *Time and Tide* offered West in the new
monthly feature announced in December 1928 is particularly significant. At around 2,000 words, each of the articles West contributed
over the next fourteen months ran to four or more columns (two
pages) of print, at least double the space customarily given to the
leading article in *Time and Tide*'s book pages, and far exceeding that
provided by the daily newspapers. Apparently West was also given a
completely free rein in her choice of subject for these contributions;
not all of them were even about books.[42] At once expanding *Time
and Tide*'s own reputation for criticism as the periodical competed
with the established intellectual weeklies in the cultural as well as
political sphere, West's contributions to the paper during this period
also consolidated her own status as a critic, and the importance of
the critical function itself.

'Notes on Books and Writers by Rebecca West' augured an elevation of criticism in *Time and Tide*'s columns at a time when the
critical apparatus for the mediation of literature was widely held to
be in a state of crisis. As Collier has discussed, many contemporary
commentators saw 'critical anarchy' in the combined conditions
of the 'emergence of newspapers as a leading publisher of reviews'
and the 'breathtaking expansion of the book market' which, even
with more reviews being written, left many books unnoticed (2006:
72–3). Literary reviews like Eliot's *Criterion* established a select field
of 'literary journalism' distinct from what modernists regarded as a
degraded journalistic world.[43] The public-orientation of West's view
of criticism, however, set both her and *Time and Tide* apart from
the 'minority culture' identified with critics like Eliot and modernist
magazines. At the same time, both she and the periodical remained
committed to a programme of educating readers up to a higher culture.[44] From January to March in 1930 *Time and Tide* ran a series of

six articles on 'The Function of Literary Criticism'. The title of the series recalls *Time and Tide*'s pedagogic feature on 'The Function of the Weekly Review' discussed earlier in this chapter; it also carries distinct echoes of two of Eliot's essays published in the *Criterion* in 1923: 'The Function of the Literary Review' (July) and 'The Function of Criticism' (October). In contrast with Eliot's essays, however, which reflect his 'need to assert the functionality of the marginal journal' (Collier 2006: 58), *Time and Tide*'s series asserts the functionality of the cultural institution of book reviewing supported by a variety of larger-circulation periodicals and newspapers.[45] Moreover, unlike Eliot's insistence on literary judgement built on external authority, evidenced in his definition of the function of criticism in the second of these two essays as 'the elucidation of works of art and the correction of taste' (Collier 2006: 58), *Time and Tide* maintained faith in an intelligent and rational public capable of forming its own literary judgements, and defended the tastes of its readers even as it worked to expand their cultural interests.

Such a complex position was enabled by *Time and Tide*'s very careful orchestration of the debate about 'The Function of Literary Criticism' in this series. Two outside contributors were commissioned for the first and third articles which consider, respectively, the topic from the point of view of the author (John Galsworthy), and the publisher (Laurie Magnus). The second article, however, which discusses the issue from the point of view of the critic, was contributed by one of the periodical's own regular columnists, Sylvia Lynd. In this article Lynd acknowledged that the conditions of modern journalism were not auspicious for the critic.[46] However, with characteristic optimism she suggests that the critic should approach his task on the assumption that it is a 'delightful' rather than 'punitive' one: 'The greatest critics have been discoverers of achievement rather than denouncers of failure. Whatever dislikes they may have had, it is for their enthusiasms that they are remembered' (7 Feb 1920: 167). Lynd goes on to define criticism as 'simply the expression and explanation of personal taste' (167) and the article concludes with a telling swipe at 'some young gentlemen newly down from Oxbridge' who, apparently forgetting that critics are the 'messengers of the arts' seem more bent on attacking literature than praising it (168). The gesture invokes growing tensions between 'amateur' and 'professional' critics as 'University English' assumed a more influential role in the cultural field: Lynd's 'enthusiasms' embody belletristic notions of 'appreciation' that would be displaced by the new Cambridge critics' emphasis on scientific 'rigour' (see Chapter 6).[47] As Cuddy-Keane notes, the institutionalisation of English within the universities 'augured an increasing gap between professional study and the general reading public' (2003: 1), and it was to this gap that *Time and Tide*'s fourth and most fascinating article in the series addressed itself.

This article was presented in the form of 'An Interview with Professor Winifred Cullis', who as *Time and Tide*'s 'Reporter' explains has been chosen as a 'laboratory specimen' of the 'general reader' who goes to books 'in leisure hours, for recreation' (21 Feb 1930: 231). A professor of physiology at the University of London, Cullis had been a director of *Time and Tide* since 1924, and in this carefully staged conversation her identity as both a 'Professor' and a 'general reader' neatly collapses a growing separation between ordinary readers and the universities, while simultaneously offering an aspirational model of the university-educated woman. The first question *Time and Tide*'s reporter puts to Cullis evidences the distinction *Time and Tide* was itself beginning to make in its books pages between 'criticism' and 'reviews'. Asking whether Cullis 'read[s] much criticism' the reporter continues: 'I don't mean just reviews. I mean, now, work by people like Edmund Gosse and Lascelles Abercrombie, and R. A. Scott James, and Rebecca West' (231). The inclusion of West in this distinguished male company provides an important cue for the promotion of *Time and Tide*'s own celebrated female critic. On answering that she does indeed 'enjoy critical writing, and at one time read a great deal of it' Cullis explains, in response to further prompts from *Time and Tide*'s reporter, that it is 'not so much the technical as the philosophic side' which interests her: 'most of all, I am interested in ideas and opinions' (231). Here Cullis's response cleverly allows *Time and Tide*'s readers to remain uninterested in the 'technical' aspects of literary style privileged in modernist criticism (later in the interview she owns that she has no interest in reading James Joyce), at the same time as it encourages them to read critical writing for the mental stimulus it provides through its 'ideas and opinions'. Significantly, Cullis suggests that criticism is also a kind of writing readers can expect to enjoy: 'For instance, in my opinion, the most delightful thing about Rebecca West's essay on art, *The Strange Necessity*, was not so much what it told me about the books she was discussing, as what it told me about her. Criticism is a tremendous revelation of the critic' (231). At once echoing the 'delight[s]' of reading expressed in *Time and Tide*'s early modern fiction reviews (see Chapter 3), it is the striking exploitation of the interview's 'atmosphere of intimacy and disclosure' (Roach 2018: 173) which makes West's essay in criticism desirable here: conjuring up the spectacular pleasures of modern celebrity culture Cullis identifies *The Strange Necessity* as a greater 'revelation' of West's mind and personality than any celebrity profile in the popular press.

Notably absent from this promotion of West's essay, however, despite its emphasis on the author's mind, is any suggestion that the critic tells the reader what to think. Throughout the interview Cullis maintains her pose as an ordinary, intelligent, cultured reader, capable of articulating her literary interests and forming her own critical judgements. Significantly, when the conversation turns to the subject of book reviews and the promotion of another of *Time and Tide*'s critics, Sylvia Lynd, Cullis states that it is the reader's knowledge of a particular reviewer's 'reactions to books in relation to your own' (232) that performs the most useful function, not the reviewer's judgement on whether a book is or is not worth reading. This faith in the reader's own evaluative capabilities is significant in the context of pessimistic views of the audience which accompanied contemporary perceptions of a crisis in book reviewing.[48] Asked whether she thinks 'that the public is in danger of losing its independence of judgment because the critics tell it what to think' Cullis replies: 'I can't think that there is much fear of that. For one thing, the reviewers disagree among themselves so vigorously. For another, I can't believe that people are altogether as docile as pessimists would have us believe' (232). Cullis goes on to suggest that critics have only an 'indirect' influence on public taste and, in a defence of the untutored mind, concludes: 'in the end, I think my favourite books are some that I have never seen reviewed, books that I read years and years ago, and have re-read and re-read, for the sake of some charm of style or mood of romance'. At this point the interview takes an unexpected turn when *Time and Tide*'s reporter asks, 'Then you enjoy romantic books, whatever the fashion of the moment?' Cullis replies: 'Oh yes. I'm afraid that the Cinderella motif always attracts me. And thrillers that are really well written.' 'Reporter' and 'Professor' then animatedly swap names of romance and thriller writers they enjoy, until they are checked by the following editorial intervention:

> (*Undeterred by fashions in literary criticism, artistic values, or the dicta of Bloomsbury, Chelsea and the* London Mercury, *Professor and Reporter relapse into the unintellectual delights of personal prejudice. The only hope for the critic which emerges from their unchecked stream of romantic reminiscence of the books they have really enjoyed, lies in the possibility of the indirect persuasion to good taste which Mrs. Lynd suggested in her article in this series and which Professor Cullis herself has admitted.*) (232)

In this mock illustration of the deterioration of public taste *Time and Tide* pokes fun at 'fashions in literary criticism' with a humour that knits the periodical's audience into its own reading community. Assuming readers' familiarity with the opinions emanating from 'Bloomsbury, Chelsea and the *London Mercury*' it allows readers to enjoy 'unintellectual delights' and expresses faith in readers' 'persuasion to good taste'.

The following week the fifth article in the series comprised a selection of comments received from readers who had been invited 'to express their own views on the question' (21 Feb 1930: 231) and several other letters on the same subject were printed in the correspondence columns. Evidence of *Time and Tide*'s continued commitment to the direct relationship it formed with its readers, they also provide a fascinating record of readers' thirst for good criticism of books. One Mrs C. C. Fraser from Liverpool states that while she gets through, on average, 'twelve new books per week', given that 14,000 volumes are published yearly she is 'dependent on reviews' to guide her selection (28 Feb 1930: 265). Another 'provincial reader' from Scunthorpe identifies him or herself as 'a greedy reader' who needs more than anything else, given time and financial constraints, 'information on what *not* to order' (270). The reader's reliance on the reviewer finds its most striking expression in the following response from a Mrs H. Gray in Hampstead:

> A reader of Catholic taste and unquenchable curiosity expects the reviewer to save him from himself. There are people for whom every bookshop is as alluring as a gin-palace. Enter and you are lost. Though you may have no money to spend and no time to waste, you are certain to emerge poorer in both than you entered. For such people, dipping into books is as dangerous as dram-drinking; for the first page is never the last.
>
> But fortified by harsh criticism you are stronger. You can pass by on the other side. Forewarned by the reviewers that your favourite novelist has fallen below his usual level, and that the biography with the exciting title is not based on any fresh evidence, you can resist temptation. In fact, the review has acted as a prophylactic. (266)

Anticipating by two years Q. D. Leavis's famous association of popular reading with the drug habit, this view of criticism resists contemporary perceptions of the reading public as passive consumers of whatever dross is offered to them, representing instead aspirational readers with a sense of standards and hungry for quality books.[49] It is, as a George Ryley Scott from Yorkshire writes, 'to the intelligent reader [. . .] [that] the literary critic becomes more and more a necessity' (270), and collectively these letters provide an endorsement of *Time and Tide*'s decision in 1928 to increase the space for book reviews in its columns. As *Time and Tide*'s assistant editor Margaret West observes in the final article of the series, for all the criticisms levelled at reviewers 'no one has questioned the necessity for the reviewer's existence' (7 Mar 1930: 299). In Chapter 6 I discuss how *Time and Tide* went on to negotiate widening tensions between highbrow intellectualism and the general reader as the periodical moved into the middle of its second decade and was inevitably drawn into the 'battle of the brows'. First, I turn in the next chapter to another pressing concern during the periodical's period of expansion: the role of male writers and critics in a magazine edited and controlled solely by women.

Notes

1. According to David Doughan and Denise Sanchez, in the 1930s *Time and Tide*'s feminism 'gradually faded away' (1987: 45). Elsewhere Doughan elaborates: '*Time and Tide* became a highly respected political/ cultural/ literary weekly [. . .] at the cost [. . .] of divesting itself of any specific feminist commitment' (1987: 268–71).
2. VB to George Catlin, 18 October 1926. VB Papers.
3. MR to DS, 28 May 1927. DS Papers.
4. Cited in Tusan (2005: 211).
5. Of the *New Statesman* Adrian Smith writes that women's 'influence over editorial content and policy was non-existent.' (1996: 59).
6. MR to DS, 9 July 1928. DS Papers. The bill was introduced in March and became law on 2 July.
7. Edward Hyams notes that the *New Statesman* was ideologically opposed to operating at a more commercial level (1963: 83).
8. Among the companies which placed advertisements in *Time and Tide* and of which Rhondda was a director were Sanatogen, Genasprin, Formamint and the British Fire Insurance Company.
9. Morrisson identifies advertising as one of the periodical codes that 'contribute to a reader's horizon of expectations for a magazine' (2001: 39).
10. For an extended discussion of *Time and Tide*'s rebranding through its advertising content, see Clay (2011).
11. The *Nation and Athenaeum* archive indicates that Keynes's periodical was still struggling to increase its circulation following the *Nation*'s amalgamation in 1921 with the *Athenaeum*. Letters dating from 1927 regarding arrangements for an exchange of advertisements with two

German journals, the *Europäische Revue* and the *Kriegschuldfrage*, show that the *Nation and Athenaeum* was also seeking to reach new audiences. JMK Papers [NS/1/2/75 & NS/1/2/81].

12. This endorsement, which appeared in the second and third advertisements *Time and Tide* placed in the *Nation and Athenaeum*, read '*Time and Tide . . . éclectique et vivante revue hebdomadaire*' ('eclectic and lively weekly review'). *Mercure de France* played a significant role in French literary life and had a wide circulation abroad. See Kalantzis (2013).

13. Ervine had been contributing articles to *Good Housekeeping* almost every month since the mid-1920s. I am grateful to Stella Deen for providing me with this information.

14. See Leiss et al. on the transition to symbolic representations in advertising during the interwar years, which they describe as a shift from 'what the product *did*' to 'what the product could *mean* for consumers' (2005: 200).

15. The event took place at the Hyde Park Hotel in West London on Wednesday, 30 November 1927.

16. MR to RW, 22 December 1927. RW Yale.

17. The cartoons, which were drawn by the artist Raphael Nelson, depicted in turn Lord Rothermere (of the *Daily Mail*), Sir William and Sir Gomer Berry (owners of *Allied Newspapers*), Lord Beaverbrook (of the *Daily Express*) and Lord Riddell (of *News of the World*).

18. *Time and Tide*'s optimism recalls a pre-war moment when, according to Morrisson, modernist little magazines willingly adopted strategies that belonged to the mass-circulating papers (2001: 5–6).

19. *Time and Tide* printed notices of its offer to existing subscribers in the four weeks leading up to its size and price increase.

20. *Time and Tide*'s Autumn Book Number of 1928 (22 Oct) contained twelve pages of book reviews and publishers' advertisements; regular issues carried between three and four pages of book-related content.

21. Dale Spender states that the periodical 'drifted more towards an arts and literary review' which is for her 'a matter of some regret' (1984: 24).

22. Daniel Tracy identifies parody as a vital component of middlebrow culture, not only satirising but also 'identifying and teaching high culture' in so far as 'All forms critiqued and parodied also get embraced as cultural reference points' (2010: 40; 55). *Time and Tide* also published several verse parodies between 1927 and 1928 by Caryl Brahms; parodies later contributed by one of *Time and Tide*'s popular writers, E. M. Delafield, will be the subject of discussion in Chapter 5.

23. Hammill observes, in her reading of this cartoon, that if Woolf's American visitors (who find her books 'most congenial') are 'Uncommon Readers' then the 'majority of people will find Woolf's work rather uncongenial' (2007: 196).

24. See Newton (2012) for a discussion of cartoons as forms of 'cultural advertisement' in 'smart magazines' including the *New Yorker* and *Vanity Fair*.

25. These caricatures were later published in book form as *Lions and Lambs* (1928) with commentaries written by Rebecca West under the pseudonym 'Lynx' (Glendinning 1987: 119).

26. I am grateful to Vike Plock for this information on Bloomfield in *Eve*; on the *London Mercury* see J. Matthew Huculak (2009).

27. On Kapp, see Bryant (2000: 131).

28. See Helen Southworth (2014) for a discussion of 'The Bloomsbury Group and the Book Arts'.

29. The extracts from *A Room of One's Own* were the passages narrating the contrasting dining experiences at a men's and women's college. They were published in *Time and Tide*'s issues of 22 and 29 November 1929.

30. Raverat's first art criticism was published in *Time and Tide*'s issue of 3 May 1929; she wrote regular art criticisms until 1940.

31. Hammill observes that *Vanity Fair* was unusual among the American 'smart magazines' in publishing avant-garde art and literature (2010: 125). Modernist materials also circulated in the British commercial women's magazine *Eve: A Lady's Pictorial* (Plock 2018).

32. 'The Bat' 4 January 1929 and 'Two Songs' 11 January 1929.

33. Introducing Stein's 'experiments in literary decomposition' in an editorial note appended to an article on 'American Newspapers', *Time and Tide* explained that it was 'very glad to give our readers a typical example of Steinway' (9 Mar 1935: 835).

34. The article is signed GREC, a pseudonym Holtby used more than once in the periodical (Clay 2010: 74).

35. Apart from Mitchison, who began but did not complete a degree in science at Oxford, all these novelists were former students at Oxford's Somerville College for women.

36. The statue (now at the Louvre Museum in Paris) is commonly regarded to depict Aphrodite, the Greek goddess of beauty and love.

37. See Spender (1984: 240–1) for *Time and Tide*'s coverage of this debate.

38. The article is reprinted in Bonnie Kime Scott (1990: 587–92).

39. The poem was 'The Devil in Seven Shires' from Wylie's collection *Trivial Breath* (1928).

40. Sylvia Lynd wrote an enthusiastic review of *The Strange Necessity*, published in *Time and Tide*'s issue of 27 July 1928. Naomi Royde-Smith lauded West's modernist novel *Harriet Hume* in *Time and Tide*'s columns, describing it as 'one of the sensations of the Autumn publishing' (27 Sep 1929: 1148).

41. Archival evidence confirms the marketability of West's signature. In a letter dated 22 February 1929, *Time and Tide*'s assistant editor Margaret West informed Rebecca West that her March article would be advertised in the daily press and Rhondda wanted to know if she could

'write us an article on some subject of wide topical interest, which would be a good publicity draw'. West's article, published in *Time and Tide*'s issue of 15 March 1929 ('A Jixless Errand') took up the subject of literary censorship, following the high-profile *Well of Loneliness* trial and the recent seizure of D. H. Lawrence's poems *Pansies* by the British Home Office. Rhondda wrote on 17 March to thank West for her 'perfect article!! It ought to sell the paper from Land's End to John O'Groats.' RW Tulsa.

42. Her contribution for April 1929 took the form of an allegory about Empire ('General Dyer' 19 Apr 1929); in June her article was on the subject of the new Labour government and the feminist movement ('The Inconveniences of Power' 21 June 1929).

43. See Collier for a discussion of the distinction Eliot set up between 'mainstream and "minority" journalism' (2006: 68).

44. See Collier (2006: 169–200) for a discussion of West's view of the critic's intermediary function in assisting public appreciation and understanding of art.

45. As *Time and Tide*'s assistant editor Margaret West clarified in her concluding article 'Summing-Up' the series: 'it is not the higher branches of criticism we have been discussing, but that which Edmund Gosse called "the pedestrian criticism that bears the name of 'reviewing'"' (7 Mar 1930: 299).

46. Lynd's article contains the main complaint against newspaper book reviews, namely their brevity.

47. Hermione Lee describes how, at the height of her fame and confidence, Virginia Woolf felt threatened by the younger generation of male writers 'rushing out of public school and Oxbridge into the literary scene and the publishing houses' (1996: 611).

48. Collier argues that even Virginia Woolf, whose engagement with 'common readers' is indicative of her democratic instincts, had concerns about the audience, worrying 'that they were ill-equipped to sort through the ever-increasing number of books on the market' (2006: 98).

49. Q. D. Leavis's *Fiction and the Reading Public* was published in 1932.

Chapter 5

'A Common Platform': Male Contributors and Cross-Gender Collaboration

This chapter examines another key element in *Time and Tide*'s rebranding as a more general-audience weekly review: the increase of male writers within its contributor base. As the journal moved into its second decade Lady Rhondda deliberately sought to achieve a balance between the number of male and female signatures in its pages, and its bills frequently advertised articles by prominent men.[1] Early accounts of the periodical suggest that the increased visibility of men and male perspectives in its pages from the early 1930s represents a weakening of *Time and Tide*'s feminism.[2] However, Rhondda never advocated a separatist position, and her idea of *Time and Tide* as a 'common platform' for 'thinking men and women' (see Chapter 4) was consistent with her conviction that collaboration between the sexes was essential for the rebuilding of society and the survival of civilisation itself (John 2013: 431). In the years immediately following the passage of the Equal Franchise Act in July 1928 Rhondda gradually withdrew from active leadership of the feminist societies she had been so instrumental in forming, but only to devote more of her energies to *Time and Tide* (John 2013: 401). In 1930 she told the American feminist Doris Stevens: 'If I can make the paper go in a big way (as is beginning to seem possible) I shall have done a big a thing for feminism as I am capable of.'[3] Continuing to pioneer a new field for women, the paper broadened its scope to address issues of international importance, and peace, constructing 'modern women' as 'both national and global citizens' with responsibilities alongside men in the public sphere.[4] However, this expansion into traditionally male territory inevitably involved challenges. In a letter to Rebecca West in June 1931 Rhondda admitted that while *Time and Tide*'s circulation and prestige continued to grow 'we still suffer slightly from the fact that we are known to be a paper run by women', a reminder of the prejudices that remained against women's advances in public life.[5]

As Julie Gottlieb has discussed, 'one of the main objections to women's enfranchisement was on the grounds that as a sex they were not suited to decide foreign and imperial affairs' and this 'distrust of women's political judgement on matters of war and peace' persisted after the war and extended through the political crises of the 1930s (2013: 159). In November 1934 *Time and Tide* drew attention to this prejudice with reference to a recent dinner given by the Royal Institute of International Affairs at which the South African statesman General Smuts had 'made a speech of world importance'. Under the heading 'For Men Only' *Time and Tide* noted that 'no women' had been invited to the event, and challenged the Royal Institute's apparent assumption that only men are interested in international affairs (17 Nov 1934: 1463). The rise of fascism in the 1930s served to harden these traditional gender ideologies still further, and provides an important context for understanding the ways in which male and female contributors interacted in the pages of this modern feminist magazine during its second decade. Following Ann Ardis's call for more attentive readings of the 'deliberately and complexly performative authorial environments' of periodical texts (2008: 31), this chapter demonstrates that while male signatures played an instrumental role in promoting the paper for a wider audience it was strategically necessary *not* to advertise women's contribution to what Rhondda once described as 'the soul of the paper': the weekly notes and leaders which shaped *Time and Tide*'s political standpoint.[6] With particular reference to the less visible role of Winifred Holtby, whose anonymous writing for the journal far outweighed her signed contributions, I show that it was women who maintained ownership and control of the periodical during these crucial years.

A second key context for *Time and Tide*'s careful management of its public image in this period is the prosecution and ban in 1928 of Radclyffe Hall's lesbian novel, *The Well of Loneliness*. *Time and Tide*'s expansion in the autumn of 1928 coincided with the high-profile obscenity trial, which had significant implications for the public association of women whose relationships could become subject to scrutiny and suspicion.[7] Several of *Time and Tide*'s core collaborators (including Rhondda) conducted their most intimate relationships with women, and according to one contemporary of the period the periodical was known in some circles as the 'Sapphic Graphic'.[8]

Earlier the same year, just days after the publication of Hall's novel, the *Manchester Guardian* threw a spotlight on *Time and Tide*'s core group of female collaborators in an article announcing that 'Viscountess Rhondda has initiated a new vogue – that of business colleagues and friends spending holidays together.' Identifying Lady Rhondda as 'a director and editor of the woman's paper "Time and Tide"' the article reported that: 'Accompanied by several of her fellow-directors, including Professor Winifred Cullis, Miss Cicely Hamilton, and Miss Winifred Holtby, a party has left London for a village on the Riviera for their holidays together' (3 Aug 1928: 9).[9] The article went on humorously to relate that '[w]hen a number of men directors were asked if they had thought of going away with their colleagues of the boardroom they nearly dropped their cigars in horror. "Good heavens. No!" replied one. "I don't want my holiday to be turned into a directors' meeting a month long"' (9). The contrast drawn between the glamour associated with the French Riviera and the stuffy atmosphere of the boardroom emphasises both the combined pleasures of work and friendship enjoyed by *Time and Tide*'s women (Clay 2006) and the gulf between male and female professional cultures that would need to be bridged to achieve gendered cooperation in the public sphere. In the second part of this chapter I explore how *Time and Tide* articulated and mediated tensions between the sexes in its lighter content (specifically, a series of parodies contributed by one of the paper's regular staff writers, E. M. Delafield, and several short stories by a new contributor from 1928, Naomi Mitchison), and how this creative work underscores the uniquely female-centric culture of this modern magazine.

Male signatures and anonymous women

Writing for a special twenty-first birthday issue of *Time and Tide* in 1941 Rhondda recalled how she and Winifred Holtby decided one winter 'to change the slant of the paper a bit, to give it a rather broader base', and planned a bumper number featuring, if they could get him, George Bernard Shaw (17 May 1941: 398). It had been the winter of George V's first serious illness and Shaw generously provided a sketch called 'The King and the Doctors' which was published in *Time and Tide*'s issue of 22 February 1929.[10] *Time and Tide* spent over £1,000 advertising the issue, increased its order to four times its usual size and, according to Rhondda, 'within an hour of publication there wasn't a copy to be had anywhere'.[11] 'That issue with that grand G.B.S. in it', Rhondda wrote, 'put *Time and Tide* on the map. And remembering how he came to our help when we needed it so badly, we have always regarded him as a kind of patron saint of the paper' (17 May 1941: 398). Shaw's cultural stature as Britain's greatest living playwright and leading public intellectual on the left made a valuable imprint on *Time and Tide* as the periodical worked to increase its prestige and influence and rebrand itself for the 'keystone public' it aimed to reach (Eoff 1991: 18). As Rhondda acknowledged, in a later letter to Shaw, 'even mentioning your name has a wonderful effect on sales', and Holtby, writing to him with a new proposition in October 1929, stated that: 'to have your name on one or two of our bills is more likely than anything else in England, America or the Irish Free State to appeal to the particular kind of public which reads the weeklies'.[12] With the explanation that she had been given '*carte blanche*' by Lady Rhondda 'to go ahead with the autumn arrangements', Holtby proceeded to offer Shaw £2,000 – a sum put aside for the autumn campaign – 'for whatever you choose to sell us, if you can consider such a proposition at all'. Apparently, Shaw did not sell any of his work on this occasion; his signature did not appear on *Time and Tide*'s contents bill again until 1931.[13] However, less than two weeks later his name and image were splashed across the periodical's pages in an illustrated feature article which, with Shaw's tacit approval, functions as a form of celebrity endorsement promoting the rebranded paper within its existing circle of readers, and beyond.

This feature article, entitled 'Saint Bernard on All Saints Day, Bernard Shaw drinks our Health', marked the first of two 'House-Warming Luncheons' held in *Time and Tide*'s new Bloomsbury offices 'to celebrate the new chapter in its history' (8 Nov 1929: 1332). The affectionate caricature of Shaw in the drawing which accompanies it underlines *Time and Tide*'s adoption of the famous playwright as a figurehead or 'patron saint' for the journal: dressed in long flowing robes and sandals he appears to bestow a blessing upon the open volumes of *Time and Tide* depicted beside him and, it is implied, to transfer to the periodical some of his own political and intellectual qualities (Figure 5.1). As the article text observes:

> It was a pleasant custom which in the Ages of Faith made men feel that a building was unfit for any serious purpose until it had received the blessing of a saint. There was a feeling that, with the act of benediction, certain qualities of the saint might pass into those who worked henceforth under his shadow. (1332)

SAINT BERNARD COMES TO BLOOMSBURY
ALL SAINTS DAY, 1929

Figure 5.1 'Saint Bernard on All Saints Day', *Time and Tide* 8 Nov 1929: 1888. Reproduced with the permission of The William Ready Division of Archives and Research Collections, McMaster University Library.

For all *Time and Tide*'s new orientation towards literary modernist cultures associated with Bloomsbury (see Chapter 4), as a representative of the Edwardian generation Shaw preserves an important link with the past and with a tradition of socially and politically engaged writing eschewed by a new generation of modernists. In the illustration, he is positioned by a window overlooking the British Museum with an enormous quill in his hand (a writing instrument associated with the past, not the present) and a copy of his latest play, *The Apple Cart: A Political Extravaganza*, under his arm. Shaw's endorsement of *Time and Tide* as 'an extraordinarily able review' (1334) had enormous value beyond the circle of the periodical's own readership. His presence at the house-warming luncheon attracted notice in the national press (his speech provided a headline for the *Manchester Guardian*: 'Mr. Shaw on "Men and Gossips." "Women Get Things Done"') (2 Nov 1929: 13), and a little more than two years later Rhondda told Doris Stevens that '*Time and Tide* mounts in prestige – it has now been publicly stated by Bernard Shaw (in the *Observer*) to be the best thing of its kind & is getting recognition all round.'[14]

Another guest at *Time and Tide*'s house-warming luncheon was one of the periodical's earliest male associates – Mr St. John Ervine – whose own 'happy little speech', according to *Time and Tide*, was 'pursued by many of the paper's male contributors, who often provide its most feminine elements' (8 Nov 1929: 1334). Following on from Shaw's inversion of the age-old stereotype of the female gossip to underline the productive capability of the women who control *Time and Tide*, this comment on Ervine is a reminder of how periodicals are gendered not by the sex of their contributors but by textual performances (see Chapter 1). Earlier the same year, Ervine had come up with the idea for a new weekly feature, 'Notes on the Way', which he wrote every week himself for over two years.[15] Positioned between *Time and Tide*'s leading articles and the periodical's expanding book reviews section, its subtitle 'Men, Women, and Events' invites comparison with the 'society' or 'gossip' column, a feminised genre which flourished in the popular press during the interwar period (McNamara 2014: 46). An illustration accompanying the third article with the caption 'St. John Ervine's Pen is Famous for its Point' (21 June 1929: 747) captures the cut-and-thrust spirit of this column. Depicting the popular journalist brandishing an enormous quill on which a startled and diminished figure is impaled, the cartoon emphasises the provocative nature of the writing that flowed from what one reader described as Ervine's 'dagger-pen' (10 Jan 1930: 47). Frequently stirring up fresh controversies Ervine entertained and infuriated readers alike, and in early

1930 'Mr. St. John Ervine and His Critics' was the subject of *Time and Tide*'s correspondence columns for several weeks. A letter from Rhondda to Stevens in 1931 highlights Ervine's usefulness for circulation and sales: 'My view of St. J. E. in *Time and Tide* is that however irritating (& indeed the more irritating, the better) he is worth some hundreds of readers a week to us for his own sake alone!'[16] At the same time, his column performed an important symbolic function in *Time and Tide*'s construction of itself as a leading 'journal of opinion' (see Chapter 4). From the issue carrying the illustrated article which identified Ervine as author of the column (the first two pieces were published pseudonymously), *Time and Tide*'s front cover sported a new slogan in the periodical's masthead: 'The Review with Independent Views' (14 June 1929: i). Responding later the same year to a reader who 'marvelled that such opinions as [Ervine's] should be published in an organ of independent views', Ervine stated that: 'In this article, I say what *I* think about anything and everybody that interests me. [. . .] To be independent *in* your views is not to be independent *of* views, as some simple souls seem to imagine' (11 Oct 1929: 1203). Ervine's distinction performs a valuable function for the whole paper which defined itself as 'independent' and 'non-party', and shows how closely even *Time and Tide*'s lighter elements worked with its overall aims.

The extent to which *Time and Tide* was prepared to print opinions with which it did not agree is illustrated by its publication in early 1931 of a series of articles on 'Hitlerism – Man and Doctrine' by a man who constructed a public image of himself as 'The Enemy': Wyndham Lewis.[17] These articles, in one of which Lewis described Hitler as 'a man of peace', would present 'a near-fatal blow' to Lewis's political and intellectual reputation (Moses 2010: 147); revised and published in book form in April the same year, their misguided estimation of Hitler and Nazi Germany is a sober reminder of the perils of being misinformed.[18] Significantly, *Time and Tide* distanced itself from the opinions expressed in the articles, printing an editorial note which read:

> Whilst we do not find ourselves in agreement with Mr. Lewis's attitude towards the German Nationalist-Socialist Party and the political situation generally, the vivid picture of present-day Germany which he gives in this series of articles seems to us of such unusual interest that we do not hesitate to publish them. (17 Jan 1931: 59)

Time and Tide was fully aware of the threat that Hitler posed to peace in Europe, and stands out among the British intellectual weeklies for its early understanding of the meaning and perils of Nazism (Morris 1991: 21; 23). In a 'Personalities and Powers' feature published four months earlier it identified Hitler as 'the German Mussolini' (20 Sep 1930: 1169), and the journal turned much attention on Germany from the beginning of this decade, from its editorial columns and leader pages, to a special German Supplement published with its issue of 17 September 1932, and the reproduction from March 1933 of cartoons from Germany's most prominent satirical political journal *Simplicissimus*.[19] The publication of Lewis's 'Hitler' articles must be seen, therefore, in the context of *Time and Tide*'s commitment to representing a broad range of opinion, and its belief in readers' abilities to think critically and independently themselves. Indeed, Lewis's concern for 'the continued viability of independent critical thinking and the future role and status of the "public intellectual"' is one that was shared by *Time and Tide*, and he found 'long-standing and public (though sometimes critical) supporters of his literary work' in such women as Naomi Mitchison and Rebecca West (Hallam 2011: 57).[20] His writing found less favour with Rhondda who, in an undated letter to Holtby, owned that she had been 'bored stiff' by his latest contributions to the paper, while admitting that 'he's a very good name'.[21] Lewis was one of the 'celebrities' who delivered speeches at a *Time and Tide* reception for readers and writers at the Dorchester Hotel, London, in June 1932 (Brittain 1986: 52), and while he is more commonly identified with 'the men of 1914' (Lewis's own promotional phrase in his 1937 memoir *Blasting and Bombardiering*) his public association with *Time and Tide*'s women in this period points to the value placed by this periodical on cross-gender collaboration with even the most unlikely of men.[22]

The increased deployment of male signatures in *Time and Tide* was an important part of the periodical's strategy for moving into the forefront of the weekly reviews. Operating in the form of celebrity branding, agents provocateurs and marketable commodities, the signatures of Shaw, Ervine and Lewis played an instrumental role in advertising the paper beyond its core readership and attracting new audiences. However, it was the less visible role of *Time and Tide*'s all-female board of directors, and of the women who occupied key editorial and staff positions, that exerted the main shaping influence on the periodical during this period of expansion. One of *Time and Tide*'s most important core collaborators in this respect was Winifred Holtby, who began writing regularly for the paper in 1924 and joined its board of directors in 1926. In an obituary essay published in *Time and Tide* soon after Holtby's death in September 1935, Rhondda wrote:

I doubt whether TIME AND TIDE would be in existence now if it were not for Winifred. Certainly she had as large a share in building it as it is today as anyone in the world. . . . It was not only what she wrote; though during those eleven years she wrote almost every week (far more anonymous than signed stuff). We discussed every detail of the paper. I consulted her and valued her opinion immensely. (5 Oct 1935: 1391)

Rhondda's tribute is an important record not only of intra-gender collaboration which remained central to *Time and Tide*, but also of a large body of anonymous writing contributed by Holtby to the periodical. Holtby's signed contributions alone make her one of *Time and Tide*'s most prolific writers during her eleven-year association with the journal; that she wrote 'far more anonymous than signed stuff' points to an even greater imprint on the periodical, added to which were contributions Holtby made under at least two pseudonyms 'Corbin H. Wood' and 'GREC'.[23] Holtby's anonymous contributions brought a different kind of value to *Time and Tide*, one that had less to do with the sales and circulations with which Shaw's, Ervine's and Lewis's signatures were associated, and more to do with the intellectual and political grounds of the paper that she inhabited as *Time and Tide*'s youngest director and one of Rhondda's closest confidantes.

Holtby joined *Time and Tide*'s board of directors shortly after her return from a six-month lecturing tour in South Africa for the League of Nations Union (LNU).[24] As her biographer Marion Shaw discusses, the racism of white South African society 'provided her with the cause that would dominate the rest of her life' (1999: 92) and back in London she threw herself into political work in support of black people in Africa, as well as interracial initiatives at home, in the company of other committed internationalists and anti-colonialists on the left. In early 1927 *Time and Tide* apparently issued as a supplement the January issue of another periodical, *Foreign Affairs* (organ of the Union of Democratic Control, and edited by the feminist, pacifist and internationalist Helena M. Swanwick) which contained an article by Holtby on South Africa, illustrated with a head-and-shoulders photograph of the young writer and activist (Figure 5.2).[25] This supplement represents a significant departure from supplements *Time and Tide* issued in earlier years, which tended to be on more feminine-coded topics (for example, the 'Domestic' and 'Education' supplements it issued in February and May 1921) or to have a more overt feminist agenda (as in its Six Point Group supplements of 1923). As such it signals *Time and Tide*'s ambition to expand beyond traditionally female territory and on December 17, 1925,* pledging each other to friendly neutrality in case of any military attack or hostile alliance or agreement by a third party or parties against either ; and providing means for amicable settlement of disputes between themselves. Notwithstanding this gesture of cordiality, and subsequent recent conversations between M. Chicherin and Tewfik Rushdi Bey on questions of mutual interest, there remains a definite opposition of viewpoint between Westward-

* *Times*. Dec. 29, 1925. (Text.)

looking Turkey and the Eastward Asiatic Russian position.

The settlement of the age-old question of the Straits has favoured Turkey and the West ; while it has not pleased Russia. As long as the Soviet Republic remains unimportant in a naval or military sense, this diversity will not be dangerous ; but there still remains the potential problem arising from the anomalous situation in which Russia holds the house and Turkey, supported by an international Commission, holds the entrance hall.

NATIONALISM AND EMPIRE IN SOUTH AFRICA

By WINIFRED HOLTBY

" **O**N behalf of the Nationalist Party . . . I wish to say that we are absolutely satisfied . . . There is no question of secession in South Africa, no question of republicanism, and no constitutional question of any kind like those raised in the past.

We fully accept what is freely given us by the British Government." Mr. Tielman Roos, acting Prime Minister and reputed die-hard of the Nationalist Party in South Africa, has thus echoed General Hertzog's expressed satisfaction with the results of the Imperial Conference. This, for the moment, is the most striking and most cheering result of the Conference as it affects this particular Dominion.

Before the Conference, underlying almost every question of South African politics, and certainly every question concerning foreign affairs, was the problem of Dominion Status. Because the Union Act bore the strain of 1914, we are apt in this country to forget its hazardous and experimental character. As the flag controversy and Mr. Roos' recent attack upon the " Sons of England " organisation has shown, the sensitive race-consciousness between Dutch and English frequently resulted in what General Smuts called " the inferiority-superiority complex," which added emotional tension to all political questions. Before the Conference, the Nationalist Party, now in office as a result of its pact with Labour, had adopted an ambiguous attitude towards the demand for sovereign independence and republicanism, formerly part of their election manifestoes, but on the whole the Dutch distrusted the vague empiricism of British constitutional tradition.

General Hertzog came to the conference as the spokesman of a party that demanded before all else certainty upon three issues : First, a clear pronouncement on the equality and freedom of the Dominions within the Commonwealth. On May 28, at Cape Town, he had declared : " It is in the League of Nations, and the League of Nations alone, that we are known as international States." Otherwise the different parts of the British Empire were too often considered, by the outside world, *en bloc:* In Part II of the Balfour Report he has what he wanted : " They are autonomous communities within the British Empire, equal in status, in no way subordinate to each other in any aspect of their domestic or external concerns."

He wanted some official diplomatic channel through which South Africa could establish direct relations with London and with foreign government centres, instead of having to rely solely upon the reports of the London High Commissioner, the Foreign Trade Commissioners, and the diplomatic reports and letters sent to the

Governor-General. Part V, sections (*b*), (*d*) and (*e*) of the Balfour Report facilitate such communications and clear up many obscurities in the technique of Dominion diplomacy.

Thirdly, South African Nationalists wanted a Nationality Act, such as that introduced by Dr. Malan last May, which would follow the example of Canada in conferring a definite South African nationality as distinct from British nationality, and which would solve such difficulties as at present are felt, for instance, in the election of judges to the Permanent Court of International Justice. Before the Conference, this Bill, combined as it was with the unfortunate flag controversy, had aroused the warmest suspicion in the country and recalled the bitterest of the divisions separating the Dutch and English sections. If, as General Hertzog has said, " nothing has ever before been accomplished so calculated to lay a deep and enduring foundation for national co-operation between members of the British Commonwealth of Nations " as the Conference, then perhaps the constitutional difficulties of the Nationality Bill can be solved without the acrimony of national division.

So much appears to be pure gain, but there are parts of the Balfour report and other conclusions of the Conference less helpful to South African policy. The section of the Report dealing with Locarno declared the conference to be satisfied with the efforts of the Secretary of State for making peace in Europe ; but it cannot so simply eliminate the divergencies between South Africa and Great Britain on certain fundamental questions of foreign policy. Since the Armistice England has drawn more and more towards the Continental idea of security through mutual guarantee ; South Africa feels strongly the attraction of the American idea of security through isolation. The Monroe doctrine exercises a fascination upon the South African mind, which is increased by the possible shifting of the world's gold centre from London to New York. If Dutch South Africans feel no pressing necessity for the protection of the British Navy—and the Opposition paper, the *Cape Times*, frequently castigates their indifference to questions of national defence—neither do they feel the same urgent need for British capital now that American tourists, with immense publicity, are investigating the resources of their country.

It is partly this instinct towards isolation, partly distrust of " veiled imperialism," partly dislike of European entanglements, and partly sheer ignorance, which has led South Africa to neglect in the past the opportunity which the League of Nations offered her for asserting her national personality before the world. The League had become mixed up with party politics. The followers of General Smuts boomed his part in the making of the Covenant after his return from Paris, and the Nationalists retaliated by calling it an Imperialistic camouflage, a creature of the Allies for crushing Germany, " another little stunt of Slim Jannie." Delegations to Geneva from South Africa had been either non-South African or of minor importance.

Figure 5.2 *Foreign Affairs* Supplement to *Time and Tide* 1927. Reproduced by kind permission of the Syndics of Cambridge University Library. Classmark: L900.a.39.

to engage its readership with international politics. Feminist internationalists attached great importance to the education of public opinion in the principles of internationalism (Haslam 1999: xxiii), and as Helen McCarthy notes, 'women, with their newly won political rights, were identified as an especially crucial target group for political education of this kind' (2013: 146–7). In April 1931 *Time and Tide* announced a new development in its columns: its incorporation of *Foreign Affairs* (now edited by the leading peace campaigner Norman Angell) which from May 1931 was published as a monthly supplement to *Time and Tide* (11 April 1931: ii).[26] The earlier *Foreign Affairs* supplement appears to have been a one-off, supporting Marysa Demoor and Kate MacDonald's idea of the supplement as an 'experimental zone' which has the potential to expand the scope of the parent publication but can also 'be risked on a new venture and abandoned if it fails' (2010: 100). But if in January 1927 *Time and Tide*'s readers were not yet ready to embrace a regular digest of international news and comment, just five months later the periodical developed a new initiative which worked in a more indirect way to extend women's interests beyond Britain's national borders and educate them in their responsibilities as global citizens.

This initiative was the publication of a special Travel Number in June 1927, the first of several Travel Numbers and Supplements issued by the periodical at regular intervals well into its second decade.[27] In the context of increased overseas tourism after the war which saw more middle-class women travelling abroad, these special travel issues made *Time and Tide* an attractive vehicle for a new set of advertisers (see Figure 5.3), but they also played an important part in shaping the periodical's more international focus. The first Travel Number opened its 'Summer Travel Section' with an article on 'The Pleasure of Travel', which appeared immediately after an article making 'A Case for the League of Nations' in its regular columns on the adjacent page (10 June 1927: 542–3). The juxtaposition is suggestive of the ways in which *Time and Tide* capitalised on a new vogue for travel in order to educate readers in the principles of internationalism. While subsequent articles on 'Ireland and France', 'Czecho-Slovakia', and 'Alpine Motoring' also promote the pleasures of travelling to European destinations, the concluding article, about travelling in South Africa and written by Holtby, not only resists travel as a form of consumption, but also evidences a distinctive anti-imperialist vision. The article's title, 'For Next to Nothing', immediately dismisses the pursuit of luxury as travel's primary object, and in contrast to high-class magazines like *Vogue* in which 'the colonies

Figure 5.3 Travel Advertisements in *Time and Tide* 15 Nov 1929: 1389.
Reproduced with the permission of The William Ready Division of
Archives and Research Collections, McMaster University Library.

are imaginatively possible as tourist attractions only because England has made them habitable' (Garrity 1999: 44), Holtby's piece challenges perceptions of Africa as backward and inhospitable as she tells readers to 'disregard the warnings of your friends':

> 'Nobody travels second class, in South Africa,' they tell you. Of course they do. All the best people do. I did. And though I have by no means travelled on all the railways in the world, I am willing to take a sporting bet that there are none more delightful than the leisurely, convivial, comfortable trains of the South African Railways. (10 June 1927: 547)

Holtby's play with the idea of 'the best people' is a delightful riposte to the racially inflected snobbery of high society. Recasting her experience of South Africa in a more popular form than her political analysis for *Foreign Affairs*, it is no less effective in its undermining of imperial ideology.

Other evidence demonstrates *Time and Tide*'s conscious attempt to challenge contemporary racism as it worked to educate readers in the principles of internationalism. Indeed, *Time and Tide*'s move from Fleet Street to Bloomsbury not only registers the periodical's close proximity to the cultures of literary modernism, but also to the networks of anti-colonialism associated with the Hogarth Press. As Anna Snaith discusses, the Woolfs' press was 'a key disseminator of anti-colonial thought in the interwar period' (2010: 103), and two of its most prominent authors on Africa, Norman Leys and Lord Olivier, were also contributors to *Time and Tide*. In 1929 *Time and Tide* published an unprecedented number of creative pieces by writers of colour, including two short stories by the Indian writer Cornelia Sorabji, and four poems by one of the most celebrated poets associated with the Harlem Renaissance, Countee Cullen.[28] Also in 1929, a short story about lynching treated in unflinching terms one of the most horrific aspects of the African American experience.[29] The following year a drawing by Edmond Xavier Kapp of a man of African descent reading *Time and Tide* on the train is the most visually arresting example of the way this periodical acknowledged the exchange between colonial and British subjects as black intellectuals and writers travelled from the periphery of the empire to its core in the interwar years (Figure 5.4).[30] Countering dominant representations in popular culture of black London as an underworld (Bush 1999: 211), the drawing simultaneously presents the African subject as cultured and civilised, and *Time and Tide* as the progressive weekly for London's non-white inhabitants.

Drawings by Kapp, No. 21

Time and Tide, July 12, 1930

Figure 5.4 Drawing by Edmond Xavier Kapp, *Time and Tide* 12 July 1930: 893. Courtesy Chris Beetles Gallery, on behalf of the Kapp Estate.

Time and Tide's travel supplements, and also features on black culture and experience, thus worked to extend readers' knowledge of the world beyond their own country in advance of the periodical's incorporation of *Foreign Affairs*. Technically the new *Foreign Affairs* maintained a level of independence from *Time and Tide*; it was presented as a separately numbered four-page sheet and in the first issue Angell reassured readers that his comment would remain 'as free and untrammelled' as before (2 May 1931: 4). In fact, such was the harmony between Angell's political standpoint and that of *Time and*

Tide's core collaborators that the supplement and parent publication effectively spoke as one voice.[31] This is particularly evident in the paper's position on peace and disarmament where *Time and Tide* closely followed the policy of the LNU and the opinion of Angell who chaired its Publicity Committee. In 1931 the LNU 'campaigned more vigorously than ever before for disarmament' (Birn 1981: 90) alongside leading women's organisations including the Women's International League for Peace and Freedom (WILPF).[32] In May 1931 *Time and Tide* joined the other leading weeklies in protesting against Lord Beaverbrook's *Daily Express* when it attacked the League, and it continued to support and promote the LNU's Disarmament Campaign even after the withdrawal from the League of first Japan and then Germany in 1933.[33] Leading articles such as 'Where *Time and Tide* Stands' published in the lead-up to the 1931 General Election (3 Oct 1931: 1128) show how closely *Time and Tide* followed the LNU on matters of economic and foreign policy, as does its publication, on the eve of the second Disarmament Conference at Geneva, 'A League Foreign Policy' supplement (23 Sep 1933).

Time and Tide's arrangement with Norman Angell over the publication of *Foreign Affairs* can be seen as a model of gendered cooperation in the public sphere. However, a fascinating exchange between Rhondda and Holtby preserved in and outside the pages of the periodical reveals that *Time and Tide*'s idea of a 'common platform' for men and women was an ongoing process of negotiation. In 'Some Letters From Winifred Holtby', edited and published in *Time and Tide* after Holtby's death, Rhondda includes an excerpt from a letter dated 22 September [1933] which begins: 'Slight ruction last week. R- displeased with my leader on Disarmament and the League called *Is it War*. Said it cut across his, and that all my leaders on his subjects should be signed' (18 Apr 1936: 553). 'R' (as Rhondda's unpublished reply to Holtby reveals) was C. Patrick Thompson, one of *Time and Tide*'s regular staff writers on the political side of the paper, and on its finance page where he signed himself 'Securitas'.[34] Earlier the previous year Holtby described to Vera Brittain how Thompson had been the subject of endless discussion at board meetings ('his payment, his views, his leaders, everything he does') while she and her colleagues 'trained [him] to the paper's ways'.[35] Her confidence, however, that they had 'at *last* converted him to internationalism and Norman Angellism' is undercut by Thompson's displeasure at her unsigned leader (published in *Time and Tide*'s issue of 16 September 1933) which highlights tensions between the sexes as women advanced into what was traditionally male territory. In her letter to Rhondda,

Holtby went on humorously to relate how she had defused the situation: 'Rang him up and went all feminine. Immediate sweetness and light from R-, who is really rather a lamb. When in doubt Gaye [Rhondda's assistant editor, Phoebe Fenwick Gaye] and I are going to go all over weak-womanish' (553). Holtby's banter with Rhondda highlights the female camaraderie enjoyed by women working in *Time and Tide*'s professional environment. But a few weeks later '[a]nother little office blow-up with R' over 'a too, too Beaverbrookian leader' illustrates women's ongoing battle for recognition as authorities on international affairs. Apparently Holtby took it upon herself to rewrite the leader; in her letter to Rhondda she writes:

> I hope that is all right; but I felt that in times of real crisis, when a lead must be given if ever, it was rather silly for an independent weekly review to follow the crowd and play for safety [. . .] when it comes to a show-down, I really believe I know now as much C20th and infinitely more C19th history than he does, and . . . anyway, I took the responsibility into my own hands, [. . .] and R- is full of amiability though I expect he thinks me a fanatical hag. (18 Apr 1936: 554)[36]

Holtby's tone remains light, but her suspicion that Thompson privately thinks her a 'fanatical hag' is a reminder that men's acquiescence to women's advances in the political sphere was by no means certain or assured.

The potential for gender conflict in modern magazine culture is dramatised by *Time and Tide*'s encounters with one of the most legendary male figures of this era, Ezra Pound. Pound had been reading *Time and Tide* since at least January 1930, but in 1933 Holtby's unsigned leader 'Is It War?' seems to have prompted him to seek greater involvement with the paper.[37] In a letter to *Time and Tide* (printed in its columns on 30 September 1933) Pound responded to the case made by Holtby against private arms manufacturers, and at around the same time sought an introduction to *Time and Tide* via Theodora Bosanquet for some articles on economics.[38] Passing the letter on to Holtby, Rhondda commented: 'He has a certain name I think, if his views are not too fantastic?'[39] To which Holtby replied (as presented in one of the letters Rhondda later published in *Time and Tide*):

> P—'s letter is most amusing. He sent one in to *Time and Tide*; we gathered that it was a letter and not an article. Most of it was so full of obscene words that we couldn't possibly have printed it, but we

extracted a few decent sentences and, as his name carries a certain amount of weight, printed the emasculated version which will no doubt infuriate him, but what can one do? (18 Apr 1936: 553)

Supporting Jayne E. Marek's claim that 'no doubt Pound's letters amused editors' (1995: 180), Rhondda's and Holtby's exchange also shows that *Time and Tide* was perfectly capable of exploiting the value of Pound's 'name' even as it refused him an entry for writing on economics. *Time and Tide* returned the next item he sent (an article entitled 'INSULARITY, INSULATION & DEATH') confessing that despite careful reading 'we simply hadn't the slightest idea what it was all about!'[40] This drew an infuriated response from Pound who complained: 'I don't see why I sh'd be "played for a sucker" or why I shd. Supply free copy to a Brit. weekly paper.' Stating that the question now is 'WILL YOU PRINT the facts referred to, in what you call my unintelligible three pages', he continued:

A toady to banks/ to a system that MADE the war//
to stay in the letter col/ fan mail alond with the
blok's who write about odog biscuit and the first cuckoo . . .
          Not good enough, ladies,
For 20 years Brit. lit/ crit/ has refised to look at know
facts/
For 100 years birt. Economists go on as if Ad/ Smiff were the
first man who ever heard of the subject . . .
As I have writ/ this you can print it if you like. But for
the next I am either a contributor or not.[41]

Time and Tide did not print this letter, and Pound never became a regular contributor (although he would appear briefly in the periodical's books pages as a reviewer the following year, as we shall see in Chapter 6). His displeasure at being confined to *Time and Tide*'s correspondence pages produces the aggressive, bullish tone, and it would be easy to read this letter as an example of what some scholars have described as Pound's fundamental misogyny (particularly its patronising 'Not good enough, ladies'). But as George Bornstein discusses, 'Pound could be abrasive to both men and women, and was' (2001: 88), a fact to which *Time and Tide*'s own pages attest in its publication of a letter of Pound's forwarded to the paper in April 1935 by Norman Angell (Figure 5.5). Less maverick than the language of much of his correspondence, the letter still bears the hallmarks of Pound's 'aggressive epistolary conduct' (naming Angell, for example, as a 'banker's pimp') and in an editorial note *Time and*

LETTERS TO THE EDITOR

Sir,—As the writer of the enclosed letter—whom I have never seen or communicated with in any way—would presumably like his views to have a wide publicity, I send the enclosed to you for publication if you deem it of any interest.   It is addressed to me at the Bank of England (which I have never entered) in " Thread and needle street."   I am, etc.,

                                             NORMAN ANGELL.

[We do indeed deem that the communication sent to us by Sir Norman Angell is of considerable interest, literary and psychological, and we feel that only facsimile reproduction can do it justice. —Editor, TIME AND TIDE.]

           E. POUND   RAPALLO

Norman Angell

                 Sir / a s a man who has exploited pacifism ,

who has ma de money and a career bleating about pacifism but

contributed nothing to the knowledge of the economic causes of

war . You merit not only contempt but loathing when you bleat

publicly of things you and your accomplices have been too lazy

to s tudy.

    I regret that you are too cowardly to meet me , and that

dueling in prohibited in yr/ enslaved country.

However a s a banker's pimp , please consider yourself slapped.

               And may hell rot your bones.

    I am glad to inform you that Nic Butler has been called a

traitor in the American House of Representatives. The lot

of you fakers will be known in due time.

            And now , go lick someones' boots

               yrs

Figure 5.5 Facsimile of Letter from Ezra Pound to Norman Angell, *Time and Tide* 11 May 1935: 685. By Ezra Pound, from EZRA POUND'S POETRY AND PROSE: CONTRIBUTIONS TO PERIODICALS, copyright © 1991 by the Trustees of the Ezra Pound Literary Property Trust. Reprinted by permission of New Directions Publishing Corp.

Tide stated its agreement with Angell that the letter 'is of considerable interest, literary and psychological, and we feel that only facsimile reproduction can do it justice' (11 May 1935: 685). *Time and
Tide*'s publication of this letter without Pound's permission was a
risky move, and in a letter to the London-based publisher Stanley
Nott Pound deliberated over whether he should strike back at the
periodical or 'preserve diggyfied [*sic*] silence' (Hickman 2011: 131).
However, in his letter Pound twice returns to the fact that *Time and
Tide*'s editorial note is 'ambiguous' (the second time, 'pleasantly' so),
observing that 'there was a very good review of *Cantos* 31/41 in the
same issue', and allowing for the possibility that the periodical took
the 'only way' possible to get the 'facts' he privately communicated
to Angell into print (Hickman 2011: 131–3). Much more likely is
that *Time and Tide* was interested in printing the letter as a historical
document of the Pound personality itself. Just as Pound valued letters as 'vital historical documents – fugitive textual productions that
could catch a historical figure in motion' (Hickman 2011: 304), so
Time and Tide places on record its encounters with one of the most
controversial men in twentieth-century English letters.

However, another letter of Pound's, this time addressed to Rhondda,
is a reminder of the 'atmosphere' of anti-feminism identified by Virginia
Woolf in *Three Guineas* as 'one of the most powerful [. . .] enemies
with which the daughters of educated men have to fight' (1938 [2015]:
135). Still denouncing Norman Angell as a 'blithering imbecile' Pound
cannot understand why *Time and Tide* should be so identified with
his views 'unless you specifivly want to make an ass of as much of the
relicts of the feminist movement as yr/ weekly publication can be supposed to represent'. He concludes:

> Skirts are no protection when they have voting right. Fluttery society
> women dabblin in literature, orthology and politics can not claim
> those antient consideration which were accorded etc. the etc. and
> Victorian etc.
>
> It is really time for you run a paper for honest thought, or else
> get out of business, and leave the really dirty work to the men who
> frankly want to debauch England and rot the Empire from its centre.[42]

In this letter, the force of Pound's criticism remains chiefly directed
at Angell, and one could argue that the communication evidences
a degree of respect for Rhondda and her paper; as Miranda Hickman argues, Pound's 'abbreviations and telegraphic style suggest he
believes his interlocutors are [. . .] astute enough [. . .] to decipher his
half-formulated language' (312). However, it is impossible to ignore

the anti-feminism which flavours his words, even if he doesn't sub-scribe to it wholesale himself. Crucially, although Pound distinguishes between a pre-modern era, in which women were 'protected' from responsibility in the public sphere, and the present moment, in which Rhondda and her colleagues claim their rights to active citizenship, the direction in which he himself was going (fascism) betrays the very real threat posed to women by the connections between patriarchal and fascist ideology.[43] As Johanna Alberti summarises, the fascist view as understood by British feminists at this time 'focused on the returning of women to the home, the controlling of the populace by propaganda which highlights the position of a leader, and the glorification of militarism'. Moreover, 'many feminists of the period understood that behind those policies and practices lay a deep fear and even hatred of women' (1994a: 111). In the remainder of this chapter I explore the ways in which *Time and Tide* dealt with this perceived fear and hatred of women in some of its lighter content which articulates *Time and Tide*'s sustained desire to transform gen-der relations and cooperate equally with men in the public sphere.

Sexual difference and female culture

In its issue of 1 November 1929, the same day that 'Saint' George Bernard Shaw blessed *Time and Tide* in its new Bloomsbury offices, *Time and Tide* carried a letter in its correspondence columns from another Edwardian giant, H. G. Wells. Reviving debates about *Time and Tide*'s use of the editorial 'Sir' (see Chapter 1) the letter begins: 'MADAM, – *I* address you as "Madam". Why did you alter the address of my last letter to "Sir" and so rob my opening sentence of its venom?' Underneath *Time and Tide* printed an editorial note re-stating its 'usual practice of having all letters to the Editor addressed "Sir"' and commented:

> Mr. Wells began his letter to us last week: 'Madam, Forgive me if I find your paragraph . . . a trifle cattish.' We fail to see why the substitution of 'Sir' for 'Madam' should rob this sentence of its venom. We had sup-posed that cats belonged to both sexes.' (1 Nov 1929: 1305)

Time and Tide's response and the laughter it elicits highlight the way in which humour can function as 'an indicator of the tensions and contradictions existing in a given society' and enable us to 'critically analyse social situations and mechanisms' (Pailer et al. 2009: 25).

Specifically, Wells's insistence on addressing *Time and Tide*'s editor as 'Madam' and the periodical's entertaining push back against the sexism implied in his use of the word 'cattish' illustrate the tension *Time and Tide* continued to negotiate over its identity as a paper run by women who, according to traditional gender ideology, were supposed to stay out of public affairs. According to Merry M. Pawlowski, it was Wells's apparent assumptions about female inferiority that provided Woolf with one of the earliest impetuses for writing *Three Guineas* (1938) which controversially made connections between the rise of fascist states in Europe and the 'domestic fascism of her literary friends and acquaintances' (1994: 46). Eight years earlier, Rhondda too placed on public record her perception of Wells's sexism and misogyny in a series of four articles published in *Time and Tide* in October and November 1930.

Entitled 'Wells on Women', this series is an early example of feminist literary criticism that sets out to analyse 'images of women' in male-authored texts. Accusing Wells of being 'quite incapable of knowing anything at all about women' and of being interested 'only in man's needs' (25 Oct 1930: 1327), in the final article of the series Rhondda concluded:

> He [Wells] could scarcely at this late hour set to work to learn that oddly difficult lesson that human beings are – regardless of sex – human beings, and that the most important thing about the human being, even the female human being, is not its sex but its humanity. [. . .] Under the circumstances by far his wisest plan is to leave the women he does not know how to draw out of his books altogether. (15 Nov 1930: 1428)

Wells, who was capable of 'inspiring and infuriating women' (Hall 2011: 68), has an ambiguous status among feminists. Writing in *Time and Tide*'s correspondence columns after Rhondda's series concluded, the feminist and socialist Winifred Horrabin reminded readers that women owed a debt to Wells's early 'trumpet-blasts' in support of feminism (22 Nov 1930: 1463), and Winifred Holtby penned a glowing review of Wells's powers as a journalist in a review published by *Time and Tide* earlier the same year.[44] Rhondda, however, believed that Wells confused sexual freedom with women's rights (John 2013: 427) and later told Shaw that 'when Wells either talks or writes about women he does make me see red'.[45] In the remainder of this chapter I discuss two key figures in *Time and Tide*'s feminist community – E. M. Delafield and Naomi Mitchison – whose creative contributions to the periodical in the early 1930s mediate the risks of cross-gender collaboration and the dangers of essentialist models of gender which both contain and limit women. At once restaging debates between 'old' and 'new' feminists about women's equality and difference (see Chapter 1), this material also shows how different modes of writing (specifically, parody and historical fiction) could address, negotiate and alleviate difficult tensions between the sexes as the periodical worked towards gendered cooperation in the public sphere.

Delafield, who joined *Time and Tide*'s board of directors in 1927, was one of the periodical's most popular writers and is best known for her comic novel *The Diary of a Provincial Lady* which was first serialised in *Time and Tide* in 1930. Her role in sustaining the magazine's relationship with women readers will be the subject of extended discussion in Chapter 6. Here, I discuss some parodies Delafield contributed to the periodical in the early 1930s which, further evidence of *Time and Tide*'s new investment in parody as a form for promoting a variety of aesthetic discourses (see Chapter 4), also reveal the periodical's use of humour for confronting and negotiating male attitudes and assumptions about women. The subject of Delafield's first parody for the paper was *The Autocracy of Mr. Parham* (1930), the latest novel by the male figure framed as an antagonist in the periodical's correspondence columns less than a year earlier: H. G. Wells. In this now largely forgotten satirical novel 'Mr. Parham' is an Oxford don who has a dream in which he is invaded by a spirit from Mars and transformed into a fascist dictator. Looking for a rich benefactor to finance a review he can edit, he believes he has found such a man in 'Sir Bussy Woodcock', recognised by contemporaries as a caricature of the newspaper baron Lord Beaverbrook (Hammond 1979: 116).[46] In Delafield's parody, 'Mr. Parham' becomes 'Mr. Ponds' and 'Sir Bussy Woodcock' becomes 'Sir Woodcock Wells' in a recognisable caricature of the author himself. At once imitating and transforming the plot of Wells's novel, Delafield has Mr. Ponds and Mr. Woodcock succeed in taking over the whole of Fleet Street, with the exception of *Ebb and Flow* (a thinly disguised *Time and Tide*) which is the only weekly to hold out. Intending to overpower the 'feminine' Board of Directors with 'the extraordinary quality of his sex-appeal', Mr. Ponds talks at them incessantly and first the 'Direct Subscribers' and then the 'Office Staff [. . .] drop away'. The 'Directors and the Editor' stay, however, '[r]ather like mastodons' until Sir Woodcock reappears carrying a glass retort of microbes which, if released, will 'devastate the universe'. While Mr Ponds is still deliberating the glass retort breaks and the whole of Fleet Street, including *Ebb and Flow* along with its editor and directors, are obliterated. The parody concludes with Sir Woodcock cheeping '[l]ike a canary' and Mr. Ponds expostulating:

> 'The *Ebb and Flow* people. What-I-mean-to-say, where *are* they? You've been in too great a hurry. Exterminating them like that.'
>
> 'What-I-mean-to-say, take Work. If you and I are talking all the time, who's to *do* it?'
>
> Sir Woodcock glanced at Mr. Ponds.
>
> '*Cheep*,' he said at last.
>
> Never before had Mr. Ponds heard a 'Cheep' so fraught with indecision, so unconvincing.
>
> 'It isn't,' said Mr. Ponds, 'good enough.'
>
> The illuminating word flashed upon him.
>
> 'Not Woodcock,' said Mr. Ponds. '*Poppycock*.' (16 Aug 1930: 1041–2)

The force of this comic denouement lies in Delafield's use of condensation in the final 'illuminating word' '*Poppycock*' which works to deflate male self-importance and render attempts to eliminate women from spheres of influence as ludicrous.[47] Well-known for his fictions which involve 'getting rid of people' (Carey 1992: 118), in Delafield's parody it is Wells himself who becomes the target of attack. The woodcock is, of course, a popular gamebird hunted for sport, and, like the woodland bird, in life Wells had a short, stocky figure, and a high, piping voice which is caricatured in his repeated utterance 'Cheep!'[48] The main force of the joke, however, lies in the self-defeating foolishness of Sir Woodcock's haste to 'exterminat[e]' *Ebb and Flow* and all its hard-working staff. In an echo of Shaw's house-warming speech, about men as gossips and women who get things done, Delafield's parody replays the argument that women – and, importantly, *Time and Tide* – have a vital role to play in the world of public affairs, and in the survival of civilisation itself.

Two more parodies Delafield produced for *Time and Tide* in 1930 and 1931 target prominent male authors: Arnold Bennett, another influential writer of the Edwardian generation, and Beverley Nichols, a prolific novelist and popular journalist. The first, a parody of Arnold Bennett's bestselling novel *Imperial Palace* (1930), mocks the perennial pursuit of the female by the male as a romantic and sexual object in novels written by men, and in its repeated refrain 'women were all alike' challenges the homogenisation of women as a group (1 Nov 1930: 1370–1). Men's presumption to know and understand women also comes under fire in Delafield's parody of Nichols's volume of short stories and sketches *Women and Children Last* (1931). A popular contributor to women's magazines and newspapers (several of the sketches first appeared in the *Daily Mail*, *Nash's Magazine*, the *Woman's Journal*, *Britannia and Eve*, *Harper's Bazaar*, *Sketch* and the *London Magazine*) Nichols was well known for his controversial statements about women, and the title of Delafield's parody indicates that the target of her satire is not only the book, but the personality: 'Beverley Nichols, According to E. M. Delafield. Women and Children Last *(but journalistic gentlemen don't, for very long)*'. The joke turns, of course, on Delafield's pun on the word 'last' where Nichols's deliberate attack on the chivalric notion 'women and children first' is transformed into a delicious exposure of the journalist's own vulnerability to ridicule and censure. Imitating Nichols's prose style and mannerisms Delafield renders comically visible not only the questionable validity of such judgements as 'women cannot possibly have souls', but also his reputation for anti-feminism:

> Contrary to what is believed all over the world, I am not a woman-hater. It is because I want to give women a chance of earning my approval that I write the truth about them. Sometimes, after I have written the truth, I have been called vulgar, and at other times I have been called vulgar without my having written anything at all. But I have never known why. (11 Apr 1931: 439)

Our enjoyment of these lines has everything to do with intonation, and the plaintive quality of Nichols's alleged inability to understand public reactions to his work. In this instance (and throughout the piece) Delafield repeats select utterances from Nichols's text almost verbatim (one sketch titled 'For Husbands Only' opens: 'Do not, please, accuse me of being a woman hater') (1931: 217), and it is the way they function in relation to the 'evaluative attitude' adopted in their new context (*Time and Tide*'s columns) that humorously contradicts the assertions and assumptions they contain.[49]

Delafield's parodic treatment of these male writers and their work exhibits what early theorists of women's humour writing have described as comedy's subversive power (Barreca 1988; Walker 1988) and invites comparison with Katherine Mansfield's use of satire as a weapon to mock the chauvinism of the male literary establishment in her parodies for the *New Age* nearly twenty years earlier' (Snyder 2010). But while Nichols admits in his foreword to *Women and Children Last* that the 'woman gets it, as far as I can give it to her, in the neck' (1931: 15), Delafield's parodies are striking for their avoidance of aggressive and abusive forms of satire. Indeed, her strategy in the Nichols parody is similar to that Virginia Woolf would use in *Three Guineas* where she 'allows men to incriminate themselves by quoting them at length' (Zwerdling 1986: 256). Through a process of repetition, exaggeration and transformation, men's attitudes towards women are exploded from within, rather than by an assailant from without. As such, Delafield's parodies might be seen as continuing in the tradition of New Woman comic writers whose work, according to Margaret Stetz, was 'far less vituperative and fierce than the comedy directed at them'. Positing that this earlier generation of feminists rejected on 'both moral and practical grounds' the 'no-holds-barred satire' of masculine posturing, Stetz argues that while the New Woman was herself the subject of numerous misogynistic comic attacks, the comedy she produced 'seldom went for the kill. More often, it kept intact the Meredithian tradition of using laughter merely to inspire change and improvement' (2001: 2; 9). This approach was led, argues Stetz, partly by an 'awareness of the moral complexities that ringed round the act of targeting an enemy for ridicule' (the link Freud established between comedy and aggression) but even more by their 'doubts about the effectiveness of laughter as a concrete political strategy' (46). The 'limitations [of laughter] for guaranteeing survival' (Stetz 2001: xiii) are thrown into dramatic relief by Delafield's parody of a book by the leader of the British Union of Fascists (BUF), Oswald Moseley, *The Greater Britain* (1932). In a paragraph that mimics a section of the book in which Mosley discusses 'Women's Work' Delafield writes:

> WOMEN. – It has been suggested that hitherto, in the New Movement, too little attention has been paid to the position of women. *But every member of our organization has, at one time or another and sometimes at both, had a woman for a mother.* Therefore, the part played by women in the Movement is important, although different from that of the men.
>
> To many the idea may seem fantastic, but *men will always be men, and women still more always be women.* In the New Movement, women will be mothers as well, continually and all the time. In this way, the problem will be solved.
>
> *Woman's place is the cradle.* (29 Oct 1932: 1183)

Laughter here is tempered by an awareness of the very real dangers posed to women in the 1930s by the rise of fascism. Delafield's subtle transformation of Moseley's statements (notably in her reworking of his famous assertion '*we want men who are men and women who are women*') highlights how gender essentialisms stick more to the female than the male in Mosley's 'New Movement' and its cult of motherhood, even as the caricature renders his thinking fatuous.

In light of this growing evidence of domestic fascism, the temperate tone of Delafield's parodies reflect a pragmatism *Time and Tide* shared with its New Woman ancestors that was born of the need to allow for continued relations between the periodical's core group of female collaborators and the men who are the object of mockery in these columns. As Stetz observes, 'no New Woman writer [. . .] could afford to alienate her masculine targets completely', and as a group 'New Woman writers tended not to expend their energies on abusive and alienating forms of satire, favouring instead a version of humour that recognized the inevitability of an ongoing relationship with the masculine objects of laughter, as well as the need to reform and improve the character of that relationship' (2001: 9; 11). In the pieces discussed, Delafield's attack on male anti-feminism is clear, but as a means to negotiate male hostility towards women parody is an effective strategy for undermining and disagreeing with male authority, yet in a good-humoured way. Two more parodies by Delafield published in *Time and Tide* in early 1933 stage a 'conversation' between various men and 'Ourselves' and evidence the periodical's desire to move beyond the sex-antagonism of the suffrage era through civilised dialogue and debate. In the first, Delafield presents a 'Totally Imaginary Conversation between Ourselves and Mr. Sinclair Lewis' in which America's most famous novelist suggests that *Time and Tide* 'might be interested in a book all about a Feminist' (18 Feb 1933: 178). The piece refers to Lewis's recently published *Ann Vickers* (frequently compared by reviewers with H. G. Wells's 1909 novel about a suffragette, *Ann Veronica*), and the force of its satire lies in the disjunction between Lewis's idea of feminism and that of *Time and Tide*'s. First, the fictional dialogue ruthlessly exposes his assumption that only women (not men) can be feminists, and then his inability to relinquish traditional stereotypes of women as primarily interested in love (for a man) and motherhood. The parody presents a conversation that is polite, civil and committed to hearing Lewis's point of view, but concludes comically in disagreement:

Mr. Lewis said Why shouldn't a True Woman be a Feminist too, and that was a question to which he thought his book, if he might say so, supplied an answer.

And so it did, because there are, after all, two answers to every question – one right and one wrong. (178)

One can almost hear the 'laughter of the group' that for Henri Bergson performs a corrective function in society (Pailer et al. 2009: 31). Pitted against the authority of 'Ourselves' Lewis is reported to exit with a 'slamming of the door' that admits his defeat (178). Two weeks later *Time and Tide* printed 'Another Totally Imaginary Conversation' by Delafield, this time between 'Ourselves' and the publishers, 'Mr. Chatto' and 'Mr. Windus'. Chatto & Windus had recently published Richard Aldington's third novel *All Men are Enemies* (1933), a social satire set in the aftermath of the First World War. The parody opens: "". . . The only thing is," we said, trying to word it as pleasantly as possible; "the only thing is, what made you publish it? And why is it called *All Men are Enemies*?"' (4 Mar 1933: 247). In a further display of 'pleasant[ness]' by *Time and Tide*'s female collaborators who remain 'kind to the last', the question evidences the periodical's reluctance to regard men as enemies. Countering perceptions of feminism as perpetuating a 'sex-war', the parody emphasises *Time and Tide*'s desire for gendered cooperation in the public sphere.[50] This goal was underpinned by *Time and Tide*'s equalitarian feminism, based on a view of men and women's common humanity (rather than sexual difference) as we have seen in earlier chapters of this book. However, like the 'in-jokes' of *Time and Tide*'s 'Weekly Crowd' column discussed in Chapter 2, the humour of Delafield's parodies also relies on a sense of belonging to a community of women readers whose shared interests belie women's sameness or identity with men. As such these pieces gesture towards Joan W. Scott's re-evaluation of the 'equality-versus-difference' debate and her argument that 'the critical feminist position must always involve *two* moves'. Identifying the first as 'the systematic criticism of the operations of categorical difference' she maintains that a refusal of the hierarchies that a binary model of sexual difference constructs should not be made 'in the name of an equality that implies sameness or identity, but rather (and this is the second move) in the name of an equality that rests on differences – differences that confound, disrupt and render ambiguous the meaning of any fixed opposition' (1988: 48). This second move is central to the creative contributions of another key member of *Time and Tide*'s periodical community, Naomi Mitchison, whose historical short fictions I examine next.

First attracting *Time and Tide*'s attention in 1928 with her letters to the editor on the subject of birth control (one of the key concerns of 'new' feminists), Mitchison's writing for the paper demonstrates that 'equality requires the recognition and inclusion of differences' (Scott 1988: 48) and at the same time challenges essentialist and constraining constructions of difference as normatively constituted. Most of Mitchison's stories for *Time and Tide* appeared during a two-year period between June 1929 and June 1931 and thus overlap with the writing of her best-known work of historical fiction, *The Corn King and the Spring Queen* (1931). Based on accounts of ancient rituals in James Frazer's influential *The Golden Bough* (1890) this ambitious novel challenges the way male modernists – particularly D. H. Lawrence – had used Frazer to define sexuality in phallocentric terms, and as Ruth Hoberman observes 'allows to surface the story both Frazer and Lawrence disavowed, a story of female power, autonomy and fecundity' (1997: 35). The title of Mitchison's second story in *Time and Tide*, 'A Little Girl Lost' (19 July 1929: 876–8), suggests her intended dialogue with Lawrence, whose first post-war novel, *The Lost Girl* (1920), represents issues of self and sexuality in terms of 'a highly self-conscious primitivism' (Beckett 2002: 50). Mitchison's story, which is set in pre-Romanised Britain, shares Lawrence's fascination with ancient ritual rooted in the earth's natural rhythms, but in contrast with his narratives, which depend on submission to the male by the female, it is centred on female independence and agency. Using third person limited narration and free indirect discourse Mitchison establishes an intimate relationship between the reader and protagonist, a little girl who becomes lost on the moor and, catching sight of the advance of her township's enemies, realises that she is to blame for the impending attacks as that morning 'she had gone the wrong way round the Spotted Stone' (877). Managing to outwit her pursuers the little girl reaches her town in time to issue the warning and then returns to the Spotted Stone where she kneels and repents and then begins 'to run round it again, the right way' (878). The story, which ends reassuringly with the statement 'It would be all right now' (878), is clearly influenced by the prominent role accorded to ritual in Frazer's *Golden Bough*, but it also appears to borrow from the so-called Cambridge Ritualists and the feminist classical scholar Jane Harrison's notion 'of a Greek religion based on the propitiation of nonanthropomorphic forces' (Hoberman 1997: 22). As Hoberman has discussed, following late nineteenth-century excavations revealing a Mycenean Age quite distinct from fifth-century Athenian culture the idea that there could be 'power, even domination, associated with specifically female body parts working in alliance with nature was an appealing notion to many women' (19). In contrast with male theorists including Frazer and Freud who 'regarded the movement from matriarchy to patriarchy as an inevitable movement toward civilization', for women writers like Mitchison the myths and rituals of ancient Greece provided a means to explore and challenge their own culture's assumptions about gender and sexuality (Hoberman 1997: 19; 22–3).

In another story published in *Time and Tide* in 1929, 'Nothing Over Much' (22 Nov 1929: 1405–6), Mitchison chooses the Greek island of Kos in the Hellenistic period as a setting to continue her dialogue with Lawrence, which here engages explicitly with public debates about female sexuality. The central protagonist in this story, Metriche, is a married woman who commits adultery with an Olympian athlete, Grulos, while her husband Mandris, a trader, is away in Egypt and presumed to be enjoying the pleasures, including the women, at King Ptolemy's court. The story's radicalism lies not only in its explicit representation of female sexual desire as Metriche, shy but 'determined to have the courage and if possible the pleasure of her own adultery', finds that '[a]bruptly and comfortingly her body took charge, stirred and prickled her' (1406). Even more challenging to male narratives about sex is its representation of female sexuality that is autonomous and not focused on the needs or desires of a man. Towards the conclusion of the story Metriche turns down the opportunity to meet Grulos again, explaining that 'it was he who was in love with me, not I with him', and when the return of her husband is announced she is unafraid and has no regrets: 'It's a thing for me alone, now, isn't it, for me myself? [. . .] I'm not a bit sorry. If I ever have a little girl I'll be able to tell her all about it when she's grown-up' (1406). Mitchison would later claim (in her 1934 feminist polemic, *The Home and a Changing Civilisation*) that 'It must be fairly obvious that Lawrence could never really stand the idea of a woman enjoying herself sexually' (141). Inserting into dominant narratives a female protagonist who asserts her right to sexual pleasure, Mitchison challenges the ways in which Lawrence used Frazer to define sexuality in phallocentric terms and frees her (as she would free Erif Der, her heroine of *The Corn King and the Spring Queen*) from patriarchal scripts.

Like Wells Lawrence has a controversial status among feminists, and his novels met with a mixed reception among *Time and Tide*'s early fiction reviewers.[51] He was championed, however, by Rebecca West, who just months after the prosecution of Radclyffe Hall's *The*

Well of Loneliness defended him when he came under fire over his new collection of poems, *Pansies*, confiscated on the way to his publisher (15 Mar 1929). Between July and November 1929 *Time and Tide* published five poems from the suppressed manuscript, and in April 1930 (a little more than a month after Lawrence's death) published a poem from his 1930 collection *Nettles*: 'Father Neptune's Little Affair with Freedom', a stinging satire of Britain's censorship laws.[52] In January 1933 *Time and Tide* announced that it had secured for first printing in England a selection from the last poems of D. H. Lawrence, and in March 1934 it issued a special D. H. Lawrence supplement comprising a 'hitherto unpublished story'.[53] *Time and Tide*'s promotion of Lawrence evidences the strong stand this periodical took against Britain's censorship laws. As Adam Parkes observes, by the time of his death 'Lawrence's name was virtually synonymous with scandal and censorship' (1996: 109), and while the periodical was necessarily circumspect about lesbianism, male writing about sex arguably provided *Time and Tide* with a vehicle for signalling its resistance to repressive sexual ideologies.[54] By the mid-1930s, however, Mitchison and also Holtby were each openly criticising Lawrence for his representations of male mastery and female submission, and associated his social and political vision with the rise of fascism.[55] As Alex Zwerdling summarises, an essential part of both Italy's and Germany's fascist regimes was 'a return to absolute sexual divisions': Mussolini would declare in 1934 that 'war is to man as maternity is to woman', while Hitler's 'twin cults of the army and motherhood' similarly revived ancient divisions of labour and 'virtually eliminated the common ground that a century of feminism had won' (1986: 264–5). The fascist construction of women was 'energetically resisted' in *Time and Tide*'s pages (Alberti 1994a: 114), and four more stories Mitchison contributed to *Time and Tide* in 1930 and 1931 participate in the paper's examination and critique of naturalised assumptions about sexual difference. But they also complicate the equality-versus-difference debate, and the periodical's strategic emphasis on 'humanity' rather than sex and gender. At once highlighting the dangers of gender essentialisms, they also preserve a notion of women's different values and perspectives which (as I will argue in the final part of this book) would remain distinctive of *Time and Tide*'s culture and standpoint throughout the interwar years.

The first of these stories, 'The Prince' (4 Oct 1930: 1226–9), is set in the great Palace of Knossos, the centre of Minoan civilisation around 2000 BC. Believed to be a peaceful and possibly matriarchal society (Freeman 2004: 124), Minoan Greece in Mitchison's story emphasises a culture without sex-segregation. While it is a male prince who provides the narrative focus of the story, Mitchison uses the iconography of recent archaeological finds to represent gender equality: notably the famous bull-leaping scenes in the frescoes at Knossos in which both princes and princesses take part, and the potent symbols of the 'double axe' and 'a curious flower' which are 'the signs of power, male and female' (1228).[56] The story also blurs rigid gender lines in its representation of the prince in what would be seen by early twentieth-century audiences as more feminine terms: his clothes are brightly coloured and 'embroidered', and his 'long black hair' is 'curled with a hot iron and laid carefully in five tresses over his shoulders' (1227). This gender ambiguity contrasts with the two male protagonists of Mitchison's next story, 'To the Glory of Ashur' (13 Dec 1930), which draws explicit links between masculinity and militarism. Set in the ancient city of Ninevah during the rule of King Ashurbanipal (the last of the great leaders of the Assyrian empire) this story centres on two boys, brothers, who 'long for the time when they, too, could be soldiers' (1568) and whose bloodlust is presented in deliberately shocking terms when they exult triumphantly at the 'bouncing heads' of the decapitated prisoners 'tossed over to the crowd' (1569). Together these stories belong to a body of anti-fascist writing by women in the 1930s.[57] 'To the Glory of Ashur' makes connections between rigid sexual divisions, the rise of militarism and the emergence of fascist states; the gender-fluidity of 'The Prince' offers a utopian vision of a world that is not organised by sexual difference.

Two further stories published in *Time and Tide* in January 1931, however, bring different perspectives to the idea implicit in many equalitarian feminist arguments that the elimination of difference is a necessary and desirable goal. The first of these, 'The War Ship Sails *(12th Century B.C.)*', is set in Mycenaean Greece, a civilisation which in contrast with the Minoan civilisation that preceded it was more 'outward-looking and often aggressive' (Freeman 2004: 125). The story opens with the departure from an unnamed island of all the menfolk engaged on a raiding expedition, but the narrative focuses centrally on the women and children who are left behind and will wait several months for their husbands and sons to return. Foregrounding what Mitchison's narrator describes as 'the women's time on the Island' (3 Jan 1931: 10) the story presents one positive consequence of a society organised by sexual difference: the development of a separate female culture with its potential for growth and empowerment. Returning from the jetty with their mother, two little girls – Phylo and Aktoris – feel 'twice as important as they had been yesterday' (10), and in a striking Woolfian echo talk excitedly about having this year 'a loom of our very own' (10). For Phylo, this will enable her to 'begin weaving for [her] wedding', but the declaration from Aktoris that 'I don't want to get married' places marriage, as the natural destiny of women, under question. Wishing instead for the stewardship of two white kids (baby goats) Aktoris looks to her mother as the new figure of authority: 'But it's you now, Mother [. . .] you'll do things now that father's gone off again' (10). The importance of preserving women's difference is central to Mitchison's story 'At Plane Tree Grove' (24 Jan 1931: 92–4) which is set in the ancient Greek state of Sparta, renowned for its military pre-eminence (the story opens with the line 'Everybody was going to see the boys fight'). Uniquely in Sparta women as well as men identified with the state, not family, and as a result they had more physical freedom, more shared interests with their husbands, and little in common with Athenian wives (Hoberman 1997: 31). In Mitchison's story the girls are like the boys in their determination to see the fight, as they push and shove through the crowd and are 'prepared to fight anyone else who wanted to take their places. They were Spartiate girls' (92). However, the thoughts of one of the girls, Alkathoa, register uncertainty about the Spartan belief that the greatest glory is to die in the service of the state. Losing sight of her brother she grows anxious, knowing that 'sometimes fighters were knocked into the ditch and drowned before anyone noticed', and official discourse rubs up against her own resistance: 'A good death, the elders said, almost as good as a death in battle, but Alkathoa was not looking at it that way' (93). Here a different, feminine point of view casts doubt not only on Sparta's military ethos, but (anticipating the arguments made by Woolf in *Three Guineas*) also on the value of seeking equal status in a society organised and run by men.

These and other short stories by Mitchison published in *Time and Tide* thus acknowledge and value women's different experiences and perspectives, and a separate female culture, even as the periodical's own official discourse worked to downplay differences between men and women and sought cross-gender collaboration in the public sphere. In the next chapter, I examine *Time and Tide*'s creation of a new space in the periodical for creative content that specifically addressed itself to women, and – with reference to gender conflict in *Time and Tide*'s book reviews section – explore the implications of increasing tensions between 'high' and 'middlebrow' spheres for *Time and Tide*'s circle of women writers and critics.

Notes

1. In October 1932 Rhondda explained in a letter to Vera Brittain that she was holding her story for a future issue as the paper aims 'to achieve some kind of balance between the number of men and women writers' and the next already had several women contributors in it. MR to VB, 4 October 1932. VB Papers.

2. David Doughan, for example, has argued that *Time and Tide*'s acceptance 'into the world of "reputable" periodicals' was achieved 'only by losing most of its female organisation, to the point where a feminist of the standing and commitment of Cicely Hamilton could [. . .] contribute a regular review column "Men and Books"' (1987: 261).

3. MR to DS 2, September 1930. DS Papers.

4. Ellen Ross discusses as a distinctively modern phenomenon the extension of women's earlier entrance into the public sphere through education and employment to international movements and causes (2015: 66).

5. MR to Rebecca West, 1 June 1931. RW Tulsa.

6. Letter from Rhondda to Holtby, September 1933, WH Collection [WH/5/5.17/04/01a].

7. In its own coverage of the trial *Time and Tide* adopted a liberal line in defence of Hall's novel, and was vocal in its condemnation of literary and press censorship. See articles collected in Oram and Turnbull (183–90).

8. Diana Hopkinson, secretary to the Labour MP Ellen Wilkinson, refers to *Time and Tide* in these terms in her memoir *The Incense-Tree* (1968: 151).

9. The village was Agay, near Cannes, where another of *Time and Tide*'s directors, Rebecca West, had also rented a villa (Glendinning 1987: 123).

10. King George V fell seriously ill in November 1928 and never fully recovered.

11. Letter from Margaret Rhondda to Rebecca West, 1 June 1931. RW Tulsa.

12. MR to GBS, 2 March 1930 and WH to GBS, 21 October 1929. GBS Collection.

13. In its issue of 14 March 1931, *Time and Tide* carried an article on theatre reform based on an interview with Shaw conducted by Winifred Holtby.

14. MR to DS, 10 January 1932. DS Papers.

15. See Rhondda's 'Reminiscences of an Editor' in *Time and Tide*'s twenty-first birthday issue (17 May 1941: 398).

16. MR to DS, 8 March 1931. DS Papers.

17. Lewis launched his magazine *The Enemy* in 1926.

18. Lewis wrote the articles following his visit to Berlin in November 1930, not long after the Nazi success in the elections of 14 September. As Alan Munton observes: 'the alarm felt throughout Europe apparently didn't reach Lewis, whose tendency to get his information almost exclusively from newspapers did not do him a service' (2010: 486–7).

19. See Otto M. Nelson (1978) for a discussion of this magazine. Rhondda stated in an interview with the *Observer* that rights to reproduce these cartoons had been sought 'in order to get the German standpoint on international affairs' (26 Feb 1933: 8). The first cartoon from *Simplicissimus* appeared in *Time and Tide*'s issue of 4 March 1933, less than two weeks before the magazine's offices were sacked by Nazi storm troopers.

20. Both Mitchison and West reviewed Lewis's work in *Time and Tide*.

21. WH Collection [WH/5/5.17/05/015].

22. In the same summer Lewis was working to complete his drawings for his 'Thirty Personalities' exhibition at the Lefevre Gallery in October that year, and among his sitters were Mitchison, Rhondda and West.

23. Vera Brittain also records that sometimes Holtby 'would have several contributions in one weekly issue of *Time and Tide* alone – an unsigned leading article, two or three unsigned notes, a signed essay or story, a book review inscribed "W.H.," and even, for about a year between 1929 and 1930, dramatic criticisms under the pseudonym of "Corbyn H. Wood"' (1940: 302).

24. The LNU was created to popularise the League of Nations (formed at the Paris Peace Conference of 1919) and the new principles of international relations that came with it. It became the largest and most influential society in the British peace movement (Birn 1981: 1–3).

25. This issue of *Foreign Affairs* is preserved loosely inside the 1927 volume of *Time and Tide* held by the University Library of Cambridge. Other supplements survive among library holdings of *Time and Tide* in this way (such as the Regent Institute leaflets discussed in Chapter 6), and according to library staff this is the most likely explanation for the preservation of the *Foreign Affairs* issue here.

26. Angell approached Rhondda early in 1931 to propose this 'mutually beneficial arrangement', suggesting that *Time and Tide* might pick up 6,000 or so of his nett sales and subscriptions while he would be relieved of editorial work for which he had no time. NA to MR, 2 January 1931. NA Papers.

27. The first Travel Number was published with *Time and Tide*'s issue of 10 June 1927. The periodical initially published two travel supplements a year (Spring/Summer and Winter), and from 1930 one annually (in April or May) until 1935.

28. Sorabji's 'The Sweetstuff in-the-Mouth Ceremony' appeared in *Time and Tide*'s issue of 9 August 1929, and 'Maiji Sahiba. A Jat Princess' in its issue of 6 September 1929. Cullen's poems were from *The Black Christ and Other Poems* (1929).

29. 'The Negro' by David Stewart was published in *Time and Tide*'s issue of 27 September 1929 and was collected in a *Time and Tide Album* (1932) edited by E. M. Delafield (see Chapter 6).

30. As Sara Blair notes, many of these visitors made their headquarters in Bloomsbury, drawn by the University College in Gower Street and by the reading room at the British Museum (2004: 821).

31. In a letter dated 5 November 1931 Rhondda told Angell: 'I shall do all in my power to back you in other parts of the paper since I so thoroughly believe in what you have to say.' NA Papers.
32. See Haslam (1999: 173–210) for a discussion of the leading role of women's organisations on disarmament.
33. Japan withdrew from the League of Nations in March and Germany in October. 'A Programme for Peace' published in *Time and Tide*'s issue of 30 December 1933 evidences the periodical's efforts to keep the Disarmament Conference alive.
34. MR to WH, 6 October 1933. WH Collection [WH/5/5.17/04/01f].
35. WH to VB, 8 March 1932. WH Collection [WH/6/6.1/13/05g].
36. The letter is dated 20 October 1933.
37. *Time and Tide* printed a letter from Pound on the subject of Married Women's Nationality in its issue of 31 January 1930.
38. EP to TB, 23 September [1933], WH Collection [WH/5/5.20/04/01f]. Pound's profound opposition to war, and to economic systems which encourage it, would have resonated with Holtby and others among *Time and Tide*'s core collaborators, though the faith he placed in C. H. Douglas's theory of Social Credit would not. See Leon Surette (2010) for a discussion of Pound and economics.
39. MR to WH, 6 October 1933. WH Collection [WH/5/5.17/04/01f].
40. This letter, dated 9 November 1922, is signed by *Time and Tide*'s assistant editor, Phoebe Fenwick Gaye. EP Papers.
41. EP Papers, n.d.
42. EP to MR, 1 September [1935]. EP Papers.
43. See Serenella Zanotti (2010) for a discussion of Pound and fascism.
44. See Clay (2010: 83–5) for a discussion of this piece.
45. MR to GBS, 1 November 1934. GBS Collection.
46. This novel was in fact the occasion of Wells's letter quoted above: the paragraph Wells objected to was an item in *Time and Tide*'s 'Review of the Week' which noted the resemblance between Sir Bussy Woodcock and Lord Beaverbrook.
47. See Lisa Colletta (2003: 28) for a summary of Freud's theorisation of condensation and displacement as two major features of the joking process.
48. See Patrick Parrinder's entry on Wells in *The Oxford Dictionary of National Biography*.
49. See Simon Dentith (2000: 1–9) for a discussion of the part played by intonation in parody's adoption of an 'evaluative attitude' in relation to precursor texts.
50. Susan Kent notes that 'postwar feminism, both "old" and "new," eschewed even the slightest hint of sex war' (1993: 136).
51. Rose Macaulay was unappreciative. Reviewing *Women in Love* she noted 'the beauty of some of his prose rhythms' but ultimately declared him 'absurd' (1 July 1921: 629). Mary Agnes Hamilton, reviewing *Aaron's Rod*, acknowledged that Lawrence 'undoubtedly possesses

a streak of that thing we call genius' but was put off by what she described as 'his intensely irritating mannerisms' (7 July 1922: 641).

52. The first poem from *Pansies*, 'When the Ripe Fruit Falls', appeared on the very day (5 July 1929) that thirteen of Lawrence's paintings were seized in a police raid.

53. *Time and Tide* printed one poem a week from 28 January to 22 April 1933. The story 'Two Marriages' was published as a supplement to *Time and Tide*'s issue of 24 March 1934.

54. In June 1933 *Time and Tide*'s printers refused to print a story treating the subject of prostitution ('I Wanna Woman'), submitted to the paper by the Irish playwright Sean O' Casey. Rhondda discussed the controversy in the periodical's 'Notes on the Way' and the printers' decision was criticised by many respondents in *Time and Tide*'s correspondence columns.

55. In *Home and a Changing Civilisation* Mitchison charged Lawrence's *Fantasia and the Unconscious* with being 'really about men owning women, men being leaders and masters' (1934: 142). In her own contribution to John Lane's Twentieth-Century Library series, *Women and a Changing Civilisation*, Holtby compared the character Lilly in Lawrence's *Aaron's Rod* with the leader of the German Nazi party, General Goering, and the leader of the British Union of Fascists, Oswald Mosley (1934: 159).

56. See Charles Freeman (2004: 123) for a discussion of these symbols and their significance in Minoan ritual and worship.

57. Discussions of this literature include Joannou (1995), Montefiore (1996) and Suh (2009).

Chapter 6

'The Enjoyment of Literature': Women Writers and the 'Battle of the Brows'

In March 1928, just seven weeks after *Time and Tide* published its first contribution from Virginia Woolf and while readers continued to debate 'The Future of the Press' in the periodical's correspondence pages (see Chapter 4), the author of *Time and Tide*'s regular 'In the Tideway' feature reflected ironically on the changes currently taking place in the paper: 'Of course what is really wrong with TIME AND TIDE is that it is too Highbrow. I mean what we all really want is more *Social News*' (23 Mar 1928: 294). Proceeding to list numerous examples of 'Social News' presented by the newspapers this week (from the departure for the Near East of a Mrs Routledge due to an attempted burglary on her Hyde Park home, to the names of the guests at a recent At Home to discuss the organisation of a charity matinee in aid of a 'Lost Cats' Home') 'North Wind' concludes teasingly: 'We are terribly remiss. I mean, these are really important things, aren't they?' As discussed in the previous two chapters *Time and Tide* was working energetically in this period to move out of the 'women's paper' category and in this piece *Time and Tide*'s columnist both identifies and dismisses the risk the periodical ran of appearing 'too Highbrow' in the eyes of its target audience as it moved towards the intellectual sphere. The readers *Time and Tide* addresses here will, it is assumed, recognise the *un*importance of such items of 'Social News' compared with the periodical's own coverage of important developments in politics, literature and the arts, and thus share a common interest in accessing the perceived higher culture. At the same time the humour negotiates an element of uncertainty about the periodical's reception in the context of an evolving discourse about brows. By 1928, as Melissa Sullivan points out, 'the initial wave of the "battle of the brows" [had] commenced in full force' with the publication of Leonard Woolf's *Hunting the Highbrow* (1927) and J. B. Priestley's 'High, Low, Broad' (1927), and *Time and Tide*'s editors and contributors were inevitably 'plunged into' this battle (2011: 97–100). With particular reference to the ways in which these culture wars were manifest in the world of books, this chapter explores how *Time and Tide* navigated increasing tensions between 'high' and 'middlebrow' spheres, and succeeded in straddling both.

I begin by discussing a new 'Miscellany' section introduced by *Time and Tide* in January 1927 which housed, between its political pages and expanding book reviews section, the periodical's 'lighter' content. With particular reference to E. M. Delafield's *The Diary of a Provincial Lady* (1930), first serialised in these columns in 1929 and 1930, I argue that *Time and Tide*'s Miscellany created and legitimised a place for the 'feminine middlebrow', both promoting celebrated women authors and offering publishing space to aspiring women writers. According to Rosa Maria Bracco, in the 1930s 'middlebrow fiction enjoyed unprecedented prestige', boosted by a range of middlebrow institutions and practices (including Book-of-the-Month clubs, reviewing and advertisement) geared towards its wider distribution (1990: 62; 48). However, in the same decade the institutions and practices of 'University English' assumed a new authoritative role in the cultural field, passing critical judgements on the middlebrow and redefining literary criticism. As Tory Young observes, 'English literature as a university subject was constructed *against* middlebrow fiction' (2004: 187), and while the interwar period produced a large number of well-regarded and commercially successful authors, their works have not endured like those of their modernist contemporaries. The years between 1932 and 1935 represent a period of instability in *Time and Tide*'s book review pages as the periodical sought to satisfy the needs of both highbrow intellectuals and general readers. With reference to a new feature from 1932 entitled 'Men and Books' and the contributions of *Time and Tide*'s first two literary editors, in the second part of this chapter I explore the periodical's negotiation of a widening schism between an older 'amateur' critical tradition identified with the Victorian sage or 'man of letters' and the new professionalisation of criticism concomitant with the development of English as a university subject.

Miscellany and the 'feminine middlebrow'

At the end of January 1927, just three issues after the paper began to appear in its new format (see Chapter 4), *Time and Tide* introduced a new heading in its contents page: 'Miscellany'. Positioned between the periodical's political pages and expanding book reviews section these columns typically comprised one or two 'light' contributions, usually in the form of short stories, sketches or familiar essays. *Time and Tide*'s chief competitor, the *New Statesman*, also carried a named Miscellany section, and this formal designation of space for lighter fare is thus another marker of the periodical's rebranding by association with the leading weeklies. In contrast to the *New Statesman*, however, where women's fiction was 'severely underrepresented' (Abu-Manneh 2011: 121), *Time and Tide* is striking for the prominence it accorded to leading women writers of the period.[1] In May 1927 *Time and Tide*'s Miscellany contained a short story by the late Katherine Mansfield, and over the next few years these pages hosted short stories by a growing number of respected and popular women writers including Stella Benson, Elizabeth Bowen, E. M. Delafield, Winifred Holtby, Naomi Mitchison, Kate O'Brien, Jean Rhys, Vita Sackville-West, Sylvia Townsend Warner and Dorothy Whipple.[2] Revisionist accounts of modernism, feminist publishing and recent recuperative scholarship on the 'middlebrow' have done much to restore these writers to visibility among present-day readerships.[3] In their own time these writers were widely read, particularly by middle-class women who formed the largest constituency within this sector of the fiction-reading public. My argument here is that in the space it created for contemporary women writers *Time and Tide*'s Miscellany negotiated a position for the 'feminine middlebrow', defined by Nicola Humble as 'works largely read by and in some sense addressed to women readers' (2001: 14). Thus, at the very same time that the periodical was seeking access to the highbrow sphere (literary and political), and working to rebrand itself as a general-audience intellectual weekly, its Miscellany section defended and promoted middlebrow culture and operated to attract, and sustain its relationship with, its core female readership.

Time and Tide's first Miscellany section, in its issue of 28 January 1927, contained a short story by Sylvia Townsend Warner ('I am Come into my Garden') who contributed several stories, poems and light articles to the periodical in the late 1920s and early 1930s. The leading item, however, was contributed by a writer who would play a far larger role in *Time and Tide*'s development, the novelist E. M. Delafield. Delafield, who joined *Time and Tide*'s board of directors in December 1927, had been a contributor of book reviews and occasional short stories and sketches since 1922 (her value to the paper as a skilled parodist, too, has been discussed in Chapter 5). According to Rhondda, writing later in *Time and Tide*'s columns, she was 'the perfect provider of good "lights"' (13 Dec 1947: 1346) and from 1927 until her death in 1943 something by Delafield appeared in the periodical virtually every week. Delafield's contribution to *Time and Tide*'s inaugural Miscellany pages illustrates the direct appeal she had for women readers. The first in an eight-part series entitled 'Imperfect Recollections from the Library of my Youth' the piece offers a humorous account of the famous gibbet scene of Martha Mary Sherwood's *The History of the Fairchild Family*, one of the most popular books for children in the Victorian period. Establishing for the series a tone of wry affection for the books of her childhood, the piece gently mocks the strong moral overtones of the feminine didactic tradition and at the same time draws her own modern-day audience into intimate relation through a shared literary heritage. As one reader wrote, in a letter of appreciation, 'they were the books of my (long past) childhood also' (25 Mar 1927: 290). As Sullivan observes, Delafield's enthusiasm for popular Victorian women's and children's literature is a hallmark of her middlebrow identity (2011: 106). But in her work for *Time and Tide* she also expanded the middlebrow as 'an alternative arena of "legitimate culture"' alongside the highbrow, resulting in 'a lively evolution within both her own writing and that of the periodical' (Sullivan 2011: 97–9). This dynamic relationship between the writer and the magazine is particularly evident in the series which was later published in book form and remains her best-known work, *The Diary of a Provincial Lady* (1930).

This quintessentially 'feminine middlebrow' fiction began as a series in *Time and Tide*'s Miscellany pages in December 1929. As Delafield later recalled, the title of 'Diary of a Provincial Lady' presented itself following a *Time and Tide* luncheon she had come from her Devonshire home to attend, almost certainly the housewarming luncheon held in *Time and Tide*'s new Bloomsbury offices in November 1929 and presided over by George Bernard Shaw (see Chapter 5).[4] 'My experiences at the luncheon were a little strange', she writes. Placed beside 'a well-known actor' on one side, who conversed in disconcertingly familiar terms about the marital affairs of some mutual acquaintances, and a woman on the other who apparently mistook her for the popular romance novelist Ethel M. Dell,

Delafield left early for a sale of sponges at a shop in High Holborn, a detail she remembers because while one or two others left early 'to meet an editor, or call on a publisher, or go to a symphony concert, or sit on a committee [. . .] Nobody, excepting myself, was going to buy a household article – and try to buy it cheaply, at that' (1937: 124–5). The anecdote illustrates a key tension which is the source of so much of the humour in the Diary: that is, a tension between the everyday concerns of the ordinary woman, a mother and housewife, beset by household responsibilities and difficulties, and the supposedly superior concerns of those with loftier ambitions (political and cultural) represented by *Time and Tide*'s distinguished guests and London set. While the luncheon, as discussed in Chapter 5, was part of the periodical's strategy for expanding its scope, readership and brow, Delafield's early departure in order to buy a sponge highlights the more mundane preoccupations of the everyday with which *The Diary of a Provincial Lady* is so centrally concerned. According to Delafield, her idea was to write 'a perfectly straightforward account of the many disconcerting facets presented by everyday life to the average woman' (1937: 125). As such the series worked to bridge what Barbara Green has described as 'the gap between the ideals of modern feminism and the distractions of daily life' (2017: 243) while forging an important connection between the London-based periodical and provincial middle-class women.

As a housewife and mother living in rural Devon, Delafield was the ideal contributor for widening *Time and Tide*'s reach amongst ordinary women readers outside London. Moreover, as an active member of the National Federation of Women's Institutes (WI), one of the largest and most influential organisations representing housewives and mothers in this period (Beaumont 2013: 3), she was ideally placed to mediate *Time and Tide*'s feminism for women who may never have questioned traditional gender roles or envisioned themselves as feminist, but who were committed nonetheless to improving the position and status of women in society.[5] As Caitríona Beaumont has shown, the WI along with other major voluntary and popular women's organisations attached great importance to the concept of active citizenship, encouraging members to participate in local and national politics and involve themselves in public life.[6] With its housewife heroine, whose literary ambitions and activities with her local Women's Institute extend the traditional female role beyond exclusively domestic concerns, 'The Diary of a Provincial Lady' worked consistently with *Time and Tide*'s feminist discourse by expanding women readers' social and political horizons. At the same time, *Time and Tide*'s own feminist ideals are not immune from the Provincial Lady's humorous treatment, as in the following characteristically wry aside: '(Query, mainly rhetorical: Why are non-professional women, if married and with children, so frequently referred to as "leisured"? Answer comes there none.)' (29 Nov 1930: 1494). In this direct echo of *Time and Tide*'s 'leisured women' articles and ensuing high-profile public debate (see Chapter 1), the Provincial Lady's 'query' operates as an in-joke which relies for its meaning both on the periodical's feminist community of readers with shared interests in the professional sphere *and* on a female constituency of non-professional women. This is a kind of self-referentiality which works to build *Time and Tide*'s readership base from across different women's groups or communities of interest, and contributes to what Green describes as Delafield's 'complex dialogue with feminist thinkers on the relationship of women's domestic and professional life' (2017: 246). The instalment continues with 'Miss P.' remonstrating that the Provincial Lady has 'no *right* to let [her]self become a beast of burden, with no interests beyond the nursery and the kitchen', and the series ended two weeks later with an entry full of intended irony:

> All so-called leisure hours spent in reading aloud, telling stories, measuring out half-teaspoonfuls of Dinneford's Magnesia, sorting and mending clothes, and looking for the Iodine.
>
> Can therefore only decide, however reluctantly, to lay aside Diary for present, it being well known that primary duty of every woman, however inefficient, is to be a Wife and a Mother. THE END. (13 Dec 1930: 1570)

As Green notes, 'Laying aside the Diary in order to perform the duties of Wife and Mother [. . .] is most certainly not a sincere gesture' (2017: 262). This entry did not appear in the book version which, advertised in the same issue, testifies to the possibility for achievement beyond the domestic sphere.

As well as mediating *Time and Tide*'s modern feminism, Delafield's 'Diary of a Provincial Lady' also mediated the periodical's new orientation towards the highbrow sphere in its coverage of literature and the arts. More than once the Provincial Lady registers anxiety about high culture, as in this example from the very first instalment:

> Am asked what I think of *Harriet Hume* but am unable to say, as I have not read it. Have a depressed feeling that this is going to be

another case of *Orlando* about which was perfectly able to talk most intelligently until I read it, and found myself unfortunately unable to understand any of it. (6 Dec 1929: 8)

Harriet Hume, often described as Rebecca West's most modernist novel, had been reviewed prominently in *Time and Tide*'s pages a few weeks earlier.[7] Its alignment in the Provincial Lady's mind with Virginia Woolf's *Orlando* conveys her unease about highbrow literature in general; as Faye Hammill observes, as a reader Delafield's heroine is defined by her middlebrow tastes, finding modernist writing difficult, and displaying a strong preference for realist fiction (2007: 194). But here and elsewhere Delafield uses the multi-layered form of her text to open up an ironic space, and in this gesture of self-deprecation she is both allowing her readers to be more highbrow than the Provincial Lady is, and comforting those who aren't. This is particularly evident in a sequence of references to an exhibition of Italian Art at the Royal Academy, the first of which comes as the Provincial Lady, in the middle of organising a game of 'Oranges and Lemons' at a children's party, tries to give 'intelligent attention to remarks from a visiting mother concerning Exhibition of Italian Pictures at Burlington House. Find myself telling her how marvellous I think them, although in actual fact have not yet seen them at all' (31 Jan 1930: 139).[8] Just three weeks earlier *Time and Tide* had carried a full-page article on the exhibition by its new art critic, Gwendolen Raverat. Positioned on the facing page to Delafield's 'Diary of a Provincial Lady' the article declared that: 'now we have in London masterpiece after masterpiece of the very greatest painters that ever have been in all the world' (10 Jan 1930: 49) (Figure 6.1). Four weeks later *Time and Tide* printed a second article by Raverat on the exhibition (7 Feb 1930), equally fulsome in praise and indicative of the periodical's new critical interest in the visual arts as well as literature. Delafield's heroine, however, is strangely reluctant to visit the exhibition despite all her intentions to do so, and in the following excerpts her predicament builds to great comic effect.

The first excerpt, from an instalment of the Diary published two months after Raverat's second review, locates the Provincial Lady in London in search of a new maid:

In the meantime, says Rose, what about the Italian Art Exhibition? She herself has already been four times. I say Yes, yes – it is one of the things I have come to London *for*, but should prefer to go earlier in the day. Then, says Rose, the first thing to-morrow morning? To this

48 TIME AND TIDE JANUARY 10, 1930

DIARY OF A PROVINCIAL LADY

By E. M. DELAFIELD.

December 11th. Robert, this morning, complains of insufficient breakfast. Cannot feel that porridge, scrambled eggs, toast, marmalade, scones, brown bread, and coffee give adequate grounds for this, but admit that porridge is slightly burnt. How impossible ever to encounter burnt porridge without vivid recollections of Jane Eyre at Lowood School, say I parenthetically! This literary allusion not a success. Robert suggests ringing for Cook, and have greatest difficulty in persuading him that this course utterly disastrous.

Eventually go myself to kitchen, in ordinary course of events, and approach subject of burnt porridge circuitously and with utmost care. Cook replies, as I expected, with expressions of astonishment and incredulity, coupled with assurances that kitchen range is again at fault. She also says that new double-saucepan, fish-kettle, and nursery tea-cups are urgently required. Make enquiries regarding recently-purchased nursery tea-set and am shown one handle without cup, saucer in three pieces, and cup from which large semi-circle has apparently been bitten. Feel that Mademoiselle will be hurt if I pursue enquiries further. (Note: Extreme sensibility of the French sometimes makes them difficult to deal with).

Read Life and Letters of distinguished woman recently dead, and am struck, as so often, by difference between her correspondence and that of less distinguished women. Immense and affectionate letters from celebrities on every other page, epigrammatic notes from literary and political acquaintances, poetical assurances of affection and admiration from husband, and even infant children. Try to imagine Robert writing in similar strain in the (improbable) event of my attaining celebrity, but fail. Dear Vicky equally unlikely to commit her feelings (if any) to paper.

Robin's letter arrives by second post, and am delighted to have it as ever, but cannot feel that laconic information about boy—unknown to me—called Baggs, having been swished, and Mr. Gompshaw, visiting master, being kept away by Sore Throat—is on anything like equal footing with lengthy and picturesque epistles received almost daily by subject of biography, whenever absent from home.

Remainder of mail consists of one bill from chemist—(*Mem*: Ask Mademoiselle why *two* tins of Gibb's Toothpaste within ten days)—illiterate postcard from piano-tuner, announcing visit to-morrow, and circular concerning True Temperance.

Inequalities of Fate very curious. Should like, on this account, to believe in Reincarnation. Spend some time picturing to myself completely renovated state of affairs, with, amongst other improvements, total reversal of relative positions of Lady B. and myself.

(*Query*: Is thought on abstract questions ever a waste of time?)

December 12th. Robert, still harping on topic of yesterday's breakfast, says suddenly Why Not a Ham? to which I reply austerely that a ham is on order, but will not appear until arrival of R's brother William and his wife, for Christmas visit. Robert, with every manifestation of horror, says Are William and Angela coming to us for *Christmas*? This attitude absurd, as invitation was given months ago, at Robert's own suggestion.

(*Query* here becomes unavoidable:—Does not a misplaced optimism exist, common to all mankind, leading on to false conviction that social engagements, if dated sufficiently far ahead, will never really materialize?)

Vicky and Mademoiselle return from walk with small white-and-yellow kitten, alleged by them homeless and starving. Vicky fetches milk, and becomes excited. Agree that kitten shall stay "for to-night," but feel that this is weak.

(*Mem.*: Remind Vicky to-morrow that Daddy does not like cats).

Mademoiselle becomes very French, on subject of cats generally, and am obliged to check her. She is *blessée*, and all three retire to schoolroom.

December 13th. Robert says out of the question to keep stray kitten. Existing kitchen cat more than enough. Gradually modifies this attitude under Vicky's pleadings. All now depends on whether kitten is male or female. Vicky and Mademoiselle declare this is known to them, and kitten already christened Napoleon. Find myself unable to enter into discussion on the point in French. The gardener takes opposite view to Vicky's and Mademoiselle's. They thereupon re-christen the kitten, seen playing with an old tennis-ball, as Helen Wills.

Robert's attention, perhaps fortunately, diverted by mysterious trouble with the water-supply. He says The Ram has Stopped. (This sounds to me Biblical.)

Give Mademoiselle a hint that H. Wills should not be encouraged to put in injudicious appearances downstairs.

December 14th. Ram resumes activities. Helen Wills still with us.

December 16th. Very stormy weather, floods out, and many trees prostrated at inconvenient angles. Call from Lady Boxe, who says she is off to the South of France next week, as she Must have Sunshine. She asked Why I do not go there too, and likens me to piece of chewed string, which I feel to be entirely inappropriate and rather offensive figure of speech, though perhaps kindly meant.

Why not just pop into the train, enquires Lady B., pop across France, and pop out into Blue Sky, Blue Sea, and Summer Sun? Could make perfectly comprehensive reply to this, but do not do so, question of expense having evidently not crossed Lady B's horizon. (*Mem.*: Interesting subject for debate at Women's Institute, perhaps: That Imagination is Incompatible with Inherited Wealth. On second thoughts, though, fear this has a socialistic trend.)

Reply to Lady B. with insincere professions of liking England very much even in the winter. She begs me not to let myself become parochially-minded.

Departure of Lady B. with many final appeals to me to reconsider South of France. Make civil pretence, which deceives neither of us, of wavering, and promise to ring her up in the event of a change of mind.

(*Query*: Cannot many of our moral lapses from Truth be frequently charged upon the tactless persistence of others?)

JANUARY 10, 1930 TIME AND TIDE 49

First Impressions

The Italian Exhibition

By GWENDOLEN RAVERAT.

LAST week, in a train, two perfectly beautiful young men got into my carriage—I think because all the first-class carriages were full. "Well, you know Bill," said one lovely creature, as he put his bunch of pheasants in the rack, "I don't think I shall like this Italian Exhibition as much as I did the Dutch one: all these Primitives, you know; I'm so *bored* with 'em." "So am I" said the other perfect one, "dead sick of 'em." But then a low-class little man in the corner suddenly struck in, and in the best foreign English told them how wrong they were, and began an immense list of all the wonders that were to be at Burlington House. I think he was German; and though we really were a pretty well-educated carriageful, his knowledge was so prodigious that Bill was obliged to change the subject as soon as he could.

Well, at the moment when Bill spoke, I felt that I agreed with him—hopelessly inferior as I felt, I agreed with him, and I had long agreed with him. A vision rose before me of rows and rows of pale, stiff madonnas; unpleasant, microcephalous infants; ill-articulated angels; damp piety. It was more than enough to quench the spark of religious fire which burns precariously in my breast. "They ought to be left in the churches", I thought, "Religion alone isn't art. However, there'll be other things: there'll be some Titians." And in this state of mind I went to the Exhibition. I had no doubts about the later men, but I did feel there might be too many angels for me in the earlier rooms. I think some other people may have felt the same. I suppose we have seen too many second-rate Primitives, second-rate both in execution and in fervour; for second-rate fervour is rather hard to bear. Dutch painting is nearer to us; it is easier to admire a good dull picture of a cook and a carrot, than an unsuccessful angel on a gold background. Angels are rather a bore, but cooks are eternally interesting; for we are very far away from mediæval faith.

But when the faith has fired the painter and the real thing is there, then we know it at once. For as usual I was quite wrong, and I knew it as soon as I got inside Burlington House. Here is the real thing; and if my friend Bill has been yet, he too will have recanted. For here there is no doubt at all. These Primitives are the real thing. And the splendours of the whole show simply take away one's breath. It is far finer than even the Dutch Exhibition, and I did not think it would be possible to say that. But while the Dutch have only one supreme genius—for I cannot quite put Vermeer into the highest class of all—*all* the other greatest painters of the old world, except Rubens and Holbein, were Italians; and now we have here in London masterpiece after masterpiece of the very greatest painters that ever have been in all the world. It is impossible to write about it, and it would be as ridiculous to attempt it, as it would be to write one paragraph about the whole of European literature. One passes from the half-articulate passion of the Primitives, to Pagan beauty-worship, and then into the gorgeous life of the full Renaissance: a life so rich that poverty or sickness seem not to exist; a life where men were so sure of themselves, that if they happened to have a broken nose they felt it a distinction to be emphasized and envied. And the power of the Renaissance seems to last, altered but hardly lessened, right through the eighteenth century down to the death of Longhi in 1813. He is the last great painter, and that is the end—for the present.

I think that the best thing to do is simply to write about a few of the less obvious or less-known things which struck me on my first visit—for one can safely leave the well-known pictures to themselves.

In the second room, the spiritual passion of the Masaccio Crucifixion (lent by Naples) makes it one of the finest things in the whole exhibition. Here are two small Castagnos, very much to be noticed. Castagno was a very wicked man, he used to poison his enemies; and in his painting there always seems to be a kind of devilish fierceness, such as there is in some Spanish work. It is most terribly alive. Here, too, are some surprising Botticellis: a very beautiful small Annunciation, the Virgin in a cool, arched loggia, in which the tone and light are lovely; and then the very unexpected Derelitta. There is always in the tender-hearted Botticelli a possibility of sentimentality and over-prettiness, kept in check by his decorative qualities. But La Derelitta, the forlorn girl weeping outside the palace door, is painted without sentimentality—it is only surprising that anyone at that time should have chosen such a subject. In the great room the Birth of Venus does not look quite happy. It is the only picture which somehow does not look in e. (The Michael Angelo David looks far more beautiful here in the Central Hall, than ever it did in the Bargello.) But certainly Venus was not born in England, so perhaps it is natural that the picture should look a little lost.

In this long room, the masterpieces are in rows; I will only note how wonderful are the Raphael portraits. I spent a long time, too, wondering why the Titian portraits are the most tremendous in the world; what is there in the placing of the subject on the canvas which makes just all the difference between these Titians and the extremely fine Tintoretto portraits? It is the placing and the pose which makes the difference, restrained and subtle as it is. But where Tintoretto would have painted a wonderful but straightforward portrait, Titian's Paul III glows and glowers for ever like a vulture, imprisoned in the cage of his weary flesh. The Duke and Duchess of Urbino, by Piero della Francesca, are extremely fine, and the little pictures on the other side may perhaps give some faint idea of his frescoes. In the next room, are Cosimo Tura, and some very interesting fragments of a large picture by Signorelli. In room No. V, is a screen on which are hung some of the most important things here, collected from the ends of the earth: two small Mantegnas from private collections, very beautiful; a lovely Masaccio birth-scene; a Ghirlandaio portrait; four little Botticellis (from Philadelphia) and a most exquisite tiny Raphael from Budapest. In room VI, mor Titians, splendid Tintorettos—a great, noble Deposition, an Adam and Eve and several very exciting small compositions (the Marriage of Cana, and the death of St. Mark). In room VII is a charming Shepherd and Cattle by a doubtful hand, and then one of the great surprises: a self-portrait by Coreggio, which in depth of feeling and perfection of execution is better than any portrait here, except one or two of Titian's. And it is as good as they are, in its own, astonishingly modern, way.

Figure 6.1 'The Diary of a Provincial Lady' and 'The Italian Exhibition', *Time and Tide* 10 Jan 1930: 48–9. Reproduced with the permission of The William Ready Division of Archives and Research Collections, McMaster University Library

> I reply, with every sign of reluctance, that to-morrow morning *must* be devoted to Registry Offices. Well, says Rose, when *shall* we go? Let us, urge I, settle that a little later on, when I know better what I am doing. Can see that Rose thinks anything but well of me, but she is too tactful to say more. Quite realise that I shall have to go to the Italian Exhibition sooner or later, and am indeed quite determined to do so, but feel certain that I shall understand nothing about it when I do get there, and shall find myself involved in terrible difficulties when asked my impressions afterwards. (11 Apr 1930: 476)

The next day the Provincial Lady continues her round of more mundane pursuits: visiting Registry Offices, shopping for dresses, treatment at a Beauty Parlour and the purchase of 'Foundation Cream, rouge, powder and lipstick'. The Italian Art Exhibition, however, remains 'unvisited,' a shortcoming that is emphasised when on returning to Rose's flat in time to dress for dinner Rose tells her 'that she spent the afternoon at the Italian Exhibition' (476). She is temporarily let off the hook when she discovers at a dinner party with Rose's friends that the 'Editor of well-known literary weekly [. . .] has *not* visited the Italian Exhibition' (18 Apr 1930: 506), a thinly veiled reference to Rhondda and *Time and Tide* which permits both the Provincial Lady (and, importantly, the readers of the periodical in which the serial is published) *not* to participate in a cultural experience otherwise presented as mandatory. But this comfort is short-lived. In the following instalment:

> Rather painful moment occurs when I suggest the Italian Exhibition to Rose, who replies – after a peculiar silence – that is now *over*. Can think of nothing whatever to say, and do not care for Rose's expression, so begin at once to discuss new novels with as much intelligence as I can muster. (25 Apr 1930: 536)

The Provincial Lady's quandary in relation to the Italian Exhibition provides a leitmotif for the middlebrow which *Punch* famously defined as 'people who are hoping that some day they will get used to the stuff they ought to like' (Brown and Grover 2012: 4), and reveals both the 'aspirational and disciplinary dimensions of middlebrow values' (Carter 2015: 352). Through its humour, however, and its sympathetic rather than condescending attitude towards its heroine, the Diary mediates potential anxieties among *Time and Tide*'s own readership as the periodical adopted a more highbrow position in its coverage of literature and art.

At the same time, in common with other middlebrow texts, Delafield's fictional diary makes distinctions between discriminating and undiscriminating readers, and works as a form of internal advertisement for the rebranded *Time and Tide* which it consistently positions as the superior weekly for the modern woman. For example, in one early instalment of the series, Delafield's heroine invokes an ongoing dialogue in *Time and Tide* about contemporary journalism:

> Immerse myself in illustrated weekly. Am informed by it that Lord Toto Finch (inset) is responsible for camera-study (herewith) of the Loveliest Legs in Los Angeles, belonging to well-known English Society girl, near relation (by the way) of famous racing peer, father of well-known Smart Set twins (portrait overleaf.) (*Query*: Is our popular Press going to the dogs?) Turn attention to short story, but give it up on being directed, just as I become interested, to page XLVIIb, which I am quite unable to locate. Become involved instead with suggestions for Christmas Gifts. (17 Jan 1930: 75)

In this humorous reflection on not only the content but also the form of the 'popular Press' Delafield's text invites readers to take up a position against 'Social News' and gossip typically associated with women readers, and to resist reading materials that are structurally designed to prevent serious and sustained engagement. As Green has argued, in Delafield's text periodicals repeatedly 'invite inattentive, scattered reading' (2017: 251); key here is that this critique also functions as an indirect promotion of the periodical in which the Diary was published. In its 1924 Publicity Week *Time and Tide* had prided itself on the fact that 'there is no searching among a maze of advertisements for the end of every article' (15 Aug 1924: 793), and an emphasis on solid reading matter for the 'thinking' woman reader was central to its repositioning as a leading 'journal of opinion' as we have seen (Chapter 4). Early in the second series 'The Provincial Lady in London' contains a more direct promotional reference to *Time and Tide* in a sequence which involves its heroine in the quest for a suitable school for her daughter. When eventually the 'Perfect school is discovered' it is the school's subscription to *Time and Tide* that provides the final seal of approval: 'Favourite periodical *Time and Tide* lies on table, and Rose, at an early stage, nods at me with extreme vehemence behind Principal's back' (7 Nov 1931: 1276). This use of the periodical as a signifier for educational and cultural distinction recalls *Time and Tide*'s deliberate promotional work on behalf of the intellectual weeklies which in the future, it claimed, would be found on the reading tables of all houses with 'any pretensions to culture' (28 Oct 1927: 956). Working with *Time and Tide*'s editorial discourse, Delafield's Diary once again operates as a form of internal marketing as the periodical worked to access the highbrow sphere.

While it is impossible to quantify the actual impact of the Diary on circulation and sales, *Time and Tide*'s correspondence columns provide material evidence of its popularity. In one letter of appreciation 'A Country Reader' asked that Delafield 'continue for many weeks to make helpless tears of merriment course down my cheeks' and in a compelling vindication of *Time and Tide*'s size and price increase declared: 'Your paper is the cheapest sixpennyworth on the market' (11 Apr 1930: 479). Another letter, in which a reader in India writes that she 'fl[ies] to read "the Diary" on mail days' evidences the periodical's global reach: 'The Provincial Lady is even my guide over gramophone records!' (18 Apr 1930: 509). When the series initially drew to a close in June 1930 it was attended, in Delafield's words, by a 'chorus of lamentation from readers'. This convinced both her and her publisher (Macmillan) that it would be worth issuing in book form, and on learning from her agent that the Book Society wished to make it a Book-of-the-Month choice Delafield agreed to write another 20,000 words to bring it to the required length (Delafield 1937: 128). In its issue of 27 September 1930 *Time and Tide* announced that it would be publishing further extracts from Delafield's 'Diary of a Provincial Lady'; these ran from 11 October to 13 December. In its 20 December issue both the published volume and Delafield's dramatic talents were afforded publicity in *Time and Tide*'s review columns; readers were also given a portrait of the author by Edmond Kapp, and treated to more of her humour in a parody of the novel by Delafield herself. The success of *The Diary of a Provincial Lady* marks the beginnings of Delafield's transformation into a literary celebrity (Hammill 2007), but it also provided more publicity for *Time and Tide*. Among the final diary entries in the extended book version (but *not* in *Time and Tide*), Delafield's heroine records the following:

Unknown benefactor sends me copy of new Literary Review, which seems to be full of personal remarks from well-known writers about other well-known writers. This perhaps more amusing to themselves than to the average reader. Moreover, competitions most alarmingly literary, and I return with immense relief to old friend *Time and Tide*. (1930: 117)

Appearing in a novel which was selected by the Book Society and went on to be a bestseller, this product placement advertises for an even larger audience that *Time and Tide* is not 'too Highbrow' for the average reader, unlike the 'new Literary Review' received by the Provincial Lady which seems to operate as an exclusive club and intimidates her with its 'most alarmingly literary' competitions. Invoking the tradition of women's magazines with their address to the reader as friend (Beetham 1996: 208), the Provincial Lady's 'immense relief' when she returns to *Time and Tide* also reassures the audience of this magazine that in its own literary turn the periodical hasn't parted with its core readership.

The Diary of a Provincial Lady was followed by three sequels, the first of which, 'The Provincial Lady in London' (published in book form as *The Provincial Lady Goes Further* in 1932), also saw its original publication in *Time and Tide* in a series which ran from October 1931 to April 1932. In this series Delafield's heroine is now the author of a successful first book, and as Sullivan observes the text continues its investigation of the relationship between 'high' and 'middlebrow' spheres by placing her 'within the depths of highbrow London' (2011: 113). Mirroring Delafield's own life, the Provincial Lady rents a flat on Doughty Street, Bloomsbury, and her accounts of the literary soirées and dinner parties she attends in this artistic neighbourhood provide another important means of mediating *Time and Tide*'s own Bloomsbury affiliations for ordinary readers in the provinces. In one of the funniest accounts among these, a story about a man who has 'written a book that will [. . .] undoubtedly be seized before publication and burnt' is told repeatedly by different guests to the point that the Provincial Lady has to fake astonishment, and her poise as she listens to another story (about the extraordinarily complicated marital affairs of several unknown persons) compares favourably with the increasingly bizarre behaviour of the bohemian 'Emma Hay' whose appearance in 'rose-coloured fish-net, gold lace, jewelled turban and necklace of large barbaric pebbles' marks her eccentricity (13 Feb 1932: 171). According to Humble, '[m]iddlebrow fiction laid claim to the highbrow by assuming an easy familiarity with its key texts and attitudes, while simultaneously caricaturing intellectuals as self-indulgent and naïve' (2001: 29). As a narrative strategy, it works well to embrace the full spectrum of high and middlebrow: the Provincial Lady, it is intimated, is knowing enough not to be fazed by Bloomsbury's literary culture, and to maintain an ironic distance from its self-regarding aspects. 'For Delafield', argues Sullivan, 'middlebrow writing should be [. . .] intelligent without being elitist' (2011: 108), and her perspective on Bloomsbury joins other elements of the periodical's discourse which challenged highbrow attitudes and assumptions about literature and art. In particular, Delafield's fictional diary resists a modernist discourse of creative genius as belonging to a natural elite, and participated – with *Time and Tide* – in what Christopher Hilliard (2006) has described as 'the democratisation of writing' in Britain between the wars.

According to Hilliard, 'if anything makes the place of literature and the arts in a society "democratic" it is a shared sense of the entitlement to participate in cultural activities' (2006: 6). Early in the first series the Provincial Lady muses incredulously 'Could I write a play myself? Could we all write plays, if only we had the time?' (24 Jan 1930: 109), and her literary success as the sequels unfold strongly suggests a reply in the affirmative.[9] As Sullivan notes, 'it is through her relationship with *Time and Tide* that the Provincial Lady first considers positioning herself as an author' and '[p]ossible ideas for more "professional" writing in her diary nearly always cast *Time and Tide* as her intended place of publication (aside from the occasional consideration of the Parish magazine)' (2011: 112). *Time and Tide*'s weekly competitions were one important way in which the periodical involved its readers as writers. Inviting readers to write on a given topic, usually in the form of a short story, prose piece or verse, these competitions actively encouraged women to extend their talents beyond the domestic sphere, and performed a pedagogical role through the competition page's editor who educated the reader in, for example, the intricacies of such verse forms as the triolet and commented on the merits and limitations of entries received.[10] In Delafield's 'Diary' the Provincial Lady frequently goes in for, and often wins, *Time and Tide*'s competitions; another example of the way in which the series functioned as a form of internal advertisement for the periodical, these references had the potential to materially boost not only readership but sales.[11] Moreover, the Diary itself served as inspiration for new topics, for example, a competition at the close of the first series which asked for 'A Page from the Diary of the Provincial Lady's Husband' (5 July 1930: 876).[12] Delafield's 'Diary of a Provincial Lady', therefore, as well as selling *Time and Tide* to ordinary women readers also positioned *Time and Tide* as a periodical for aspiring women writers. In a new series beginning in February 1931 on the subject of 'Women in Fiction' Delafield remarks:

> For the benefit of those who wish – however mistakenly – to become authors, the Editor of TIME AND TIDE has consented to publish a few examples of the kind of thing that readers expect, and authors supply, where women are concerned. (7 Feb 1931: 158)

At once satirising the presentation of female stereotypes and conventional plot-lines in varieties of contemporary fiction (in the first article, the dialect novel), the series also contributes to a discourse in *Time and Tide* that actively encouraged women to seize opportunities to write for publication within the literary and journalistic sphere.[13]

From the late 1920s *Time and Tide* frequently carried advertisements for schools and correspondence courses in journalism with such straplines as 'Wanted – Women Writers!' and 'Write Your Way to Success!'[14] With testimonials from women, and claims that 'hundreds of publications need the work of women contributors', some of this advertising specifically targeted *Time and Tide*'s female readership while publicising a real growth in opportunities for aspiring writers to receive financial remuneration for articles and short stories as the newspaper and periodical press expanded between the wars.[15] The key concept running through these advertisements was that of *learning* to write, as the following text from a leaflet promoting a free booklet on 'How to Succeed as a Writer' proclaims: 'You need not be a genius to become a successful writer. Many contributors who find a ready market for their articles and stories are men and women of average education. Training was the short cut to their mastery of the rules of effective writing.'[16] Directly opposing a modernist conception of authorial genius as belonging to a natural elite, the idea of 'training' to write encourages an egalitarian view shared by amateur writers' groups of the period 'that almost anyone could write creditably if willing to work at it' (Hilliard 2006: 7). Hilliard's reconstruction of an aspiring writers' movement which began in the 1920s and grew in tandem with the exponential rise of an entire literary advice industry provides an important context for *Time and Tide*'s address to readers not only as consumers but also producers of publishable writing.[17] Predominantly middle class in composition this movement attracted women in large numbers, many of whom lived outside the metropolitan centre in Britain's provincial towns and cities (Hilliard 2006: 4–8). According to Hilliard, a huge volume of copy published by London-based media 'came from outside the metropolitan neighbourhoods of Grub Street and Fleet Street from freelance writers in the provinces' (2006: 8). Although *Time and Tide* contains little in the way of biographical information about its more obscure contributors, undoubtedly its readers also became writers in the periodical's Miscellany columns which often carried pieces by 'unknown' aspiring writers alongside established literary figures.

In early 1932 *Time and Tide* announced, in a full-page publisher's advertisement in its 20 February issue, the publication of *The Time and Tide Album*, an anthology of short stories which had made their first appearance in the pages of this periodical. The volume was edited by E. M. Delafield, and of the thirty-seven stories collected, twenty-eight were by women writers and most of them date from the inauguration of *Time and Tide*'s Miscellany section in 1927. At once promoting the authors whose stories were collected here in book form (among them Stella Benson, Eleanor Farjeon, Cicely Hamilton, Winifred Holtby, Sylvia Lynd, Naomi Mitchison, Sylvia Townsend Warner and E. M. Delafield herself) the *Album* also promotes *Time and Tide* as a publisher of quality short fiction. Writing in a foreword to the collection, John Galsworthy is struck by 'the galaxy of names!' represented, and remarks that the book is surely 'calculated to make the reader say: "But why don't I take in *Time and Tide*?"' (Delafield 1932: 10). Capitalising on a 'boom' in short story anthologies to make the periodical's name more widely known (Baldwin 2013: 112), *The Time and Tide Album* is further evidence of *Time and Time*'s 'courage to advertise' and sophisticated use of modern publicity methods (see Chapter 4). It also consecrates and celebrates the middlebrow and *Time and Tide*'s circle of leading women writers at the start of a decade in which middlebrow fiction 'enjoyed unprecedented prestige' (Bracco 1990: 62). Over the next few years, however, the middlebrow was progressively subjected to assault and ridicule by a powerful group of intellectual critics. In 1932 F. R. Leavis launched his Cambridge literary journal, *Scrutiny*, which played a crucial role in the establishment of University English, and his wife Q. D. Leavis published *Fiction and the Reading Public* with its famous attack on the middlebrow and its indictment of public taste. Virginia Woolf's response to the middlebrow, in her letter addressed but never sent to the *New Statesman*, was also penned in this year.[18] In the second part of this chapter I explore how *Time and Tide* negotiated growing tensions between 'high' and 'middlebrow' spheres as it advanced further into its second decade.

'Men and books' and University English

In early 1932 an unsigned leader on 'The Book Society' in *Time and Tide*'s issue of 13 February produced a flurry of responses in the periodical's correspondence columns. The Book Society, as Nicola Wilson discusses, 'both epitomised and celebrated the middlebrow' though it is 'perhaps now best remembered for the withering attack it receives as one of the most offending "Middlemen" responsible for the "standardization" of second-rate taste in Q. D. Leavis's *Fiction and the Reading Public*' (2012: 245). Established in 1929 in imitation of America's successful Book-of-the-Month club, it was part of a 'virtual industry' that had grown around middlebrow fiction by the early 1930s, 'with Book of the Month Clubs, and with reviewing and advertising geared to the wider distribution of these novels' (Bracco 1990: 48). The concerns of intellectuals like Leavis 'sprang from the predominant place of middlebrow fiction in the literary world;' in her opinion, 'selection committees and middlebrow reviewers had contributed [. . .] to a standardization of literary values which precluded even the will to acquaint oneself with something more difficult but of higher quality' (Bracco 1990: 48). As such, these concerns return us to modernism's 'doxa of difficulty' and 'problem with pleasure' discussed in Chapter 3: unlike highbrow critics the Book Society was, as Wilson notes, 'proud [. . .] to validate the authors that the majority of people most enjoyed reading' (2012: 245). *Time and Tide*, from its earliest fiction reviews to its consecration of the 'feminine middlebrow' in its Miscellany columns, both defended and promoted the work of middlebrow women writers, as we have seen. This commitment to the middlebrow did not mean, however, a disregard for high 'standards' of judgement and taste. In its leading article *Time and Tide* took up the chief criticism of the Book Society, namely that in its choices and recommendations 'literary merit [. . .] has not always been given its due weight' and went on to examine the selections made by the Book Society since January 1930. Commending some choices and disagreeing with others, *Time and Tide* charged the Book Society with a certain unevenness in its selections and suggested that in some months 'it might well consider the desirability of protecting its own prestige and maintaining the necessary standard by refusing to make a choice at all' (13 Feb 1932: 166–7).

Over the next four weeks the Book Society was the subject of several letters from readers printed in *Time and Tide*'s correspondence columns.[19] Among these was a letter from Sylvia Lynd, one of *Time and Tide*'s early fiction reviewers and a founding member of the Book Society's Selection Committee. In this letter Lynd challenged *Time and Tide* on a number of points stated or implied in its article, from the 'special significance' it seemed to attach to the fact that the Book Society chooses more books from some publishers than from others, to its criticism of the Book Society's selection of unremarkable books which, if published alongside something better another month, may not have been thus recommended. Pointing out that these results are in fact no different from those which must inevitably arise in *Time and Tide*'s own reviewing space, Lynd went on to correct the misperception that the Book Society claims to choose 'the "best" book of the month', stating that: 'Our object was to extend the pleasure of reading and possessing books.' Her letter concludes:

> Might it not be more sensible to question the disinterestedness of the anonymous critics of the Book Society Committee rather than to question the integrity of Mr. Hugh Walpole, Professor Gordon, Miss Clemence Dane, Mr. J. B. Priestley, and, in all humility, your old contributor? (27 Feb 1932: 227)

Lynd's question contains more than a hint of reproach. She had stopped writing regular reviews for *Time and Tide* by the end of 1929, presumably on account of her new responsibilities with the Book Society. But it is also possible that she felt squeezed out as *Time and Tide* sought more access to the highbrow sphere. In addition to an editorial note, which explained that Lynd's letter was printed in full despite the fact that it 'exceed[ed] by a considerable amount' the space *Time and Tide* usually devoted to any one correspondent (227), Rhondda felt it necessary to write privately to Lynd to assure her that '*Time and Tide*, at least, has *never* either "questioned your integrity" or suspected you of "dark practices"'. She went on: 'Did you not take our leader for more of an attack than it actually was? It was intended rather as a critical analysis of what is for all people who read an extraordinarily interesting project'.[20] What is clear is that fault lines were opening up within *Time and Tide*'s periodical community as writers and critics felt compelled to take up positions on one side or other of the highbrow/middlebrow divide. In a letter from another 'old contributor', Rose Macaulay wrote in defence of both Lynd and the Book Society but concluded:

> Dark suggestions have been made that the Book Committee are paid for their services. But why not? If they are not, they are in a very odd position, quite unlike that of most literary critics and judges. For my part, it would require all the gold of France and America to induce me to sample more than an occasional new book, and these five intelligent and unfortunate people must dive continuously in the insipid flood that ceases not by day or night. (5 Mar 1932: 261)

With a characteristic mimicry of highbrow intellectualism that works to defuse contemporary anxieties about the mixing of literature and commerce, Macaulay also distances herself from the messiness of middlebrow culture that the Book Society represents.

In an editorial printed a few weeks after its Book Society article, *Time and Tide* noted that the correspondence it had received revealed 'a deep discontent in the book world at large'. Acknowledging that the 'Book Society has, perhaps, borne an undue share of the criticism', the item drew attention to a feature article by Wyndham Lewis discussing 'other aspects of the question' including the 'note of extravagance in present criticism, its degeneration to the standard of the publishers "blurb"' and the 'growing tendency [. . .] for publishers to appoint as their readers the star-reviewers on the big papers' (19 Mar 1932: 311). Lewis's article (published in two parts in this and the following issue) was written in response to the publication of *Authors and the Book Trade* by the writer, critic and 'impassioned upholder of the middlebrow philosophy' Frank Swinnerton (Bracco 1990: 52). In satiric mode Lewis dealt ruthlessly with Swinnerton, and also Arnold Bennett (for many years a star reviewer on the *Evening Standard*) whom he maliciously credits with what he calls the 'Tipster Technique' in an extended analogy between the book trade and gambling.[21] Most provocative of all, however, is his direct address to an implied reader who will share a highbrow attitude towards the literary marketplace: 'Now the sort of "authors" of whom Mr. Swinnerton writes are, heaven knows, not the sort of crowd it is my business or yours (when I say you I mean You) to defend' (19 Mar 1932: 323). With this calculated taunt of middlebrow writers Lewis proceeds to draw a line 'between *their* world and *our* world', and with reference to publishers' advertisements in the popular newspapers he concludes: 'The only sort of books that you and I (and when I say you, I do mean You) are at all interested in are such as do not as a rule recommend themselves to those vast distributive machines' (324). The 'sort of books' Lewis is referring to here, of course, are those rarefied modernist commodities which circulated amongst a more select public. His pose is deliberately antagonistic, stylistically reinforcing his opinion 'that a bitter struggle for power of some sort is in progress' (323). As Melba Cuddy-Keane has discussed, the hostilities that arose in the 'battle of the brows' were 'fuelled by perceived or feared injustices in the distribution of power', the compelling issue being 'a fight for readership, on one side, and a fight for respect and legitimization, on the other' (2003: 21). Literary criticism was one key site for this 'struggle for power', including in *Time and Tide*'s own book reviews section as the periodical sought to establish its direction and identity in this increasingly contentious terrain.

In September 1932 *Time and Tide* introduced a new feature 'Men and Books' (initially 'Books and Men'), which was announced in the periodical's columns as 'a literary causerie' to be contributed 'by the distinguished critic RICHARD SUNNE' (10 Sep 1932: 969). 'Richard Sunne' was in fact very likely a pseudonym for R. Ellis Roberts who had recently left the Books pages of the *New Statesman*.[22] A High Anglican, who had worked for many years on the *Church Times*, Roberts was a critic in the 'man of letters' tradition (Hyams: 161), a 'belletrist' to use the more pejorative Victorian and Edwardian term. Certainly, the feature as it appeared weekly under this signature contains what Josephine M. Guy and Ian Small identify as the 'basic elements' of the amateur critic: its grounding in non-specialist knowledge, its appeal to common experience, and assertions regarding the 'truth' of literature (2000: 384). As such the feature addressed the general reader, not the intellectual or specialist, and in an important refutation of recent and 'severe denunciations of the reading habit' the inaugural article defended 'reading for pleasure' (17 Sep 1932: 1000). This positive identification with one of the hallmarks of the middlebrow is matched by the capaciousness of this column. In contrast with the virtue modernism made of selectivity, 'Richard Sunne' states that the 'business of the critic is to remind his readers how wide is the world of literature', and unappreciative of modernist linguistic experiment ('the lost forest into which Mr. Joyce has wandered' and 'the blinding, glittering sands of the desert which Miss Stein has never abandoned') he argues that: 'Today many set too high a value on ingenuity, on method, on the craft of writing.' His claim that 'what is true of all art is [. . .] that its only ultimate reason is the passion for communication' could also stand in for his view of criticism. Eschewing technical language privileged in the newer academic discourses, the column reaffirms *Time and Tide*'s commitment to the ordinary, intelligent reader with its informal, conversational style.

The risks of the amateur tradition, however, were brought into sharp relief only a few weeks later when *Time and Tide* published a review by Gwendolen Raverat of Elizabeth Bowen's new novel *To the North* (1932). The review drew a storm of protest from some of Britain's leading women writers, Raverat's offence being a flippant paragraph in which she stated: 'I can say very little about *To the North*. I have tried to read it: at the beginning, at the end, and in the middle, and it simply won't bite. But I can't see why it won't [. . .] it is quite well-written. So why can't I read it?' (22 Oct 1932: 1144). The following week *Time and Tide* printed a letter signed by Margaret Kennedy, Marie Belloc-Lowndes, Theodora Bosanquet, Rose Macaulay, Naomi Royde-Smith and Helen Simpson which stated:

> We cannot tell Mrs. Raverat why she is unable to read books which she has undertaken to review, but we would suggest that a critic suffering from such a disability had better hand over her task to someone else. It is a pity that readers of *Time and Tide*, who are accustomed to expect a very high standard of criticism, should be denied even an adverse review of a book which has received considerable notice elsewhere, simply because Mrs. Raverat cannot discover why she is unable to read it.
>
> Miss Bowen is recognized as a brilliant young novelist and we, who have followed her career with the greatest interest, feel that any new book of hers demands considered attention. (29 Oct 1932: 1181–2)

In *Time and Tide*'s next issue E. M. Delafield joined the protest, in a letter stating that she was 'a good deal surprised and shocked' by Raverat's 'airy dismissal' of Bowen's new novel. Also testifying to Bowen's importance 'as a serious and extremely competent artist' she described reading *To the North* 'with an admiration that I fear bordered on the envious, for its subtlety, its brilliant flashes of wit [. . .] and its admirable characterization' (5 Nov 1932: 1214). Underneath Delafield's letter *Time and Tide* printed a reply from

Raverat who defended her review stating that: 'I think all my stern critics would agree that there is no use in reviewing books unless one says what one really thinks about them.' Standing by her view that the novel had 'every good quality, except that of being interesting', she concluded:

> I think that books are very often praised by other writers, because, as fellow-craftsmen, they appreciate the technical qualities which are less obvious to the layman [. . .]. I know that I [. . .] can find interest in almost any picture whatever, from a technical point of view [. . .]. But I should not expect the public to see these qualities. And as far as books are concerned, I write as an ordinary reader. (5 Nov 1932: 1214)

Not only does the controversy expose the high stakes involved in the periodical's reception of such important women writers as Bowen, it also highlights the challenges posed by a growing tension between generalist and specialist approaches to criticism. The following week *Time and Tide* printed a letter from a reader who wrote in defence of Raverat: 'Surely most of us are tired of hearing the senseless praise of competent novelists by other competent novelists. Let the novelist stick to his novel-writing, and leave an honest reviewer to do her job without fear or favour' (12 Nov 1932: 1250).

The upset over Raverat's review of Bowen's novel appears to have revealed the need for closer management of *Time and Tide*'s Books pages. In March 1933, the periodical announced that Mr R. Ellis Roberts had joined its staff as literary editor (4 Mar 1933: 249), and Raverat, though she continued to write as *Time and Tide*'s art critic, contributed only the occasional book review from this point. As I have indicated, Roberts had probably already been trialled on the paper's new 'Men and Books' column as 'Richard Sunne'. Outside the paper, his wide popular appeal apparently commended him further to the post: announcing the appointment of Roberts in an interview for the *Observer* Rhondda commented that his talks on the radio about new books had 'endeared him to countless thousands of listeners' (26 Feb 1932: 8). Like the Book Society the BBC was regarded as a middlebrow institution, and *Time and Tide*'s first literary editor thus marks the periodical's allegiance to the middlebrow sphere. However, unpublished evidence suggests that Roberts was found to be too populist, not discriminating enough for the intellectual audience *Time and Tide* was also seeking to reach. In October 1933 Rhondda wrote a congratulatory wire to the office for its recent literary number, but privately confessed to Holtby that some of its content was not 'good enough for a literary number which all the high-brows read and criticise'.[23] Apparently proving difficult to manage in the office, Roberts also became unpopular with Rebecca West and Naomi Mitchison, and by late spring of the following year *Time and Tide* was looking for a replacement.[24] One candidate considered was Gerald Bullett, who contributed regularly to *Time and Tide*'s review columns for a time from early 1934.[25] But in the summer of this year the literary editorship passed from Roberts to a man called John Beevers who had recently graduated from Queens College, Cambridge, with a First Class degree in English.[26] As a product of the new Cambridge English and '"academicization" of English literary studies' (Matthews 2009: 848), Beevers's university background seems to have promised the kind of access to the highbrow sphere that *Time and Tide* needed to secure its reputation for a high standard of criticism. As we shall see, his appointment inaugurated a shift in the periodical's book reviews section from 'amateur' criticism associated with belles-lettres to 'professional' criticism associated with the rise of University English, a shift we might expect to sit well with *Time and Tide*'s faith in the value of professionalism. However, *Time and Tide*'s second choice of literary editor was also followed by difficulties, though these were of a different kind from those that accompanied the first.

Among the people Beevers first contacted in his new position as *Time and Tide*'s literary editor were Wyndham Lewis and Ezra Pound. Reviews by both men were published in *Time and Tide*'s book pages in August 1934, but unpublished letters reveal even greater designs Beevers had upon the paper. Apparently responding to a query from Pound as to how free a hand he could expect to be given (presumably in light of *Time and Tide*'s reluctance to publish his articles on economics the previous year, see Chapter 5), Beevers wrote 'You can write what you like provided it isn't libellous or obscene' and intimated that he was in a position to ensure Pound's publication in the periodical now that he was in employ there: 'It's quite certain that everything you've written for the *New English Weekly* would go in here now I'm looking after the review columns.'[27] A few days later Beevers wrote about the books he was sending Pound for review and issued more advice:

> Foibles of the paper: I should keep off Orage and the *New English Weekly* [. . .]. And there is the minor foible about women – keep them out of everything. I think it would stand your use of CAPITALS – but not too much. I'm all for your saying what you want and how you

want – and I can do a good deal to [ensure] you this. I want to get T&T into the position of a really 1st rate review – no bunk anywhere in the reviewing section, at any rate.[28]

Beevers's self-aggrandising and his bombastic language ('no bunk') are very Poundian, and his instruction to 'keep [women] out of everything', though ostensibly given to caution Pound against giving offence betrays a misogynistic desire to wrest control over the magazine from *Time and Tide*'s female directors and staff who, it is implied, are incapable of making it a '1st rate review'. Indeed, the correspondence itself was conducted in such a way as to circumvent *Time and Tide*'s office. Handwritten (i.e. not dictated) on *Time and Tide* notepaper this letter was marked 'Personal', while in his next letter Beevers gave Pound his home address (26 Great James Street, London) and closed with the instruction: 'I should send letters here in future – more convenient and private.'[29] With this deliberate subterfuge Beevers thanked Pound for his reviews and assured him that they would be printed with his full name at the bottom ('be damned to E. P. or anonymity') and drew attention to this week's issue where 'Wyndham Lewis is in [. . .] at my petitioning.' Explaining that he hoped to put Pound in next week, he concluded with reference to *Time and Tide*'s plans for a monthly book supplement 'which will make it possible for us to get some selection, some order, some planning into the business'. Beevers's use of the personal pronoun here is revealing, the 'us' seeming to refer not to the collective body behind *Time and Tide* but the would-be usurpers: himself, Pound and Lewis.

Beevers's scheming with Pound (and, apparently, Lewis) reveals the risks involved in the periodical's commitment to cross-gender collaboration, examined in Chapter 5 of this book.[30] His actual control over the magazine, however, was limited, as his next letter to Pound reveals:

> The powers that be are VERY restive about your economic reviews – so I'm only venturing to print the Warburg one. I'm sorry – but there are some things I can't do – not yet anyhow. People are frightened of letting you have your head in matters economical – I'd let you write what the devil you wanted if I were the EDITOR – but I'm only the *literary* editor.[31]

Rhondda and her female colleagues were clearly keeping a close eye on their new literary editor, and maintaining their embargo on

Pound's economic writings. Beevers was not one to give up, however, as the continuation of his letter reveals:

> But the value of your name is appreciated – so can't you manage to do some other kind of work – anything except economics. I know that it must sound bloody silly to you – asking you to do anything BUT the things you most want to. But if you started appearing regularly here – it would be the thin end of the wedge. Let me know.[32]

In the event Beevers's plot backfired; Pound was furious at his name being used while being asked to write 'anything except economics', and Beevers was able to get only a very little more work for Lewis.[33] The names of both men, however, were featured in the first of *Time and Tide*'s new monthly double numbers launched in October 1934 which contained a newly defined 'LITERARY SECTION' comprising thirty-two pages. Leading this section was *Time and Tide*'s weekly 'Men and Books' column (now written by Beevers under the pseudonym 'Roderick Random') and most of the first article under its new signatory was devoted to a discussion of Lewis's *Men Without Art*, with a final paragraph on Pound's essays *Make it New*.[34] A clear signal of a new orientation in *Time and Tide*'s columns towards the 'Men of 1914' (Beevers's 'Men and Books' article in the next issue began with a discussion of T. S. Eliot), this discussion of Lewis and Pound also sounded a new note for the feature 'Men and Books'. In contrast with the generalist interests and catholic taste exhibited in these articles under 'Richard Sunne', Beevers's first contributions in this column participated in the processes of canonisation that elevated a select group of male modernist writers to the forefront of literary history and English literary studies.

Time and Tide's new monthly double numbers were announced with the declaration that they did 'not represent a new departure but a necessary extension of our functions' (29 Sep 1934: 1195). However, the explanation that the new literary supplements would include 'a vigorous series of new scrutinies of literary reputations' (1195) suggests that, in cooperation with its new literary editor, the periodical was deliberately repositioning itself in relation to the highbrow sphere. As in its 1926 commissioning of articles on 'present-day literary tendencies' echoing T. S. Eliot's *New Criterion* manifesto (see Chapter 3), here *Time and Tide* reveals itself as being in dialogue with another powerful literary force: F. R. Leavis's Cambridge journal *Scrutiny* launched in May 1932. This monthly periodical took its name from the 'Scrutinies' Comments and Reviews section of an earlier, short-lived journal, *The Calendar of Modern Letters* (1925–7), and in its own judgements on contemporary literature *Scrutiny* had 'a significant influence on the establishment of a modernist canon of both literary and critical work' (Matthews 2009: 838). Beevers claimed in *Time and Tide*'s columns not to be a follower of Leavis.[35] However, his writing for the periodical was very Leavisite, not only in his promotion of male modernist writers, but also in his attitude towards mass cultural forms. For example, in early 1935 Beevers used his 'Men and Books' column to attack the contemporary phenomenon of the bestseller, identifying Dennis Wheatley as 'one example of a vicious tendency in contemporary life' (12 Jan 1935: 49).[36] The bestseller occupied a position at the centre of the book trade, 'the publishers' and booksellers' most important business, and the goal of most writers' (Bracco 1990: 13). Beevers's chief charge against such fiction is that it 'calls for no intellectual response on the part of its readers', and his assertion that 'this vulgarization of literature is going on everywhere' is strongly reminiscent of Leavis's indictment of 'mass society' in *Mass Civilization and Minority Culture* (1930).[37] In an important sense, Beevers's concern about the evolution of 'a type of fiction that may be read with the minimum of mental effort' (50) accords with *Time and Tide*'s statements about the popular press and its failure to provide 'solid reading matter' (see Chapter 4). In the same issue *Time and Tide* announced that from February 1935 it would be issuing *two* double numbers a month: in addition to its monthly literary number, in the fourth week of every month it would issue a University Supplement. *Time and Tide*'s University Supplements are a further indication of the more intellectual audience the periodical was seeking to reach in these years. But the new authority of academic discourses would also have implications for other core constituents in its contributor and readership base.

As Sean Matthews has discussed, as a product and achievement of the Cambridge English tripos *Scrutiny* was 'both a medium for, and an exemplification of, the gradual professionalisation, indeed institutionalisation, of literary criticism'. Insisting upon 'a distinctive conception of the discipline of English studies, combining scholarship with judgement' *Scrutiny* 'oppose[d] what it saw as the *belle-lettrist*, journalistic [. . .] and coterie tendencies within contemporary academic and newspaper criticism, tendencies which its contributors regularly castigated as a betrayal of the critical function' (2009: 849). The influence of *Scrutiny* and the new University English is evident in Beevers's onslaught in another 'Men and Books' column on a recently published book of essays in criticism, *The Enjoyment of Literature* (1935) by Elizabeth Drew. Drew's first book on the *Modern Novel* (1926) had been reviewed positively in *Time and Tide*'s pages some years earlier by Sylvia Lynd (see Chapter 3). Her latest volume, which extends to discussions of drama and poetry as well as fiction, is a further testament to the value she placed on the pleasure of reading and on sharing that enthusiasm with others. In Beevers's estimation, however, *The Enjoyment of Literature* is 'a type of book I shall never cease to attack whenever and wherever I meet it'. Dismissing certain passages as 'nonsense' and 'utter balderdash' he describes the book as merely offering readers 'anecdotes and gossip about dead writers, extremely inaccurate generalizations [. . .] and pages of emotional gush certain to do infinitely more harm than good' (27 Apr 1935: 623). Beevers's chief complaint against Drew is that her criticism lacks disciplinary rigour. As Francis Mulhern observes, an 'emphasis on "rigour"' in the writing of leading Cambridge academic I. A. Richards was 'a deliberate repudiation of the amateurism of *belles lettres*, and thus a symbol of the intellectual professionalism to which the rising generation aspired' (1979: 28). Richards's influence on Beevers is further evident in the singling out of Drew's discussion of poetry as a particular target of attack:

> Reading lyric poetry is not easy. To read it properly – i.e., to get the maximum possible enjoyment out of it – needs on the part of the reader an acute sensibility, a very well-read mind and the power to achieve a quick and intense concentration on a handful of images [. . .]. How many people do you imagine possess these qualities? Not many. (623)

Richards's concern with 'the proper reading of good poetry' was an important part of the development of Cambridge English (Heath 1994: 27), while in *Mass Civilization and Minority Culture* Leavis asserted that: 'In any period it is upon a small minority that the discerning appreciation of art and literature depends' (Matthews 2009: 840). Beevers's review was published in one of *Time and Tide*'s monthly double numbers issuing a University Supplement. Disqualifying Drew from the profession he lays claim to, Beevers declares that: 'She would do well to leave criticism alone' (623).

The violence of Beevers's attack on Drew's book is testament to the struggle for power that took place in the development of English as a university subject. As Carol Atherton states, 'what was being contested was the nature of the authority that underwrote the critical process, and whether this belonged to the "amateur" or the "professional":

what was at stake was nothing less than the ownership of literary knowledge' (2005: 24). Drew herself was university educated (at Oxford) and began a career as a university lecturer in English at Girton College, Cambridge, during the First World War. After leaving this position (on account of the College not allowing its teaching staff to live out) she went on to give many lecture tours at American universities, and for most of the period between the wars continued to reside in Cambridge after her marriage to an English academic, Brian Westerdale Downs. Drew joined the Cambridge Faculty of English under her married name in 1936 but she never held an established university post.[38] Author of several books on literary subjects, but positioned on the margins of the new Cambridge English, she is one of many dissenting voices which, according to Guy and Small, 'historians of the universities and of university education have tended to ignore' in their description of the 'transition to professionalisation as an inevitable and smooth progression'. But as Guy and Small contend: 'in English studies at least the resistance of the amateur critic, although historically unsuccessful, is still significant; indeed, it raises serious issues about the function of criticism in society, and the relationship between professional critics and the public' (377–8). These are precisely the issues *Time and Tide* was grappling with in its Book criticism of the 1930s as it sought to achieve a high standard of criticism and serve the needs of multiple target groups. Two letters of protest against Beevers's review were published in *Time and Tide* the following week. In the first, 'Joan Bennett' writes from a Cambridge address to say that: 'He [Beevers] cannot bear that the path he has found so hard and strange should be made easy and attractive. Literature must be nothing but a discipline' (4 May 1935: 652). In the second, 'Edgar Appleton' from Hull writes that the review left him 'gasping':

> Though a provincial, I am quite aware that there are gentlemen in Cambridge, Leavis-led, who preach that to enjoy literature is to commit the unforgivable sin. To them, literature is an excuse for mental gymnastics. They have taken the wrong train. *Tristam Shandy* did not become a classic because it provided intellectual exercise, but because people enjoyed reading it. (652)

Invoking once again an interwar conflict around pleasure, these letters clearly evidence 'an increasing gap between professional study and the general public' that was augured by the institutionalisation of English studies as a university subject (Cuddy-Keane 2003: 1).

The implications of this gap for *Time and Tide* were significant. As noted by Erica Brown and Mary Grover, 'the pejorative connotations of the term "middlebrow" rapidly intensified in ways often connected with the professionalisation of literary criticism' (2012: 6), and the imprint of University English on *Time and Tide*'s book reviews section during Beevers's literary editorship not only risked alienating the periodical's core readership, but devaluing the work and reputations of its own celebrated female authors and critics as well. At the beginning of June 1935 *Time and Tide* published a provocatively titled article 'The Yellow Peril in Publishing' as a means of airing controversy and debate over a supposed disregard for standards behind what it called the 'Book Ramp' (1 June 1935: 816). A number of prominent women writers (Phyllis Bentley, Winifred Holtby, Sylvia Lynd, Rose Macaulay, Dorothy Sayers) were drawn into the periodical's correspondence columns in defence both of the middlebrow fiction market and of their own standing as professional authors and critics, while a 'competition in book Blurbs', issued in association with the article, injected humour into mounting tensions surrounding publishers' advertising methods.[39] In these and other features *Time and Tide* shows its continuing affiliation with the middlebrow promoted and celebrated in its Miscellany columns, and it seems that on these grounds the suitability of its second literary editor was tested. Within four months of his attack on *The Enjoyment of Literature* Beevers had tendered his resignation, and he contributed his last 'Men and Books' article in *Time and Tide*'s issue of 5 October 1935. It is unclear whether Beevers left voluntarily or was pushed.[40] Among his supporters was Edith Sitwell, who intimated in a letter to Beevers's wife that his articles had been criticised:

> I really am so furious that Roderick Random [i.e. Beevers] is going to leave *Time and Tide*. Lady R. must be mad not to see how perfectly admirable his critical articles are. I am not exaggerating when I say that almost everybody I know has said to me that he has been the making of that paper, and that it is quite unrecognisable since he joined it. Now, of course, it will become an owl's nest and a rest-home for old ladies once again.[41]

Sitwell's letter is a reminder that intra-gender relationships are no guarantee of solidarity, and shows that *Time and Tide*'s female culture could produce hostilities among women as well as men. If the male pronoun in *Time and Tide*'s 'Men and Books' column was designed to strategically dissociate the periodical's book reviews section from the 'feminine middlebrow', under Beevers the column perhaps showed too much 'masculine' combative spirit.[42] By the end of 1935 the literary editorship had passed to Theodora Bosanquet, a contributor since 1927, restoring both ends of the paper to female control. Bosanquet's shaping influence on the periodical's next stage of development is the focus of the final part of this book.

Notes

1. See Clay (2018) for an extended discussion of *Time and Tide*'s short fiction content.
2. First published in 1915 under the title 'Autumns I' in the anti-war little magazine *Signature* Katherine Mansfield's story appeared in *Time and Tide*'s 'Miscellany' section as 'The Apple Tree' in its 20 May 1927 issue. The same story was reprinted in *Woman's Home Magazine*, an American monthly, in the same year.
3. Some of these writers (e.g. Bowen, Rhys) have been recuperated within an expanded modernist sphere, others (e.g. Delafield, Holtby) have been identified as leaders within middlebrow culture. Whipple is one of the most popular authors published by Persephone Press, the London publisher and bookseller of neglected mid-twentieth-century fiction.
4. Delafield dates the luncheon, which she 'think[s] [was] in honour of Bernard Shaw', in 1929 (1937: 124).
5. Delafield was elected President of her local Women's Institute in the village of Kentisbeare in 1924, a position she retained to the end of her life (Powell 1988: 61).
6. The other organisations in Beaumont's study are the Mothers Union, the Catholic Women's League, the National Council of Women and the National Union of Townswomen's Guilds.
7. It was reviewed by Naomi Royde-Smith in *Time and Tide*'s issue of 27 September 1929.
8. This exhibition ran from January to March 1930.
9. Hammill observes that Delafield's narrator articulates 'a democratic concept of authorship', and that as the sequels unfold the Provincial Lady is 'increasingly identified with her professional role' and 'treated as a professional writer by those she meets' (2007: 185; 181).
10. Commenting on the results of the 'Triolet' competition, the editor of the competition page remarked that 'a large number of the entries are not triolets at all' and went on to explain 'that slight change and corresponding intensification of meaning in the line repeated three times, which is the real secret of the triolet' (14 June 1930: 780).
11. As Stephanie Rains has discussed, by requiring readers to submit a coupon with each entry, magazine competitions were extremely valuable in boosting sales (2015: 140).

12. Another competition, in association with a one-off instalment on the occasion of a *Time and Tide* party at the Dorchester Hotel, London, invites readers to imagine themselves as 'a gossip-writer hard up for copy' who has followed George Bernard Shaw to the event (25 June 1932: 728).

13. Hammill has remarked on the possibility that this first article may have influenced the composition of Stella Gibbons's first and successful novel *Cold Comfort Farm* (2007: 179).

14. The first strapline is from a leaflet issued by the Regent Institute and distributed as a supplement to *Time and Tide* at least twice, with its issues of 21 September 1928 and 2 March 1929. (These leaflets are preserved in bound volumes of *Time and Tide* at Cambridge University Library and the National Library of Scotland respectively.) The second strapline is from an advertisement for the London Editorial College which appeared on the front cover of *Time and Tide*'s issue of 22 February 1929.

15. Regent Institute leaflet.

16. Regent Institute leaflet.

17. From the late nineteenth century onwards, various guidebooks to writing were published, for example Arnold Bennett's *How to Become an Author* (1903). Hilliard identifies three major commercial dispensers of advice which came into their own during the interwar years: writers' magazines, correspondence schools, manuscript criticism and placement-advice services or 'bureaus' (2006: 20).

18. See Melba Cuddy-Keane (2003: 22–34) for a discussion of this essay.

19. Several of these congratulated *Time and Tide* on the article and issued further questions about the Book Society's methods on which they wished to be informed.

20. MR to SL, 28 February 1932. Private Collection.

21. The article is called 'A Tip from the Augean Stable', a classical reference to the Twelve Labours of Hercules which insinuates the degradation into which the Book World is perceived to have fallen, and the Herculean nature of the task at hand for cleaning it up.

22. Roberts joined the *New Statesman* under Clifford Sharp's editorship, but didn't long survive the journal's merger with the *Nation*. Kingsley Martin, editor of the newly amalgamated title *New Statesman and Nation*, later admitted that Roberts was the only writer whose style and opinions he found intolerable; following a period of constant quarrels Roberts left the paper in 1932 (Smith 1996: 187).

23. MR to WH, 17 October 1933. WH Collection [WH/5/5.17/04/01h]. This was the 14 October 1932 issue of *Time and Tide*.

24. In a letter to Holtby written on the same day that the appointment of Roberts was announced in *Time and Tide*'s columns, Rhondda admitted that 'for all his feminism, I fear he many not find it easy to take detailed orders from a woman'. MR to WH, 4 March 1933.

WH Collection [WH/5/5.17/03/01r]. West recorded in her diary on 13 April 1934: 'Wrote long letter attacking Ellis Roberts "Time and Tide."' RW Yale. In an undated letter to Wyndham Lewis, Mitchison refers to the 'cattishness' with which her book has been received at *Time and Tide*, 'especially from that nasty man Ellis Roberts'. WL Cornell [Box 126].

25. Rhondda asked Holtby for her opinion on Gerald Bullett's suitability for the post in a letter dated 26 May 1934, and added anxiously: 'Is he too much of the R.E.R. type?' WH Collection [WH/5/5.17/05/01g].

26. The exact date of the changeover, which passed unannounced in *Time and Tide*'s pages, is unclear, but in a letter to Ezra Pound dated 19 June 1934 Beevers declared that he was now *Time and Tide*'s literary editor. EP Papers. There seems to have been a period of overlap. Writing to Mary Butts on 13 August, Roberts explains that he has delayed writing until he could say with certainty that he is no longer acting as *Time and Tide*'s literary editor which is now in the hands of John Beevers. MB Papers.

27. JB to EP, 23 July 1934. EP Papers.

28. JB to EP, 27 July 1934. EP Papers.

29. JB to EP, 3 August 1934. EP Papers.

30. Letters from Lewis to Beevers in the Harry Ransom Collection record their association in the mid-1930s; one letter refers to 'enjoy[ing] our pub talk extremely'. WL HRC, 1934 [n.d.]. According to Beevers (in some notes he sent to Cornell University in 1975 on reading of the Lewis Collection) he and Lewis enjoyed regular lunchtime meetings at the Horseshoe Pub on Tottenham Court Road (a few minutes' walk away from the *Time and Tide* office) where they would 'sit & drink & talk'. WL Cornell [B51/F8].

31. JB to EP, 8 August 1934. EP Papers. Pound's review, of *The Money Muddle* by J. P. Warburg, was published in *Time and Tide*'s issue of 11 August 1934.

32. JB to EP, 8 August 1934. EP Papers.

33. Pound wrote angrily to Norman Angell: 'Time and Tide having printed me, has also asked if I couldn't write "anything EXCEPT economics." The lot of you DARE not look into this subject.' EP to NA, 6 May 1935. EP Papers. Beevers records in his notes on Lewis that Rhondda 'did not care for Lewis, so I could give him no more work – or very, very little'. WL Cornell [B51/F8].

34. 'Roderick Random' was identified as John Beevers in a letter from Edith Sitwell published in *Time and Tide* in its issue of 26 October 1935.

35. In *Time and Tide*'s correspondence columns he declared that he had 'spent a deal of time damning Dr. Leavis and his men' (20 Apr 1935: 8).

36. The article refers to Wheatley's *The Devil Rides Out* (1934), a super-natural thriller on which the author's reputation rests. See Bloom (2002: 162–3).

37. Leavis states in this essay that 'mass-production and standardization [. . .] is rapidly enveloping the whole world'. Cited in Matthews (2009: 841).
38. I am grateful to archivists at Girton College Library, Cambridge, and at Cambridge University Archives, for their assistance in establishing this information.
39. For an extended discussion of this material see Clay (2011: 80–2).
40. In a letter dated 25 August 1935 Rhondda told Holtby that Beevers had given *Time and Tide* three months' notice with effect from 1 September. WH Collection [WH/5/5.17/05/01r].
41. ES to Mrs Marjorie Beevers, 5 September 1935. ES Collection.
42. A swipe at Geoffrey Grigson in Beevers's 'Men and Books' of 7 September 1935, itself made in retaliation against an unflattering reference to himself in Grigson's journal, *New Verse*, led to an extended spat between the two men until *Time and Tide*'s editor announced that '*This correspondence is now closed*' (21 Sep 1935: 1334). Such a visible editorial intervention of this sort in the paper was unusual, and perhaps suggests an irritated impatience with the male infighting exhibited here.

Part III

Reorientation, 1935–1939

Chapter 7

A New Partnership: Art, Money and Religion

Readers of *Time and Tide*'s contents from the mid-1930s onwards can be forgiven for thinking that this modern feminist magazine became 'less feminist' as it moved towards the end of its second decade. Early notes I made when first researching this periodical register my own disappointment at the increasingly scarce signs of *Time and Tide*'s feminist mandate which was stamped so visibly on its earlier issues. In the few years leading up to the Second World War there are markedly fewer female and feminist signatures, and leading articles are more internationally than woman-focused. In the same period *Time and Tide*'s exuberant celebration of female literary celebrities and middlebrow culture disappears; while the periodical continued to publish some short stories and poems by women, in May 1936 it dropped its 'Miscellany' section which, I argued in Chapter 6, created a home for the 'feminine middlebrow'.[1] Gone, too, are regular advertisements for other women's periodicals such as the *Woman Engineer* and *Jus Suffragi*, which had marked *Time and Tide*'s participation in the networks associated with interwar feminist print culture. Indeed, a developing relationship with a new set of advertisers shows how the periodical was seeking to alter its readers' 'horizon of expectations' for the magazine (Morrisson 2001: 39) once again. From July 1935 publishers' advertisements alternated on *Time and Tide*'s front cover with advertisements for a range of financial services and products, and in October *Time and Tide* issued a special Insurance and Finance Supplement. From 2 November to 14 December 1935 a large advertisement for 'First Provincial Fixed Trust Ltd' appeared on the front page of *Time and Tide*'s advertising wrapper every week, and the masculine-coding of this advertisement, with its head-and-shoulders drawing of a man smoking a cigar in the top-right corner, is striking (Figure 7.1). Dismantling the periodical's association with the 'women's paper' category the advertisement explicitly addresses a male rather than a female reader. This change was also effected on the inside pages of the periodical. By 1936, advertisements for fashions and fabrics promoted by the London department stores which had formerly dominated *Time and Tide*'s advertising space had completely disappeared.

Discussing this material elsewhere I have argued that while *Time and Tide* may appear by the mid-1930s to have severed its connections with feminism, we may instead consider the repackaging of this periodical as 'a strategic response to the difficulties faced by a female-run weekly review in a world still hostile to women's participation in the political sphere'. Furthermore, with specific reference to the new prominence of financial products and services in its advertising content, I have suggested that while it may look as though *Time and Tide* had moved away from its feminist and female readership, what it was actually doing was 'refashioning an image of the modern woman in terms of her economic power as professional worker, rather than domestic consumer, in the context of middle-class women's large-scale professionalisation in this period' (Clay 2011: 85).[2] Arguably the periodical's new bright red cover, adopted as a permanent feature in February 1935, encodes *Time and Tide*'s still radical affiliations – not only with socialism (red being the traditional colour of the left) but also with feminism: any long-standing feminist readers would likely recall the red covers of the monthly journal the *Englishwoman*.[3] In the final chapter of this book I present two case studies which explore how *Time and Tide*'s seemingly non-feminist veneer is disrupted, first in its book reviews section, and second in its political and correspondence pages. In the present chapter, I consider the significance for the periodical of the new partnership that was formed between *Time and Tide*'s political editor, Lady Rhondda, and its literary editor from October 1935, Theodora Bosanquet.

Bosanquet, a critically marginalised figure and best known for her association with Henry James (she served as his amanuensis during the last years of his life), had been a contributor of reviews and other articles to *Time and Tide* since 1927. Her appointment as literary editor in the autumn of 1935 (a position she retained until 1943) restored both ends of the paper to female control, and testifies to the strong female culture that continued to shape the periodical from within despite surface appearances. By 1935 Bosanquet was author of three critical books, the first a study of Henry James published

TIME AND TIDE

THE INDEPENDENT WEEKLY REVIEW

Vol. XVI. No. 50 *(Registered as a Newspaper)*   SATURDAY, 14th DECEMBER, 1935   PRICE 6d

---

OUR GRAVE RESPONSIBILITIES

Other Contributors include :

NORMAN ANGELL   **STEPHEN GWYNN**

MALCOLM MUGGERIDGE   **H. M. TOMLINSON**

ELLEN WILKINSON, M.P.

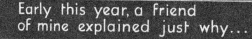

Figure 7.1 *Time and Tide* front cover, 14 Dec 1935. Reproduced by kind permission of the Syndics of Cambridge University Library. Classmark: L900.a.39.

by the Hogarth Press in 1924 (and reprinted in 1927), the second a study of the nineteenth-century feminist and woman of letters, *Harriet Martineau* (1927), and the third, a study of the French symbolist poet, *Paul Valery* (1933). Following the instabilities in *Time and Tide*'s book reviews section under its two male literary editors R. Ellis Roberts and John Beevers (see Chapter 6), Bosanquet's 'highbrow' literary interests appear to have brought the kind of qualities the periodical needed as it engaged in the mid-1930s with the 'battle of the brows' while sustaining its commitment to women's achievements in intellectual and creative spheres. Her positive review in 1933 of Elizabeth Drew's *Discovering Poetry* (22 July 1933: 886) contrasts markedly with Beevers's attack on the same author's later book of criticism, *The Enjoyment of Literature* (discussed in the previous chapter), and her first 'Men and Books' article lauded what has proved to be a landmark text in Shakespeare criticism, *Shakespeare's Imagery* by the female Cambridge academic, Caroline Spurgeon (2 November 1935: 1582). University-educated, and for many years the executive secretary of the International Federation of University Women (IFUW), Bosanquet was not – as Beevers was – a product of 'Cambridge English', and she would conduct *Time and Tide*'s books pages along much wider lines than those of her immediate predecessor.[4] At the same time, under her watch *Time and Tide*'s review pages paid increasing attention to books on spiritualism, mysticism and religion, subjects which seem at odds with the more materialist concerns of this secular periodical.

A convert to Christianity in 1933, Bosanquet was also a long-standing member of the Society of Psychical Research, and her involvement in the practices of mediumship will be the subject of further discussion both here and in Chapter 8. Lady Rhondda, according to her most recent biographer, was 'nominally Church of England but did not see herself as a religious person' (John 2013: 479), and it is the tension and dialogue between these two apparently opposing forces – material and spiritual, secular and religious – that is the focus of this chapter. In the first section, I explore a conversation between Rhondda and Bosanquet about the idea of 'work' that exposes the limits of *Time and Tide*'s feminist discourse of professionalism and highlights a tension between material and spiritual interests. In the second section, I read the new religious influence in the periodical under Bosanquet's literary editorship alongside content contributed by a new generation of artists and writers on the left, and argue that *Time and Tide*'s dialogue between 'radicals' and 'mystics' may not be as oppositional as it seems.

The 'idea' of work: professionalism, amateurism, and 'literary service'

Rhondda and Bosanquet probably first became acquainted as early as 1922 through their mutual acquaintance with Professor Winifred Cullis, co-founder of the IFUW (and its President from 1929 to 1932) and a director of *Time and Tide* from 1924 (Eoff 1991: 113). According to Shirley Eoff, their early contacts were 'limited and tense'; Rhondda considered Bosanquet's political position to be too narrowly focused on the interests of an elite group of university women, and worked for several years to persuade Bosanquet to support and lobby her membership for a broader commitment to a treaty on equal rights (1991: 113). By the end of 1933, however, the two women had formed a close companionship that would endure until the end of Rhondda's life. As Angela V. John documents, in the spring of this year Bosanquet accompanied Rhondda on a cruise on the *Homeric* to Madeira, Tenerife, Morocco and Gibraltar, one of several journeys abroad taken by Rhondda following some severe health problems in 1931 (2013: 472; 316), and in the autumn of 1933 the two women embarked on another voyage together, this time a tour of the Mediterranean taking in Greece, Palestine and Egypt. As John observes, this five-month cruise was a 'turning-point' for relations between the two women (2013: 365). Unpublished letters from Rhondda to Winifred Holtby indicate that by October she and Bosanquet had decided to set up house together on their return, and over the next twenty-five years the two would share a house in Hampstead, a country home in Surrey, and in the last years a flat overlooking Green Park (Eoff 1991: 114). In these same letters Holtby was instructed on the proper line to take when their intentions became known, namely, that the new home Rhondda had been seeking for some time was too large for her own needs, and that she had persuaded Bosanquet to take a couple of rooms in it (Eoff 1991: 114; John 2013: 365–6). They would explain to people at home, Rhondda communicated to Holtby, that it was a temporary arrangement while she and Bosanquet completed a book they planned to write together, adding that: 'We really have thought of rather a fascinating book on the different means of influencing public opinion (bringing in weeklies strong of course) and are tempted by it (done in dialogue form perhaps, for we seldom agree [. . .]).'[5] This book was never written (Rhondda admitted to Holtby her doubts that there would really be time for it), but its existence as an idea offers an illuminating perspective on the new partnership that would shape *Time and Tide* during the second half of the 1930s. Specifically, the disclosure that 'we seldom agree' points to differences of view between Rhondda and the paper's future literary editor that would play out in fascinating ways in the periodical in the years to come.

A rare glimpse of the private exchanges that took place between Rhondda and Bosanquet is preserved in two documents produced during the Mediterranean cruise of 1933, the second dated less than ten days before Rhondda's letter to Holtby outlining her and Bosanquet's plans for their return. The first, in Bosanquet's handwriting, bears the title 'Credo', and as a statement of religious belief reflects not only her recent conversion to Christianity, but also her passionate view of the value of art to society. Opening with the words 'I believe in Eternity' it identifies 'contemplative saints and artists' as people who 'live more in eternity than other kinds of people, who have their mind more constantly on the clock', and continues:

> I believe that contemplative saints perform real work – but that their work takes effect in an invisible non-material part of the universe. I believe that artists too perform real work. I think one might perhaps say that a difference between the saint and the artist is that the saint creates in eternity while the artist creates in time what he sees in eternity. Artists [. . .] are distinguished from other people in two ways. First because their work has aesthetic value and need have no other (that is to say it reveals beauty and need have no other function whatever). Secondly because as far as they are real artists they are disinterested.[6]

This 'Credo' carries all the hallmarks of a high modernist sensibility (particularly in its assertion of art's value for its own sake, and of the artist's disinterestedness) and is consistent with views expressed in Bosanquet's book reviews for *Time and Tide*, many of which were of works by French as well as Anglo-American modern and contemporary writers who played a part in modernism. Stating in a review of *Le Temps Retrouvé* (the final volume in Marcel Proust's monumental novel *In Remembrance of Things Past*) that 'whatever aspect of the world is seen by the great artist is translated into universal values' she asserts that the author [Proust] has 'accomplished something which, even in these days of utilitarian ethics and counting-house ideals, may still be recognised as a service to humanity' (24 Feb 1928). Bosanquet's comments here invite comparison with Ezra Pound, whose critical writings of this period consistently support his enduring belief that the artist should serve the public (Moses 2010: 146). Bosanquet was a reader of Pound's early little magazine enterprises, and it was Bosanquet whom Pound contacted in 1933 when seeking an entry to *Time and Tide* (see Chapter 5). The closing lines of Bosanquet's 'Credo' also contain a distinctly Poundian flavour:

> I believe obstinately and persistently that art is a real necessity for the life of educated men and women. And the first reform we need is a chance of a true education for everyone. And because I honestly believe that the art of a country is its most valuable possession I hate the attitude of my country and its schools to aesthetics. And because I love my country this scornful attitude is a constant distress and irritation.[7]

As we saw in Chapter 5, Rhondda was only interested in Pound for the value of his name, and in general she was unreceptive to the works of modernist authors, admitting in a letter to Holtby while reading *Night and Day* by Virginia Woolf (on board the *Homeric* with Bosanquet in April 1933): 'I don't get what you people see in her.'[8] As John notes, however, Rhondda 'recognised the need for her paper to reflect modern taste and originality' (2013: 320) and apparently Bosanquet presented qualities that could serve *Time and Tide* well. A second document originating from their Mediterranean cruise in the autumn of 1933, this one in Rhondda's handwriting, was clearly produced as a response to Bosanquet's 'Credo'. It begins with a qualification ('This is not a Credo really at all – not a whole confession of faith [. . .] merely a statement of how I see my own duty so long as I'm alive') and goes on to explain that 'there is one definite thing I have to do in life' and that this has 'always, or almost always, to do with women (directly or indirectly)'. Rhondda continues:

> *Time and Tide* is merely an instrument, a dozen other instruments would have served as well no doubt, & it is largely chance that this particular instrument shaped itself. [. . .] I believe that everything I possess, my brains, my strength, my health, my money, my reputation have to go to this one end [. . .] I believe that insofar as I use, or waste, these things for any other purpose or fail to take care of them so as to be able to give them at their best to this, that is for me the one real Sin. No, it's more than belief: I know.[9]

As John astutely observes, Rhondda's own passionate and heartfelt credo 'reaffirmed her feminism at a time when it was no longer so prominent in her paper', and importantly she believed that Bosanquet could help her (2013: 473–4). Her credo ends: 'I want you to understand this more than I want most things. It would make a big difference. Partly because you can help me so much [. . .] partly just that it would make me happy.'

Both handwritten statements appear to participate in an extended conversation between the two women about their convictions, motivations, and especially their ideas about the nature of 'work' and the relative value of the different ways in which a person might contribute to society. As Krista Cowman and Louise A. Jackson discuss in their introduction to a collection of essays on *Women and Work Culture*: 'what officially counts as "work" has been subject to definition'; further, what paid and unpaid labour has meant to individual women has varied considerably with different forms of work being viewed in terms of 'economic necessity, social aspiration (status), self-fulfilment, vocation, duty or service (or indeed any combination of these)' (2005: 6). For Rhondda and Bosanquet, the orientation in their credos to an ethic of public service marks the legacy of Victorian liberal feminism which, as Joyce Senders Pederson argues, 'was closely attuned to emergent professional ideals' and 'part of a general "culture of altruism"' that flourished in the Victorian period (2005: 28; 39). However, while feminists of this generation 'invested work with existential hopes that were both religious and secular in character', 'in the late nineteenth and early twentieth century, more materialist outlooks gained ground' and 'the "idea" of "worthy" work was increasingly coming to be associated with paid employment' (Pederson 2005: 28; 43–4). Bosanquet's statement in her credo that 'artists too perform real work' joins the voices of other writers concerned in this period (in the context of the economic depression) with justifying the function of art (Karshan 2011: 112) and asserts art's spiritual rather than monetary value. The language of self-sacrifice in Rhondda's credo is suggestive of a similarly religious vision of work, but the emphasis in her paper on women's advances in the professional sphere reflects her more materialist interests that are a key marker of the differences between the two women.

These differences are highlighted by the very provenance of the two credos discussed above, which are preserved among Bosanquet's papers in the archives of the Society of Psychical Research (SPR).[10] Bosanquet's interest in psychical research dates to the time she spent working for Henry James immediately before and during the early years of the First World War. But it was in 1933 (the same year she and Rhondda began their lifelong companionship) that an experiment in mediumship led to a more active interest in spiritualist phenomena and a commitment to one of its signature practices: automatic writing. Bosanquet's archive contains scores of automatic scripts she produced from the early 1930s well into the 1940s, and the significance of this material for her reviewing and literary editorship of *Time and Tide* will be the subject of further discussion in Chapter 8. Here, I consider its significance in relation to Bosanquet's and Rhondda's conversation about 'work', and the ways in which this writing itself performed a function in their new partnership. As Bette London has discussed, mediumship had an important place in women's culture of the modernist period. In particular, it attracted women from middle-class backgrounds with 'intellectual, artistic, and professional aspirations', and as 'occupations' and 'points of entrée into exclusive intellectual and artistic circles' modern practices of mediumship were 'important avenues for women's professionalization and mental development' (2007: 625–6). At the same time, as an amateur practice mediumship was predominantly the preserve of leisured middle-class women (London 2007: 631), and it is this tension between amateurism and professionalism that provides another marker of the different priorities and interests of Rhondda and *Time and Tide*'s future literary editor.

Bosanquet's experiment in mediumship began under the auspices of one of London's leading female mediums, Mrs Hester Dowden, who had a reputation for being able to contact literary figures (Sword 2002: 57; London 2007: 627). At an anonymous sitting in February 1933 'Henry James' communicated through the Ouija board that he wished to write a 'literary work' through Bosanquet, and much of Bosanquet's early automatic writing – which she began to practice regularly at home – is dominated by communications purporting to come from Henry and also William James concerning plans for this literary project.[11] This other-worldly commission, undertaken by Bosanquet with a certain amount of scepticism, was not an isolated phenomenon. As both London and Helen Sword have shown, the interwar years saw a publishing boom in spiritualist communications via automatic writing, the majority transmitted 'via female mediums from the proverbial company of "dead white men"' (Sword 2002: 42). However, it soon becomes apparent that Bosanquet wants to be more than a 'secretary' to James or any other dead male author; she desires to write something of her own.[12] Bosanquet's literary ambition is dramatically illustrated by some automatic writing produced, unusually, neither at a public séance, nor in the privacy of Bosanquet's home, but during the course of a meeting of the British Federation of University Women's 'Committee on International Relations'.

According to this script, while the committee discussed agenda items ranging from the 'dismissal of married university lecturers' to more mundane matters such as 'double voting' and the 'balance sheet', Bosanquet was conducting a conversation with 'William James' who tells her at one stage of the proceedings: 'I think that you personally do not take it all seriously, and I am very glad to sense that for you have a very much more important work to fulfil.'[13] Here, Bosanquet's psychic conflict between competing regimes of work is writ large. Boredom with her work as secretary of the IFUW fuels her fantasy of having 'more important work to fulfil', and it is significant that earlier in the script, during a discussion of the committee's selection of books for 1932, Bosanquet records having pointed out a title to 'William James' and written 'Virginia Woolf is very good'. Woolf's works attracted special attention from Bosanquet, as we will see in Chapter 8. But in contrast to Woolf, whose private income released her from the need to work, Bosanquet reminds her spirit communicators that 'I have to earn my living.' Work as economic necessity, we can infer, is an obstacle to the 'literary work' that is her real ambition.

This tension between work that performs a purely utilitarian function and work that has a higher value or importance for the individual lies at the heart of a letter Bosanquet wrote to *Time and Tide* in August 1934 in response to a series of articles recently published in the periodical's columns on 'The Debutante Market'. Contributed by Dorea Stanhope (an 'ex-Deb' now serving on the staff of the paper) and *Time and Tide*'s youngest director Winifred Holtby, the articles roundly debunked a social system devoted to parading women in the 'London Show-Ring' and failing to train them for more meaningful work and public service. Disrupting the assumptions on which their critique was based, Bosanquet writes:

> The assumption – I think I might say fallacy – which seems to me to underlie part of their argument is that *joie de vivre* is more likely to be found in what Miss Holtby calls 'the rigid routine of the professional job' than in amateur activities. Frankly, I do not believe it. There are some professional jobs which enhance life – among those one might class literary work (above a certain level of mediocrity) [. . .]. But large numbers of routine workers, male and female, do not find life in their work but in their leisure. All they get from work is the means for living. [. . .]
>
> Nor does what I have seen of voluntary activities carried on by the leisured permit me to share Miss Holtby's condemnation of these pursuits as lacking the 'fierce joy, absorbed interest and gaiety' of

professional work. [. . .] Is it worthwhile to discourage the amateur now, when with any luck we shall all within the next fifty or a hundred years be living mainly as leisured people? Are Miss Stanhope and Miss Holtby entirely justified in telling débutantes that the panacea for all their troubles is to find a grindstone and apply their noses to it? (11 Aug 1934: 1005)

The publication of Bosanquet's letter in *Time and Tide* is striking. As we have seen in earlier chapters of this book, *Time and Tide*'s promotion of professional opportunities for women and its strong espousal of a feminist 'duty to work' formed a core part of the periodical's identity and reflected a wider shift in feminism from the political to the economic sphere in this period.[14] Contesting the idea that professional work is necessarily liberating for women, Bosanquet's defence of the debutante and assertion of the value of voluntary and amateur activities also runs counter to the view propounded by Rhondda in the series of articles that launched her career as editor of the paper in 1926 that the 'leisured woman' posed 'a serious menace to society' (see Chapter 1). Bosanquet's critique of *Time and Tide*'s work ethic echoes socialist demands for less work and more leisure that Eleanor Farjeon's contributions to the paper had made visible nearly a decade earlier (see Chapter 2), and is also part of the legacy of aestheticism that would gain more prominence in the paper under Bosanquet's literary editorship (see the second section of this chapter).[15] Her final question regarding the value of telling young women to 'find a grindstone and apply their noses to it' might recall, for example, Oscar Wilde's assertion in 'The Soul of Man under Socialism' that: 'Man is made for something better than disturbing dirt' (cited in Karshan 2011: 117).

It was, however, *Time and Tide*'s professional environment that liberated Bosanquet from the 'very dull work' she did out of necessity for the IFUW.[16] In a letter to Henry James scholar, Leon Edel, in November 1935, Bosanquet declared:

I have changed my way of life . . . having migrated from SW3 to NW3 in close proximity to Hampstead Heath. I've left off being Secretary to the University Women's Federation too. Fifteen years of it was, I thought enough. I'm hoping to do a little study and writing in what leisure years human mortality and the European situation may permit . . . I'm busy being literary advisor (and pro tem acting as literary editor) to the weekly review *Time and Tide*. (Powers 2006: 124)

The new postcode refers to the home Bosanquet now shared with Rhondda in Hampstead, and her temporary position as *Time and Tide*'s literary editor was one she would in fact retain for the next eight years. But what is most striking about this letter is the way it positions the 'busy' nature of her advisory/editorial duties alongside the 'study and writing' she aspires to, and which remains identified with 'leisure' rather than work. Another typescript preserved among her papers in the SPR archive illuminates the importance for Bosanquet of preserving leisure. Entitled 'Plan of Work (Ideal)' and reflecting Bosanquet's developing spiritual and mystical interests, it charts a day that begins after breakfast with 'meditation and translation' and ends with 'healing passes and mental practice' (Figure 7.2). In between, 'literature of light kind' and 'more literary light work' is punctuated by regular lunch, tea and rest breaks, creating an 'ideal' day that is extraordinarily leisured compared with a typical day experienced by Rhondda who was accustomed to spending 'at least fourteen hours a day at her job' (Eoff 1991: 127). It is unlikely, of course, that this 'ideal' was habitually realised in practice. However, some sentences added in red pencil at the top of the page are suggestive of the kinds of negotiations she and Rhondda were involved in when they embarked on their personal and professional partnership. They read: 'This is our plan. It does not include line of social work. But this personality is no use in the plan of the world unless she is allowed literary line of service. She is seriously spearing a true literary link' (emphasis in original). Remobilising an idea of work as public service these lines insist on Bosanquet's contribution to the literary sphere, but their performative quality also evokes the idea that art is a form of play – a view that had become one of the main theories in European aesthetics by the beginning of the twentieth century (Karshan 2011: 6). Indeed, in two further sentences hand-printed in red towards the end of the typescript Bosanquet playfully invokes well-established literary associations between sleep and creativity (and developed by the surrealists, in whom Bosanquet also took an active interest): 'But I can make the night fertile. Tricks can be performed and immense privileges obtained.'[17]

In October 1935 *Time and Tide* announced 'A New Departure' in its columns, and this especially in its book reviews section. 'The progressive review in 1935', stated the editorial, 'has [. . .] to be radical in its book-out-look. It exists not to draw attention to styles which have arrived, but to symptoms which, though today slight, may indicate radical change soon.' Identifying 'Sociology' as one such symptom, *Time and Tide* continued:

THIS IS OUR PLAN ⓒ IT DOES NOT INCLUDE LINE OF SOCIAL WORK
BUT THIS PERSONALITY IS NO USE IN THE PLAN OF THE WORLD
UNLESS SHE IS ALLOWED LITERARY LINE OF SERVICE,
SHE IS, SERIOUSLY SPEAKING, A ~~Powerful~~ TRUE LITERARY ALL LINK.

PLAN OF WORK. (Ideal)

SPR. MS 7/11/16

7. Leave bed.

8. Breakfast.

8.30–10. Plane. Meditation and translation.

10. Pause, talk.

10.15– 12. Literature of light kind. This can go on with interval
till lunch.

1 – 2   Lunch and leisure.

2 – 3   Rest on bed.

3 – 4   Take plenty of air and exercise.

4.30   Tea.

5 – 7   More literary light work.

7 – 10   Dine, talk, read light and easy literature. Play with
young cat. Amuse Margaret. (This requires no effort)
Sometimes do little experiments in mental contact.

10 – 11   Prepare for Margaret's plane. By healing passes and
by mental practice. The actual passes over the afflicted
mentalities may take about ten minutes.

11 – 12   Make my own preparations. Bath. Hair tone. Bathing in
lamp rays. Malkuth in the plane of Netzach.

12 – 7   ~~Absent~~. Sleep supervenes. I leave my plan in the
hands of the higher powers. BUT I CAN MAKE
THE NIGHT FERTILE. TRICKS CAN BE PERFORMED
AND IMMENSE PRIVILEGES OBTAINED.

This plan is free. Should plane lift it will become superfluous.
Plenty of liberty is needed for friends. They will be best in the
moment of the evening light literature.

Figure 7.2 'Plan of Work (Ideal)'. Reproduced by kind permission
of the Syndics of Cambridge University Library. Classmark: SPR
MS 7/11/16.

TIME AND TIDE is therefore going, for the time being, to have a
sociological outlook and this particularly in its book section. Men
and Books will no longer be devoted purely to matters of literature.
Interspersed with Roderick Random's literary articles we shall publish others commenting freely on significant sociological and other
books and saying why we think such books should be watched, and
where we believe they tend. For we believe that this new science of
human society is not only the most important, but is, because of its
present transitional state, the peculiar concern of the review which is
really progressive. (12 Oct 1935: 1422)

From 1933 Bosanquet's own reviews for the paper were increasingly on such subjects as science, religion, spiritualism, mysticism and psychical research, and it is fascinating to read *Time and Tide*'s 'sociological turn' alongside an unclassified item among Bosanquet's papers in the SPR archive comprising notes of a sitting in which the spirits of the next world purportedly communicate to Rhondda through Bosanquet as their medium. The manuscript is undated, but was certainly produced after October 1933 as it refers to Rhondda's definition of *Time and Tide* in her credo as 'one of many possible instruments', and its early lines contain the statement: 'we want to give Margaret a new point of departure'.[18] Apparently, mediumship provided a way for Bosanquet to negotiate with Rhondda the future direction of *Time and Tide*, at least so far as the book reviews section was concerned. Although it is clear from the lengthy script that Rhondda remained extremely sceptical regarding the spirit controls' ontological existence, prior to *Time and Tide*'s 'new departure' she wrote on the subject of 'survivalism' in one of her signed articles for the paper, and observed that there were now a growing number of intellectuals who were keeping 'an open mind' on the question of survival after death (23 Feb 1935: 267). Among those she identified were Aldous Huxley, novelist, philosopher and close associate of the Bloomsbury Group, and the influential religious and science writer Gerald Heard. Both men were given a platform in *Time and Tide* in early 1936 (see Chapter 8), evidence of the ways in which the religious interests of the periodical's literary editor also fed into the front political pages of the paper. It is this dialogue between the secular and religious, material and spiritual, that I discuss next.

Radicals and mystics: Christianity, class and commitment

Time and Tide's announcement in its columns of 'A New Departure' (12 Oct 1935: 1422) coincided almost precisely with an event that is widely regarded as marking the beginning of the crisis in European democracy that would culminate in the Second World War: Italy's invasion of Abyssinia on 3 October 1935. In the same issue *Time and Tide*'s regular 'Review of the Week' opened on the conflict, and in its two leading articles the periodical called on the League of Nations to stand firm on collective security and advocated an immediate and co-ordinated response with respect to economic sanctions. As the deepening horror confronting Europe continued to unfold during the rest of this decade *Time and Tide* was vigilant in its coverage of political developments. Writing in the paper's 'Notes on the Way' column in May 1938 Lady Rhondda commented 'I [. . .] cannot keep my thoughts from the world situation' (14 May 1938: 663) and the periodical continued to extend the international outlook it had been developing since 1928 (see Chapter 5). The crisis in Europe also profoundly affected the literary landscape. Cultural historians of the era have emphasised the widespread politicisation of art and literature in the 1930s, most famously in the work of figures identified with the 'Auden Generation' who consciously rejected an earlier high modernist aesthetic. The rise of this new generation of writers was registered visibly in *Time and Tide*'s columns during the second half of this decade. In May 1936 *Time and Tide* published a poem by W. H. Auden, 'Europe 1936' (23 May: 754), and later the same year its 'Notes on the Way' feature was contributed by Stephen Spender who used the column to defend 'the political writer' following his recent lecture tour in the north of England on the subject of 'Writing and Politics' (19 Dec 1936: 1803). In April 1938 C. Day Lewis contributed a poem to *Time and Tide*'s spring book number, which also carried advertisements for books by Louis MacNeice, Christopher Isherwood and Edward Upward.[19] As a women's periodical *Time and Tide* tends to be overlooked in accounts of the 'literary left'. Andy Croft's important survey of the period *Red Letter Days* (1990) does not include *Time and Tide* in its index, although *Time and Tide*'s chief competitor the *New Statesman* is frequently cited, as is *Left Review* (1934–8). However, that many artists and writers published in *Left Review* also contributed to *Time and Tide* is a further reminder that this modern feminist magazine inhabited – in Lucy Delap's terms – 'overlapping periodical communities' (DiCenzo 2011: 174). For example, Naomi Mitchison, Winifred Holtby, Phyllis Bentley, Storm Jameson and Sylvia Townsend Warner all wrote for both periodicals, and *Time and Tide*'s graphic content during this period included lithographs by Pearl Binder and James Fitton, both contributors of artwork to *Left Review* and founding members of the Artists International Association (A.I.A.) which was formed in 1933 to mobilise 'the international unity of artists against Imperialist War on the Soviet Union, Fascism and Colonial oppression' (Morris and Radford 1983: 2).

That *Time and Tide*'s cultural pages should reflect the radical currents of this decade is not surprising given the periodical's strong political commitment, particularly with regards to feminism, from its inception. More unexpected, however, is the increasing prominence given simultaneously in this decade to a modernist view of art from which the *Left Review* writers and artists were turning away. In January 1935 *Time and Tide*'s 'Notes on the Way' were contributed by T. S. Eliot who, in his first article, questioned 'whether any of the social causes agitated in our time is complete enough to provide much food for poetry' (5 Jan 1935: 7). This was the first time that Eliot's signature appeared in the periodical, and it highlights a second line of influence in *Time and Tide* that seems to directly compete with 'radicals' on the literary left. In the same article Eliot goes on to articulate his different response to a world in crisis: 'I believe we need, on the one hand, a rigorous study and practice of Christian ethics, and, on the other, such economic changes as will tend to make it impossible for any nation to have anything to *gain* by war' (7). That Eliot's Anglo-Catholicism has become almost synonymous with his conservative, anti-democratic politics has arguably lent force to the persistent view that modernity and religion are at odds.[20] Indeed, in contrast with Eliot's advocacy of 'the just impartiality of the Christian philosopher' and his *Criterion*'s stance of detachment (Harding 2002: 198–9), *Time and Tide*'s claim to be a 'progressive review' is supported by its books pages which were joined by an increasing number of writers and critics on the left, some of them committed political party members, activists and organisers, and including Ralph Bates, Phyllis Bottome, Lettice Cooper, James Hanley, Malcolm Muggeridge, George Orwell and Raymond Postgate.[21] At the same time, under the literary editorship of Theodora Bosanquet there grew a small nexus of reviewers who shared her more esoteric interests in spiritualism, mysticism and religion, among them the religious writer Evelyn Underhill, the poet, novelist and theologian Charles Williams, the anthropologist Geoffrey Gorer (whose interest in religion and magic in *Bali and Angkor* attracted Bosanquet's notice), and Renee Haynes (Tickell) who, like Bosanquet, was a member of the Society of Psychical Research and later wrote a history of the organisation, published in 1982. Since the relationship between feminism and religion has also often been assumed to be an antithetical one, this 'religious turn' in the periodical might appear to represent a conservative shift away from the paper's more radical commitments.[22] However, it is my aim to show that *Time and Tide*'s dialogue between 'radical' and 'mystics' may not be as oppositional as it first appears.

I begin by presenting, in full, a poem written by Bosanquet and published in *Time and Tide*'s issue of 22 February 1936. Its rather laboured lines and forced symbolism go some way to illustrating why Bosanquet never established herself as a poet. However, as a cultural artefact it is interesting for the position it takes up in relation to debates about art and politics in this decade. The poem is entitled 'Art for Life's Sake' and reads:

> By graven metal,
> By chiselled stone,
> Touched strings – or the breath
> Through a hollow reed blown,
>
> By the pattern of word
> Black on the page,
> We may assure
> Love's heritage.
>
> Only the image
> Bound by no art
> Fades and is lost
> In the changing heart.
>
> The voice whose music
> Moves tears and laughter
> Will stir no echo
> In days hereafter.
>
> And the form beloved,
> The lighted eyes,
> We shall encounter
> Without surprise.

Appearing in the periodical exactly three months before Auden's 'Europe 1936', Bosanquet's poem couldn't be more at odds with the work then being produced by the younger generation of left-wing poets. In contrast with Auden's poem, where references to 'poverty', 'weapon-making' and terrified crowds underscore the 'violent features' of contemporary Europe, Bosanquet's poem is completely emptied of any reference to the present political moment, seemingly existing on an entirely different plane and enacting high modernism's declared separation of art and politics. 'Art' is the poem's central subject: in whatever form – sculpture, music or poetry – art makes permanent and immortal the process of change that defines human experience, and as such it subscribes to a high modernist regard for universal values. But at the same time the poem's title presents a subtle challenge to formalist approaches to art, captured most influentially in Roger Fry's claim (in 'An Essay on Aesthetics') that 'in art we have no moral responsibility' (Berman 2011: 49). In its deliberate reworking of the famous slogan of late nineteenth-century aestheticism ('Art for Art's Sake') the title 'Art for *Life's* Sake' suggests that art's search for pure form is not a retreat from the experience of living in a world of crisis, but necessary for the preservation of life itself. With this move the poem thus revives an earlier nineteenth-century emphasis on art's social function, and its vision of eternity recalls Bosanquet's belief (articulated in her 'Credo') that by revealing beauty the artist performs a service to humanity. As previously noted, this idea also runs through her early book reviews for *Time and Tide*; indeed, a 1930 review of essays by Katherine Mansfield apparently gave her the title for her 1936 poem:

> Katherine Mansfield was in love with life and with art for life's sake. She believed that artists are people moved more deeply and continuously aware of the wonder and glory of life than others, and she saw it as the duty of the kind of artist who uses words to communicate some at least of the wonder and the glory to readers. (25 Oct 1930: 1342)

Again, in language similar to her 'Credo' Bosanquet elevates the artist's role as a special kind of 'duty' to reveal the 'wonder and glory of life'; several years later, in a review of Woolf's novel *The Years*, she would assert even more boldly: 'It is not a poet's function (*pace* Mr. Auden & Co.) to offer a sociological tract but to give us more abundant life' (13 Mar 1937: 353). This statement clearly aligns her with aestheticist approaches to Woolf that defined early Woolf criticism. However, as I show below, this does not mean that she was politically unengaged.

Jessica Berman, in her important book *Modernist Commitments*, has shown that 'our continuing assumption that modernist aesthetics of the sort Woolf espoused were antithetical to overt political engagement' has obscured an alternative view of modernism in which ethics, politics and aesthetics combine (2011: 49). Her analysis of 'the interconnection of ethics and aesthetics' in Woolf's novels (62) builds on feminist readings of a 'political Woolf' which have largely displaced earlier views of Woolf as 'excessively private, unconcerned with and divorced from politics and the public realm' (Snaith 2000a: 2). Bosanquet, too, was not unconcerned with or divorced from the most urgent social and political questions of her time. Through her work for the IFUW she was very well travelled, and outside *Time and Tide*'s book review columns she more than once contributed articles and letters to the periodical reflecting her international interests and anxiety about Europe.[23] In her 'Credo' Bosanquet also stated her belief 'that Ethics should be linked to Aesthetics' and *Time and Tide*'s positioning of her poem 'Art for Life's Sake' directly alongside its correspondence columns highlights a conversation between art and politics in this periodical in which its author was an active partici-pant (see Figure 7.3). The leading items on this page were several letters from readers written in reply to Gerald Heard, who (as previ-ously noted) had been given a platform in *Time and Tide* in early 1936. Among these is a letter bearing the signature 'Martin Tindal' which – as I have discovered among Bosanquet's papers at Harvard University – was one of two pseudonyms Bosanquet began using for some of her contributions to *Time and Tide* from 1936.[24] This star-tling find – a letter submitted pseudonymously by the same author of a signed poem printed on the previous page – not only sheds more light on Bosanquet's political engagement, but is also highly sugges-tive of the complex ways in which ethics and aesthetics intercon-nected in this periodical.

In this letter Bosanquet (writing as Martin Tindal) conceded that Heard's articles 'leave us in no doubt about our almost certain fate', but she questioned his definition of 'civilization'. Observing that if he means by this 'a standard of living dependent on applied science, a matter of gas and electricity, railways, motor-cars and ships [. . .] that [. . .] will hardly be destroyed by a conflagration of the capital cities of Europe'; in a few years 'the world would probably recover its civilization' in such new centres as New Zealand and the United States. She continues:

> If, on the other hand, Mr. Heard means a social organization based on the principles of justice and freedom and offering its members security for the exercise of their finer capacities, the thing is non-existent. The vast majority of people live under the constant menace of poverty, and nothing, not even the threat of incendiary bombing, is so destructive to civilized life. (22 Feb 1936: 264)

Submitted under a pseudonym this letter preserves Bosanquet's stance of 'detachment' which Fry argued to be 'the supreme necessity of the artist' (there is no reason for the reader to identify its writer with the author of the poem printed overleaf), but it also reveals the impossibility of remaining silent or apart from the most pressing political and social issues of the day. Its searing condemnation of the conditions under which the majority of people in the so-called 'civi-lized' world are forced to live evidences Bosanquet's understanding dragged herself to her feet and staggered to where the baby lay, pitifully limp in the dust. She half lifted the child, then fell forward herself, throwing it from her with one last desperate motion.

This time the girl lay still, but the little black baby threshed the air with tiny, stick-like arms.

"Damn!" muttered the military correspondent. "War's hell!"

Hello! Not the planes back already?

Dark shapes showed in the sky again. Some more of Africa's birds. Vultures—five of them. Trust them to know where the dead lay!

But the baby had moved its arms. . . . Birds of prey began with the eyes as a rule. . . .

"Hi! Shush! Get off, you brutes!" the military correspondent shouted absurdly, waving his arms at the great, evil-looking birds, which could not see or hear him, and would not have minded if they had.

Then, because he did not like to think of a not-quite-dead baby being finished off by those fiercely hooked beaks set in the repulsive bald heads, he fixed his mind determinedly again on the memory of old Jim and the swallow's nest.

"That is that person's house. . . . You cannot break up a person's house."

Well, the poor devils who had left their houses and lives down there wouldn't find much when they returned.

As the military correspondent sat waiting for the return of the departed planes, a preposterous idea took possession of his mind. Wasn't that good-for-nothing old Kaffir Jim, with his kind old eyes, in his tattered shirt and deplorable trousers, perhaps a finer human being than the representative of Power and Might and Honour and Glory who had sent those death-dealing machines up the valley?

An absurd thought, yet it persisted.

"Oh, thinking's a mistake!" grunted the military correspondent, and, drawing a pad from his pocket, began to write rapidly and with scarcely a pause.

"An aerial reconnaisance was carried out by a squadron of bombing planes with entire success. Bombs were dropped on enemy encampments. No casualties are reported, but it is believed that the enemy's losses were severe. . . . "   G. HARVEY.

Art for Life's Sake

By graven metal,
By chiseled stone,
Touched strings—or the breath
Through a hollow reed blown,

By the pattern of words
Black on the page,
We may assure
Love's heritage.

Only the image
Bound by no art
Fades and is lost
In the changing heart.

The voice whose music
Moves tears and laughter
Will stir no echo
In days hereafter.

And the form beloved,
The lighted eyes,
We shall encounter
Without surprise.

THEODORA BOSANQUET.

LETTERS TO THE EDITOR

Letters, which should preferably not exceed 300 words, must be written on one side of the paper only, and should reach TIME AND TIDE offices not later than first post on Tuesday morning. They should, if possible, be typewritten, and must be accompanied by the name and address of the writer, which will not, however, be published if a request is made to that effect.

REPLIES TO GERALD HEARD

SIR,—It is with great interest and appreciation that I have so far followed Gerald Heard's masterly analysis of the present world situation. I should have thought that "muddled thinking" would be the last possible offence of which we could accuse him.

Philip Jordan disputes the statement that "the real sources of war, we all know, are not arms, but passions. The real reasons for fighting are no longer economic." The only part of that sentence of Mr. Heard's which is not true is "we all know"; but for that lapse, the essence of the statement is true. I fear that Mr. Jordan's purely materialistic diagnosis will not do, for is man conditioned by economic forces or is he largely himself to blame for the present world chaos? I incline to the latter view. It is almost impossible to over-estimate the extent to which man has created his own economic environment.

I would also express my entire agreement with Gerald Heard in tracing the primary cause of world trouble to that final particle of the world community—the individual. Is not the chaos without merely the vast, magnified, projection of the sum total of all the moral chaos within?

In modern weapons and warfare, I see nothing but the logical working out of man's attempt, throughout history, to bring about, by force, the morality which is necessary to his civilization.

It is apparent that all the most learned arguments of the psychological and sociological sciences are merely leading us to conclusions and decisions, known, and acted upon, by Jesus Christ, nearly two thousand years ago.

I am an eager and appreciative reader of TIME AND TIDE, and fully realize the sincerity and good intention of your support of the "collective security through the League of Nations" theory. The successful working of such a scheme, however, depends principally upon the integrity and moral capacity of each and every one of the members of the League to respect and honour all their Treaty obligations.

I would suggest that when that moral stage is reached, by all the Nations of the League, that the collective security clause will no longer be needed.

Surely, then, in view of these facts, we are at present, in our efforts to save civilization "putting the cart before the horse."

Those who, like Mr. Lansbury, hold the Christian view of life, in peace and war alike, are everywhere accused of being mere impractical idealists, but the time has come when we must be prepared to take risks for peace—those risks which Mr. Heard tells us that the modern anthropologist takes, when he sits unarmed, outside the village of an angry wild tribe—those risks which the staff of a modern asylum take, where the lunatic is no longer bound, but treated "as though he were one of us seized with a convulsion which will pass and leave him."

I am, etc.,

GEORGE J. GARTON.

35 Hallstile Bank,
Hexham, Northumberland.

SIR,—May I correct Mr. Gerald Heard on one small point? He says we shall win if "we use the method of an alienist helping and curing a paranoiac." Recorded cures of full-blown paranoia do not amount to more than half-a-dozen.

I am, etc.,

J. I. STURGES.

Blagdon, Somerset.

SIR,—Whether my analysis of the causes of war is Marxian, or Humpty-Dumptyan is beside the point, so long as it is correct. What is not beside the point is to make clear which is the cart and which the horse—

Figure 7.3 'Art for Life's Sake', *Time and Tide* 22 Feb 1936: 263. Reproduced with the permission of The William Ready Division of Archives and Research Collections, McMaster University Library.

that 'poverty' poses as significant a threat to human life as fascism and war, and invites comparison with writing produced by the radical left in this decade. Indeed, the substance of this letter introduces another context for interpreting the title of her poem which resonates with the manifesto of an American radical magazine of the period *Rebel Poet* (1931–2): 'We ridicule the musty echoes of the fin de siècle slogan "Art for Art's Sake" and inscribe on our banner: "ART FOR HUMANITY'S SAKE"' (Conroy and Johnston 1973: xiii). Co-founded by Jack Conroy, one of the most prominent and influential working-class writers in early 1930s America, *Rebel Poet* (and the Rebel Poets organisation from which it emerged) represented an eclectic grouping of writers on the left including anarchists, liberals, communists and Christian socialists whose goal, as Berman summarises, was 'to create a decentred, anti-foundationalist community of radical writers around the world' (2011: 253). Its successor, the *Anvil* (1933–5), became one of the most significant little magazines of the left in the period and 'circulated widely in the United States and abroad, and not only in communist circles' (Berman 2011: 249). Given Bosanquet's international connections and interest in new literary movements it is unlikely that she would have been unfamiliar with these periodicals and their distinctive Midwestern vernacular modernism.

In Britain, reports of mass unemployment and poverty, and the highly visible hunger marches of this decade, brought the class-nature of society to the surface of middle-class consciousness. In early 1934 *Time and Tide* printed articles by Walter Greenwood and Winifred Holtby on a national hunger march organised by the National Unemployed Workers Movement (NUWM) that year, one of several hunger marches in the interwar period.[25] In September 1935, just two weeks before *Time and Tide* announced its 'New Departure', Rhondda invited a new attention to class in the periodical's pages:

> We have found the courage during the past thirty years to look sex in the face. We have in fact looked it in the face so much and so often that a change would be welcome. What about dropping sex for a year or two and picking up class instead? What about trying to achieve as purely an objective attitude towards it as during the past fifteen years or so we have tried [. . .] to achieve towards sex? (28 Sep 1935: 1360)

Rhondda went on in this article to state that she could 'find no kind of theoretical justification for the class-system as we know it today', though her reluctance to 'follow the true Left-Winger' all the way registers the limits of her radical commitment. Distancing herself from the position of communists and Marxists her doubt concerning how deep class feeling goes ('I feel that there are limits, beyond which one is merely human, neither capitalist demon nor proletarian angel') (1362) drew a spirited response from the left-wing radical Ellen Wilkinson who, in a letter published in *Time and Tide* the following week, pointed out that 'class is not a matter of [. . .] personal emotions' but determined by one's place in the scheme of production and therefore 'part of our life pattern, deeper than consciousness itself' (12 Oct 1935: 1434). Wilkinson, who re-entered Parliament as Labour MP for Jarrow in the general election of November 1935, was a regular contributor to *Time and Tide* during the 1930s and became a close friend of Rhondda who, despite their differences, valued her ideas and advice and considered her one of the paper's 'best friends' (John 2013: 485). Given Wilkinson's involvement in revolutionary politics (she was a member of the Communist Party and joined and helped found other communist-led organisations) this association is evidence that the periodical continued to include political radicals among its core collaborators as it advanced through its second decade.[26] Though *Time and Tide* never adopted the revolutionary language of a periodical like *Left Review*, its publication in March and April 1935 of a series of articles on 'The Abolition of Poverty' demonstrated a campaigning zeal to tackle a problem regarded by the writers 'to transcend all others in importance at the present time' (9 Mar 1935: 331).[27] *Time and Tide*'s 'discovery' in the same year of a northern writer Winifred Williams, who contributed a number of hard-hitting short stories on various aspects of working life between 1935 and 1939, evidences the interest this periodical shared with other journals and publishers on the left in working-class writing.[28]

Bosanquet, as her comment on 'Auden & Co.' reveals in her review of Woolf's novel *The Years* (cited above), was herself uninspired by the new work being produced by the next generation of British writers. She also seems to have shared with Rhondda, early in their new partnership, a scepticism towards Communism as the answer to the world's problems. In a piece published in *Time and Tide*'s 'Miscellany' section in June 1934 she defends individualism over collectivism and the group lauded in left-wing writing of this period, and apparently accepts the association frequently made between 'Bolshevism' and 'Fascism' as twin forms of 'totalitarianism'.[29] As a recent convert to the Christian faith, the Communist Party's hostility to the Church no doubt reinforced the distance Bosanquet felt between

herself and writers associated with the new political movements on
the left. Later in 1934, in a review for *Time and Tide* of a book
on the Austrian philosopher and theologian Friedrich Von Hügel,
Bosanquet remarks on 'How very odd it is to be a Christian!' when
belief in the supernatural 'is out of favour just now among the intelligentsia' and 'scores of passionate young men and women are out
to exorcize a religion that is posed as a baleful bogey blocking the
march to humanity to the proletarian paradise of the good life for
all' (24 Nov 1934: 1512). However, by the spring of 1937 Bosanquet appears to have revised her position. In a review of *Christianity
and Communism*, a symposium of articles and letters first published
in the *Spectator* (Harris 1937), she states that while 'there can be
no final synthesis' between Marxism and Christianity 'there can
be some temporary tolerance'. She observes: 'The less intransigent
Christians are ready enough to admit that the Communists have stolen an ethical march on the Church' (13 Apr 1937: 524). Bosanquet's
review, and the volume which is its subject, registers the emergence
of new strategic alliances which formed between communists and
Christians from the mid-1930s, particularly in the context of peace
and anti-fascist movements, as progressive religious leaders emphasised 'the revolutionary character of the Christian faith' (John Lewis
1935: 28).[30] In the second half of this decade Bosanquet was reviewing far more books for *Time and Tide* on religious subjects than
on literature, and contrary to the influential notion 'that religion
promoted a political passivity and a concern with otherworldliness
among women' (Dixon 2010: 191), her faith appears to have provided the primary context for the growth of more radical instincts.
Bosanquet's automatic writing, which she continued to practise regularly throughout the 1930s, shines a light on this, evidencing that
what might appear to be a mystical turn inward was actually more
socially and politically engaged.

By the end of 1935 Bosanquet's automatic writing was most commonly 'dictated' by a spirit (or internal) communicator simply identified as 'O.' and explained in one script to be her 'guardian'.[31] A
significant number of these scripts seem to take the form of Christian
meditations, mirroring Bosanquet's increasing preoccupation with
religious over literary subjects in this period. Some deliberately reflect
upon parables or other passages from the Bible, such as the following
transcript of some writing produced between 9.50 and 10.05 a.m.
on 25 March 1937 which I present in full, including Bosanquet's
explanatory note:

'The Ointment of Spikenard'

(Yesterday, as I was watching Margaret being fitted for her Coronation robes, I had my usual mild socialist reaction against these prices and these luxury shops. As I was inwardly protesting, the words 'Why was not this ointment sold for three hundred pence and given to the poor' flowed into my head. T. B.)

O. Coronation robes are provided at a monstrous cost. Really, the fancy price represents symbolically the gulf between day labourer and princely liver.

But in this event it would be wrong to restrain peers.

All must bear their symbol.

As for the ointment which Mary sacrificed:

Isolation. Devotion.

Heavily perfumed ointment was poured about the feet of the Lord Jesus Christ.[32]

The occasion for this meditation, as Bosanquet's note reveals, was Rhondda's preparation to attend the Coronation of King George VI and Queen Elizabeth which took place at Westminster Abbey on 12 May 1937. In an account of the ceremony, published as a special supplement to *Time and Tide*, Rhondda described her robes as 'very solid red velvet', emphasising the luxury of the garments which she wore with 'tiara, and [. . .] such further pearls and diamonds as I possessed' (15 May 1937: no page). What is striking about Bosanquet's inward protest against the 'monstrous cost' of the robes is the Christian context provided by the Gospel story that frames her 'mild socialist reaction'. Just as the onlookers in the Gospel of St John question Mary's extravagance in using so costly an ointment to anoint Jesus's feet, Bosanquet's reflection on the extreme disparities between rich and poor, highlighted by Rhondda's expenditure, registers her discomfort. Interestingly, a tension between material and spiritual values finds its way into Rhondda's account of the Coronation which opens by presenting the words of the Gospel read at the Coronation service: 'Render therefore unto Caesar the things which are Caesar's: and unto God the things that are God's'. In a fascinating hint at the cross-currents influencing *Time and Tide* under the direction of the new partnership forged between its political and literary editors, Rhondda writes that the words 'forced upon one the clash of two different and opposing sets of values, the glittering values of Caesar's empire and the invisible values of another kingdom' (15 May 1937: no page).

It is this 'clash of [. . .] values' that prompts a dialogue between the religious and the secular which I am arguing to be an underlying feature of *Time and Tide* in the latter part of its second decade. Rhondda's account of the Coronation conscientiously reminded readers 'that the Abbey, in which the brilliant glittering crowd was assembled, had been built for another purpose [. . .] than to serve as the perfect background for a pageantry which symbolized all the might of a great Empire' (15 May 1937: no page), but as John observes it also 'carefully stressed her rank as a viscountess' in the context of her long battle to secure the admission of women to the House of Lords on the same terms as men (2013: 466). In Bosanquet's 'Ointment of Spikenard' script, the words 'in this event it would be wrong to restrain peers. All must bear their symbol' carry an acknowledgement of the importance for feminism that lay in Rhondda dressing in full regalia and taking a position 'on a level' with the peers seated around her, their own 'crimson velvet robes only visible here and there beneath the white ermine' (15 May 1937: no page). In the context of this modern feminist magazine, forged in an equal-rights tradition, Rhondda's peerage claim had wider implications for the status of women. However, it was precisely *Time and Tide*'s materialist emphasis on women's advances in the physical world that concerned its literary editor. Among Bosanquet's papers preserved in the SPR archive are several items which suggest that, in addition to her private meditations, she was using her spirit communications to negotiate her relationship with Rhondda and the direction of the periodical. In the manuscript cited earlier (in which it is communicated through Bosanquet that spirits in the next world wish to give Rhondda 'a new point of departure') the controls elaborate:

> To us you seem to be living in a very dark world. And we don't know where you think you are trying to lead your free men and women. We don't believe in freedom and responsibility unless they are combined with a view which takes account of the possibility at least of the universe being as much man's abode as the planet earth is. [. . .] We do want the leaders to have more light. That is why we want Margaret to be determined to free women for something more than material work.[33]

In another echo of Bosanquet's 'Credo' the central message is that Rhondda (and by extension *Time and Tide*) is too much caught up with women's employment and (professional) work in the present life at the expense of their spiritual development in preparation for the life hereafter. At the end of the script, before its descent into an illegible page of writing, the spirits conclude: 'We think that all Communists, all Socialists, all Feminists, all Sex Reformers, all Religions are mistaken if they think that success along material lines will bring the world peace'.

According to Joy Dixon 'opposition to materialism was a central concern of spiritualists' (2010: 216), but it was Rhondda's materialist feminism which continued to wield the greater influence on *Time and Tide*, particularly in relation to women's new economic earning power as we have seen (Chapter 1). As early as 1923 *Time and Tide* published a series of articles on 'Women and their Money' which showed Rhondda's willingness to violate what Jean Mills describes as 'one of the most enduring tenets of Victorian etiquette – ladies do *not* talk about money', just as Woolf would do in *A Room of One's Own* and *Three Guineas* (2016: 222). More than ten years later Winifred Holtby gave a humorous account in *Time and Tide* of a recent encounter with 'a middle-aged business man' who declared that papers such as the *Financial Times* 'should be forbidden to Ladies. A bit strong meat for them' (11 May 1935: 678). Economics, like Foreign Affairs, was a masculine field, and one Rhondda considered it important for women to enter. As noted at the outset of this chapter, by the autumn of 1935 *Time and Tide* had established relationships with another important group of advertisers promoting financial services and products, and in an automatic script dated 11 September 1935 Bosanquet's irritation with Rhondda's exertions 'in a hard-hearted business direction with her eye glued to the progress of the advertisement revenue of *Time and Tide*' is palpable.[34] However, as I have argued above, Bosanquet's greater preoccupation with men and women's spiritual progress does not represent a retreat from material realities, but a context for the growth of radical sympathies. Indeed, in 1937 she participated in the Mass Observation Day-Surveys coordinated by the project's communist co-founder Charles Madge, and in 1939 responded to its Directives on 'Class' and 'Race'.[35] In contrast with T. S. Eliot, whose religion is virtually synonymous with his conservatism, Bosanquet's religious conversion seems to have led her in more democratic directions.

In December 1936, in response to a request from the Artists International Association, Woolf developed her most candid statement on the relation between aesthetics and politics in 'Why Art Today Follows Politics' published in the *Daily Worker*, the newspaper of the Communist Party of Great Britain. In this essay Woolf states that '[t]he practice of art, far from making the artist out of touch with his kind, rather increases his sensibility', and suggests that since it 'breeds in him a feeling for the passions and needs of mankind in the mass [. . .] even if he be ineffective, he is by no means apathetic'. She continues:

> [I]t is clear that that artist is affected as powerfully as other citizens when society is in chaos, although the disturbance affects him in different ways. His studio is now far from being a cloistered spot where he can contemplate his model or his apple in peace. It is besieged by voices, all disturbing, some for one reason, some for another. (2008: 215)

One of the enduring fascinations of mediumship is, as London observes, 'the way it literalizes things' (1999: 23). In Bosanquet's automatic scripts of the mid-1930s onwards the 'chaos' of society is registered in innumerable references to war, violence and the build-up of armaments under the darkening shadow cast by Hitler and Mussolini across Europe, while the 'voices' of intellectual figures including Gerald Heard and Aldous Huxley present a different kind of 'disturbance' with their appeals and political programmes in the name of peace. Bosanquet's partnership with Rhondda gave her a room of her own (two, in fact, in the home they shared in Hampstead), and an earned income of around £500 a year (the figure Woolf calculated as necessary for a woman to write), but this was no mystic's withdrawal to the peaceful silence of the cloister.[36] Far from representing a retreat from the world, Bosanquet's automatic writing advocates ever-greater attention to it – as will be seen in the next chapter.

Notes

1. *Time and Tide* registered this loss in a pair of verses printed in its correspondence columns in 1937: 'The Plaint of a Middlebrow Novelist' and 'A Reply to the "Middlebrow Novelist"'. See Clay (2011: 87–9).
2. In January 1936, the overt male encodings in the periodical's cover image were removed: the front advertising wrapper still carries an advertisement for financial services, but without the male head-and-shoulders image.
3. *Time and Tide* adopted red covers for its monthly double numbers dating from 13 October 1934, and moved permanently into red covers with its issue of 9 February 1935. Leila Ryan and Maria DiCenzo note that the *Englishwoman* (1909–21) 'sported a red cover throughout its run which was remembered fondly by its supporters' (DiCenzo et al. 2011: 128).

4. Bosanquet obtained her BSc from University College, the University of London. She served the IFUW for fifteen years from 1920 to 1935.
5. MR to WH, 17 October 1933. WH Collection [WH/5/5.17/04/01h].
6. TB SPR MS 7/11/15.
7. According to Michael Valdez Moses 'From his earliest political essays and journalism Pound judges the worth of a political regime [. . .] according to whether it promotes culture, arts, and letters in the broadest sense' (2010: 143).
8. MR to WH 11 April 1933. WH Collection [WH/5/5.17/03/01s].
9. TB SPR MS 7/11/15.
10. The Society of Psychical Research was founded in 1882 with the stated aim to study objectively claims for the existence of supernatural phenomena.
11. See Chapter 4 in Pamela Thurschwell (2001) for a discussion of this material.
12. See Thurschwell 2001 (101–6) for an account of this material.
13. TB SPR 7/2/32.
14. As Johanna Alberti explains, economic independence became the 'new morality' in 1920s feminism; 'the post-war feminist believed that it was her duty to find professional work which would provide her with an income' (1989: 132).
15. In a study of the Russian novelist Vladimir Nabokov, Thomas Karshan traces this development of aestheticism in the work of modernist authors who resist work (2011: 116–20).
16. In a letter dated 25 September 1932 to Henry James scholar Leon Edel, Bosanquet explains that it is her 'very dull work' for the IFUW that has delayed her response to his interesting letter of 1 August (Powers 2006: 116).
17. Bosanquet took an active interest in surrealism long before the movement was taken up by British culture in the London Surrealist Exhibition of 1936. In 1926 an article she had submitted to the *Criterion* was returned to her by T. S. Eliot who, with an unusual lack of critical judgement, did not consider the surrealists important enough to justify the care with which she had approached the subject. TSE to TB, 21 June 1926. TB Harvard. [MS Eng 1213.3.81] Later Bosanquet discussed the surrealists in a 'Men and Books' essay for *Time and Tide* where she notes André Breton's discovery 'that the threshold of sleep is also the threshold of inspiration' (28 Dec 1935: 1931).
18. TB SPR MS 7/8.
19. Lewis's poem 'Self-Criticism and Answer' was published in *Time and Tide*'s issue of 9 April 1938 (494).
20. Recent scholarship has challenged the secularisation thesis: that is, the idea that secularity is constitutive of modernity. In modernist studies, too, scholars have challenged the consensus that modernism was secular. See especially Suzanne Hobson (2011), Pericles Lewis (2010), Leon Surette (1993), Helen Sword (2002), and Leigh Wilson (2013).

21. Bates was an organiser of the International Brigades in the Spanish Civil War; Bottome helped to secure the safe transport of Jews from Nazi Germany; Cooper was a committed socialist and Labour Party activist; Hanley was a proletarian novelist; Muggeridge was writing in the 1930s as an independent socialist (though he later moved to a right-wing religious stance); Postgate was a lifetime socialist and former communist.

22. This consensus has also been challenged by recent scholarship on gender and religion. See especially Joanna DeGroot and Sue Morgan (2015) and Sue Morgan and Jacqueline DeVries (2010).

23. For example, in a three-part series on 'The Concert of Europe' in May 1929 she discussed the importance of promoting good international relations, and in 1931 she entered *Time and Tide*'s correspondence columns to express her concern about the rise of nationalism across Europe and the failure of the leaders of public opinion to take action against 'a common danger threatening all their countries' (3 Jan 1931: 14).

24. Several of her book reviews in the second half of the 1930s were published under this and another pseudonym, Egon Heath.

25. These articles were printed in *Time and Tide*'s issues of 24 February 1934 (Greenwood) and 3 March 1934 (Holtby).

26. See Paula Bartley for a discussion of Wilkinson's radical politics.

27. These articles, written by 'two students of the economic problem' under a joint pseudonym 'Duplex', ran from 9 March to 13 April 1935.

28. *Time and Tide* claimed its 'discovery' of Winifred Williams in its 'Notes on Some Contributors' on 12 October 1935.

29. 'Go to the Swan' (23 June 1934: 798). The argument is made by way of an analogy between the social behaviour of the bee and the ant which is compared with that of the swan.

30. John Lewis, a former minister who became a communist in 1938, played an important role in mediating between the Communist Party and the Anglican Church in the mid-1930s. Another key figure was the 'Red Dean' of Canterbury, Hewlett Johnson. In another volume of 1937, founding Communist Party member T. A. Jackson stated, in an essay on 'Communism, Religion and Morals', that between Marxism and religion 'there is more room for agreement [. . .] than might seem possible' (227). I am grateful to Ben Harker for sharing his knowledge of this subject with me.

31. TB SPR MS 7/5/100 (11 Oct 1935). On the connections between spiritualism and Catholicism, Jenny Hazelgrove observes that 'mediums often spoke of their "guardian angel" and prayed to their spirit-guides as one would pray to a favourite saint' (2000: 67).

32. TB SPR MS 7/6/44.

33. TB SPR MS 7/8.

34. TB SPR MS 7/4/22.

35. Mass Observers would not usually be identified, but given the significance of Bosanquet's involvement for the subject discussed here it is necessary to do so and relevant permissions have been obtained.
36. In her response to the Mass Observation Directive on 'Class' in June 1939, Bosanquet states that her 'earned income has varied, but for the greater part of the time it has been about £500'. MOA, DR 2033, reply to June 1939 Directive. For more on Mass Observation, see Hinton (2013) and Hubble (2006).

Chapter 8

'A Free Pen': Women Intellectuals and the Public Sphere

Towards the end of 1935, shortly after the re-election of Britain's National Government under the leadership of Conservative Prime Minister Stanley Baldwin, *Time and Tide* reminded readers that it was 'part of our deliberate policy to allow "Notes on the Way" writers an entirely free pen, however much we may disagree with them'. Declaring that 'under no other condition than that of the consciousness of perfect freedom' could the kind of notes it wanted be written, *Time and Tide* went on to introduce its Notes writer this week, the nonconformist journalist Malcolm Muggeridge, with the editorial explanation that: 'We, ourselves, disagree with quite nine-tenths of what he has to say. [. . .] Nevertheless, he seems to us the kind of person who should – occasionally – be heard. He is think-ing hard' (30 Nov 1935: 1735). Originally conceived of and writ-ten by one of *Time and Tide*'s most provocative writers, St. John Ervine (see Chapter 5), since 1932 'Notes on the Way' had hosted many writers of different political persuasions, and *Time and Tide*'s restatement of 'Our Policy' in this piece is consistent with the peri-odical's commitment from its inception to fostering open dialogue and debate between 'thinking' men and women. Nearly three years later, at the height of the Munich Crisis, another of *Time and Tide*'s 'Notes on the Way' writers, Edward Thompson, stated that: 'These Notes are the greatest opportunity in current journalism. Nowhere else are you free of the censorship clamped down, with increasing firmness, on newspaper column and broadcast talk' (24 Sep 1938: 1307). Thompson's praise for the 'opportunity' afforded by *Time and Tide*'s columns for unfettered opinion and comment is a further testament to the reputation the periodical had by now established among men as well as women as a leading weekly review. However, the freedom exercised in the periodical's pages must be qualified by the fact that by 1938 the vast majority of *Time and Tide*'s Notes writers were men. To be sure, the column continued to host such distinguished figures as Odette Keun, Rose Macaulay and Ellen Wilkinson, as well as the periodical's political and literary editors Lady Rhondda and Theodora Bosanquet. But the marked decline in women's contributions inevitably raises questions about the extent to which women enjoyed 'perfect freedom' in *Time and Tide*'s columns as the periodical moved into the second half of its second decade.[1] In a letter to Virginia Woolf in June 1938 Rhondda made the following startling admission: 'I go through the paper every week taking out women's names & references to matters especially concerning women because if I left them in it would soon kill the paper' (Snaith 2000b: 22).

Rhondda's disclosure to Woolf was made in the course of a private exchange between the two women over Woolf's latest book, *Three Guineas* (1938). Most often viewed as a book opposing war, *Three Guineas* is also, as Naomi Black convincingly argues, 'the best, clearest presentation of Woolf's feminism': not only does it document details of continuing sexism which prevent women's full and free participation in public and professional life, it also makes the argument, unpalatable to many (especially male) readers at the time, that fascism and war had their roots in the patterns of power and domination that characterise men's oppression of women in a patriarchy (2004: 1). With reference to Woolf's much-discussed 'Society of Outsiders', Rhondda writes (immediately before the sentence quoted above):

> No woman who tried to run a Weekly Review could remain unaware of how much she was an Outsider.
>
> It's not only that to run that kind of paper one must know something of the inside gossip that is going on & almost all the Official Gossip Centres are closed to women. [. . .] It is also that the presumption amongst the average general public is that that kind of paper can't be run by women & all the advertisers belong to the general public. Also the general public is convinced that what women have to say on public affairs cannot have any real weight, so that if one uses many women's names one's circulation & – again – one's advertising are affected.[2]

Rhondda's letter makes it quite clear that she was all too familiar with the anti-feminist 'atmosphere' in public life that Woolf identifies in *Three Guineas* as 'one of the most powerful [. . .] of the enemies with which the daughters of educated men have to fight' (2015: 135). The revelation that she was deliberately removing women's names from *Time and Tide* does not represent a willing neutralisation of the paper's content (she writes to Woolf that to do so is 'maddening'); rather, it is a lamentable but necessary compromise with both 'advertisers' and the 'general public' in order to preserve women's participation – however invisibly – in political affairs. Indeed, it is this letter's intimation of the continuous if anonymous presence of women behind this modern feminist magazine that proves particularly suggestive for present-day readers of its contents during the period 1936–9. If on the surface *Time and Tide* appears to have almost entirely severed its ties with women's culture and feminist politics, something much more complex was going on underneath.

A striking example of this is the removal from *Time and Tide*'s masthead, in November 1936, of the drawing of Big Ben and the Houses of Parliament overlooking the River Thames which had been so central to the construction of the periodical's early feminist identity (see Chapter 2).[3] With its new banner stripped bare of all decorative content *Time and Tide* appears to have finally cut loose from its feminist origins, discarding a label that Woolf famously consigns to the bonfire in *Three Guineas* (see Figure 8.1).[4] The eradication of the feminist label was a goal of the periodical from its earliest years, as we have seen in earlier chapters of this book. This goal is not equivalent, however, to an abandonment of feminist commitment, although some contemporaries saw it this way. In October 1937 *Time and Tide* printed a letter from Monica Whateley, secretary of the Six Point Group, who criticised the paper for failing to give even a brief account of discussions relating to 'the Status of Women' at the Eighteenth Assembly of the League of Nations. In a fascinating (and lengthy) editorial note *Time and Tide* defended the omission, arguing that Mussolini's visit to Munich was 'the most momentous event of the week' and necessarily overshadowed those at Geneva. Acknowledging that the work of equalitarian societies was 'undoubtedly still necessary' the paper questioned the wisdom of that work 'being too widely advertised', stating that: 'There appears [. . .] to be actual danger in too much publicity on that score, since it must tend to perpetuate in the mind of the younger generation a picture of women as a class apart and inferior, always knocking outside the door, never doing, but always claiming the right to do.' *Time and Tide*'s own stated position was that:

DOUBLE
BOOK NUMBER

TIME AND TIDE, 14th November, 1936

TIME & TIDE

THE INDEPENDENT WEEKLY REVIEW

Vol. XVII. No. 46 (*Registered as a Newspaper*)   SATURDAY, 14th NOVEMBER, 1936   PRICE 6d

Figure 8.1 *Time and Tide* Masthead, 14 Nov 1936. Reproduced by kind permission of the Syndics of Cambridge University Library. Classmark: L900.1.39.

better results can at the present time be obtained if as many women as possible use the powers which they have already acquired [. . .] since by using them they are not only enabled to do good work in the world but also to familiarize the general public with the idea of men and women working side by side regardless of sex and on equal terms for the general good. (23 Oct 1937: 1402)

In this response *Time and Tide* publicly distanced itself from the equalitarian societies with which it had been so closely identified in former years. However, against early assessments of this periodical which conclude that 'in the 1930s [its] feminism gradually faded away' (Doughan and Sanchez 1987: 45), I contend that *Time and Tide* – like Woolf – 'does not so much reject as reach beyond a certain narrow definition of feminism [. . .] concerned solely with the status of women' (Black 2004: 24). As the above correspondence reveals, international affairs defined the priorities and anxieties of *Time and Tide*'s core group of feminist collaborators, and the removal of the drawing from its masthead, like Woolf's burning of the word feminism, can be read as a 'celebrat[ion] [of] the ability of women to use their newly acquired economic autonomy not to advance their own rights, narrowly described, but to advance the larger goals that subsume their own needs' (Black 2004: 24; 28).

In this chapter, I examine two examples of how *Time and Tide*'s seemingly non-feminist veneer is disrupted, first in its book reviews section, and second in its political and correspondence pages. In the first section I argue that the surface appearance of a less feminist engagement with literature and the arts is called into question by the archive of Theodora Bosanquet's automatic writing (introduced in Chapter 7). Building on Bette London's work on female medium-ship, I show how Bosanquet's automatic scripts re-situate her pub-lished reviews, and reveal a mode of feminism that Barbara Green has theorised as 'a form of attention' (2017: 273). In the second section I show how *Time and Tide*'s apparently non-feminist veneer is disrupted much more overtly when all the leading feminists of the period emerge publicly in the paper at the outbreak of the Second World War. With reference to the function of *Time and Tide*'s corre-spondence columns, I explore the contribution this periodical made – as the only female-edited intellectual weekly in Britain – to public debates about war and peace.

'Ambiguous professionalism': feminism as a 'form of attention'

A reviewer for *Time and Tide* since 1927, Theodora Bosanquet took over the periodical's literary editorship after a period of instability in its book reviews section. Under its first two literary editors, both men (R. Ellis Roberts, 1932–4, and John Beevers, 1934–5), *Time and Tide* negotiated a deepening tension between generalist and special-ist approaches to criticism, as the authority of the amateur critic or Victorian 'man of letters' was gradually replaced by that of a new generation of professional critics spawned by the rise of University English (see Chapter 6). In her years as literary editor (1935–43) Bosanquet restored order and control in the back half of the paper, which in format and appearance was now virtually indistinguishable from any other leading weekly review. However, Bosanquet's papers preserved in the archives of the Society of Psychical Research (SPR) reveal something very atypical and unorthodox going on under-neath. Among these a typescript dated 30 March 1933 evidences a direct relationship between Bosanquet's experiment in mediumship (see Chapter 7) and her reviewing for *Time and Tide*, and is worth quoting at some length.

> The controls promised help in writing the review of 'New Country.'
> [. . .]
>   It was not easy for them to write about the book. They tell me I must do exercises in concentration, which I know very well, and I will try and perhaps with this powerful aid I may do it better than I expect.

The 'Arnold Bennett' control wrote a bit this evening. He said he knew I couldn't believe it was himself (and I can't) but he would give me a convincing test in a few days' time if I did effective concentration exercise in the meantime. Speaking about the book, he said the truest thing I could say was that these Communists were the biggest fools on earth and that they have no business to make the earth an even worse place that it is. He added that I shouldn't think of saying such a thing because Communists are the fashion and I am a modernist and wouldn't dream of coming out as a new Christian. [. . .] Henry James wrote for a moment to say he couldn't make out what the Communists were driving at but that they are not worth much trouble for they will soon be swept away like the dust of last year.[5]

This text has to be one of my most extraordinary discoveries in the literary archive. The book Bosanquet is referring to here ('New Country') was the second volume of poetry and prose edited by Michael Roberts which, with *New Signatures* (1932) before it, played a pivotal role in launching the Auden Generation. Bosanquet's review of the book appeared in *Time and Tide*'s issue of 22 April 1933, and while it is fairly clear from the material I have examined that Bosanquet did not really conceive of her writing for the periodical as some form of cosmic dictation from another realm (indeed, the quotation marks around Arnold Bennett's name and admission of disbelief alert us to her incredulity), the suggestion that this review was in some psychic sense co-authored by the surviving spirits of Bennett and Henry James who 'control' her hand raises fascinating questions about what the structures of automatic writing facilitated for her.[6]

According to Bette London, one of the most interesting aspects of mediumship's attraction for women is the way its fantasies 'consistently return to the problem of intellectual and cultural authority'. 'Mediumship problematized even as it represented women's agency, displacing women's authority (including her authority to mediate) onto a host of other mediators' (1999: 148). This problem is writ large in Bosanquet's private notes about her *New Country* review, where the displacement of her authority onto the powerful male figures of the late Arnold Bennett and Henry James suggests anxiety about passing judgement on her male contemporaries, and also that as a female mediator of culture in *Time and Tide*'s book review columns she does not enjoy the 'consciousness of perfect freedom' celebrated by the periodical's policy (in relation to its 'Notes on the Way' feature) of a 'free pen'. As we saw in Chapter 7, as both a 'modernist' and a 'Christian' Bosanquet found herself at odds with the fashionable new generation of writers on the left, and the publication of her critical book on the symbolist poet Paul Valery earlier in 1933 aligned her with an aesthetics that Auden and his followers defined themselves against. Situated on a new frontier between high and late modernisms, Bosanquet negotiates the problem of intellectual and cultural authority from the position of the 1910 generation confronting the new generation of 1932, just as Virginia Woolf had done one year earlier in her essay 'Letter to a Young Poet' (Brosnan 1997: 127–9). However, while Woolf's joint ownership of the Hogarth Press with her husband Leonard Woolf afforded her great freedom of self-expression, Bosanquet was also negotiating material changes in *Time and Tide*'s periodical environment. In March 1933, the same month Bosanquet recorded the communications purporting to come from Bennett and James about the *New Country* review, *Time and Tide* appointed its first literary editor, R. Ellis Roberts, a well-known 'man of letters' in London literary circles and former literary editor of the *New Statesman*.

I have come across no evidence to indicate whether Bosanquet was considered for the literary editorship at this point (or in 1934, when Roberts was succeeded by John Beevers). But that Bosanquet's experiment in mediumship took place at the very moment when Auden and his peers (notoriously hostile to women) arrived as a force in the cultural landscape, and when even the feminist *Time and Tide* appointed a man as its first official literary gatekeeper, is a coincidence too striking to ignore. More than once during this period her automatic writing engages explicitly with the exclusion of women from culture, and registers her battle for recognition as a female author and critic. For example, one lengthy script dated 17 March 1933 circles around the question of who is controlling Bosanquet's hand as she moves between the grip of 'men of the present day, men of the past, men of tomorrow', amid which Bosanquet interjects: 'No women?' The reply comes 'No women are in this group' but a script produced the following day opens with an ambiguously gendered spirit 'Manetom' saying: 'Have I told you that I want you to be the first woman of the new' [. . .]. Here the communication breaks off and, according to Bosanquet, is followed by 'exercises in curving lines' (18 March).[7] Crucially, for all its association with amateurism and the leisured classes, Bosanquet's practice of automatic writing appears to have brought a new kind of attention to her work as a professional reviewer and critic. As I discuss below, in the instruction purporting to come from Arnold Bennett that she 'do exercises in concentration' Bosanquet appears to have found a technique that aided her in the reviewing process, lending support to one of London's central claims about mediumship that 'what looks like an amateur practice often turns out to be deeply professional' (1999: 23). The automatic scripts in Bosanquet's archive often refer to books and authors she was reviewing for *Time and Tide*. Most striking of all are a series of scripts produced in association with her review of Woolf's 1937 novel *The Years*, which I discuss next.

Woolf's eighth novel had its origins in a lecture she delivered in 1931 to the Junior Council of the London and National Society for Service, later published in essay form as 'Professions for Women' (Wood 2013: 32). As critics have noted 'professionalisation' is one of the most central preoccupations of *The Years*: whether women should enter or stay outside the professions, and whether the 'professional system' might be redeemed, are questions which pervade this novel, though less explicitly than in *Three Guineas* (1938) which Woolf was working on simultaneously during this period.[8] Bosanquet's review of the novel appeared in *Time and Tide*'s issue of 13 March 1937. While her glowing discussion of the book highlights the periodical's continuing promotional value for women writers publishing between the wars, it also appears to support Alice Wood's observation that although *The Years* is 'now commonly read for its feminist critique of patriarchy' its feminist outlook 'was obscured from its first readers' (2013: 27–8). Anticipating, correctly, the 'reaction of the class-conscious and guilt-ridden propagandists of the present age' as one of 'indignation', Bosanquet's review contributes squarely to early aestheticist approaches to Woolf:

> Life is a fountain of living water within us. What will it profit us if we eliminate all the causes of war, equalize everybody's income [. . .] if the jet of that fountain is plugged up?
>
> In *The Years*, celebrating the recurrent rebirth of the beauty of the visible world and the marvel of the minds that recognize it, we are in contact not only with a first-rate novelist [. . .] but also with a great lyrical poet. It is not a poet's function (*pace* Mr. Auden and co.) to offer us a sociological tract but to give us more abundant life. (353)[9]

Bosanquet's emphasis on Woolf's qualities as an artist or 'poet' is consistent with her view of aesthetics examined in Chapter 7. Her automatic writing, however, offers a different perspective on the novel, revealing a feminist layer of interpretation of *The Years* which is unexpressed in the published review. Disrupting the seemingly non-feminist veneer of *Time and Tide*'s book reviews section, this material both illuminates the 'thinking' female mind at work, and registers what might be lost in the adoption of professional male standards in literary criticism.

Bosanquet's papers in the SPR archive contain five pieces of automatic writing pertaining to *The Years* which she produced over a six-day period from 24 February to 1 March 1937. 'Pre-texts' to Bosanquet's published review they all carry a heading which identifies *The Years* as the object of her contemplation, and all but one record the exact time that the automatic writing took place, typically ranging between ten and twenty minutes.[10] The original handwritten scripts don't appear to survive, but it was Bosanquet's custom to transcribe her own automatic writing, as can be illustrated by another automatic script produced on Armistice Day later the same year. In this example, the handwritten original has a line drawn through it and the word 'copied' noted at the top (Figure 8.2); preserved in the same folder in the archive is a typewritten copy, and it is reasonable to conclude that Bosanquet's automatic writing on *The Years* has been through the same process. The scripts I discuss here, therefore, are the typewritten copies, and are remarkable not so much for their content but for the spotlight they shine on the processes Bosanquet engaged in in her reviewing for *Time and Tide*. Regular and structured they take on the character of a discipline, and as evidence of the concentrated energy Bosanquet poured into reading and reflecting on Woolf's novel they hold special significance in the context of what Jonathan Crary has described as a 'crisis of attentiveness' in the modern period (cited in Green 2017: 266). As Patrick Collier has discussed, the newspaper press was believed by social commentators to have had a deleterious effects on modern reading habits (2006: 14–17). For example, according to Q. D. Leavis the appearance of the printed page had so changed in the direction determined by the *Daily Mail* press baron Lord Northcliffe 'that its contents are to be skimmed: the temptation for the modern reader is *not* to read properly – i.e. with the fullest attention' (1932: 226). Bosanquet's automatic scripts on *The Years* draw attention to the attention she gave to the books she undertook for review, and as such they are also testament to the '*work* of valuing' that the institutions of book reviewing and criticism perform (Madelyn Detloff 2016: 1). With book reviewing also seen to be in a state of crisis in this period (according to Collier, in the daily newspapers 'a column covering 10 to 12 books in 1,000 words was not uncommon' and 'accusations that reviewers were not reading the books they critiqued' were rife)

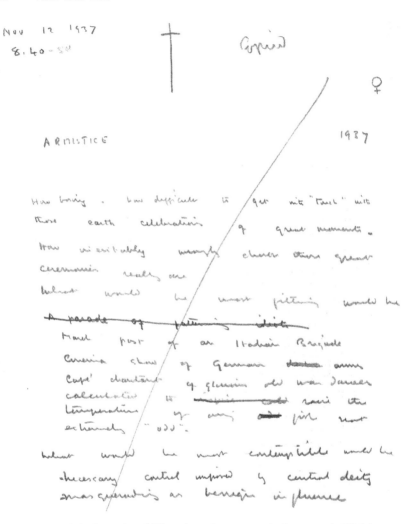

Figure 8.2 Sample of Theodora Bosanquet's Automatic Writing, 1937. Reproduced by kind permission of the Syndics of Cambridge University Library. Classmark: SPR MS 7/6/109.

(2006: 81–3), Bosanquet's singular practice foregrounds the value of 'deep attentive reading practices' associated with the rise of University English (Detloff 2016: 12) while circumventing the profession of literary criticism as established by educated men.

In a fascinating discussion of 'Distraction and Daydream' in *Time and Tide* and E. M. Delafield's *Diary of Provincial Lady*, Barbara Green argues that 'instead of a secure position, an identity, or a cause, feminism in Delafield's writings might very well be a form of attention, a perspective on everyday life' which she locates in the Provincial

Lady's 'daydreams': 'the internal and inward-turning memoranda' that punctuate the text (2017: 273, 268). For Green, these daydreams suggest that Delafield notices 'a continuing disparity between a feminism that addressed woman's inner life (the advanced or avant-garde feminism of the Edwardian period that Lucy Delap traces in her reading of the *Freewoman*) and a feminism that addressed social and political advancement', allowing for the development of 'an internal transformation of feminine self-regard' that was essential for true equality (2017: 265). Green's reading of Delafield provides a stimulating context for thinking about the private automatic writing of Bosanquet, for whom, as we saw in Chapter 7, women's mental and spiritual development was as important as (or even more important than) their material advances in economic and political terms. Like Delafield's heroine, for whom the daydream functions as 'stolen time' from the demands and routines of everyday life (Green 2017: 268), Bosanquet defends the supposedly non-productive hours of leisure as a vital resource for individual maturation and growth. In a book review that echoes an early *Time and Tide* editorial expressing concern about modern reading habits, Bosanquet writes:

> [E]ach year diminishes the number of persons who have leisure enough to try to understand anything really difficult, for the enjoyment of leisure is falling into such disrepute that few of us can resist the hypnotic persuasion that it is somehow nobler to bustle about for sixteen hours a day than to sit still to read, mark, learn and inwardly digest the fruits of other people's more competent work. (6 Jan 1928: 8)[11]

At once embracing a 'doxa of difficulty' that Laura Frost argues was central to modernism's redefinition of pleasure in this period (see Chapter 3), Bosanquet's advocacy of 'leisure' simultaneously resists the notion that 'difficult' texts can only be understood by professional and university-trained critics. With a commitment to the ordinary intelligent woman reader *Time and Tide* addressed from its earliest issues, Bosanquet wrote in a review of Paul Valery in 1932: 'He [Valery] is not easy to read, and he is difficult to translate. But no writer yields a finer or more rewarding response to the pressure of attention' (3 Sep 1932: 952).

Virginia Woolf was also widely regarded as a 'difficult' author, but the automatic scripts Bosanquet produced in association with her reading of *The Years* evidence the 'fine' and 'rewarding' response Woolf yields to the attentive reader willing to engage deeply with her work. Indeed, one of the most fascinating aspects of these scripts is the way in which they enact Woolf's own theorisation of the reading process in 'How Should One Read a Book?' Each script might be conceptualised as a receptacle for receiving and storing what Woolf describes in this essay as the 'impressions' that form in 'quick succession' in the first stage of reading, and which must be allowed to sink into the unconscious mind before the literary work can 'floa[t] to the top of the mind complete' (2008: 71). Predominant among these impressions are contrasts between light and shadow, youth and age, and, of course, the passage of time: 'Minute by minute continue the years – the centuries – billions of centuries – aeons.'[12] Also preserved are perceptive insights that would preoccupy later Woolf criticism, such as Woolf's vision of androgyny ('a masculine intelligence running through feminine intuition', 25 February) and her interest in varieties of mystical experience ('A partial mystical consciousness pervades', 1 March).[13] Above all they capture the changing emotional currents experienced by Bosanquet as a reader: in the first script the novel bears down on her in a series of questions ('Nothing but dust? Is there really no light? Is decay, frustration, darkness, death, interment all the answer?'); in the second it seems to have produced a lighter mood ('Proximity of this volume releases a flood. Light springs').[14] However, as Melba Cuddy-Keane discusses, 'experience at this level is not easily conveyed in standard critical prose', and Woolf 'objected to the new academic criticism because it suppressed the personal and emotive dimension of literature and its rich pluralities of affect'. Sensing in the new professional discipline of English studies 'a declining appreciation of literature's appeal to the associative powers of the unconscious mind', for Woolf '[a]ddressing the unconscious [. . .] functioned as a crucial antidote to the scientific model that privileged the conscious alone' (2003: 122).

Considering this, Bosanquet's fourth script (produced on 28 February) is particularly fascinating for the 'metacommentary' it offers on reviewing and professional criticism.[15] It opens:

How to review a real living expression. How to talk about a <u>thin</u> perception. How to encourage people to see through this porous outgrowth. How to preserve the purity, the clarity, the delicious nonconformity, the graceful disdain, the patriarchal disposition. How, in short, to preserve the true discipline and yet sensitize the world. Men of letters are too ambitious, she thought, guarding unspoken her delicate intuition. They fling words like gauntlets to the four winds of destiny. Whereas we, women, listen. Our power is the truth of our perception. What we make is the Word Incarnate.[16]

Here, the repeated question of 'how' to write a review which will 'preserve the true discipline and yet sensitize the world' seems to reflect the difficulty of writing professionally about literature without robbing it of its affective power. Several years later, as she prepared to write a review of Woolf's posthumous collection of short stories, *A Haunted House* (1944), Bosanquet asked in her diary 'How can anyone "review" Virginia Woolf?' – a question which resonates with Woolf's own view 'that the task of reviewing was severely limited by [. . .] having to make definitive pronouncements in a meagre few lines of print' (Cuddy-Keane: 169).[17] Importantly (and contrary to dominant contemporary perceptions of Woolf's supposed insularity) Bosanquet recognises that *The Years* is 'a real living expression' of an author who desires to connect with the world around her: in her own desire to 'encourage people to see' she mirrors Woolf's now widely recognised commitment to the ordinary reader and the public sphere.

It is striking, however, that Bosanquet's most prescient insight regarding *The Years* does not find its way into her published review of the book: namely her perception in Woolf's novel of a feminist viewpoint connected to the power of the feminine. While the novel's feminism appears to have eluded most contemporary readers, in the contrast Bosanquet draws between the 'ambitious' and combative nature of male critics, and the 'intuition' and perceptive powers of women who 'listen', the script bears a striking resemblance to the links Woolf would later make more explicitly in *Three Guineas* than in *The Years* between masculinity, education, the professions and militarism, and her insistence that women's difference must be preserved in order to effect a 'complete overhaul of the patriarchal cultural values by which Britain's social and political institutions are shaped' (Wood 2013: 49). The mystical claim in Bosanquet's text that women 'make the Word Incarnate' not only reinforces a view of women's alterity, but also produces the idea that the professional system might be transformed and redeemed when imbued by feminine values. Other female modernists, too, drew inspiration from mysticism and religion in their visions of female creativity and empowerment (Ingman 2010). But it is precisely this statement of women's difference that *Time and Tide* publicly disavowed in its editorial content. That Bosanquet's feminist reading of *The Years* is supplanted in her review by aestheticist criticism is a further illustration of the way in which *Time and Tide*'s emulation of masculine standards eclipsed more overt feminist concerns. But her archive is a potent indicator of the female perspectives which continued to inform the periodical from beneath.

The fourth script quoted above concludes: 'There is little or nothing to remark, except that V.W. is a wood [*sic*] author. She is of another order from Simple Simon. Dazzling complexity.'[18] Here, the banality of the critical judgement which invokes a nursery rhyme ('Simple Simon') as a foil for the superior qualities of 'V[irginia] W[oolf]' satirically demolishes the idea that the book review can say anything meaningful about literature, and while the word 'wood' (where Bosanquet surely means 'good') may be a typing error, it might also be read as a critique of the conditions of reviewing which incur haste and slipshod thought. However, if the value of the book review is flawed by its limited capacity to convey the 'dazzling complexity' of so great a literary artist, its promotional value, as we have seen, is great. Moreover, as Woolf would concede in *Three Guineas*, women must enter the professions to work for change, and by joining *Time and Tide*'s columns as a reviewer and editor Bosanquet was a key participant in this feminist periodical's contribution to the public sphere. Yet her experiment in mediumship also makes her an 'outsider' to the academic cultures of contemporary literary criticism, and to consider her automatic writing as part of her practice of reviewing is to recognise that she became a professional critic (to borrow London's words) 'in ways not institutionally legitimated' (1999: 8). As such Bosanquet's work for *Time and Tide* represents an 'ambiguous professionalism' that London argues was part of mediumship's appeal, providing women with a place 'to be simultaneously amateurs and professionals' (1999: 161–2). As Anna Snaith observes, Woolf's 'Outsiders' Society' is not, as some critics have assumed, an argument for female separatism, but a means for 'enter[ing] the public sphere [. . .] while maintaining difference', a model for operating 'simultaneously within and without' the professional system (2000a: 127). At once working with *Time and Tide*'s policy of assimilation into the male-dominated field of interwar journalism, Bosanquet's automatic writing also suggests that the private space (in another echo of Woolf) provides a vital resource for the growth of female autonomy and power. According to Woolf, writing in *Three Guineas*, for such work 'Secrecy is essential. We must still hide what we are doing and thinking even though what we are doing and thinking is for our common cause' (2015: 195). However, as Britain moved closer towards the outbreak of another world war *Time and Tide*'s female voices would break out volubly in the periodical's columns, as we shall see next.

'Agenda for peace': letter writing and public debate

In early 1936, as the probability of Germany's remilitarisation of the Rhineland was watched anxiously by the British weekly press, *Time and Tide* announced that starting from its issue of 8 February it would be giving a platform to 'two writers whose views on world affairs to-day are of special significance': Aldous Huxley and Gerald Heard.[19] These views, *Time and Tide* declared, 'constitute a NEW APPROACH to the whole position of International Relations and to the possibility of securing peace' and the periodical hoped that they would 'provide an open forum for discussion by others' (1 Feb 1936: 148). While Aldous Huxley's reputation has survived better than that of his friend and fellow writer Gerald Heard, both men were influential figures within London's intellectual circles between the wars. Fêted in the 1920s by Bloomsbury Huxley's critical reputation as a novelist was by the mid-1930s at its peak, and it was his turn towards religion and mysticism in this decade that brought him into closer association with Heard, whose own writings on science and religion had a formative influence not only on Huxley but also on other literary figures including W. H. Auden and Christopher Isherwood.[20] By the time *Time and Tide* was offering them 'A Platform for Some New Ideas' in its columns (8 Feb 1936: 174) both Huxley and Heard had become leading members of Canon Dick Sheppard's Peace Movement which in May 1936 became the Peace Pledge Union (P.P.U.), Britain's leading pacifist society.[21] Pacifism in Britain had been growing in popularity during the last months of 1935, and given the prominence of women in the interwar peace movement, along with common assumptions about women as the 'naturally' pacific sex, it is striking that *Time and Tide* should give a platform to two leading male intellectuals on the question of how to secure peace.[22] By employing Huxley and Heard in its columns *Time and Tide* was deliberately *not* framing peace as a feminist or women's issue, thus resisting gender essentialisms that equated women with pacifism and men with bellicosity. Indeed, the Sheppard Peace Movement was initially a male-only organisation, and according to one of Theodora Bosanquet's automatic scripts, in looking to Heard in early 1936 Rhondda 'will[ed] to take his <u>male</u> influence' (emphasis in original).[23] But the backlash against feminism is also important here, and Rhondda's comment to Woolf (quoted at the start of this chapter) that 'the general public is convinced that what women have to say on public affairs cannot have any real weight', provides a context for understanding why she and her female collaborators would strategically use prominent men to address the most urgent issues of the time. However, the significance of the fact that women continued to direct and control what was the *only* female-edited intellectual weekly of its time should not be underestimated, and their shaping influence, however invisible, is one of the under-examined histories of this periodical I seek to uncover here.

In April 1936, two weeks after the conclusion of Heard's and Huxley's pacifist contributions to the paper, *Time and Tide* announced that it would be publishing 'a series of articles on the agenda for a World Conference' to avoid war (18 Apr 1936: 552). The pacifist Labour leader George Lansbury had called for a world conference in an influential letter to *The Times* in August the previous year (Ceadel 1980: 189), and in a foreword to the series *Time and Tide* identified 'six essential points on the Agenda which in broad outline the World Conference might follow' (25 Apr 1936: 586). The presentation of this 'Agenda for Peace' in 'six essential points' is distinctly reminiscent of *Time and Tide*'s earlier Six Point Group manifesto (see Chapter 1), and the echo is suggestive of the feminist commitment that continued to direct and shape the periodical as it adopted an increasingly international outlook (see Figure 8.3). Constructed in seemingly gender-neutral terms *Time and Tide*'s 'Agenda for Peace' avoids advertising women's presence in politics, but it in fact evidences the participation of women in international affairs and their influence on public opinion in relation to matters of world importance. If *Time and Tide*'s core female personnel were less publicly visible than in earlier years, its editorial policy and agenda were still controlled by an all-female board of directors: among them (in addition to Rhondda) Winifred Cullis, Cicely Hamilton and Rebecca West. (Winifred Holtby, who played such a pivotal role in *Time and Tide*'s expansion – see Chapter 5 – died tragically young in October 1935; *Time and Tide*'s first chairman,[24] Mrs Chalmers Watson, died a few months later in August 1936.)[25] Although the articles in the 'Agenda for Peace' series are unsigned, of the fact that they represented the views of *Time and Tide*'s core feminist collaborators there can be no doubt. In its issue of 13 June 1936, the periodical drew special attention to the concluding article, stating that while it has 'made a special point of continuing to publish signed articles of various shades of opinion which have on numerous occasions not agreed with our editorial policy [. . .] the article we publish this week [. . .] does embody our own views on the present world situation, and on the chief hope of remedy' (833).

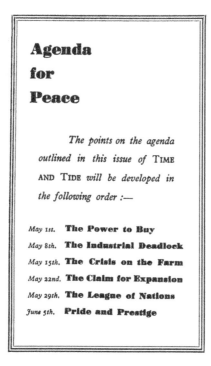

Figure 8.3 'Agenda for Peace', *Time and Tide* 25 Apr 1936: 586. Reproduced with the permission of The William Ready Division of Archives and Research Collections, McMaster University Library.

Time and Tide's 'own views' as outlined in its 'Agenda for Peace' belong to a 'pacificist' (rather than a 'pacifist') tradition, which 'pinned its hopes successively on disarmament, collective security, and peaceful change' (Ceadel 1999: 141).[26] Rhondda stated publicly in the paper in May 1936 that '[u]rgently as I want peace I do not know that I could call myself a pacifist' (9 May 1936: 662), though the periodical continued to debate the case for and against pacifism in the context of deepening divisions within the peace movement over whether and in what circumstances the use of force might be justified.[27] However, as Beryl Haslam summarises, the debate in the 1930s 'was not simply between the absolute pacifists who opposed all war and the internationalists (or pacificists) who wished to outlaw war, but within this last category. The debate resolved into a clash of principle between the sanctionists and anti-sanctionists, or as some preferred, between the "realists" and "idealists"' (1999: 193). In the summer of 1936 which (after Italy's invasion of Abyssinia and German's remilitarisation of the Rhineland) saw the League of Nations put to a further test with the outbreak of the Spanish Civil War, this 'clash of principle' between supporters of, and opponents to, the strengthening of League sanctions struck a fault line down the middle of *Time and Tide*'s own inner circle. In a leading article on 'Pacifists – and Peace' *Time and Tide* acknowledged that the paper had been 'bitterly assailed by correspondents because of our doubts about the whole Sanctions policy of the League of Nations' and drew attention to a letter printed in its columns this week written by Miss Phoebe Fenwick Gaye who 'from comparatively sheltered Chelsea, derides deliciously as moonstruck faith-fakirs, those who have decided that when they have said "No More War" during the last twenty years they happened to mean it' (11 July 1936: 984). Explaining that the paper was not committed 'either to the Peace Pledgers or to all the opinions of Mr. Gerald Heard', *Time and Tide* went on to place 'against the opinions of a sheltered inhabitant of Chelsea' the opinion of a communist involved in underground work in Germany (whose reported view was that if the Powers could avoid a war for two or three years, Hitlerism would collapse) and repeated its call for a World Conference (984–5).[28] This 'sheltered inhabitant of Chelsea' was in fact Rhondda's former assistant editor who, as *Time and Tide* explained two weeks later, 'resigned from the political side of the paper in June because she was not wholly in agreement with our editorial policy, especially as regards Sanctions, which she was prepared to push to very much greater lengths than was advocated in *Time and Tide*' (25 July 1936: 1067). The undisguised superior tone in this repeated framing of Gaye as 'sheltered' and uninformed provides a glimpse of the charged atmosphere in *Time and Tide*'s offices as it steered a course through complex political issues. But this internal disagreement also presented the periodical with an opportunity to publicly defend its own position, and its handling of Gaye's resignation demonstrates its commitment to *open* dialogue and debate.

Significantly, *Time and Tide*'s explanation regarding Gaye's resignation was made in an editorial note accompanying its 'Notes on the Way' column which was written this week by Gaye herself. Possibly the offer of a 'free pen' in this column was part of the terms on which Gaye remained a contributor of the paper but agreed to stay out of its political news and comment.[29] What is clear is that *Time and Tide* aimed to deal with the dispute fairly and democratically: 'In the circumstances, we feel that it is due to Miss Gaye that she should have the space to put her point of view upon the recent trend of opinion on international relations' (25 July 1936: 1067). In her article Gaye continued to level criticism at Gerald Heard and his

'Tree-shrew' followers: a reference to Heard's 1935 book *The Source of Civilization* in which he traced all humanity back to a small, sensitive, adaptable tree-shrew and argued that violence always gives rise to more violence (Falby 2008: 80). In its editorial note *Time and Tide* again distanced itself from the absolute pacifist position, stating that 'we could not go so far as to describe ourselves as complete members of Miss Gaye's Tree-shrew group', but also admonished Gaye in the same superior tones as before: 'On the other hand, we very definitely wish to dissociate ourselves from the Nursery Governess School of Thought which is apparently prepared to go to war in order to teach benighted foreigners to observe the British Public School Code' (1067). *Time and Tide*'s mockery of Gaye's thinking as rudimentary, immature and, importantly, related to the feminised private sphere, is a measure of the periodical's investment in expert knowledge and opinion of the kind it now regularly attracted to its pages. But there is perhaps a hint in the language that this dressing-down of Gaye was also partly staged. The following week *Time and Tide* printed a letter from one of its readers, a Mr David A. Peat, who wrote:

> I enjoyed Phoebe Fenwick Gaye. We are all guessing now and she guesses with humour. What I like about *Time and Tide* is that it gives the impression of being produced for the interest of its staff as much as for the sake of being a highly successful weekly – well, that may be too strong, but it is not metallic and machine-like.
>
> I earned my living for a long time as a second-rate journalist on cheap and 'popular' papers [. . .] and we were all impressed with this: 'Don't let the public see the wheels go round.' That is just what *Time and Tide* does, and it is pleasant – it lets us see the wheels. (1 Aug 1936: 1098)

This insight as to the way *Time and Tide* allows its public to 'see the wheels' highlights the periodical's willingness at this moment to make its internal disagreements public.[30] Arguably it is the gravity of the world situation that motivates *Time and Tide* to air publicly its own conflicts in an amicable way: the observation that *Time and Tide* is 'not metallic and machine-like' suggests a mode of operation that is not authoritarian or dogmatic, but firmly committed to the free circulation of competing opinions and ideas which it believes is essential for preventing war and securing peace.

At the same time, Gaye's resignation seems to have occasioned a moment of critical self-reflection in the periodical regarding its responsibilities as a leader of public opinion and its relationship to its readership. On the same page carrying the former journalist's letter about *Time and Tide* letting its public 'see the wheels', a letter from the feminist, pacifist and former editor of *Foreign Affairs*, Helena Swanwick, accuses Gaye of 'smudg[ing] the records of the [First] World War's beginnings' (1 Aug 1936: 1098). Swanwick was an absolute pacifist who 'remained consistently opposed to collective security based on sanctions' (Elgin 1999: 155), and in printing her letter *Time and Tide* couldn't have found anyone more politically engaged and informed to position against Gaye. However, directly alongside Swanwick's letter, a letter signed 'Rosa Dartle' represents a readership in danger of being alienated by *Time and Tide*'s orientation from the mid-1930s to the intellectual and political highbrow sphere. Printed under the heading 'Miss Dartle Wants to Know' the letter opens:

> Sir, – It is well known how ignorant I am and that I only ask for information; but since, in my old age, I have been given a vote I do try to understand things that, when I was younger, were left entirely to the gentlemen.
>
> Some time ago we had a war to end war, and though this was not successful, I did see why we took part in it. Now, I am told, we are to have a war to end Civilization, which does not seem a very sensible object. (1 Aug 1936: 1098)

Apparently the voice of a mature but naive woman reader who, as a result of her Victorian upbringing, is 'ignorant' of public affairs, this letter is the very opposite of the expert knowledge and opinions expressed in Swanwick's. But contrary to dominant assumptions, in contemporary discussions of the press, that the general populace preferred simplicity and amusement to the presentation and digest of complex issues (Hampton 2004: 158), 'Miss Dartle' 'wants to know' and 'tr[ies] to understand' issues and debates that used to be left entirely to men. The letter functions as a reminder, therefore, of *Time and Tide*'s responsibility to women readers still becoming active citizens, ordinary women who, as Julie Gottlieb discusses, were attempting to 'make sense of the "international" – a vantage point that was increasingly intruding into [women's] lives whether they were committed and well-informed feminist internationalists or housewives with a vote and with a voice' (2012: 203). The positioning of these letters alongside each other is not accidental, and highlights the very different readerships *Time and Tide* was still trying to address as it mediated very fraught political debates. It is also a juxtaposition that makes visible the feminism lying beneath *Time and Tide*'s surface. As well as a pacifist, Swanwick had been a leading feminist figure before the war, and would have been recognised as such in the inter-war years.

Further examination of *Time and Tide*'s letters columns reveals that 'Miss Dartle' was, in fact, a fictional correspondent. Through October 1936 *Time and Tide* printed four more letters from 'Rosa Dartle' under the same heading 'Miss Dartle Wants to Know', and, like the letter quoted above, the first of these reveals more intellectual acumen than her pose as an 'ignorant woman' suggests. Presenting in simple terms what she has learned about Europe's 'Race for Rearmament', 'Miss Dartle' likens it to the 'Caucus Race' in Lewis Carroll's *Alice's Adventures in Wonderland*, in which participants have to run around in circles until an arbitrary end is called and everyone is declared a winner. The letter concludes: 'I only ask for information, but I am really most anxious to know how long this race will last and who is going to decide when the general level of disarmament has risen enough for us to begin disarming? I do hope that, when it does stop, everybody will have won, as if everybody loses there is bound to be widespread discontent' (10 Oct 1936: 1385). The guise of innocence is in fact a vehicle for more searching questions that cut through the more impenetrable aspects of current debates (while satirising the futility of the political response to the crisis in Europe), and relies on more common points of reference (a much-loved children's book) among ordinary women readers. Some of Miss Dartle's requests for information elicited responses from 'real' readers who apparently took her at face value, for example a Herbert A. Tressider who, in a letter printed in *Time and Tide*'s issue of 24 October 1936, dismissed as nonsense the idea that collective tax resistance could prevent another European war. But the same week *Time and Tide* printed the suspicions of another reader, G. G. Coulton, who wrote from St John's College, Cambridge, to ask 'What is Miss Dartle's real name and address?' and suggested that the disclosure would bear out his experience that 'not all old women [. . .] are of the feminine sex' (24 Oct 1936: 1474). *Time and Tide* declined to supply the requested information and two weeks later printed another letter from the same Mr Coulton who offered a lengthy and abstruse response to the question in the latest letter from what he described as 'this interesting literary hermaphrodite' (7 Nov 1936: 1548).

These letters from this Cambridge academic draw attention to the complexity of *Time and Tide*'s textual performances, and apparently prompted a more overt declaration of the periodical's commitment to the ordinary reader. In the issue carrying Mr Coulton's second letter there was no letter from 'Miss Dartle' in *Time and Tide*'s correspondence columns, but a new feature called 'Miss Dartle's Diary' appeared instead. The following week *Time and Tide* printed a letter in its correspondence columns under the heading 'Miss Dartle's Diary' and signed 'CLASSICUS'. I present the letter in full:

> Sir, – I should like to express my appreciation of Miss Dartle's Diary, which more than relieved my disappointment over her absence this week from your correspondence columns. Like Miss Dartle, I am only an ignorant person, and I accordingly appreciate the fact that she 'tells me the story simply, as to a little child' – unlike her latest critic who deluges me with his ponderous learning, without, in my humble opinion – and I have consulted his erudite authorities – offering an adequate answer to Miss Dartle's question. So I still put my trust in Miss Dartle, and I care not whether 'she' be male, female, or, as your learned correspondent indelicately (I think) suggests, epicene; and I look forward to his/her (or its) future contributions, in whatever column, with pleasurable anticipation. (14 Nov 1936: 1587)

This letter – undoubtedly also invented by *Time and Tide* – makes it very clear that 'Miss Dartle' was created to negotiate the widening gap between intellectual and general readers discussed in earlier chapters of this book, and reveals much about the periodical's sense of responsibility to explain the complexities of current events to the uninitiated. Indeed, *Time and Tide*'s rebuke to the Cambridge University scholar who 'deluges' his readers with his 'ponderous learning' publicly registers resistance to the authority of the university as the sole arbiter of knowledge, and the reference to the hymn 'Tell me the old, old story' invokes more popular forms of education and learning.[31] The use of a Latin declension ('Classicus') in the signature of this letter belies, of course, the fictional letter-writer's claim to ignorance, and is a reminder of the knowledge, wit and sophistication with which *Time and Tide*'s highly intelligent female personnel operated. Though 'Miss Dartle's Diary' didn't achieve the success of some of the paper's longer-running lighter elements, it may have motivated the inauguration of a new 'Time and Tide Diary' column dating from 23 October 1937 which offered readers something 'lighter and more personal than our Editorial Notes on politics, though not necessarily less significant' (16 Oct 1937: 1359).[32]

As a correspondent, 'Miss Dartle' made occasional further appearances in *Time and Tide*'s letters columns, generally at key flashpoints such as Germany's annexation of Austria (the *Anschluss*) in April 1938, the Munich Crisis in October 1938, and soon after the start of the Second World War. As Leila Brosnan observes in a discussion of Virginia Woolf's use of the letter format: 'inventing the reader at the other end allows for a degree of self-controlled re-invention of the self. Creating, shaping, or even implying a recipient, whose characteristics, although created by the writer, determine the tone and manner of the letter, thus enabling the writer to create herself in response to the fictionalised reader' (1999: 124). Following Brosnan, *Time and Tide*'s invention of 'Miss Dartle' is thus a re-invention of itself as a periodical that is still addressed to a readership of ordinary women readers, as well as to the growing number of intellectuals and specialists contributing to its pages. She is, in fact, part of the periodical code that, as Lynne Warren writes of the appearance of the reader in magazine texts, 'serves both to specify and consolidate the readership, in much the same way as the encoded discourse of, for example, the front cover or the material format' (2000: 123).

As well as reaffirming *Time and Tide*'s commitment to the ordinary woman reader, 'Miss Dartle' – in her letters and her diary – also plays an important symbolic function in women's move from the private to the public sphere. Historically both the letter and the diary have been considered a woman's medium, but *Time and Tide*'s fictional use of these forms is atypical of what might have been considered the private dimension of women's letter- and diary-writing.[33] In contrast with the predominantly domestic concerns of E. M. Delafield's fictional *Diary of a Provincial Lady*, 'Miss Dartle's Diary' opens with reference to a long letter she has received regarding the 'Race for Rearmament' (7 Nov 1936: 1546) and it is the public discourse of militarism and war that shapes her letters, too, as we have seen. The invented 'Miss Dartle' is thus another example of the way in which *Time and Tide* worked to engage ordinary women with international issues, refashioning their identities in the context of interwar gender ideologies which apparently limited the range of topics on which they felt able to write or speak. In all the 'Replies to Gerald Heard' published in *Time and Tide*'s columns in early 1936 it is striking that the only female signature was that of Naomi Mitchison, herself an intellectual, a friend of Heard's and an insider to *Time and Tide*.[34] Furthermore, of the total number of letters printed over the same period, less than 20 per cent bore women's names, and of these two thirds were letters on what might traditionally be described as women's topics (subjects include children, abortion, education and equal pay for equal work). Woolf's *Three Guineas*, which opens with its narrator's surprise at a barrister asking a woman's opinion on what can be done to prevent war, is centrally concerned with the long-term effects of gender inequalities which 'impede women's political agency' (Snaith 2015: xxvi). But the reception of this text, as Snaith has shown, also demonstrates the readiness of ordinary women to 'defin[e] and express [. . .] intellectual opinions' and to 'engag[e] with issues of culture and politics' (2000b: 8). In *Time and Tide*, 'Miss Dartle' advertises a space for ordinary women to engage with debates of the public sphere, and the periodical's letters pages also played an important part in mobilising its female readership. For example, appeals for Aid for Spain signed by figures including Sylvia Townsend Warner and Ellen Wilkinson were printed in its columns, and in December 1938 a letter from E. M. Delafield explicitly addressed *Time and Tide*'s women readers with the suggestion made by one 'Provincial Lady [. . .] to others' that housewives of provincial households offer their guest room(s) 'to one or two Jewish refugees in need of rest and country quiet, for a month's hospitality or more' (31 Dec 1938: 1871).[35]

By the end of 1938, the broad consensus supporting appeasement in the British weekly press had been irreparably undermined by the Czech crisis which culminated in the Munich Agreement signed on 30 September of that year. According to Angela V. John, for Rhondda this betrayal of Czechoslovakia 'represented Britain's most shameful hour' (2013: 487), and although like everyone else *Time and Tide* breathed a sigh of relief at war having been (temporarily) averted, 'that Britain would come to "wholly regret" [the settlement] was more than implied if less than definitively stated' (Morris 1991: 139–40). In March 1939, following Germany's occupation of Prague, the paper finally relinquished any lingering hopes that Hitler was someone who could be negotiated with, and when Britain declared war on Germany, on 3 September 1939, *Time and Tide* gave the government its unqualified support. However, debates about war, fascism and the merits of fighting a war against Hitler continued in the paper, and most heatedly in its correspondence columns. Here, for all the neutralising of women's voices in the paper in the late 1930s, *Time and Tide*'s engagement of women in international politics is loud and clear.

Two months into the start of the Second World War Naomi Mitchison wrote to *Time and Tide* 'with a certain horror and astonishment' at what she called the paper's 'present attitude of blind acceptance of war', and suggested that the periodical had been taken in by war-time propaganda and was failing to provide the kind of 'analytical and intelligent' journalism that readers had come to expect (11 Nov 1939: 1436). In a lengthy editorial note appended to this letter *Time and Tide* expressed its own bewilderment at what Mitchison could mean 'by "blind" acceptance of war. If she imagines that we loathe the war one whit less wholeheartedly than she does herself she is wrong.' Defending its view that it would not be wise in the current circumstances to press for an official statement of Franco-British war aims, *Time and Tide* agreed with Mitchison that 'we cannot be too carefully on guard' against infringements of civil liberties, but laid out in very clear terms what it believed the country was fighting for: the prevention of further atrocities perpetrated by the Nazis against innocent German citizens (1436). The following week *Time and Tide* printed a long letter from Rebecca West, who, grieved by Mitchison's letter, accused her of expressing 'entirely contrary and inconsistent ideas' which she regarded as typical 'of the fatuity and confusion noticeable in the Left-Wing today' (18 Nov 1939: 1466).[36] Less cynical than Mitchison about the government's war aims West asserted in a subsequent letter (in an exchange which continued in *Time and Tide*'s columns for a further seven weeks) that 'this is a war fought by all concerned "for *some* freedom and against Fascism"' (2 Dec 1939: 1519). This correspondence is a vivid illustration of the splits that had opened between feminists as well as on the Left by the eve of the Second World War. As Gottlieb observes, the situation for feminists at this juncture was 'far messier' than that which divided the women's movement in the wake of the First World War; 'in the late 1930s there were endless shifting alliances, making shrapnel of once united political formations, and throwing political identities into confusion' (2012: 215–16). But the correspondence also evidences the level of energy and commitment with which feminists were engaged in public debates about such important issues as peace and war. In her final letter on the subject Mitchison asserted: 'My job as a writer [. . .] is to be critical, and as far as possible sane, in a world swirling with emotionalism and lies, and to try and induce a certain clearheadedness in others' (30 Dec 1939: 1651); West, responding to Mitchison's charge of 'muddl[ed] [. . .] thinking' (1651) concluded: 'I was trying, when I entered this correspondence, to ascertain what thoughts it was right to think if we wanted to keep the good people of all nations safe from persecution and death' (6 Jan 1940: 7).

What this exchange demonstrates, therefore, is that *Time and Tide* truly had achieved its aim of providing a 'common platform' for women as well as men 'trying to think things out', as Rhondda described her vision for the paper in her letter to the American feminist Doris Stevens in July 1928 (see Chapter 4). While her removal of women's names from the paper in the late 1930s served to disguise women's influence in the face of persistent prejudices against their participation in public life, in *Time and Tide*'s letters pages female as well as male intellectuals took a prominent place. In addition to Mitchison and West other well-known figures entered the debate about 'War Aims', including Cicely Hamilton, Sylvia Lynd and Odette Keun. But they were also joined by other 'unknown' women readers who contributed to this and other mainstream political debates in larger numbers than those writing letters to the editor during *Time and Tide*'s publication, in early 1936, of 'Replies to Gerald Heard'.[37] Two further letters from 'Miss Dartle' in October 1939 demonstrate that at this time of international crisis *Time and Tide* remained conscious of its loyalties towards this ordinary readership, and in December a letter simply signed 'A Yorkshire Woman' highlights the voice of the 'common' reader it also sought to represent:

> Sir: I have read the published letters of our intellectuals on war aims and ask that you will find space for the common-sense standpoint of the vast majority of the people in Britain.
>
> We may have our opinions concerning events which led to this war. We may think a wiser Government could have tamed the eagle and the bear. The plain fact remains that we are committed to the struggle and are now fighting to preserve our most precious possessions – liberty of thought and speech. (9 Dec 1939: 1585)

While it is possible that 'A Yorkshire Woman' is another invented correspondent, in language and tone this letter sounds more authentic than the self-consciously styled prose of 'Miss Dartle' and it is equally likely that this was the letter of a real woman from Yorkshire who desired to remain anonymous.[38] Whether fictional or not, it underlines *Time and Tide*'s belief that ordinary women 'have [their] opinions', and that the periodical had a duty to them as much as to female intellectuals as it sought to extend women's influence in the public sphere.

The protracted exchange between Mitchison and West ended in *Time and Tide*'s first issue of 1940 (6 January). The following week, immediately before its 'Letters to the Editor', *Time and Tide* printed a full-page contribution from the periodical's most influential male supporter from its early years, George Bernard Shaw. The piece is titled 'Danakil Women': a reference to what is now more properly known as the Afar people, an ethnic group inhabiting the Danakil Desert of Ethiopia where traditionally (according to Shaw's source) 'no decent Danakil woman would marry a man who could not produce trophies proving that he had killed at least four adult males' (13 Jan 1940: 29). Referring to the recent correspondence on 'War Aims' in *Time and Tide*'s columns, Shaw writes:

> [T]he moment there is a threat of war, or a declaration of it, the suppressed Danakil breaks loose, and the women are all for the slaughter. Just now, whilst the male-controlled weeklies have become unreadable with their cacklings as of scared ganders [. . .] TIME AND TIDE, woman-controlled, hurls itself into the fray with a clear conscience, an impatience for battle and victory, and a generous and unashamed militancy. The men's speeches and articles sicken me: the women's delight me in spite of my loathing of the war [. . .]
>
> There is no hypocrisy about the editorials, or about Naomi Mitchison, Rebecca West, and Odette Keun, who have played the men off the stage. (29)

Shaw's article represents, at one important level, a further endorsement of *Time and Tide*. His applause for the courage, decisiveness and conviction of its female staff and contributors elevates this 'woman-controlled' weekly review above its 'man-controlled' rivals, and despite his 'loathing of the war' its attitude earns his respect. At the same time, the gender essentialisms implicit in his words run counter to the ideals the periodical pronounced from its earliest issues. In an editorial note appended to the article *Time and Tide* responded:

> It was Bernard Shaw who, more than any other one person, exploded the Dickensian Nineteenth Century view that 'women must be admitted to the fellowship of the Holy Ghost on a feminine instead of a human basis'. It is queer to find him now attempting to sustain the archaic and quite untenable proposition that it is possible to generalize on men's versus women's attitude towards war.
>
> The view of *Time and Tide* upon this war is just the same as the view of the vast majority of people in this country, whether men or women. (13 Jan 1940: 30)

Entirely consistent with its earlier refusals of generalising statements about men and women, here *Time and Tide* reasserts women's claim to participation in the public sphere on the basis of common humanity rather than sexual difference. While it yokes itself, as a leader of public opinion, to 'the view of the vast majority of people in this country', its 'War Aims' correspondence demonstrates that there was, as Gottlieb observes, 'clearly no one quintessential feminine or feminist pathway through the storms of international affairs in this period' (2014: 459). For all the constraints upon women still 'in the process of proving themselves in the realm of international politics and foreign affairs' (Gottlieb 2012: 201), *Time and Tide*'s letters pages during this crucial period are testament to the periodical's lasting commitment to dialogue and debate between 'thinking men and women' (both intellectuals and general readers) that was central to its feminism from its earliest years.

Notes

1. For a while in the early 1930s *Time and Tide* maintained a fairly even balance between the number of male and female signatures in its 'Notes on the Way' column; though there were more men contributing, they were usually commissioned for single articles rather than for a whole month at a time. From 1936 onwards a much greater proportion of this feature across any one year was written by male writers.
2. Woolf outlines in *Three Guineas* her idea for a Society of Outsiders that will operate without leaders, laws, honour or ceremony.
3. The drawing appeared in *Time and Tide*'s banner for the last time in its issue of 7 November 1936.
4. Woolf writes controversially: 'What more fitting than to destroy an old word, a vicious and corrupt word that has done much harm in its day and is now obsolete? The word "feminist" is the word indicated. [. . .] Since the only right, the right to earn a living, has been won, the word no longer has a meaning' (2015: 179). This is in fact a later iteration of a view espoused in *Time and Tide* as early as 1926 when Winifred Holtby stated in her much-quoted article 'Feminism Divided': 'Personally, I am an Old Feminist, because I dislike everything that feminism implies. I desire an end of the whole business, the demands for equality, the suggestions of sex warfare, the very name of feminist' (6 Aug 1926: 714). Holtby's article is reprinted in Berry and Bishop 1985: 47–50.
5. TB SPR MS 7/2/9.
6. Bette London clarifies that in her research on women's mediumship her question 'was not whether mediums really talked to the dead but what the structures of automatic writing facilitated for them' (1999: 27).
7. TB SPR MS 7/2/2 (ix). While Bosanquet's notes clarify that 'Manetom' (who does later appear as 'Manet') is 'not really the soul of the departed painter but a kind of being of tomorrow' (SPR MS 7/2/15), the unmistakable allusion to the great modernist artist seems to signify

Bosanquet's desire to be recognised as someone who is conversant with the modern and the 'new' in the world of art and letters.

8. According to Evelyn T. Chan 'the vision which underlies *The Years* [. . .] is possibly even more sweepingly radical than the solutions provided in *Three Guineas*'. Rather than encouraging women to enter the professions in order to change them (as she does in the later text) in her novel Woolf 'steadfastly refuses to promote women's entry into the professions' and 'questions the validity of certain types of professional service' (2010: 604; 613).

9. The novel met a negative reception in other contemporary highbrow literary periodicals (Wood 2013: 28), part of 'a series of class-based attacks on Woolf' in the 1930s onwards (Snaith 2007: 3).

10. The term 'pre-texts' is used in genetic criticism; see Alice Wood (2013: 18–23) for a discussion of genetic approaches to Woolf.

11. Shortly after the death of Lord Northcliffe *Time and Tide* lamented the habits of modern readers who 'turn the pages, skim the headlines, glance at the pictures, but [. . .] rarely read and, most certainly, neither mark, learn, nor inwardly digest' (25 Aug 1922: 804).

12. TB SPR MS 7/6/27.

13. TB SPR MS 7/6/26 and 7/6/29.

14. TB SPR MS 7/6/26.

15. London (1999: 170) describes automatic writing as a kind of 'metacommentary' on authorship.

16. TB SPR MS 7/6/28.

17. TB Diary, Harvard. 13 February 1944. [MS Eng 1213.1.17]

18. TB SPR MS 7/6/28.

19. Benny Morris notes that through January and February 1936 the British weeklies displayed awareness of the probability of a German march into the Rhineland (1991: 99).

20. See Paul Eros (2002) and David Garrett Izzo (2002) for discussions of Heard's influence on Auden and other literary and intellectual figures.

21. Heard recruited Huxley to the Sheppard Peace Movement in October 1935 (Falby 2008: 83).

22. Julie Gottlieb observes that 'the proliferation of women-led internationalist and pacifist groups was a notable feature of the first part of the twentieth century'. The Women's International League for Peace and Freedom (WILPF) is the best-known of these, but there were many others, including the Women's Peace Crusade, the Women's International Alliance, The Women's Peace Pilgrimage, the Women's Advisory Committee to the Labour and Socialist International, and Women Against War and Fascism (2010: 105).

23. TB SPR MS 7/5/22. Sheppard's first letter to the press published on 16 October 1934 called on all men to send him a postcard indicating that they would be ready to renounce war (Ceadel 1980: 177). Women were invited to join the P.P.U. in July 1936; a letter to this effect was printed in *Time and Tide*'s correspondence columns in its issue of 4 July 1936.

24. *Time and Tide* always used the male-gendered term 'chairman' even though this position was occupied by a woman. Like *Time and Tide's* use of the 'editorial Sir', discussed in Chapter 1, this is another example of the way in which the periodical neutralised its identity as a 'women's' or 'feminist' paper.

25. *Time and Tide* no longer printed the names of its directors as it had done in earlier years, and lack of evidence makes it difficult to establish exactly when old members left and new members joined.

26. Ceadel defines pacifism as 'the belief that all war is *always wrong*, and should never be resorted to, whatever the consequences of abstaining from fighting' and pacificism as 'the assumption that war, though *sometimes necessary*, is always an irrational and inhumane way to solve disputes, and that its prevention should always be an over-riding political priority' (1980: 3).

27. For example, in November and December 1936 *Time and Tide* published articles by Rose Macaulay and Malcolm Muggeridge for and against pacifism respectively.

28. Like the rest of the British weekly press *Time and Tide* protested loudly against Mussolini's invasion of Abyssinia, Hitler's remilitarisation of the Rhineland and Franco's war in Spain, but showed itself extremely reluctant to back verbal protest with a firm response. As Morris discusses, the posture adopted by the British weekly press was one of appeasement, and *Time and Tide's* repeated calls for a World Conference are evidence of its continued insistence 'that the door of discussion must be left open' (100). In November 1935 *Time and Tide* revoked its earlier call for military as well as economic sanctions to be applied against Italy; in March 1936, it warned against the employment of force against Germany maintaining that negotiation was the way forward; and in August 1936 the paper unequivocally came out in support of the government's policy of Non-Intervention in Spain. See Morris 1991: 87–120.

29. Gaye continued to contribute lighter features to the paper, including book and theatre reviews, sketches and gardening notes. She later joined *Time and Tide's* board of directors, indicating that she remained on good terms with the periodical's core personnel.

30. *Time and Tide's* public notice of Gaye's resignation contrasts with the silent departure of the periodical's first political editor, Helen Archdale, ten years earlier (see Chapter 2).

31. In this well-known hymn, the speaker asks that the 'old, old story [. . .] of Jesus and His glory' be told 'simply, //As to a little child, // For I am weak and weary, // And helpless and defiled.'

32. 'Miss Dartle's Diary' ran for a few weeks until early December 1936, then resumed (intermittently at first) in March 1937, becoming weekly for a short time until July 1937.

33. Naomi Black (2004: 75) makes this point about Virginia Woolf's use of letters in *Three Guineas*.

34. Sixteen 'Replies to Gerald Heard' were printed in total. One of these was the letter submitted by Theodora Bosanquet under a male pseudonym, discussed in Chapter 7. In four instances, the sex of the letter-writers cannot be determined as they provided only initials in their signatures. Most of the letters (ten) were printed above male signatures.

35. Warner's appeal on behalf of the Spanish Intellectuals Fund, Writers Association, was printed in *Time and Tide*'s issue of 7 May 1938; Wilkinson's appeal for books on behalf of the Spanish Medical Aid Committee was printed in *Time and Tide*'s issue of 11 June 1938. Women played a significant role in relief efforts for the victims of the Spanish Civil War, and were at the forefront of a range of organisations set up to help refugees (Gottlieb 2005: 85).

36. In particular West identified a contradiction between the encouragement 'Mrs Mitchison and her Left-Wing friends' gave the Spanish Loyalists to fight Franco and her unwillingness to fight against Hitler now (1466).

37. Of a total of 118 letters published in *Time and Tide*'s columns while the debate over 'War Aims' ran, just over 30 per cent (37) carried female signatures. Women readers wrote from addresses in London and the Home Counties as well as East Anglia, Yorkshire, Carlisle, Wales and the South West, and even traditionally 'women's topics' (such as children and nursing) were inflected by the public discourse of war.

38. *Time and Tide*'s correspondence pages always carried a note stating that 'letters must be accompanied by the name and address of the writer, which will not, however, be published if a request is made to that effect'.

Coda

The Second World War inevitably brought fresh challenges for *Time and Tide*. In an article published in the periodical's Twenty-First Birthday Number, just eighteen months into the war, Rhondda recorded her anxiety over 'whether we could find enough writers of the standard we needed to keep up the paper we were in the habit of producing' and the relief when not only 'old friends' but also other 'distinguished people with a thousand other calls on their time and energy' found time to write for the periodical (17 May 1941: 401–2). Among the 'old friends' who re-entered *Time and Tide*'s columns during the war were Sylvia Lynd and Rose Macaulay, but there were new figures too.[1] For example, Lettice Cooper, the Yorkshire novelist and Labour Party activist who joined *Time and Tide*'s staff in November 1939 and contributed a number of feature articles on 'Politics in the Provinces', and the poet Stevie Smith, who contributed book reviews from 1944. As Rhondda further noted in her article for *Time and Tide*'s Twenty-First Birthday Number, on the editorial side 'the heaviest weight' fell on three people: Theodora Bosanquet, in the book department; Ann Gimingham, Rhondda's assistant editor (appointed following Phoebe Fenwick Gaye's resignation in 1936); and herself (401). Through their efforts, and despite paper shortages and the loss of revenue from advertisements which 'vanished overnight' (410), *Time and Tide* managed to keep publishing every week throughout the war, albeit in a reduced 'war format' of twenty-four pages (21 Oct 1939: 1357): the same size in which the periodical was initially launched nearly twenty years earlier.[2] As discussed in Part Three of this book, by the end of its second decade *Time and Tide* no longer carried feminism overtly in its pages, and the periodical's contents pages and indexes for issues published during the war years show that there were far more men writing for the paper than women. However, women including Odette Keun, Rose Macaulay and the crime and religious writer Dorothy L. Sayers did sometimes feature prominently in *Time and Tide*'s 'Notes on the Way' column, and the periodical's Arts section continued to carry female signatures, among them Gwendolen Raverat, who remained as *Time and Tide*'s art critic, and the detective novelist Margery Allingham, who had been reviewing 'New Novels' since early 1938. The war also produced a new serial by one of *Time and Tide*'s most popular women writers, E. M. Delafield. From 7 October 1939 until 13 January 1940 the periodical published weekly instalments of *The Provincial Lady in War Time*, evidence that *Time and Tide* still consciously catered for the ordinary woman reader.[3]

As I have argued throughout, although *Time and Tide* may appear, by the late 1930s, to have cut loose from its feminist origins, its success as the *only* female-controlled weekly review in Britain is – in the context of persistent prejudice against women's participation in public life – a remarkable achievement. Auditors' reports from the mid-1940s verify that during the war *Time and Tide* was still run by an all-female board of directors: Winifred Cullis, Cicely Hamilton and Rebecca West, as well as Rhondda, Theodora Bosanquet and (until 1943) Phoebe Fenwick Gaye.[4] Although not always visible in *Time and Tide*'s columns, these women remained an important influence in the background of the paper. Another key figure was Ellen Wilkinson, a frequent dinner and weekend guest during the war at the two homes Rhondda shared with Bosanquet in London and in Surrey. Wilkinson was one of the 'Four Winds' writers of the 'Time and Tide Diary' feature, and, with the Labour politician Herbert Morrison, an important source of information from the Palace of Westminster (John 2013: 490). Rhondda, as we have seen, never espoused a separatist position, and she continued to recruit men to the paper whose views and/or writing she particularly admired. But she remained absolutely committed to the advancement of women in the journalism profession, and became first president of the Women's Press Club founded in 1943 by *The Times* journalist Phyllis Deakin (John 2013: 502). Bosanquet's private diary records that in early 1944 Rhondda lunched with and interviewed women journalists in pursuit of a substitute for her assistant editor who was suffering ill health, demonstrating her ongoing commitment to the employment of women in key staff positions on her own paper.[5] Another change of personnel in the war years took place in *Time and Tide*'s book department where, in 1943, the historian Cicely Veronica Wedgwood replaced Theodora Bosanquet as literary editor, a position she held until 1950. As Rhondda later recalled, Wedgwood was also persuaded to serve for a time as deputy editor, and though she left the paper's staff in 1949 to spend more time on her research and writing, in the mid-1950s she was still serving *Time and Tide* on its board of directors as deputy chairman (Lejeune 1956: 13).

Time and Tide thus continued to operate out of a feminist commitment to women's participation in public life long after the point at which (in the 1930s) it has been seen to have lost its identification with feminism and with women. However, by the mid-1950s *Time and Tide* was constitutionally very different. A surviving auditors' report from 1956 testifies to the continuing influence of four women on the paper – Rhondda, Wedgwood, Bosanquet and West (it also regretfully records the death of Cullis) – but these female directors were far outnumbered by as many as *eight* men.[6] Men also occupied key staff positions by this time. In 1955 the position of deputy editor was filled by a young male journalist Anthony Lejeune (son of the *Observer* film critic, Caroline Alice Lejeune) (John 2013: 524), and in the book department the literary editorship passed from Wedgwood to the poet John Betjeman and then Lord Birkenhead. The political character of the paper had also changed dramatically by mid-century. As Angela V. John has discussed, Rhondda's politics were 'transformed during the forties' (2013: 497) as she moved further to the right, and the paper was deeply critical of the post-war Labour government. Shortly before the 1951 general election *Time and Tide* stated its support for the Conservative Party, and in late 1957 'an analysis of the views of 1,374 readers revealed that thirty-seven per cent of every hundred were Tories. [. . .] Thirty per cent belonged to no party. Liberals counted for eight per cent and a mere six per cent belonged to other parties, including Labour' (John 2013: 512). By this point *Time and Tide* had travelled a very long way from its feminist and liberal-left origins. But the two factors that would irreparably alter the periodical's future were the failing physical and financial health of Rhondda herself. Rhondda's health deteriorated fast from the start of 1957 (John 2013: 527), and her finances, which had bankrolled the periodical from its inception, were fast running out too. On 15 February 1958 *Time and Tide* printed an announcement on the inside of its front cover signed by Rhondda, stating that she was no longer able to subsidise the paper and that 'unless help is available, the last issue [. . .] will appear on March 22nd next'. The response to this appeal was positive. On 5 July 1958 *Time and Tide* announced that owing to 'the wonderful generosity and loyalty shown by so many friends' the periodical would continue to be published weekly. This notice was signed by Rhondda's deputy editor, Anthony Lejeune, as Rhondda had been admitted to hospital for what the paper hoped would 'only be a short period of rest and recuperation'. Three weeks later, however, Rhondda died (from stomach cancer) in a private room at Westminster Hospital (John 2013: 531).

Tributes poured in to *Time and Tide* after Rhondda's death from readers, friends and collaborators of the paper, including T. S. Eliot, Rose Macaulay and Rebecca West whose comments testified to her 'magnanimity' (Eliot), 'courageous[ness]' (West), and her untiring 'work for women's interests' (Macaulay) (26 July 1958: 911–12). Wedgwood and Bosanquet were among those appointed in Rhondda's will as trustees for the future of the paper, and in *Time and Tide*'s issue of 23 August 1958 they announced that the periodical would continue under the ownership of Mr L. M. Skevington (a paint manufacturer) (Alvin Sullivan 1986: 451), with Anthony Lejeune continuing as editor. This final transfer of the paper was the beginning of the slow death of this once female-controlled modern feminist magazine. Over the next few years the paper was passed from one new male owner to another, and merged for a time with the literary magazine *John O'London's* before it was 'redesigned as a complete news magazine on the model of the American *Time* and *U.S. News and World Report*' (Sullivan 1986: 451). During the 1960s and 1970s it struggled on under a succession of titles until its last issue in July 1979, and the introduction of a new subtitle 'The Business Man's Weekly Newspaper' (Sullivan 1986: 452) further dramatises the changes to the paper since the days when it advertised itself in the *Woman Engineer* as 'The Modern Weekly for the Modern Woman' (see Chapter 1).

It is odd to note that a magazine called *Time and Tide* was still appearing weekly on news-stands in Britain during the height of the women's liberation movement in the 1970s, but one so utterly different from its early feminist incarnation. But what this brief survey of the periodical's history from the 1940s onwards serves to reinforce is just how important *Time and Tide* was for British feminism and women's writing between the two world wars. These two decades are indisputably the richest years of this periodical in terms of its energetic commitment to women's participation in the public sphere, and the prominence it gave to women writers and critics. Undoubtedly, too, these fertile years were the achievement not only of Rhondda, but of the many women who thrived at the heart of this periodical network. As this book has demonstrated, *Time and Tide*'s core collaborators combined political and artistic commitment with keen market sense and business acumen, a flair for courting controversy and debate, and a wit and humour that illuminates the pleasures of working in this periodical's material environment. Naomi Mitchison, despite her estrangement from *Time and Tide* during the first months of the Second World War, later described the periodical as 'the first feminist literary journal with any class, in some ways ahead of its time' (1979: 168). The claim appears in her memoir of the interwar years in a chapter called 'Why Write?' and is followed by a memory of returning home from one of Rhondda's parties 'feeling splendid, as though the whole world was opening up and everything would work out, not only for myself, but for women in general' (169). While it is sobering to reflect upon the obstacles women continued – and continue – to face through the twentieth- and into the twenty-first century, the optimism Mitchison recalls is also an answer to her question, and is clearly linked to the unique female culture that motivated and stimulated the political and creative energies of the women who gravitated towards *Time and Tide*'s pages in the interwar years.

Notes

1. Lynd wrote some literary articles in the early part of the war; Macaulay provided articles and book reviews and in 1945 served as the paper's radio critic.
2. Just two months before Britain declared war on Germany on 3 September 1939, *Time and Tide* had adopted a new format better suited for rotary rather than flat printing in order to meet the demands of its rapidly increasing circulation. In a notice printed in its columns *Time and Tide* regretted that it would no longer be possible to have the all-red cover it had been sporting since February 1935, but hoped readers would like the 'new type' that had been chosen and the 'new headings [. . .] designed for each feature' (24 June 1939: 820). The 'new war format' retained these typographical changes, and by reducing its margins and number of pages 'to an economical minimum' *Time and Tide* was able to maintain all its usual features (21 Oct 1939: 1357).

3. Delafield continued to write book reviews and light features for the periodical until her death in 1943.

4. These records are among Rebecca West's papers at the University of Tulsa.

5. TB Diary, 21–8 January. TB Harvard. [MS Eng 1213.1.17]

6. The male directors listed are: the Earl of Birkenhead, Mr W. J. Brown, the Lord Coleraine, Professor John Jewkes, Mr Eoin C. Mekie, Sir Charles Peake, Mr John H. C. Robertson, and Sir John Wedgwood.

Bibliography

Manuscript sources

Ball State University Archives and Special Collections
- Norman Angell Papers

Beinecke Rare Book and Manuscript Library, Yale University
- Ezra Pound Papers
- Rebecca West Papers

Cambridge University Library
- Society of Psychical Research Collection

Cornell University Library
- Wyndham Lewis Papers

Fales Library and Special Collections, New York University Libraries
- Elizabeth Robins Papers

Harry Ransom Center, The University of Texas at Austin
- Edith Sitwell Collection
- Elizabeth Robins Collection
- George Bernard Shaw Collection
- Virginia Woolf Collection
- Wyndham Lewis Collection

Houghton Library, Harvard University
- Theodora Bosanquet Papers

Hull History Centre
- Winifred Holtby Collection

King's College Archive Centre, Cambridge University
- John Maynard Keynes Papers

McFarlin Library, University of Tulsa
- Rebecca West Papers

McMaster University Library
- Vera Brittain Papers

Mass Observation Archive, University of Sussex

Schlesinger Library, Radcliffe Institute, Harvard University
- Doris Stevens Papers

Women's Library, London
- Records of the British Federation of University Women
- Six Point Group Papers

Periodicals and newspapers

The Adelphi
British Worker
Calendar of Modern Letters
The Criterion/New Criterion
Daily Express
Daily Herald
Daily News
The Englishwoman
Foreign Affairs
The Freewoman
G. K.s Weekly
Good Housekeeping
Labour Weekly
Jus Suffragii
Left Review
London Mercury
Manchester Guardian
Modern Woman
The Nation and Athenaeum
The New Age
The New Leader
The New Statesman
The New Statesman and Nation
The Observer
Opportunity
Saturday Review
Scrutiny
The Spectator
Time and Tide
The Times
The Vote
The Woman Clerk
The Woman Engineer
The Woman Teacher
The Woman's Leader

Selected books and articles

Abu-Manneh, Bashir. 2011. *Fiction of the New Statesman 1913–1939*. Newark: University of Delaware Press.

Alberti, Johanna.1989. *Beyond Suffrage: Feminists in War and Peace, 1914–28*. London: Macmillan.

—. 1994a. 'British Feminists and Anti-Fascism in the 1930s'. *This Working-Day World: Women's Lives and Cultures in Britain 1914–1945*. Ed. Sybil Oldfield. London: Taylor & Francis. 111–22.

—. 1994b. 'The Turn of the Tide: Sexuality and Politics, 1928–13'. *Women's History Review*. 3.1:169–90.

Ardis, Ann. 2008. 'Staging the Public Sphere: Magazine Dialogism and the Prosthetics of Authorship at the Turn of the Century'. *Transatlantic Print Culture, 1880–1940: Emerging Media, Emerging Modernisms*. Ed. Ann Ardis and Patrick Collier. Basingstoke: Palgrave Macmillan. 30–47.

Armstrong, Tim. 2005. *Modernism*. Cambridge: Polity.

Ashraf, Mary, ed. 1975. *Political Verse and Song from Britain and Ireland*. London: Lawrence and Wishart.

Atherton, Carol. 2005. *Defining Literary Criticism: Scholarship, Authority and the Possession of Literary Knowledge 1880–2002*. Basingstoke: Palgrave Macmillan.

Aynsley, Jeremy. 2007. 'Fashioning Graphics in the 1920s: Typefaces, Magazines and Fashion'. *Design and the Modern Magazine*. Ed. Jeremy Aysley and Kate Forde. Manchester: Manchester University Press. 37–55.

Baldick, Chris. 1983. *The Social Mission of English Criticism, 1848–1932*. Oxford: Clarendon.

Baldwin, Dean. 2013. *Art and Commerce in the British Short Story, 1880–1950*. London: Routledge.

Barreca, Regina, ed. 1988. *Last Laughs: Perspectives on Women and Comedy*. New York: Gordon and Breach.

Bartley, Paula. 2014. *Ellen Wilkinson: from Red Suffragist to Government Minister*. London: Pluto Press.

Beasley, Rebecca. 2007. *Theorists of Modernist Poetry: T. S. Eliot, T. H. Hulme and Ezra Pound*. London: Routledge.

Beauman, Nicola. 1983. *A Very Great Profession: The Woman's Novel 1914–39*. London: Virago.

Beaumont, Caitríona. 2013. *Housewives and Citizens: Domesticity and the Women's Movement in England 1928–64*. Manchester: Manchester University Press.

Beckett, Fiona. 2002. *The Complete Critical Guide to D. H. Lawrence*. London: Routledge.

Beetham, Margaret. 1996. *A Magazine of Her Own?: Domesticity and Desire in the Woman's Magazine, 1800–1914*. London: Routledge.

Berman, Jessica. 2011. *Modernist Commitments: Ethics, Politics and Trans-national Modernism*. New York: Columbia University Press.

Berry, Paul and Alan Bishop, eds. 1985. *Testament of a Generation: The Journalism of Vera Brittain and Winifred Holtby*. London: Virago.

Binckes, Faith. 2010. *Magazines, Modernism and the British Avant-Garde: Reading Rhythm*. Oxford: Oxford University Press.

Bingham, Adrian. 2004. *Gender, Modernity and the Popular Press in Interwar Britain*. Oxford: Oxford University Press.

Birn, Donald S. 1981. *The League of Nations Union*. Oxford: Clarendon Press.

Black, Naomi. 2004. *Virginia Woolf as Feminist*. Ithaca, NY: Cornell University Press.

Blair, Sara. 2004. 'Local Modernity, Global Modernism: Bloomsbury and the Places of the Literary'. *ELH* 71: 813–38.

Bloom, Clive. 2002. *Bestsellers: Popular Fiction Since 1900*. Basingstoke: Palgrave Macmillan.

Bornstein, George. 2001. *Material Modernism: The Politics of the Page*. Cambridge: Cambridge University Press.

Bracco, Rosa Maria. 1990. *Betwixt and Between: Middlebrow Fiction and English Society in the Twenties and Thirties*. Melbourne: History Department of Melbourne.

Brake, Laurel. 1994. *Subjugated Knowledges: Journalism, Gender and Literature in the Nineteenth Century*. London: Macmillan.

Brittain, Vera. 1940. *Testament of Friendship*. London: Virago, 1980.

—. 1986. *Chronicle of Friendship: Vera Brittain's Diary of the Thirties*. Ed. Alan Bishop. London: Victor Gollancz.

Brooker, Peter and Andrew Thacker, eds. 2009, 2012, 2013. *The Oxford Critical and Cultural History of Modernist Magazines*. 3 vols. Oxford: Oxford University Press.

Broomfield, Andrea L. 2004. 'Eliza Lynn Linton, Sarah Grand and the Spectacle of the Victorian Woman Question: Catch Phrases, Buzz Words and Sound Bites'. *English Literature in Transition* 47.3: 251–72.

Brosnan, Leila. 1999. *Reading Virginia Woolf's Essays and Journalism*. Edinburgh: Edinburgh University Press.

Brown, Erica and Mary Grover, eds. 2012. *Middlebrow Literary Cultures: the Battle of the Brows, 1920–60*. Basingstoke: Palgrave Macmillan.

Bryant, Mark. 2000. *Dictionary of Twentieth-Century British Cartoonists and Caricaturists*. Aldershot: Ashgate.

Bush, Barbara. 1999. *Imperialism, Race and Resistance: Africa and Britain 1919–1945*. London: Routledge.

Carey, John. 1992. *The Intellectuals and the Masses: Pride and Prejudice among the Literary Intelligentsia 1880–1939*. London: Faber and Faber.

Carlson, Susan. 2000. 'Comic Militancy: The Politics of Suffrage Drama'. *Women, Theatre and Performance: New Histories, New Historiographies*. Ed. Maggie B. Gale and Viv Gardner. Manchester: Manchester University Press. 198–215.

Carter, David. 2015. 'Middlebrow Book Culture'. *Routledge International Handbook of the Sociology of Art and Culture*. Ed. Laurie Hanquinet and Mike Savage. London: Routledge. 349–69.

Ceadel, Martin. 1980. *Pacifism in Britain 1914–1945: The Defining of a Faith*. Oxford: Clarendon Press.

—. 1999. 'A Legitimate Peace Movement: The Case of Britain, 1918–1945'. *Challenge to Mars: Pacifism from 1918–1945*. Ed. Peter Brock and Thomas P. Socknat. Toronto: University of Toronto Press. 134–48.

Chan, Evelyn T. 2010. 'Professions, Freedom and Form: Reassessing Woolf's *The Years* and *Three Guineas*'. *Review of English Studies*. 61. 251: 591–613.

Clark, Suzanne. 1991. *Sentimental Modernism: Women Writers and the Revolution of the Word*. Bloomington: Indiana University Press.

Clay, Catherine. 2006. *British Women Writers 1914–1945: Professional Work and Friendship*. Aldershot: Ashgate.

—. 2009. 'On Not Forgetting "the Importance of Everything Else": Feminism, Modernism and *Time and Tide*, 1920–1939'. *Key Words: A Journal of Cultural Materialism*. 7: 20–37.

—. 2010. 'Winifred Holtby, Journalist: Rehabilitating Journalism in the Modernist Ferment'. *Winifred Holtby: 'A Woman In Her Time'*. Ed. Lisa Regan. Cambridge: Cambridge Scholars Press. 65–88.

—. 2011. '"What We Might Expect if the Highbrow Weeklies Advertised Like the Patent Foods": *Time and Tide*, Advertising and the Battle of the Brows'. *Modernist Cultures* 6:1: 60–95.

—. 2018. '"The Magazine Short Story and the Real Short Story": Consuming Fiction in the Feminist Weekly *Time and Tide*'. *Women's Periodicals and Print Culture in Britain 1918–1939: the Interwar Period*. Ed. Catherine Clay, Maria DiCenzo, Barbara Green and Fiona Hackney. Edinburgh: Edinburgh University Press. 72–86.

Cockin, Katharine. 1998. *Edith Craig (1869–1947): Dramatic Lives*. London: Cassell.

—. 2001. *Women and Theatre in the Age of Suffrage: The Pioneer Players, 1911–1925*. Basingstoke: Palgrave.

—. 2015. 'Edith Craig and the Pioneer Players: London's International Art Theatre in a "Khaki-clad and Khaki-minded World"'. *British Theatre and the Great War, 1914–1919: New Perspectives*. Ed. Andrew Maunder. Basingstoke: Palgrave Macmillan. 121–39.

Cohen, Deborah Rae. 2006. 'Rebecca West and the Taxonomies of Criticism'. *Rebecca West Today: Contemporary Critical Approaches*. Ed. Bernard Schweizer. Newark: University of Delaware Press. 143–56.

Colletta, Lisa. 2003. *Dark Humor and Social Satire in the Modern British Novel*. Basingstoke: Palgrave Macmillan.

Collier, Patrick. 2006. *Modernism on Fleet Street*. Aldershot: Ashgate.

—. 2007. 'Journalism Meets Modernism'. *Gender in Modernism: New Geographies, Complex Intersections*. Ed. Bonnie Kime Scott. Urbana and Chicago: University of Illinois Press. 186–224.

—. 2015. 'What Is Modern Periodical Studies?' *Journal of Modern Periodical Studies*. 6.2: 92–111.

—. 2016. *Modern Print Artefacts: Textual Materiality and Literary Value in British Print Culture, 1890–1930*. Edinburgh: Edinburgh University Press.

Conroy, Jack and Curt Johnston, eds. 1973. *Writers in Revolt: The Anvil Anthology*. New York: L. Hill.

Corrin, Jay P. 1989. *G. K. Chesterton and Hilaire Belloc: The Battle Against Modernity*. Ohio: Ohio University Press.

Cowman, Krista and Louise A. Jackson, eds. 2005. *Women and Work Culture in Britain c. 1850–1950*. Aldershot: Ashgate.

Croft, Andy. 1990. *Red Letter Days: British Fiction in the 1930s*. London: Lawrence and Wishart.

Cuddy-Keane, Melba. 2003. *Virginia Woolf, the Intellectual and the Public Sphere*. Cambridge: Cambridge University Press.

Deakin, Phyllis A. 1984. *Press On*. Worthing, West Sussex: Henry E. Walter.

De Groot, Joanna and Sue Morgan. 2015. 'Beyond the "Religious Turn"? Past, Present and Future Perspectives in Gender History'. *Gender and History* 25. 3: 395–422.

Delafield, E. M. 1930. *The Diary of a Provincial Lady*. London: Virago, 1984.

—, ed. 1932. *The Time and Tide Album*. London: Hamish Hamilton.

—. 1937. 'The Diary of a Provincial Lady'. *Titles to Fame*. Ed. Denys Kilham Roberts. London: Thomas Nelson and Sons. 119–38.

Delap, Lucy. 2000. '*The Freewoman*, Periodical Communities, and the Feminist Reading Public'. *Princeton University Library Chronicle* 61: 233–76.

—. 2007. *The Feminist Avant-Garde: Transatlantic Encounters of the Early Twentieth Century*. Cambridge: Cambridge University Press.

Demoor, Marysa and Kate Macdonald. 2010. 'Finding and Defining the Victorian Supplement'. *Victorian Periodicals Review* 43.3: 97–110.

Dentith, Simon. 2000. *Parody*. London: Routledge.

Detloff, Madelyn. 2016. *The Value of Virginia Woolf*. Cambridge: Cambridge University Press.

DiCenzo, Maria and Leila Ryan. 2007. 'Neglected News: Women and Print Media, 1890–1928'. *Residual Media*. Ed. Charles R. Acland. Minneapolis: University of Minnesota Press. 239–56.

DiCenzo, Maria and Lucy Delap. 2008. 'Transatlantic Print Culture: The Anglo-American Feminist Press and Emerging "Modernities"'. *Transatlantic Print Culture, 1880–1940: Emerging Media, Emerging Modernisms*. Ed. Ann Ardis and Patrick Collier. Basingstoke: Palgrave Macmillan. 48–65.

DiCenzo, Maria, with Lucy Delap and Leila Ryan. 2011. *Feminist Media History: Suffrage Periodicals and the Public Sphere*. Basingstoke: Palgrave Macmillan.

DiCenzo, Maria. 2014. '"Our Freedom and Its Results": Measuring Progress in the Aftermath of Suffrage'. *Women's History Review* 23.3: 421–40.

DiCenzo, Maria, with Alexis Motuz. 2016. 'Politicizing the Home: Welfare Feminism and the Feminist Press in Interwar Britain'. *Women: A Cultural Review*. 27: 4: 378–96.

Dickens, Elizabeth. 2011. '"Permanent Books": The Reviewing and Advertising of Books in the *Nation and Athenaeum*.' *Journal of Modern Periodical Studies* 2.2: 165–84.

Dixon, Joy. 2010. 'Modernity, Heterodoxy, and the Transformation of Religious Cultures'. *Women, Gender, and Religious Cultures in Britain 1800–1940*. Ed. Sue Morgan and Jacqueline deVries. London: Routledge. 211–30.

Doughan, David. 1987. 'Periodicals by, for and about women in Britain'. *Women's Studies International Forum* 3: 261–73.

Doughan, David and Denise Sanchez. 1987. *Feminist Periodicals 1855–1984*. Brighton: Harvester.

Dowson, Jane. 2009. 'Interventions in the Public Sphere: *Time and Tide* (1920–30) and *The Bermondsey Book* (1923–30)'. *The Oxford Critical and Cultural History of Modernist Magazines. Volume 1, Britain and Ireland 1880–1955*. Ed. Peter Brooker and Andrew Thacker. Oxford: Oxford University Press. 530–51.

Elgin, Josephine. 1999. 'Women Pacifists in Interwar Britain'. *Challenge to Mars: Essays on Pacifism from 1914–1945*. Ed. Peter Brock and Thomas P. Socknat. Toronto: University of Toronto Press. 149–68.

Eoff, Shirley M. 1991. *Viscountess Rhondda: Equalitarian Feminist*. Columbus: Ohio State University Press.

Eros, Paul. 2002. 'A Provision of Agape: Gerald Heard's Importance to Auden'. *W. H. Auden: A Legacy*. Ed. David Garrett Izzo. West Cornwall, CT: Locust Hill Press. 105–19.

Falby, Alison. 2008. *Between the Pigeonholes: Gerald Heard 1889–1971*. Cambridge: Cambridge Scholars Press.

Farjeon, Annabel. 1986. *Morning Has Broken: Biography of Eleanor Farjeon*. London: Julia Macrae.

Farjeon, Eleanor, 1958. *Edward Thomas: The Last Four Years*. Oxford: Oxford University Press.

Fernald, Anne. 2013. 'Women Fiction, New Modernist Studies, and Feminism'. *Modern Fiction Studies*. 59.2: 229–40.

Flint, Kate. 1993. *The Woman Reader 1837–1914*. Oxford: Oxford University Press.

Freeman, Charles. 2004. *Egypt, Greece and Rome: Civilizations of the Ancient Mediterranean*, 2nd edn. Oxford: Oxford University Press.

Frost, Laura. 2013. *The Problem with Pleasure: Modernism and its Discontents*. New York: Columbia University Press.

Fyfe, Hamilton. 1926. *Behind the Scenes of the Great Strike*. London: The Labour Publishing Company.

Gale, Maggie B. 1996. *West End Women: Women and the London Stage 1918–1962*. London: Routledge.

—. 2000. 'Errant Nymphs: Women and the Inter-War Theatre'. *British Theatre between the Wars 1918–1939*. Ed. Clive Barker and Maggie B. Gale. Cambridge: Cambridge University Press. 119–34.

Gardner, Viv. 2015. 'The Theatre of the Flappers?: Gender, Spectatorship and the "Womanisation" of Theatre 1914–1918'. *British Theatre and the Great War, 1914–1919: New Perspectives*. Ed. Andrew Maunder. Basingstoke: Palgrave Macmillan. 161–78.

Garrity, Jane. 1999. 'Selling Culture to the "Civilized": Bloomsbury, British *Vogue*, and the Marketing of National Identity'. *Modernism/Modernity*. 6.2: 29–58.

—. 2013. 'Modernist Women's Writing: Beyond the Threshold of Obsolescence'. *Literature Compass*. 10.1: 15–29.

Glendinning, Victoria. 1987. *Rebecca West: A Life*. London: Weidenfeld and Nicolson.

Goldie, David. 1998. *A Critical Difference: T. S. Eliot and John Middleton Murry in English Literary Criticism, 1919–1928*. Oxford: Clarendon Press.

Goldman, Jonathan. 2011. *Modernism Is the Literature of Celebrity*. Austin: University of Texas Press.

Gottlieb, Julie V. 2005. 'Feminism and Anti-Fascism in Britain'. *British Fascism, the Labour Movement, and the State*. Ed. Nigel Copsey and David Renton. Basingstoke: Palgrave Macmillan. 68–94.

—. 2010. 'Varieties of Feminist Responses to Fascism in Inter-War Britain'. *Varieties of Anti-Fascism: Britain in the Inter-War Period*. Ed. Nigel Copsey and Andrzej Olechnowicz. Basingstoke: Palgrave Macmillan. 101–18.

—. 2012. '"Broken Friendships and Vanished Loyalities": Gender, Collective (In)Security and Anti-Fascism in Britain in the 1930s'. *Politics, Religion and Ideology* 13.2: 197–219.

—. 2013. '"We Were Done the Moment We Gave Women the Vote": The Female Franchise Factor and the Munich By-elections, 1938–1939'. *The Aftermath of Suffrage: Women, Gender, and Politics in Britain 1918–1945*. Ed. Julie V. Gottlieb and Richard Toye. Basingstoke: Palgrave Macmillan. 159–80.

—. 2014. '"The Women's Movement Took the Wrong Turning": British Feminists, Pacifism and the Politics of Appeasement'. *Women's History Review*. 23.3: 441–62.

Graves, Pamela M. 1994. *Labour Women: Women in British Working-Class Politics, 1918–1939*. Cambridge: Cambridge University Press.

Green, Barbara. 2009. 'The Feminist Periodical Press: Women, Periodical Studies, and Modernity'. *Literature Compass* 6.1: 191–205.

—. 2017. *Feminist Periodicals and Daily Life: Women and Modernity in British Culture*. Basingstoke: Palgrave Macmillan.

Guy, Josephine M. and Ian Small. 2000. 'The British "Man of Letters" and the Rise of the Professional'. *The Cambridge History of Literary Criticism, vol. 7, Modernism and the New Criticism*. Ed. A. Walton Litz, Louis Menand and Lawrence Rainey. Cambridge: Cambridge University Press. 377–88.

Hackney, Fiona. 2008. '"Women are News": British Women's Magazines 1919–1939'. *Transatlantic Print Culture, 1880–1940: Emerging Media, Emerging Modernisms*. Ed. Ann Ardis and Patrick Collier. Basingstoke: Palgrave Macmillan. 114–33.

Hall, Leslie. 2011. 'An Ambiguous Idol: H. G. Wells Inspiring and Infuriating Women'. *The Wellsian*. 34: 68–75.

Hallam, Michael. 2011. 'In the "Enemy" Camp: Wyndham Lewis, Naomi Mitchison and Rebecca West'. *Wyndham Lewis and the Cultures of Modernity*. Ed. Andrzej Gasiorek, Alice Reeve-Tucker and Nathan Waddell. London: Routledge. 57–76.

Hammill, Faye. 2006. 'Modernism and the Culture of Celebrity'. *Modernism/Modernity* 13.2: 389–90.

—. 2007. *Women, Celebrity and Literary Culture Between the Wars*. University of Texas Press.

—. 2010. 'In Good Company: Modernism, Celebrity, and Sophistication in *Vanity Fair*'. *Modernist Star Maps: Celebrity, Modernity, Culture*. Ed. Aaron Jaffe and Jonathan Goldman. Farnham: Ashgate. 123–36.

Hammond, J. R. 1979. *An H. G. Wells Companion: A Guide to the Novels, Romances and Short Stories*. London: Macmillan.

Hampton, Mark. 2004. *Visions of the Press in Britain 1850–1950*. Urbana and Chicago: University of Illinois Press.

Hankins, Leslie Kathleen. 2004. 'Iris Barry, Writer and Cinéaste, Forming Film Culture in London 1924–26: the *Adelphi*, the *Spectator*, the Film Society, and the British *Vogue*'. *Modernism/Modernity*. 11.3: 488–515.

Hannam, June and Karen Hunt. 2002. *Socialist Women: Britain 1880s to 1920s*. London: Routledge.

Hanson, Clare. 2000. *Hysterical Fictions: The 'Woman's Novel' in the Twentieth Century*. Basingstoke: Palgrave Macmillan.

Hapgood, Lynne and Nancy L. Paxton, eds. 2000. *Outside Modernism: In Pursuit of the English Novel, 1900–1930*. London: Macmillan.

Harding, Jason. 2002. *The Criterion: Cultural Politics and Periodical Networks in Inter-War Britain*. Oxford: Oxford University Press.

—. 2009. 'The Idea of a Literary Review: T. S. Eliot and *The Criterion*'. *The Oxford Critical and Cultural History of Modernist Magazines, vol. 1, Britain and Ireland 1880–1955*. Ed. Peter Brooker and Andrew Thacker. Oxford: Oxford University Press. 346–63.

Harris, H. Wilson, ed. 1937. *Christianity and Communism*. Oxford: Basil Blackwell.

Harvey, Anne, ed. 2013. *Like Sorrow or a Tune: Poems of Eleanor Farjeon*. Holt: Laurel Books.

Haslam, Beryl. 1999. *From Suffrage to Internationalism: The Political Evolution of Three British Feminists, 1908–1939*. New York: P. Lang.

Hazelgrove, Jenny. 2000. *Spiritualism and British Society between the Wars*. Manchester: Manchester University Press.

Heath, Stephen. 1994. 'I. A. Richards, F. R. Leavis and Cambridge English'. *Cambridge Minds*. Ed. Richard Mason. Cambridge: Cambridge University Press. 20–33.

Heffernan, Laura. 2008. 'Reading Modernism's Cultural Field: Rebecca West's Strange Necessity'. *Tulsa Studies in Women's Literature* 27.2: 309–25.

Hickman, Miranda, ed. 2011. *One Must Not Go Altogether with the Tide: the Letters of Ezra Pound and Stanley Nott*. Ithaca, NY: McGill-Queen's University Press.

Hilliard, Christopher. 2006. *To Exercise Our Talents: the Democratization of Writing in Britain*. Cambridge, MA: Harvard University Press.

Hinton, James. 2013. *The Mass Observers: A History, 1937–1949*. Oxford: Oxford University Press.

Hoberman, Ruth. 1997. *Gendering Classicism: The Ancient World in Twentieth-Century Women's Historical Fiction*. Albany: State University of New York Press.

Hobson, Suzanne. 2011. *Angels of Modernism: Religion, Culture, Aesthetics, 1910–1960*. Basingstoke: Palgrave Macmillan.

Hollis, Matthew. 2011. *Now All Roads Lead to France: The Last Years of Edward Thomas*. London: Faber & Faber.

Holtby, Winifred. 1934. *Women and a Changing Civilisation*. London: John Lane.

Hopkinson, Diana. 1968. *The Incense-Tree*. London: Routledge.

Howarth, Peter. 2005. *British Poetry in the Age of Modernism*. Cambridge: Cambridge University Press.

Hubble, Nick. 2006. *Mass-Observation and Everyday Life: Culture, History, Theory*. Basingstoke: Palgrave Macmillan.

Huculak, J. Matthew. 2009. '*The London Mercury* (1919–1939) and Other Moderns'. *The Oxford Critical and Cultural History of Modernist Magazines. Volume 1, Britain and Ireland 1880–1955* Ed. Peter Brooker and Andrew Thacker. Oxford: Oxford University Press. 240–59.

Humble, Nicola. 2001. *The Feminine Middlebrow Novel 1920s to 1950s: Class, Domesticity and Bohemianism*. Oxford: Oxford University Press.

—. 2011. 'Sitting Forward or Sitting Back: Highbrow v. Middlebrow Reading'. *Modernist Cultures* 6.1: 41–59.

Hyams, Edward. 1963. *The New Statesman: The History of the First Fifty Years 1913–1963*. London: Longmans.

Ingman, Heather. 2010. 'Religion and the Occult in Women's Modernism'. *The Cambridge Companion to Modernist Women Writers*. Ed. Maren Tova Linett. Cambridge: Cambridge University Press. 187–202.

Ingram, Angela and Daphne Patai, eds. 1993. *Rediscovering Forgotten Radicals: British Women Writers, 1889–1939*. Chapel Hill: University of North Carolina Press.

Izzo, David Garrett. 2002. 'The Incredible Gerald Heard and "This Thing"'. *W. H. Auden: A Legacy*. Ed. David Garrett Izzo. West Cornwall, CT: Locust Hill Press. 89–104.

Jackson, T. A. 1937. 'Communism, Religion and Morals'. *A Mind in Chains: Socialism and the Cultural Revolution*. Ed. C. Day Lewis. London: Frederick Muller. 205–35.

Jaffe, Aaron. 2005. *Modernism and the Culture of Celebrity*. Cambridge University Press.

James, David. 2010. 'Modernist Narratives: Revisions and Rereadings'. *The Oxford Handbook of Modernisms*. Ed. Peter Brooker, Andrzej Gasiorek, Deborah Longworth and Andrew Thacker. Oxford: Oxford University Press. 85–107.

Janowitz, Anne. 1998. *Lyric and Labour in the Romantic Tradition*. Cambridge: Cambridge University Press.

Joannou, Maroula. 1995. *'Ladies, Please Don't Smash These Windows': Women's Writing, Feminist Consciousness and Social Change, 1918–1938*. Oxford: Berg.

—. 2002. 'The Angel of Freedom: Dora Marsden and the Transformation of the *Freewoman* into the *Egoist*'. *Women's History Review* 11.4: 595–611.

—, ed. 2012. *The History of British Women's Writing, 1920–1945*. Basingstoke: Palgrave Macmillan.

John, Angela V. 2013. *Turning the Tide: The Life of Lady Rhondda*. Cardigan: Parthian Books.

Jones, Stephen G. 1986. *Workers at Play: A Social and Economic History of Leisure 1918–1939*. London: Routledge.

Kalantzis, Alexia. 2013. 'The "Little Magazine" as Publishing Success: *Le Scapin* (1885–6); *La Pléiade* (1886–90); and *Le Mercure de France* (1889–1965)'. *The Oxford Critical and Cultural History of Modernist Magazines. Vol. III, Europe 1880–1940, Part I*. Ed. Peter Brooker, Sascha Bru, Andrew Thacker and Christian Weikop. Oxford: Oxford University Press. 60–75.

Kaplan, Sydney Janet. 2010. *Circulating Genius: John Middleton Murry, Katherine Mansfield and D. H. Lawrence*. Edinburgh: Edinburgh University Press.

Karshan, Thomas. 2011. *Vladimir Nabokov and the Art of Play*. Oxford: Oxford University Press.

Kent, Susan Kingsley. 1993. *Making Peace: The Reconstruction of Gender in Interwar Britain*. Princeton: Princeton University Press.

Krasner, David, ed. 2008. *Theatre in Theory, 1900–2000*. Oxford: Blackwell.

Law, Cheryl. 1997. *The Suffrage and Power: The Women's Movement 1918–28*. London: Tauris.

Leavis, Q. D. 1932. *Fiction and the Reading Public*. London: Pimlico.

Lee, Hermione. 1996. *Virginia Woolf*. London: Chatto & Windus.

LeFanu, Sarah. 2003. *Rose Macaulay: A Biography*. London: Virago.

Leiss, William, Stephen Kline, Sut Jhally and Jacqueline Botterill. 2005. *Social Communication in Advertising, Consumption in the Mediated Marketplace*. 3rd edn. London: Routledge.

Lejeune, Anthony. 1956. *Time and Tide Anthology*. London: Andre Deutsch.

Leventhal, F. M. 1974. 'H. N. Brailsford and the New Leader'. *Journal of Contemporary History* 9.1: 91–113.

Lewis, John, ed. 1935. *Christianity and the Social Revolution*. London: Gollancz.

Lewis, Pericles. 2010. *Religious Experience in the Modernist Novel*. Cambridge: Cambridge University Press.

Littau, Karin. 2006. *Theories of Reading: Books, Bodies, and Bibliomania*. Cambridge: Polity.

Livesey, Ruth, 2004. 'Socialism and Victorian Poetry'. *Literature Compass* 1.1: 1–6

London, Bette. 1999. *Writing Double: Women's Literary Partnerships*. Ithaca, NY: Cornell University Press.

—. 2007. 'Mediumship, Automatism and Modernist Authorship'. *Gender in Modernism: New Geographies, Complex Intersections*. Urbana and Chicago: University of Illinois Press. 623–76.

Lonsdale, Sarah. 2018. '"The Sheep and the Goats": Interwar Women Journalists, the Society of Women Journalists, and the Woman Journalist'. *Women's Periodicals and Print Culture in Britain, 1918–1939*. Ed. Catherine Clay, Maria DiCenzo, Barbara Green and Fiona Hackney. Edinburgh: Edinburgh University Press. 463–76.

Low, Rachael. 1997. *The History of the British Film 1918–1939*. London: Allen & Unwin.

Lucas, John. 2000. The *Radical Twenties: Aspects of Writing, Politics and Culture*. Nottingham: Five Leaves.

Lyon, Janet. 1999. *Manifestoes: Provocations of the Modern*. Ithaca, NY and London: Cornell University Press.

McCarthy, Helen. 2013. 'Democratising Foreign Policy Between the Wars'. *The Aftermath of Suffrage: Women, Gender, and Politics in Britain 1918–1939*. Ed. Julie Gottlieb and Richard Toye. Basingstoke: Palgrave Macmillan. 142–58.

McNamara, Sallie. 2014. 'Lady Eleanor Smith: The Society Column, 1927–1930'. *Women and the Media: Feminism and Femininity in Britain, 1900 to the Present*. Ed. Maggie Andrews and Sallie McNamara. London: Routledge. 46–61.

Marcus, Laura. 2007. *The Tenth Muse: Writing About Cinema in the Modernist Period*. Oxford: Oxford University Press.

Marek, Jayne E. 1995. *Women Editing Modernism: "Little" Magazines and Literary History*. Kentucky: University Press of Kentucky.

Matthews, Sean. 2009. '"Say Not the Struggle Naught Availeth . . .": *Scrutiny* (1932–53)'. *The Oxford Critical and Cultural History of Modernist Magazines, vol.1, Britain and Ireland 1880–1955*. Ed. Peter Brooker and Andrew Thacker. Oxford: Oxford University Press. 833–55.

Messenger, Rosalind. 1967. *The Doors of Opportunity: A Biography of Dame Caroline Haslett*. London: Femina Books.

Mills, Jean. 2016. 'Virginia Woolf and the Politics of Class'. *A Companion to Virginia Woolf*. Ed. Jessica Berman. Oxford: Wiley Blackwell. 219–34.

Mitchison, Naomi. 1934. *Home and a Changing Civilisation*. London: John Lane.

—. 1979. *You May Well Ask. A Memoir 1920–1940*. London: Flamingo, 1986.

Montefiore, Janet. 1996. *Men and Women Writers of the 1930s: The Dangerous Flood of History*. London: Routledge.

Moore, James Ross. 2007. 'Girl Crazy: Music and Revue between the Wars'. *British Theatre between the Wars 1918–1939*. Ed. Clive Barker and Maggie B. Gale. Cambridge: Cambridge University Press.

Morgan, Sue and Jacqueline DeVries, eds. 2010. *Women, Gender, and Religious Cultures in Britain, 1800–1940*. London: Routledge.

Morris, Benny. 1991. *The Roots of Appeasement: The British Weekly Press and Nazi Germany During the 1930s*. London: Frank Cass & Co. Ltd.

Morris, Lynda and Robert Radford. 1983. *The Story of the Artists International Association 1933–1953*. Oxford: Museum of Modern Art.

Morrisson, Mark S. 2001. *The Public Face of Modernism: Little Magazines, Audiences and Reception, 1905–1920*. Wisconsin: University of Wisconsin Press.

Moses, Michael Valdez. 2010. 'Modernists as Critics'. *The Oxford Handbook of Modernisms*. Ed. Peter Brooker, Andrzej Gasiorek, Andrew Thacker and Deborah Longworth. Oxford: Oxford University Press. 139–55.

Mulhern, Francis. 1979. *The Moment of Scrutiny*. London: New Left Books.

Munton, Alun. 2010. 'Modernist Politics: Socialism, Anarchism, Fascism'. *The Oxford Handbook of Modernisms*. Ed. Peter Brooker, Andrzej Gasiorek, Andrew Thacker and Deborah Longworth. Oxford: Oxford University Press. 477–500.

Murray, Simone. 2000. '"Deeds and Words": The Woman's Press and the Politics of Print'. *Women: A Cultural Review* 11. 3: 197–222.

Nelson, Otto M. 1978. '*Simplicissimus* and the Rise of National Socialism'. *Historian* 40. 3: 441–62.

Newton, Leslie. 2012. 'Picturing Smartness: Cartoons in the *New Yorker*, *Vanity Fair*, and *Esquire* in the Age of Cultural Celebrities'. *Journal of Modern Periodical Studies* 3.1: 64–92.

North, Michael. 2013. *Novelty: A History of the New*. Chicago: University of Chicago Press.

Oram, Alison and Annemarie Turnbull. 2001. *The Lesbian History Sourcebook: Love and Sex between Women in Britain from 1780–1970*. London: Routledge.

Pailer, Gaby, Andreas Böhn, Stefan Horlacher and Ulrich Scheck, eds. 2009. *Gender and Laughter: Comic Affirmation and Subversion in Traditional and Modern Media*. New York: Rodopi.

Parkes, Adam. 1996. *Modernism and the Theatre of Censorship*. Oxford: Oxford University Press.

Pawlowski, Merry. 1994. 'Virginia Woolf, *Three Guineas* and Sons'. *Virginia Woolf: Emerging Perspectives, 3rd Annual Conference on Virginia Woolf*. Ed. Mark Hussey. New York: Pace University Press. 44–51.

Pederson, Joyce Senders. 2005. 'Victorian Liberal Feminism and the "Idea" of Work'. *Women and Work Culture: Britain c. 1850–1950*. Ed. Krista Cowman and Louise A. Jackson. Aldershot: Ashgate. 27–47.

Plock, Vike. 2018. '"A Journal of the Period": Modernism and Conservative Modernity in *Eve: The Lady's Pictorial* (1919–1929)'. *Women's Periodicals and Print Culture in Britain, 1918–1939*. Ed. Catherine Clay, Maria DiCenzo, Barbara Green and Fiona Hackney. Edinburgh: Edinburgh University Press. 28–41.

Powell, Violet. 1988. *The Life of a Provincial Lady: A Study of E. M. Delafield and her Works*. London: Heinemann.

Powers, Lyall H. 2006. *Henry James at Work by Theodora Bosanquet; with excerpts from her diary and an account of her professional career*. Ann Arbor: University of Michigan Press.

Prothero, Iorweth. 1974. 'William Benbow and the Concept of the "General Strike"'. *Past and Present* 63.1: 132–71.

Puchner, Martin. 2002. *Stage Fright: Modernism, Anti-Theatricality, and Drama*. Baltimore: Johns Hopkins University Press.

Purkis, Charlotte. 2011. 'Velona Pilcher and Dame Ellen Terry'. *Ellen Terry, Spheres of Influence*. Ed. Katharine Cockin. London: Pickering & Chatto.

Pursell, Caroll. 1993. '"Am I a Lady or an Engineer?" The Origins of the Women's Engineering Society in Britain, 1918–1940'. *Technology and Culture* 34.1: 78–97.

Purvis, June and Sandra Stanley Holton, eds. 2000. *Votes for Woman*. London: Routledge.

Pykett, Lyn. 2000. 'The Making of a Modern Woman Writer: Rebecca West's Journalism, 1911–1930'. *Journalism, Literature and Modernity: From Hazlitt to Modernism*. Ed. Kate Campbell. Edinburgh: Edinburgh University Press. 176–90.

Rabaté, Jean-Michel. 2009. 'Gender and Modernism: *The Freewoman* (1911–12), *The New Freewoman* (1913), and *The Egoist* (1914–19)'. *The Oxford Critical and Cultural History of Modernist Magazines, vol. 1, Britain and Ireland 1880–1955*. Ed. Peter Brooker and Andrew Thacker. Oxford: Oxford University Press. 269–89.

Rains, Stephanie. 2015. 'Going in for Competitions: Active Readers and Magazine Culture, 1900–1910'. *Media History* 21.2: 138–49.

Rhondda, Margaret. 1933. *This Was My World*. London: Macmillan.

Roach, Becky. 2018. '"The Lady Interviewer and Her Methods": Chatter, Celebrity, and Reading Communities'. *Women's Periodicals and Print Culture in Britain, 1918–1939*. Ed. Catherine Clay, Maria DiCenzo, Barbara Green and Fiona Hackney. Edinburgh: Edinburgh University Press. 170–84.

Robins, Elizabeth. 1913. *Way Stations*. London: Hodder & Stoughton.

Ross, Ellen. 2015. 'Militarism, Pacifism, and Internationalism'. *Cambridge Companion to Modernist Culture*. Ed. Celia Marshik. Cambridge: Cambridge University Press. 66–78.

St John, Christopher. 1959. *Ethel Smyth, a Biography*. London: Longmans.

Schreiner, Olive. 1911. *Woman and Labour*. London: Virago, 1988.

Scott, Bonnie Kime, ed. 1990. *The Gender of Modernism: A Critical Anthology*. Bloomington and Indianapolis: Indiana University Press.

—.1995. *Refiguring Modernism, vol. 1: The Women of 1928*. Bloomington: Indiana University Press.

—, ed. 2000. *Selected Letters of Rebecca West*. New Haven: Yale University Press.

Scott, Joan W. 1988. 'Deconstructing Equality-versus-Difference: Or, the Uses of Poststructuralist Theory for Feminism'. *Feminist Studies* 14.1: 32–50.

Sewell, Brocard. 1990. *G.K.'S. Weekly: An Appraisal*. Upton: The Aylesford Press.

Sexton, Jamie. 2002. 'The Film Society and the Creation of an Alternative Film Culture in Britain in the 1920s'. *Young and Innocent? The Cinema in Britain 1896–1930*. Ed. Andrew Higson. Exeter: University of Exeter Press. 291–305.

Shaw, Marion. 1999. *The Clear Stream: A Life of Winifred Holtby*. London: Virago.

Shaw-Miller, Simon. 2010. 'Modernist Music'. *The Oxford Handbook of Modernisms*. Ed. Peter Brooker, Andrzej Gasiorek, Andrew Thacker and Deborah Longworth. Oxford: Oxford University Press Oxford: Oxford University Press. 599–617.

Shepherd-Barr, Kirsten. 2005. 'Modernism and Theatrical Performance'. *Modernist Cultures* 1.1: 59–68.

Shiach, Morag. 2004. *Modernism, Labour and Selfhood in British Literature and Culture, 1890–1930*. Cambridge: Cambridge University Press.

Smith, Adrian. 1996. *The New Statesman: Portrait of a Political Weekly 1913–1931*. London: Frank Cass.

Snaith, Anna. 2000a. *Virginia Woolf: Public and Private Negotiations*. Basingstoke: Palgrave Macmillan.

—. 2000b. 'Wide Circles: The *Three Guineas* Letters'. *Woolf Studies Annual* 6: 1–168.

—. 2007. *Palgrave Advances in Virginia Woolf Studies*. Basingstoke: Palgrave Macmillan.

—. 2010. 'The Hogarth Press and Networks of Anti-Colonialism'. *Leonard and Virginia Woolf, the Hogarth Press and the Networks of Modernism*. Ed. Helen Southworth. Edinburgh: Edinburgh University Press. 103–27.

—. 2015. Introduction to *Virginia Woolf, A Room of One's Own and Three Guineas*. Oxford: Oxford University Press. xi–xxxix.

Snyder, Carey. 2010. 'Katherine Mansfield and the *New Age* School of Satire'. *Journal of Modern Periodical Studies* 1.2: 125–58.

Southworth, Helen. 2014. 'The Bloomsbury Group and the Book Arts'. *The Cambridge Companion to the Bloomsbury Group*. Ed. Victoria Rosner. Cambridge: Cambridge University Press. 144–61.

Spender, Dale. 1984. *Time and Tide Wait for No Man*. London: Pandora Press.

Staveley, Alice. 2008. 'Teacups and Turbines: Negotiating Modernity in the Interwar Women's Professional Magazine'. Paper given at the 10th annual conference of the Modernist Studies Association, Nashville, Tennessee.

Stead, Lisa. 2016. *Off to the Pictures: Cinemagoing, Women's Writing and Movie Culture in Interwar Britain*. Edinburgh: Edinburgh University Press.

—. 2018. '"Dear Cinema Girls": Girlhood, Cinemagoing, and the Interwar Film Magazine'. *Women's Periodicals and Print Culture in Britain 1918–1939: The Interwar Period*. Ed. Catherine Clay, Maria DiCenzo, Barbara Green and Fiona Hackney. Edinburgh: Edinburgh University Press. 103–17.

Stetz, Margaret D. 1994. 'Rebecca West's Criticism: Alliance, Tradition, and Modernism'. *ReReading Modernism: New Directions in Feminist Criticism*. Ed. Lisa Rado. New York: Garland. 41–66.

—. 2001. *British Women's Comic Fiction: Not Drowning but Laughing*. Aldershot: Ashgate.

Suh, Judy. 2009. *Fascism and Anti-Fascism in Twentieth-Century British Fiction*. Basingstoke: Palgrave Macmillan.

Sullivan, Alvin, ed. 1986. *British Literary Magazines*, 4 vols. London: Greenwood Press.

Sullivan, Melissa. 2011. '"I return with immense relief to old friend *Time and Tide*": Middlebrow Expansions in E. M. Delafield's Fiction and Journalism'. *Modernist Cultures* 6.1: 96–120.

Surette, Leon. 1993. *The Birth of Modernism: Ezra Pound, T. S. Eliot, W. B. Yeats, and Occult Modernism*. Montreal; London: McGill Queen's University Press.

—. 2010. 'Economics.' *Ezra Pound in Context*. Ed. Ira B. Naidel. Cambridge: Cambridge University Press. 106–14.

Sword, Helen. 2002. *Ghostwriting Modernism*. Ithaca, NY: Cornell University Press.

Thurschwell, Pamela. 2001. *Literature, Technology and Magical Thinking, 1880–1920*. Cambridge: Cambridge University Press.

Tracy, Daniel. 2010. 'Investing in "Modernism": Smart Magazines, Parody, and Middlebrow Professional Judgment'. *Journal of Modern Periodical Studies*. 1.1: 38–63.

Tusan, Michelle. 2005. *Women Making News: Gender and Journalism in Modern Britain*. Urbana and Chicago: University of Illinois Press.

Walker, Nancy. 1988. *A Very Serious Thing: Women's Humor and American Culture*. Minneapolis: University of Minnesota Press.

Warren, Lynne. 2000. 'Women in Conference: Reading the Correspondence Columns in *Woman* 1890–1910'. *Nineteenth-Century Media and the Construction of Identities*. Ed. Laurel Brake, Bill Bell and David Finkelstein. Basingstoke: Palgrave Macmillan. 122–34.

Wasson, Haidee. 2002. 'Writing the Cinema into Daily Life: Iris Barry and the Emergence of British Film Criticism'. *Young and Innocent? The Cinema in Britain 1896–1930*. Ed. Andrew Higson. Exeter: University of Exeter Press. 321–77.

Whitelaw, Lis. 1990. *The Life and Rebellious Times of Cicely Hamilton: Actress, Writer, Suffragette*. London: The Women's Press.

Widdowson, Peter. 1999. *Literature*. London: Routledge.

Williams, Raymond. 1989. *Politics of Modernism: Against the New Conformists*. London: Verso.

Wilson, Leigh. 2013. *Modernism and Magic: Experiments with Spiritualism, Theosophy and the Occult*. Edinburgh: Edinburgh University Press.

Wilson, Nicola. 2012. 'Virginia Woolf, Hugh Walpole, the Hogarth Press, and the Book Society'. *English Literary History* 79.1: 237–60.

Wood, Alice. 2013. *Virginia Woolf's Late Criticism: The Genesis of* The Years, Three Guineas *and* Between the Acts. London: Bloomsbury.

Woolf, Virginia. 1929. *A Room of One's Own. A Room of One's Own and Three Guineas*. Oxford: Oxford University Press, 2015.

—. 1938. *Three Guineas. A Room of One's Own and Three Guineas*. Oxford: Oxford University Press, 2015.

—. 2008. *Selected Essays*. Ed. David Bradshaw. Oxford: Oxford University Press.

Young, Tory. 2004. 'Torrents of Trash'. *The Cambridge Quarterly* 33.2: 187–9.

Zanotti, Serenella. 2010. 'Pound and Fascism'. *Ezra Pound in Context*. Ed. Ira B. Naidel. Cambridge: Cambridge University Press. 376–90.

Zwerdling, Alex. 1986. *Virginia Woolf and the Real World*. Berkeley: University of California Press.

Index